1996

Managing Credit Programs in Continuing Higher Education

Joe F. Donaldson

The Guide Series

in Continuing Education
A publication prepared by the
University of Illinois at Urbana-Champaign

Foreword

The management of credit programs in continuing higher education requires many skills, not the least of which are a well-developed political sensitivity and the ability to establish a variety of relationships. As with any complex endeavor, constant attention is needed to make sure that all aspects of every course and program offered are being handled effectively.

Joe F. Donaldson is well qualified to author this publication. He directed a complex credit program operation, in addition to studying how to gain acceptance for this form of study. In his new role as a professor of adult education, he combines practice with theory on how to effectively manage this important area of continuing education.

In addition to presenting a clear process, Professor Donaldson identifies the problem areas likely to be encountered and the staff support needed to administer different forms, levels, and modes of program delivery. For me personally, the most fascinating portions are those dealing with building and maintaining important relationships. The material on maintaining quality control is equally well done.

Those who are managing any aspect of continuing education will find this a valuable guide to the role of leadership in program development and operation. We feel that Professor Donaldson has made an important contribution to the literature of our field.

Charles E. Kozoll
Editor
Guide Series

Acknowledgments

My appreciation goes out to the many people who helped me with this book. Much of the thought behind it came through reflection on what I had learned while administering a continuing education credit programming unit at the University of Illinois at Urbana–Champaign. During my time there, I learned much from all my colleagues in the Division of Extramural Courses and from other continuing education administrators, the faculty members, department chairs, and deans with whom I had an opportunity to work on a daily basis. My thanks go to all of them for providing me with such a rich and challenging learning environment.

Charles Kozoll, editor of the Guide Series, was a constant source of support during the writing of the manuscript. I am especially grateful for his excellent suggestions about ways that the manuscript could be revised, expanded, and improved. I am also indebted to Sandra Pearce, Gary Kuhne, and Barbara LeGrand, who reviewed early drafts of the manuscript. Special thanks goes to Robert Batchellor of the University of Illinois at Urbana–Champaign, Don Gogniat of The Pennsylvania State University–York, and Kay King of the University of Illinois at Chicago, all of whom took the time to be conscientious reviewers of the manuscript. As a result of their many valuable suggestions, the manuscript has been strengthened in innumerable ways.

Finally, a word of thanks goes to my wife, Meredith, and to my children, Susie, Andrew, and Marylee. Many drafts of the manuscript have benefited greatly from Meredith's careful review. And she and the children alike have been constant sources of personal support and encouragement throughout this project.

Contents

Introduction

Credit course and degree programming is only one of several programming forms in continuing higher education. But it is an area of programming that is growing and receiving increased attention. In recognition of this development, the National University Continuing Education Association (NUCEA) established in 1985 a new Division of Summer, Evening, and Off-Campus Programs. Results of a survey (Hanniford & Basil, 1988) commissioned by this division indicate that about one-third of responding NUCEA member institutions have a summer session administrator housed in the institutions' continuing education units and that almost 90 percent of the continuing education units offer both evening and off-campus credit courses and programs.

During the last two decades, continuing education credit programming has also become more differentiated in form, level, delivery, and organization. Programs that permit credit for experiential learning and for contract learning have been developed. The number of graduate degree programs offered for part-time adult students has increased, and this trend is predicted to continue (Sonntag, 1986). Courses and programs have begun to be delivered through distance education technologies, including audio-teleconferencing, videotape, video-teleconferencing, and satellite. And institutions of higher education use a variety of organizational models (at some institutions more than one model) for the planning and delivery of credit courses and degree programs. In the most common model—the one emphasized in this book—the credit programming unit, as part of a centralized continuing education unit, works with academic departments in scheduling and delivering courses and programs. Colleges and academic departments may also house decentralized continuing education units that are responsible for the extension of their colleges' or departments' credit courses and programs. Still other institutions have fairly autonomous colleges of continuing studies that are able to award their own credit and degrees.

THEMES TO BE HIGHLIGHTED

This book is about managing credit courses and degree programs in continuing education in the various forms, levels, delivery modes, and organizational contexts in which they manifest themselves. To understand this form of continuing education programming is to appreciate the reality of the following events:

1. *Missing the Magic Moment.* An off-campus degree program is phased out because of Dr. Stone's negative interpretations of evaluation results. Dr. Stone is an influential faculty member, but he is unfamiliar with off-campus credit programming and adult instruction. The damage is

1

corrected, and the department attempts to reinitiate the degree program, only to find that another institution is now offering the same program. The department's initiative is thwarted.

2. *Are Your Bases Covered?* After making arrangements for an off-campus degree program with local school districts, superintendents, and teachers, Whipple University fails to receive state coordinating board approval for the program. School district personnel are upset, and the academic department questions the wisdom of taking initiatives in light of what it considers to be administrative and bureaucratic hassles required to serve its external constituencies.

3. *False Hopes—False Expectations.* A comprehensive survey provides evidence of a significant level of need and demand for a credit degree program. However, when credit programming unit administrators approach the academic department with this information, they are told that offering the program will not be possible. Having had their expectations raised, those who were surveyed are very upset when they learn that the institution will be unresponsive to their need. Credit unit administrators must now expend time and energy in attempting to control the damage done to the image of the unit and the institution. They are also bitter about the situation. They had committed both personal and institutional resources to designing a survey questionnaire, collecting and analyzing data, and writing a summary of results for presentation to the academic department.

4. *Understanding Constituent Clout!* A flawed needs assessment results in offering a series of courses that attracts far less enrollment than anticipated. When the history department and the continuing education office realize that their commitment of resources far outweighs the return they will receive, talk of canceling the course series ensues. Students learn of this and begin a letter-writing campaign to the institution's president, insisting that the series continue. As a result, the series is offered to completion even though enrollments are marginal at best.

5. *Skewed Priorities or Not?* After several attempts to have an academic department commit to offering a course repeatedly requested by a local professional association, the course is finally scheduled. It will be taught by Dr. Green, who is not only an excellent instructor but a nationally recognized expert in the field. Pre-enrollments are excellent, and the client group is anxiously awaiting the beginning of the semester. Three days before the course is to begin, Dr. Green calls the credit unit administrator to tell her that he has just received a project grant and the course will have to be canceled.

6. *Low Tech/No Tech—Keeping Pace.* During the past fifteen years, the continuing education credit unit's program at Omega University has

evolved from the delivery of courses to the offering of degree programs. The institution's record-keeping system has not kept pace. Resources are unavailable for the major computer programming that would be required to support degree programming for nontraditional students in the same way that programming is supported for resident, traditional students. Transcripts still identify students as "nontraditional." Reports needed by colleges and departments for curriculum planning and for reporting faculty and credit generation activity are either unavailable or must be compiled by hand.

These six vignettes illustrate some of the problems that have to be dealt with in organizing and administering credit course and degree programs in continuing higher education. Each of the vignettes also highlights several of the themes that run throughout this book. Credit programming unit administrators must constantly be aware of perceptions of many faculty and campus leaders who still consider continuing education credit courses and degree programs to be, by their very nature, inferior to resident courses and programs. There are many things over which credit unit administrators have little or no control—especially those factors and events arising outside the unit and the parent institution. Working with client groups requires sensitivity and the critical and judicious use of programming techniques advocated in much of the adult and continuing education literature. Unit administrators are heavily dependent upon (but have little authority over) others with whom they work, whether these others are faculty members, campus leaders, academic departments, administrative units, or external stakeholders. As a result, unit administrators must focus upon (1) building and maintaining relationships so that leverage and influence can be applied in programming and (2) developing expertise in continuing education credit programming and clientele interests and needs so that this expertise can be put to work fostering relationships with others.

This book grapples with some of these issues, offering practical means that have been shown to mitigate some of the obstacles and challenges inherent in this form of continuing education programming. At the same time, the book highlights the leadership opportunities that credit programming unit administration can provide for people who wish to contribute to the development of higher education in an era when the education of adults is receiving increased attention.

THE PROGRAMMING CONTEXT

Continuing education credit programming involves the extending of on-campus credit courses and degree programs to adults in ways that accommodate their many roles and responsibilities. Because programming results in the awarding of course credit, certificates, and even degrees—coins of the higher education realm second in importance only to research and publication—credit programming is a jealously guarded commodity of the higher education community.

This jealousy is compounded because faculty and the institution's academic leadership are apprehensive that continuing education credit courses and programs may fail to meet quality standards. The quality of adult students is believed to be lower than that of traditional students. Instructional resources available either for evening or for off-campus courses and programs are believed to be inadequate. The socialization process that is believed to occur only through extended periods of on-campus residency is thought to be lacking.

In this programmatic context, administrators of credit course and degree programs are faced with special constraints, demands, and choices that are distinct from those faced by administrators of noncredit programs. In addition, the credit unit administrator's role is made more difficult by the fact that he or she is often expected to oversee a comprehensive program of courses and degrees that rivals the size and complexity of most administrative functions of many small colleges.

OVERVIEW

The purpose of this book is to provide an overview of principles, practices, and procedures required in organizing and administering an effective credit programming unit in continuing higher education. The book's content is drawn primarily from administrative experience with, and observations of, off-campus credit course and degree programs offered by major research universities. The importance of different contextual factors and organizational models varies among different institutional types (as they do among institutions of like type). Even so, the principles and practices covered are applicable to all institutions of higher education (whether they are two- or four-year colleges or universities) as well as to the administration of summer, on-campus evening, and off-campus credit course and degree programs.

Topics covered include:

1. Guiding principles of leadership and coordination in credit programming (chapter 1)

2. Organizing for and coordinating a comprehensive credit program (chapter 2)

3. Developing and strengthening relationships with colleges, departments, campus leadership, and client groups (chapter 3)

4. Working with faculty and supporting faculty involvement in credit programming (chapter 4)

5. Evaluating credit courses and programs (chapter 5)

The book is intended primarily for deans and directors of continuing higher education, directors and coordinators of credit courses and programs, and continuing education field staff who work in the credit area. Deans, department heads, and faculty members involved in credit programming for adults may, however, also find much of what is covered here to be relevant to their situations, as may individuals involved in other arenas of adult and continuing education practice.

Chapter 1

Guiding Principles of Leadership and Coordination

Organizing and administering continuing education credit courses and programs requires an understanding of leadership and managerial principles, as well as specific functional areas of credit programming. This chapter briefly introduces some leadership and management principles that will be interwoven throughout later chapters.

MANAGING AND LEADING

Warren Bennis (1984) says that managers "do things right," while leaders "do the right thing." Attention to detail is undeniably critical in effective credit programming. Yet administrators must also rise above day-to-day detail to gain a view of where they are, where their total program is going, and how all courses and degree programs interplay with each other. In short, administrators of credit programming units must be both good managers and effective leaders. Leadership does not end in the continuing education unit itself. Rather, it needs to be extended to one's activities and relationships with the entire institution, client groups, the community, and the larger, external environment of the credit programming unit.

According to Bennis (1984), to be an effective leader, one must focus on four things. First, leaders must have a sense of direction, a vision of what the unit's total program is to become. This is necessary to provide leadership in directing staff activities. But it is just as necessary to have a sense of direction and vision that can be communicated to all those with whom the administrator works. Faculty members, other campus administrators, and others must be aware of the direction the credit programming unit is taking so that they can be involved in defining that direction and participating in it.

Second, leaders must manage the meaning of what their unit is about. This requires the development of a unit identity that is shared by the staff and is communicated to outsiders. A favorable identity is prerequisite to internal and external marketing, as well as to building a positive image of the unit in the minds of stakeholders (Deal, 1987). Stakeholders will see, for example, an image of (1) a unit committed to academic integrity and other institutional values that assure high quality credit courses and programs, (2) an effective and efficient unit committed to serving instructors and capable of reducing administrative hassles for them, and (3) a staff that possesses expertise in program planning, course delivery, adult learning, and marketing, especially as related to credit course and degree programming. And this image

7

will do much to foster good working relationships with others and the development of the credit programming unit's total program.

Third, leaders must be consistent, dependable, and credible. These three attributes are particularly important when dealing with faculty members, academic departments, and client groups. As noted later, much of the power that credit programming unit administrators are able to exercise within and outside the institution comes from developing good interpersonal relationships with others and from the trust others put in their ideas, judgments and recommendations. In spite of a person's interpersonal skills, without consistency in approach, without follow-through in what is promised, and without credibility, an administrator's effectiveness is severely limited.

Finally, leaders must manage themselves well. They must know their own strengths and use those strengths effectively. They must likewise be aware of their weaknesses and compensate for them in their work, even selecting staff members who have complementary strengths and weaknesses to work with them. Leaders must be committed to developing themselves. This requires them to have a positive self-concept and to develop themselves both professionally and personally. They must make time to be involved in continuing professional learning, and in learning and activities that contribute to their personal development.

Many consider leadership to be the sole dominion and responsibility of chief executives, thereby relegating managerial tasks to directors of and administrators in credit programming units. However, it is argued here that leadership by all levels of professional staff is essential to the development and administration of effective continuing education credit programming. The kind of leadership required and the groups with which it can be exercised will of course differ according to each professional's particular role in the unit. Each professional, irrespective of role or position can, however, exercise educational leadership, which requires a vision of what the unit's total program could and should be and a commitment to work toward those ideals. This form of leadership also depends heavily upon administrators' expertise and the development of expert power, a topic addressed later in this chapter (Donaldson, 1989b).

CONSTRAINTS, DEMANDS AND CHOICES

Knox (1981) writes that "the latitude for most [adult education] agencies lies between the demands and constraints of the parent organization." The concepts of constraints, demands, and choices (latitude) have also been used by Stewart (1982) in her description of managerial work. Constraints on credit programming and on the jobs of administrators in the credit programming unit come from sources external and internal to the institution. They manifest themselves in several forms:

1. State-level policies on credit programming, as was seen in the second vignette in the "Introduction"

2. Competition from other institutions in the institution's service area

3. The mission and strengths of the parent institution

4. A reward structure for faculty that does not sufficiently consider continuing education activities in promotion, tenure, and salary increase decisions

5. Requirements that course offerings fit into the academic calendar used in resident instruction

6. Resource limitations

7. The organization's definition of the credit programming unit's work

8. The inability of campus administrative units to adequately support the credit unit's programming, as described in the sixth vignette in the "Introduction"

9. Institutional attitudes about and policies on credit programming

10. The institution's physical location.

Demands come from the parent institution in the form of policies and procedures that cannot be ignored. There are expectations of self-support and high quality programming; expectations that standard accounting and budgeting procedures will be followed and that residuals (that is, revenue above expenses) will be returned to the parent organization; expectations that the programming unit will cooperate with academic departments in developing and offering courses and programs identified as high priorities by the institution's administration; role definitions that specify with whom a unit administrator may and may not work; and expectations of how an administrator and his or her staff are to carry out their unit's duties.

The latitude between constraints and demands determines the quantity, quality, and types of choices that can be made about the unit's work. Because constraints and demands can change, this latitude varies over time, but it also varies for different institutions, continuing education units, and administrative positions (see Figure 1). When demands are high and constraints tight, choices are limited and effectiveness in programming and in job performance is most probably measured in terms of meeting expectations (demands). When the latitude for choices is greater, effectiveness is measured more in terms of whether the right choices are made (doing the right things).

When choices are available, they can be made in *how* work is done and *what* work is done (Stewart, 1982, p. 2). If changes in standard operating procedures do not violate expectations and exceed constraints, changes can be made in *how* work is done. A change to computerized registration, accounting, and data management systems is an example of a choice in how work is done. Another example would be a change in the way students must register for courses and pay tuition and fees. A choice to use distance education technologies to deliver courses would also fit into this category of choices.

Making choices about *what* work is done is usually more strategically important to the administrator and to the programming unit than are decisions about how work is done. In fact, making choices about what work is done requires leadership—having vision about what work should be done or "doing the right thing," while making choices about how work is done requires a focus upon "doing things right," or management. Making choices about what work is done may involve changes in programmatic priorities, for example from undergraduate to graduate level programming, or from course to degree programming. It may also involve extending

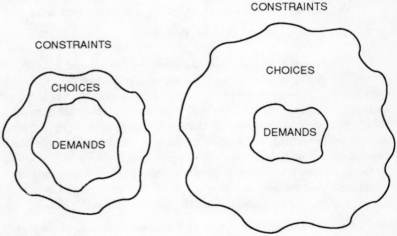

Figure 1.

Differences in the demands, constraints, and choices in what work is done and how work is done by the credit programming unit and its administrators. The wavy lines suggest the likelihood, as well as the potential, for change.

From Rosemary Stewart, Choices for the Manager, © *1982, p. 7. Reprinted by permission of Prentice Hall, Inc., Englewood Cliffs, New Jersey.*

a unit's programming domain into areas not previously addressed, for example expanding the unit's total program in order to work with an academic department the unit has not traditionally worked with, developing contract course offerings when the unit has historically offered only open enrollment courses to the general public, and beginning to work with academic departments in offering summer courses on campus when the unit has previously offered only courses located off campus.

Effectiveness in organizing and administering credit courses and degree programs requires administrators to identify and fully understand the constraints, demands, and choices in their own and their unit's work. To the extent possible, administrators should seek to push back constraints, and work to have demands relaxed, thereby increasing the quantity, improving the quality, and expanding the types of choices available to them. If, for example, campus policies do not support credit programming for adults, the administrator should work toward the acceptance of policies supportive of credit programming. If all residuals must be returned to the parent organization, negotiating some program development capital for the unit would reduce this demand on the unit and provide more choices and flexibility in programming.

FIVE PRINCIPLES OF PROGRAM COORDINATION

Directors of programming units and the administrators who work under their direction are responsible for coordinating a comprehensive program of credit courses and degree programs. Although many of the skills and tasks of program coordination are similar to those of program development, coordination differs in (1) the scope of activities that tasks must address; (2) its focus upon the interplay of individual courses and degree programs and the mutual effect they have upon one another; (3) the need to attend to the three interacting variables of people, procedures, and work (Handy, 1985, pp. 368-371); and (4) the need to achieve optimal integration of activities.

Alan Knox (1981, pp. 8-9) notes that unpredictability in funding, participation, personnel, and migratory participants and resource persons requires administrators to provide a "human glue" to hold continuing education agencies together. This is no less true for directors and administrators of credit programming units. To ensure the strength and bonding power of this "glue," however, administrators must keep in mind five key principles of program coordination.

The Helicopter Effect

To effectively coordinate a comprehensive program, administrators must be willing and able to rise above the press of day-to-day details (Handy,

1985). From this vantage point, they can get a more complete picture of their total program, the interplay of its various components, and the effect the total program has upon other factors within the institution and the unit's service area. For example, if several academic departments in the same location offer credit courses, the administrator may be able to broaden the base of electives available for clientele. A focus on the details of only one course or degree program would preclude taking advantage of this opportunity to better serve the programming unit's client groups. Administrators must constantly attend to this principle, because it takes planning, effort, and effective management of self to make the time necessary to rise above day-to-day activities and crises.

Power and Influence

Credit programming unit administrators have little if any direct authority or control over those outside their unit. This point is illustrated by the fourth vignette in the "Introduction"; here, the client group had the power to prevent cancellation of the series of courses. The point is also portrayed (vignette five) in the helplessness and frustration that the administrator must have felt when Dr. Green announced that the course he had agreed to teach would have to be cancelled. Because unit administrators are dependent upon persons over whom they have little or no control, other forms of power, especially influence and leverage, must be cultivated. This can be done by exercising whatever legitimate authority an administrator has, by developing the influence and leverage that come from others' recognition of an administrator's expertise, and by building a base of personal power.

Position Power and Status

Credit programming unit administrators must have sufficient position power (legitimate authority) and appropriate status (Handy, 1985) as viewed by campus leadership, faculty, and staff. Position power exhibits itself, for example, in control over financial resources and their allocation, in authority over the cancellation of courses and programs, and in the development of unit policies and procedures (such as those related to employment and payment of adjunct instructors, student registration, and arrangements and payment for classroom space) that directly affect program development and implementation. This form of power is either vested in the responsibilities of role incumbents or is directly or indirectly delegated to them. It is a type of power that continuing educators seldom talk about, but all continuing education administrators do have certain legitimate powers that come with their roles. These powers must be accepted and exercised if program coordination is to be effective.

Status, in contrast to position power, may come with the position, but it is as likely to be a function of the perception of others. One's status is increased to the extent that one's position is seen to be important by the people with whom one works (Handy, 1985, p. 210). The importance of the credit programming unit and of the administrator's job therefore depends on how critical the credit function is for campus and individual academic departments achieving their agendas. One's status would be increased, for example, if the credit programming unit were viewed as essential to the development of a department's relationship with a professional association. Consequently, status is closely related to the concept of internal support for the credit function, a topic considered in depth in chapter 3.

Expertise

Developing and enhancing administrators' proficiencies has become an important agenda among continuing higher education professionals. NUCEA's (1988) Continuing Higher Education Leadership (CHEL) project has developed a "Self Assessment Inventory" for practitioners to use in their professional development activities. The inventory is designed around the concept of proficiency developed by Knox (1979, 1987) and others (for example, American Society for Training and Development, 1983). Proficiency entails both understanding and experience; it is defined as the ability of a professional to perform at a desirable level when given the opportunity to do so (Knox, 1979, p. 4). Four major areas of proficiency have been identified in the NUCEA inventory for all continuing higher education administrators: (1) perspective on the field, (2) personal qualities, (3) program development, and (4) administration. A position-specific profile for directors of credit programming units has also been developed as part of the CHEL project and is available from NUCEA.

The concept of expertise as used here combines the concept of proficiency with the need for others to recognize that the person or the credit programming unit is proficient in certain areas. In this way, expertise becomes a form of power and leverage that the unit and the administrator possess. Those who recognize proficiency in others are more apt to respect and act upon their professional judgment and advice and are less apt to resent being influenced (Handy, 1985). For credit programming unit administrators, it is critical that others in the institution recognize that they possess proficiencies common to all continuing higher education administrators and unique to the administration of credit courses and programs. These unique proficiencies include understanding and managing the following:

1. Threats to the coherence of adult, part-time students' programs of study

2. Matters of degree program curricular design and implementation in off-campus, evening, and summer session settings

3. Ways the institution can adapt to adult learners enrolled in credit courses and programs

4. Ways in which credit course and program needs assessments resemble and differ from noncredit needs assessments

5. Variations among needs assessments for courses and programs and among different client groups

6. The need to administer and coordinate different forms of course and program delivery

7. Special considerations involved in credit course and program evaluation and quality control

8. Modification of approaches to marketing credit courses and programs

9. Unique dimensions in strengthening internal and external relationships in the credit programming domain

All too often continuing education units define themselves and are in turn defined by others as service units. Although the credit programming unit must provide a service (and an effective and efficient one at that), the unit must also offer educational leadership. This leadership can be accomplished only by obtaining and exercising the power that comes through others' recognition of the administrator's and the unit's proficiency and expertise in the areas outlined above.

Recognition of proficiency is also fostered by academic experience. Perceptions of expertise will be heightened if a credit programming unit administrator has not only taught credit courses but has also participated as a faculty member in an academic department's design of its program. Experience in writing and research also contributes to others' perceptions of expert power in a higher education context. Although they cannot always do so, administrators should try to gain some experience in the academic life of the institution if they do not already have it.

Interpersonal Skills

In working with others, credit programming unit administrators need skills to assist them (1) in managing conflicts that arise in their work, (2) in developing informal networks across the parent organization, and (3) in building another base of power—personal power—that can be used in persuasion. Conflict arises in all organizational contexts. If properly dealt with, however, it can be effectively managed to reduce the harm it might inflict. Or conflict can be turned into useful competition or purposeful argument, both of which can be used productively within the organization

(Handy, 1985). Administrators should know different strategies for managing of conflict and should use them in their work.

Credit programming unit administration involves the management of a continuous process of building and maintaining relationships. Interpersonal and informal communication networks help administrators to get their work done, and to develop sources of information—information that is critical to effective program coordination.

Although power can come from the position that administrators hold in the organization and from the expertise others attribute to them, it can also be derived from personal attributes—from personality and from the relationships an individual develops with others. As noted earlier, because credit programming unit administrators have little if any direct authority over those with whom they work, other forms of power must be cultivated. One of these is personal power, which contributes to the administrator's ability to be persuasive and to apply leverage when needed to coordinate the unit's total program.

Uniformity and Diversity

Credit programming unit administrators should be able to balance uniformity with diversity. Certain levels of uniformity in procedures, policies, and processes must be in place if a unit's total program is to be effectively and efficiently coordinated and managed. Yet working with different academic departments, faculty members, and client groups, and using a variety of course and program delivery mechanisms require flexibility so that the credit programming unit can attend effectively to diverse interests, needs, and motivations. Too much uniformity interferes with the flexibility needed to work with the different stakeholders of a credit programming unit. Too much diversity results in inefficiency and ineffectiveness in program coordination. Administrators should aim for an optimum balance between uniformity and diversity in their unit's operations. This optimum level will differ for each organization and will depend in part upon the constraints, demands, and choices that administrators have in their jobs.

This need for balance also applies to the arena of values. Credit unit directors, more so than those with responsibility for noncredit programming, have to be consistent in their support of key institutional values and systems in order to maintain the power described in previous sections. But consistency is not equivalent to total uniformity. Rather, while administrators and their units must support key institutional values and systems, they must also be comfortable with and supportive of some diversity in values—

especially the values unique to the academic departments and professions they work with and the values related to working with adult learners—if they are to be effective, creative, and innovative forces in their institutions. This too requires arriving at an optimum, and often delicate, balance between uniformity and diversity in dealing with the values and norms of the institution and others with whom administrators work.

People, Systems and Procedures, Work and Structure

Credit unit administrators need to manage the three interacting variables of people, systems and procedures, and work and structure (Handy, 1985). The administrator's work is not confined to external relationships. Internal coordination of the unit's people, procedures, and work is necessary for smooth unit operation. In fact, it is only through effective internal coordination that time is made available to develop external relationships, to study the unit's external environment, and to be able either to respond to changes in the environment or to be proactive and affect the environment in advantageous ways. Ineffective internal operations fraught with problems only distract administrators from other tasks that are more critical to the unit's coordination and well-being.

Handy (1985, p. 368) identifies several tasks that administrators must attend to in managing each of these three variables. In the people area, the tasks are recruitment and selection, reassignment, training and education, rewarding, and counseling of staff. In the work and structure area, the duties are organizing reporting relationships, defining job tasks, enriching jobs, and defining roles. And in the systems and procedures category, the tasks are developing and monitoring communication systems, reward systems, information systems, reporting mechanisms, budgeting systems, and decision-making systems. What must be kept in mind about these three categories of variables is that a change in one will produce changes in the other two (Handy, 1985, p. 369). Introducing a computerized record-keeping system, for example, may affect office communication channels, may raise the staff's anxiety level, and will require staff training. Therefore, each category of variables and their effect upon each other must be monitored and managed as part of program coordination.

Information Nerve Center

Credit programming unit administrators must serve as information nerve centers for their units. Information is a critically important resource for the effective operation of the unit and coordination of its overall program. The importance of information to the continuing education unit and the role of gathering information from the external environment is repeatedly addressed in the management and continuing education literature. Quality information improves decisions, assists in deciding what work is to be done, and grounds strategic planning in reality. For example, knowing what the competition is doing in a particular location will help the administrator to correctly advise an academic department about the placement of its courses and programs. Knowing about the difficulties an academic department is experiencing will allow the administrator to approach the department with a sensitivity to the ways programming might help solve its problems. Administrators must develop information sources and seek information throughout the unit's service area and the institution to have as much information as possible when decisions are made.

SIX PRINCIPLES FOR WORKING WITH OTHERS OUTSIDE THE UNIT

Managing a credit programming unit requires constant attention to building and maintaining relationships outside the unit. These relationships have to be fostered with those in the parent institution, as well as with individuals, groups, and organizations in the unit's service area. In this section, six key principles for working with others will be reviewed briefly. Building and maintaining relationships will be dealt with in greater detail in chapter 3.

Openness

Credit unit administrators need to be open to others' perceptions, problems, and ideas. Only by actively listening to and understanding others' views of reality and their perceptions of the problems that they and their units face can administrators contribute to their agendas and help solve their problems. All too often our own agendas and problems interfere with our really hearing and really understanding the perspectives of others with whom we work. Openness is required to foster effective communication, problem solving, negotiation, decision making, change, and the strengthening of relationships.

Ownership

Others must be given ownership of ideas, programs, and policies. Like most effective administrators, credit programming unit administrators must learn to live vicariously through the successes of the faculty members and academic departments they work with. Internal support of courses and programs, policies and procedures requires that others have a stake in them and have ownership of them.

Reciprocity

"You scratch my back, and I'll scratch yours" accurately communicates the concept of reciprocity. It is a basic principle of the political dimension of organizations. Credit unit administrators need to understand and act on this principle. To the extent that they can act on it in mutually beneficial ways, their work and relationships with others will be enhanced.

Logical Incrementalism

James Brian Quinn (1980) has identified "logical incrementalism" as a change strategy that many successful administrators use. To use this strategy, administrators must (1) have a sense of direction, (2) encourage experimentation, (3) collect data about the results of experiments that can be shared with others, (4) move slowly in stepwise fashion, and (5) develop pockets of support for ideas (especially with opinion leaders). Since credit programming is so carefully guarded by the academy, change in credit programming occurs very slowly. Also, if change is to be successful, it must "bubble up" within the organization. These two conditions point to the use of "logical incrementalism" as an appropriate change strategy for credit programming unit administrators. For example, change from face-to-face to mediated course delivery is usually resisted in higher education. Working incrementally has a better chance of effecting change than "laying the change" on the campus. In short, administrators will have greater chance for success by moving logically and incrementally than by attempting to effect change by grand design.

Multiple Communication Channels

Administrators of credit programming units should open channels of communication to others. They should aim toward variety in their personal contacts and in the academic departments and colleges with which they work. This is not only wise strategically, but it also allows administrators to broaden their base of understanding of and support for their total program across the institution.

Zones of Compatibility

Administrators should identify and develop zones of compatibility between their unit's goals and those of sponsoring academic departments. Compatibility can come in many forms. Academic departments may wish to participate in credit programming for a number of reasons: to maintain or to increase enrollments; to develop relationships with professional associations, businesses, school districts, or government; to contribute to broader political and strategic agendas of the institution; to provide additional income for faculty members; to contribute to social, political, and visibility agendas of their own; to foster research and development agendas; because they believe participation has intrinsic value; or any combination of these and other motives. The administrator's role is not to judge the differing motivations of academic departments and faculty, but to identify these motives and develop compatibility between these motives and the agendas of the credit programming unit. Goal compatibility and complementarity provide another basis upon which relationships can be built and fostered.

SUMMARY

This chapter has addressed some leadership and managerial principles in organizing and administering credit courses and programs. Unit administrators are encouraged to:

- Focus on four competencies of leadership: having a sense of direction, managing the meaning of the unit, being consistent, dependable, and credible, and effectively managing one's self

- Recognize constraints, demands, and choices of their unit and job, and seek to push back constraints, reduce demands, and thereby increase the number, type, and quality of choices

- Be aware and act upon five principles of program coordination

- Keep in mind the six key principles for working with others.

The next three chapters focus on specific functional areas of credit programming into which the concepts presented in this chapter are interwoven.

Chapter 2
Organizing and Coordinating a Comprehensive Program

The function of organizing and coordinating a credit unit's comprehensive program is the point at which the administrator works at the interface among the unit's staff, colleges and departments, and client groups. It involves attention to staffing (work and structure) and to systems and procedures. This chapter reviews some ways that a credit programming unit can be organized. It also addresses the implications for staffing and work that different means of course delivery have for the unit. Procedures to be employed in needs assessment, program planning, and marketing are considered as well by focusing upon distinctions in these areas for individual credit course offerings and degree programming.

STAFFING

The choices afforded in organizing the responsibilities and work of a unit's staff depend in part upon unit size and mix (professional and support staff), in part upon the nature of the unit's total program, and in part upon whether certain functions are provided by other continuing education or campus units. As Strother and Klus (1982) note, some formal structure begins to emerge in units with as few as six staff members. However, some role differentiation, even if on an informal basis, is necessary in two-person operations to prevent duplication of effort, to provide clear channels of communication for those outside the unit, and to ensure unit effectiveness and efficiency. The proportion of professional and support staff members in a unit also has implications for how the unit is organized. For example, a unit with a preponderance of professional staff members may have to assign them more of the nuts-and-bolts, day-to-day responsibilities than would be necessary with a more balanced staff.

The level of program differentiation also affects a unit's organization. As the total program differentiates, staff roles and responsibilities must likewise become more differentiated. Program differentiation increases with growth in the number of different (1) colleges and departments the credit programming unit works with, (2) program types the unit is responsible for (summer, evening, and/or off-campus), (3) program levels addressed (associate, undergraduate, and/or graduate), (4) program formats offered (course, certificate, and/or degree), (5) delivery systems used (face-to-face and different distance education methods), and (6) combinations of these factors.

21

Finally, organization of the staff is affected by the presence or absence of other continuing education or campus units that may be able to perform key programmatic functions. The existence of a marketing unit in the continuing education operation reduces, for example, the need to assign this entire complex function to unit staff. Likewise, an ability to work through the institution's registrar's office means that staff members are not needed to perform the critical function of registering course participants.

Some Principles

Although each of these factors is important, there are three principles that administrators should also keep in mind in staffing. The first principle is that the unit's staffing pattern should mirror the organization of the unit's environment. In credit programming units, this can take one of several forms: the unit might be organized to correspond to the institution's college and departmental organization, to the different client groups served, to different program types, forms, and level, or to different delivery methods employed. A mixture of these staffing patterns is usual in most credit programming units

Even though a certain level of specialization is required in all credit programming units, the second principle is that overspecialization in defining roles and responsibilities is to be avoided. Although large staff size and extensive program differentiation may point toward developing distinct roles and responsibilities and toward strict reporting and control lines, too much specialization and bureaucratization can lead to unit dysfunction. Again, uniformity must be balanced with diversity (see chapter 1). A certain level of multifunctional roles with flexible role boundaries provides for the following:

1. Staff members will have interesting, varied work. Their jobs will be enriched both in level and extent of responsibility and in autonomy, two things that contribute to intrinsic job satisfaction (Katz & Kahn, 1978, pp. 370-371).

2. A task-oriented and team culture will be developed within the unit. Such a culture is required to address the complex, people-oriented tasks associated with credit programming, to respond adequately to changes in the unit's environment, and to be innovative in programming, (Katz & Kahn, 1978, p. 283; Handy, 1985).

The third principle is that the support staff's roles must be more specialized than those of the professional staff. Although support staff do not differ from professional staff in their need for enriched and varied jobs, their roles within the programming unit must and do differ from those of the professional staff. Specialization in support staff roles and responsibilities permits them to focus upon the day-to-day tasks of the unit and allows the unit to offer effective and efficient service to faculty and students. Such assignments are in keeping with the requirement that support staff responsibilities should be more specialized than those of professional staff.

Support staff should be responsible, among other things, for arranging instructor travel, handling registrations and admissions questions (unless this is handled by the institution's registrar's office), duplicating instructional materials, initiating and following through on instructor payroll, arranging for library support, handling the details of promoting the total program, assisting with textbook orders, and handling the details of accounting and budgeting. The administrator's responsibilities with respect to the steady-state are twofold: (1) to establish routine procedures in consultation with others, including support staff, and (2) to ensure that paper flow and communications among support staff are adequate, that enough checkpoints exist so that problems and errors will be identified in a timely way, and that all details are covered.

In summary, support staff should be primarily responsible for the day-to-day service function of the programming unit. As noted earlier, all too often continuing education units view themselves primarily as campus service operations. Although service to instructors and students and a unit culture supportive of such service are critical ingredients in organizational effectiveness (Peters & Waterman, 1982), too much involvement in the nuts and bolts of service by professional staff detracts from their other responsibilities of problem solving, innovation, policy development, boundary management, and educational leadership.

This division of responsibilities between support and professional staff is illlustrated in Figure 2. As seen in this figure, the various responsibilities overlap, indicating that all staff members share some responsibility for all areas. For example—innovation (such as in record keeping) and ideas about development of policy and course and degree program delivery might arise from the support staff, and their involvement in the life of the unit should be encouraged. Likewise, while professional staff members should focus on other responsibilities, this does not excuse their involvement in steady-state operations. They must recognize that they are not only responsible for the overall coordination of the steady-state, but that their activities in other arenas also affect day-to-day operations in often subtle but important ways. In addition, sometimes the professional staff must become directly involved in steady-state activities (such as applying labels in a rush to mail promotional materials). Their involvement in steady-state activities communicates to the support staff that no work of the unit is below any member and helps engender the team culture needed to carry out the many complex tasks required.

Another view of this principle is provided in Figure 3. This figure portrays a typical staffing pattern in a medium-sized credit programming unit. Areas of primary responsibility are indicated. In addition, it should be noted that support staff have been assigned a variety of service functions, ranging from secretarial support for different professional staff members to responsibilities for travel coordination, payroll, data management, and promotion. The assignment of the varied responsibilities illustrates the principle of job enrichment discussed earlier.

WORK SYSTEMS AND PROCEDURES

In the jargon of organizational theory, a unit's technology is the way it does its work. One aspect of a unit's technology is the way it is organized or structured to do work, a topic just covered. Work procedures and systems represent another dimension of a unit's technology. These procedures and systems address the ways that a unit goes about planning and administering its total program and its component parts. The next two major sections of this chapter address some of the programmatic considerations unique to organizing and administering credit courses and programs in continuing higher education. These considerations are highlighted by focusing upon differences in the delivery of courses and programs through face-to-face and distance education methods and upon differences in organizing for courses and for degree programs.

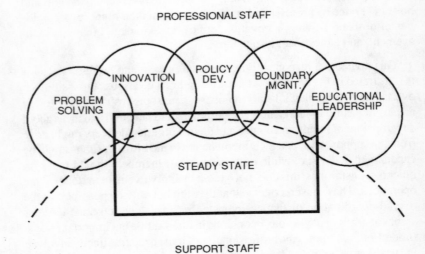

Figure 2.

Primary responsibilities of support staff and professional staff of the credit programming unit.

COORDINATING AND ADMINISTERING FACE-TO-FACE AND DISTANCE EDUCATION COURSES AND PROGRAMS

The means selected to deliver credit courses or degree programs have implications for how staff members and their work are organized. To illustrate, let's compare some of the factors involved in administering credit courses offered at a distance from campus using (1) face-to-face instruction, (2) instruction delivered through audio-teleconferencing, and (3) instruction through videotape.

ORGANIZATION OF WORK

In the face-to-face model, we are concerned most about getting people together in the same place at the same time. Transporting instructors to off-campus locations where students have gathered is the major logistical concern, and effective and efficient travel coordination is key. Once this is accomplished, instructors are relied upon to deliver instructional materials and to handle many of the administrative details (for example, registration if on site) associated with the course. With instructors and learners together

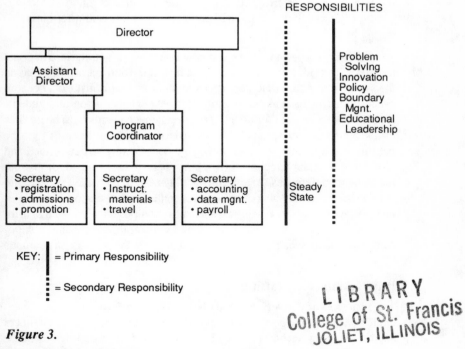

KEY: ▌ = Primary Responsibility

⋮ = Secondary Responsibility

Figure 3.

Typical staffing pattern in medium-sized credit programming unit.

in the same place and at the same time, communication, teaching, and learning can take place.

In the audio-teleconferencing model, we are concerned most about having people communicating with each other at the same time. Facilitating this communication is a major logistical concern. But in this instance, instructors cannot act as administrative agents. Additional logistical support must be provided by the credit programming unit staff and by individuals at off-campus locations. The unit staff must be responsible, for example, for handling a "call-in" or "mail-in" registration system; for mailing and receiving handouts, homework assignments, and examinations; and for maintaining regular contact with faculty members to ensure that materials are moving smoothly among sites. Individuals at off-campus sites must be responsible for facilitating the registration process, receiving materials, proctoring examinations, and returning materials to the campus. And all this must be done in a timely way to prevent delays from disrupting the teaching and learning process. In addition, the programming unit must either have the staff or arrange to use the staff of another continuing education or campus unit to set up equipment, monitor its performance, and facilitate its use by instructors and students. And times for students to talk with instructors individually must be arranged, since the public nature of audio-teleconferencing often precludes individual conferences before and after class and during breaks.

In the videotape model, we are concerned about getting instructional materials (the videotape and supporting materials) and learners together at the same time. Again (and perhaps even more so in this instance, because synchronous instructional communication between instructors and students is not characteristic of this model), people and mechanisms must be in place on and off the campus to handle logistical details. Viewing schedules and the pace at which learners proceed through a course must be determined and monitored. Regular telephone office hours need to be arranged for instructor-student conferences. Arrangements may need to be made for the entire class to meet with the instructors by using either audio-teleconferencing or face-to-face meetings on campus or at an off-campus location. And distributing and receiving materials, including the central instructional component, the videotape, must be coordinated at both on- and off-campus locations.

Implications for Staffing

Expansion of delivery methods beyond face-to-face instruction to include distance education technologies requires hiring more staff members and/or assigning current staff members additional responsibilities. Because the instructor cannot act as an administrative agent for the continuing education unit, the staff must assume these responsibilities. The staff must also directly oversee and manage delivery as it takes place. And for videotape delivery, production of instructional materials is required.

The responsibilities of staff members not directly involved in course and program delivery will also be affected.Thus the method of paying instructors may differ for mediated instruction, budgeting and accounting procedures will have to be modified to address different cost and income variables introduced by the new means of delivery, and the professional staff will have to gain additional expertise in distance education so that they can be effective in their work with colleges, departments, and instructors. Introducing distance education delivery methods therefore affects the differentiation of staff roles and the organization of a programming unit's work. Depending on the extent to which distance education delivery is used, it may also have an effect upon the total number of staff members needed to carry out the unit's work. The primary concerns and task responsibilities for these three modes of credit course delivery are summarized in Table 1.

CREDIT COURSES AND DEGREE PROGRAMS

In the types of credit programming, one major distinction is between single, unrelated course offerings and certificate and degree programs. Certificate and degree programs require programming procedures that differ both in degree and kind from those required by unrelated course offerings. These differences are evident in the needs assessment, marketing, and curricular planning and support required for certificate and degree programming.

Needs Assessment

Degree and certificate programs require a greater commitment by learners, academic departments, and the credit programming unit than do course offerings. In the case of course offerings, sunk costs are relatively low, a limited amount of coordination is required, and all parties' commitment is kept within the bounds of an academic term. In contrast, degree programs require greater up-front costs, a high level of coordination, and substantial resource commitment over an extended time period. Learners are committing themselves and their families, friends, and employers to extended use of discretionary time and dollars in pursuit of degrees. Academic departments commit both financial and human resources for the life of the program, thereby reducing budget and staffing flexibility from one term to the next. Degree and certificate programs also require the credit programming unit to commit considerable staff time and energy and financial resources not only to the coordination of each term's offering, but to the coordination and support of the program over many terms. As a result

Table 1.

Three Modes of Credit Course Delivery, Areas of Primary Concern, and Task Responsibilities

	Face-To-Face	Audio Conf.	Videotape
Primary Concern	People at the same place at the same time	People communicating at the same time	Materials and learners together at the same place at the same time
Primary Logistical Detail	Travel	Facilitation of audio communication	Material distribution
Major Tasks	Responsible Party(ies)	Responsible Party(ies)	Responsible Party(ies)
Delivery of Instructional Materials	Instructor	Unit staff[2]	Unit staff[2]
Production of Instructional Materials	Instructor	Instructor	Instructor, with unit staff
Registration	Instructor[1], if on-site	Unit staff[2]	Unit staff[2]
Course Administration, Including Scheduling and Pacing	Instructor	Instructors with unit staff	Unit staff, with instructor
Instructor-Student Communication	Instructor	Unit staff, with instructor	Unit staff, with instructor
Communication Equipment		Unit staff	Unit staff

[1]Often with the help of other staff
[2]Often with the help of off-campus coordinators

of this difference in commitment, more extensive and formalized assessments of need and demand are justified for degree and certificate programs than for a single course. Yet assessment must proceed in a way that avoids the results of the flawed needs assessment highlighted in the fourth vignette in the "Introduction."

Integrated View and Approach.

Assessment must first and foremost focus upon an integrated view of learner need, demand, eligibility, and commitment. Learners must feel that they need the program, demand for the program must be great enough, there must be enough eligible learners within the pool of those needing and demanding the program, and those eligible learners must be motivated and committed enough to exchange their time and money to pursue the degree. Seldom does one method of assessment meet the conditions of this integrated view. Rather, a number of interrelated assessment activities, using multiple methods of data collection and multiple sources of data, are required. Data must not only be more varied, but must also be as reliable and as valid as possible to support the decisions required for resource commitment

An example of how one academic unit approached needs assessment illustrates of the importance of this integrated view. The School of Social Work at the University of Illinois at Urbana–Champaign offers a combined off- and on-campus Masters of Social Work (MSW) program. Although learners can complete almost half of the program requirements off campus, they must also commit to spending one semester in on-campus study, followed by twenty-eight weeks in a supervised internship that can be in their home communities. The conditions of residence and of being away from their jobs for more than half a year require a commitment that exceeds the commitment asked of most other students enrolled in off-campus programs. As a result, the School of the Social Work is very concerned that its assessment methods accurately measure the level of motivation and commitment among potential students, as well as need, demand, and eligibility.

The needs assessment approach used is a continuous one that draws upon several sources of information and uses a number of methods. School administrators and faculty and continuing education staff members maintain informal and formal contacts with social service agencies and local professional associations to monitor the level of need and demand in a particular geographic area. These contacts are also used to determine how committed employers are to providing released time for residence study. At times, surveys are used as another source to double-check level of need and demand. Names of persons who request the program are collected, and they are kept informed of the possibility of the program being offered in their communities.

As a final step leading to an annual decision about where the program will be offered the following year, information meetings are held in communities where informal contacts, requests for the program, and surveys have indicated that sufficient program demand exists. The information meetings are publicized through (1) letters to potential students, professional associations and social service agencies, (2) contacts throughout the community, (3) press releases, (4) newspaper advertisements, and (5) fliers.

The information meeting serves four interrelated purposes. A final gauge of program demand is made through a count of people who turn out for the meeting. The program is completely described, with special emphasis on the level of commitment required of learners. Information on the eligibility of potential learners is collected through a questionnaire that addresses this variable and through later review of transcripts that those attending the meeting are asked to send the School of Social Work. The commitment level of those in attendance is also determined, but this process defies detailed description because it is based upon the professional judgments of School administrators. Through years of experience with information meetings, administrators can pick up nuances about the participants' commitment level from their attitudes, comments, and questions. This last step also illustrates the importance of informal judgments in needs assessment—judgments that are based on information gleaned through effective listening, picking up subtle cues from potential clients, and empathizing with them.

Although administrators of an academic school are used to illustrate these points, credit programming unit administrators should have the same professional and personal proclivity for informally obtaining essential information from and about potential students. The entire needs assessment process just described has evolved over many iterations and through continuously fine-tuning it. Although it is not a perfect system, problems with insufficient program enrollments have occurred very infrequently, thereby avoiding the situation described in the fourth vignette, "Underestimating Constituent Clout."

The Problem of Raised Expectations. A final thing to keep in mind about needs assessments is that care must be taken to ensure that assessment activities do not create unrealistic expectations among potential participants. Although this principle applies to a single course offering, it is particularly important for degree or certificate programs where learner commitment is extensive. The very act of assessing needs may communicate to potential learners that a course or program offering is not only possible but probable. This was the case in the third vignette described in the "Introduction." Dashing the hopes of client groups can have negative consequences, so it is better to avoid needs assessments unless realistic expectations can also be communicated to potential learners.

Clearly, credit programming unit administrators can find themselves at the center of many "tugs of war." They are expected to satisfy as many of the various unit stakeholders as often as they can. They are asked to be both responsive and responsible—responsive to clientele and responsible to the institution and its colleges and departments. Therefore, decisions about whether and how to conduct needs assessments are not to be made without seriously considering the possible consequences within and outside the parent organization. One rule of thumb is that needs assessments should not be undertaken until criteria for responding have been thoroughly worked out and are fully understood by academic departments. Even then, care must still be taken not to raise the expectations of potential clientele.

Special Programmatic Considerations for Certificate and Degree Programs

Certificate and degree programs are much more than the aggregate of single course offerings. Even in programs that require only course credits, administrators must pay attention to several issues: (1) course sequencing, (2) the mix of major, minor, and elective courses, (3) curricular choice offered students, (4) credit transfer policies, (5) provision of adequate instructional resources, and (6) program information and advisement. And in programs that require learning experiences other than course work (for example, internships, comprehensive examinations, theses, or special papers), attention to these additional requirements is essential. Programs, like wholes, are greater than the sum of their parts, and this fact must be recognized and be given full consideration in programming.

The part-time enrollment pattern of adult learners also places special demands on programming. Because adult students must fit their study into larger personal and work patterns, they have to extend their programs over several additional terms and are frequently unable to maintain a continuous enrollment pattern as most of their on-campus counterparts do. Special consideration must therefore be given to potential threats to adult students' programs and their academic progress and success. These threats include:

1. Insufficient number and type of course offerings over time

2. Improper sequencing of courses

3. Inadequate access to program advisement and to advisement related to long-range educational planning and career goals

4. Inadequate access to information about rules and requirements of specific programs and to information about course selection and scheduling

5. Inadequate attention to problems encountered in programs and courses

Faculty Program Coordinators. Dealing with these potential threats requires the concerted effort of the credit programming unit and sponsoring academic departments alike. One means of achieving full participation of academic departments in this endeavor is by appointing faculty members to program coordinator positions for their respective departments. Such an appointment should come with released time from other duties, a condition of appointment that may be achieved only through financial and other forms of support from the credit programming unit. But the support provided to release a faculty member's time to carry out program coordination responsibilities is well worth the investment.

The responsibilities of a faculty program coordinator should include (1) being in regular communication with the credit programming unit staff members with whom they work, (2) assisting in needs assessment, (3) overseeing advisement, (4) scheduling courses, (5) helping to prepare information pieces distributed to students on a regular basis, (6) assisting in developing marketing and promotional strategies for the program, (7) orienting colleagues to working with adult students, (8) dealing with students' academic problems, and (9) assisting in regular program evaluation. The major rationale for having faculty program coordinators rests less on having other persons available to assist in programming, but more on (1) faculty coordinators' knowledge of their disciplines, their departments, and their clientele, (2) their ability to work collegially with other faculty members in fulfilling their coordination responsibilities, and (3) their bringing credibility to the program.

The presence of a faculty program coordinator does not, however, excuse credit programming unit administrators from exercising leadership in ensuring that measures are taken to deal with potential threats to students' progress and success and to maintaining program quality. Rather, the faculty program coordinator should be viewed as a partner, as well as a resource, in this process. Together, they should work with others in dealing with the following issues:

Information. Adult students should be given timely and accurate information about university policies and procedures and about specific program requirements. Although some of this can be accomplished through regular promotional pieces, such as course schedules published for each academic term, other means of communication are equally important. Student handbooks that spell out policies, procedures, and requirements and that include guides to assist students in planning their programs with advisers contribute much to sharing of information, student orientation, and the preplanning of students' programs. Letters can be sent to degree candidates when changes in policies and procedures will have an immediate effect upon them. Regular newsletters can keep students up to date with program policies, procedures, and offerings. And specially developed program brochures that detail program requirements and tentative course schedules are useful communication devices if they are kept current.

Course Scheduling. Courses should be tentatively scheduled over an extended period of time (at least three to four academic terms), and this schedule should be communicated to students in newsletters, program brochures, and course catalogs. Since the number and the types of courses that can be offered part-time students will probably be limited, students need to know well in advance when courses will be offered so that they can plan ahead. Although firm schedules would be preferred, it is unlikely that this form of scheduling is feasible, given the possibilities of faculty illnesses, sabbaticals, leaves of absence, and other vagaries associated with long-range course scheduling.

Cohort versus Continuous Program Entry. Students can be admitted to part-time certificate and degree programs in one of two ways: in a specified term or at any time. In the first situation, students enter a program as a cohort, proceed through the program in lock-step fashion usually taking the same courses, and graduate together. In the second instance, each academic term is witness to new admissions, to new program graduates, and to students being at a variety of places in their programs. In some instances, programming unit administrators have no choice about the type of entry to be used; for example, in a contract program for a business offered to only a select group of employees for a specified number of academic terms, and in a program offered to a client group too small to support multiple program cycles or a wide selection of course offerings. But in most instances, administrators and departments have a choice about which form of entry to use. Each form has its own advantages and disadvantages, and understanding them is requisite to making a good decision about this program variable.

Planning for a cohort of students is generally easier than planning for students who are at different places in their programs. Courses can be scheduled well in advance for each academic term with the expectation that students will take each course in succession. The cohort approach is also very workable when no deviation from an established curriculum is permitted. Program budgeting is also facilitated, because enrollments seldom fluctuate widely which is possible in continuous entry programs. The cohort approach also contributes to the development of an *esprit de corps* among students, which in turn encourages peer teaching and support and augments the socialization process (Patchner et al., 1987). Unless the cohort is very large, however, overall program enrollment levels will usually be lower than those of continuous entry programs, and the number of different course options available to students will, of necessity, have to be more limited.

Although planning for students who are in a flexible entry program may be more difficult, there is more opportunity to offer a wider selection of courses for students, allowing them to pursue specialties of interest. Such curricular flexibility is critically important in programs leading to a variety of specializations and career tracks. Likewise, there is increased potential for establishing higher enrollment ceilings, thereby creating the potential for larger overall program enrollments than would be the case in cohort programs.

Finally, some would argue that the cohort approach is superior simply because it contributes more to the development of an *esprit de corps* among learners and to student socialization. Yet research (Donaldson, 1988a, 1988b) has shown that a community of supportive learners is just as likely to develop within single course offerings, and may in fact depend more upon the instructor and instruction than upon students being together in a group throughout their program. In other research on one university's program, the author has discovered the existence of a cohort effect within some of the institution's continuous enrollment programs. Apparently, in sensing cyclical declines in program enrollment, programming unit administrators expend added resources and effort to build enrollment levels. The result is an enrollment pattern that resembles a bell-shaped curve. Outliers—those who have just entered the program or who are graduating—are present in far fewer numbers than the bulk of students who are found in clustered groups at the curve's center. Even in continuous enrollment programs, groups of students, like their cohort program and on-campus counterparts, are taking courses together and contributing to each other's learning. The variable of cohort and continuous entry programs in continuing higher education has been the subject of frequent debate among program administrators, campus leadership, and faculty. It is a variable in need of additional analysis and research so that the programming decisions it affects can be made with better information and greater justification.

Open versus Closed Enrollment. Depending upon institutional policies and specific programming situations, a program may be open to all in the general public who meet eligibility requirements. Or it may be closed to everyone except members of an identified group who also meet eligibility requirements. Except in unusual circumstances, programs are closed only when the institution's credit programming unit and departments enter into contractual arrangements to offer programs for the employees of other organizations.

In deciding whether program enrollment should be closed or open, the credit programming unit should be especially careful to take into account institutional mission and policies, legal requirements and obligations, and program precedent. Offering a program on either a closed or an open enrollment basis when the other enrollment policy applies has much potential for creating great difficulties for and damage to the credit programming unit. Furthermore, it cannot and should not be assumed that either sponsoring academic units or client groups are familiar with the rationale for such enrollment policies. Therefore, the enrollment policy and its rationale need to be fully explained to others.

Closed and open enrollment policies may also have implications for decisions about the type of program entry (cohort or continuous) that will be permitted. A decision to limit enrollment in a program to the employees of one governmental unit, for example, may necessitate cohort program entry if there are not enough eligible employees to support a program on the basis of continuous program entry. When entering into contract negotiations, programming unit staff must fully understand the implications of one decision on the other and must thoroughly explain these implications to representatives of the other organization.

Program participants enter into a contract with the institution in one of two ways: either individually in open enrollment programs, or within the context of a contract between the university and another organization in closed enrollment programs. The implications of these different contexts of program entry cannot be underestimated. Entry into contractual arrangements usually results in additional stipulations about who is and is not eligible for admittance to a program. For example, a company may make the program available to engineers in one of its divisions and not to engineers in its other divisions. The quality of the relationship that develops between the university and the other organization also establishes a social and psychological climate that may either facilitate or create barriers to learner participation.

Curricular Integrity. Again, because most credit programs offered exclusively to part-time adult students are often restricted in the frequency and variety of course offerings, great care must be taken to ensure the curricular integrity of these programs. This requires attention to (1) the frequency with which courses are offered, (2) the number of different courses offered during each academic term, (3) the proper sequencing of courses, and (4) either offering a selection of courses over the period required for most participants to complete their program or identifying other institutions' courses for transfer into students' programs. Attention to these factors is necessary to meet students' educational interests and needs as fully as possible and to enable them to make good academic progress. Higher education's past experience with a full-time, resident student body in a continuous enrollment pattern has, in many instances, not required the same level of concern for these factors as does curriculum planning for adults. Part of a credit programming unit administrator's responsibility is therefore to be an advocate for careful curricular planning, to ensure that departments and colleges understand the potential threats to adult students' programs, and to assist colleges and departments in planning so that curricular integrity is ensured.

Adequate Instructional and Learning Resources. Credit programming unit administrators must be sure that adequate instructional and learning resources are made available at times and places convenient to learners. For on-campus offerings, this may require working with other administrators to arrange for the use of specialized classrooms and laboratory facilities. It may also require working to keep certain learning resource centers and student services offices open at times when adults can use them. For off-campus offerings, the administrator must arrange for adequate classroom and laboratory facilities with other educational institutions or organizations.

Arrangements also will have to be made with other institutions and public libraries for library support. Sometimes this may require hiring library personnel (as has been done by the University of Wisconsin–Extension, Central Michigan University, and the University of Illinois at Urbana–Champaign) to arrange for extending campus library resources to libraries near the students.

Although it is important for adequate instructional and learning resources to be available for each course offering, it is equally important for resources to be made available to help students complete other program requirements, whether internships, theses, seminar papers, or comprehensive examinations.

Communication with Faculty. Students need to communicate regularly with faculty members about course work and their programs. For on-campus programs, faculty members should hold office hours at times convenient for adult students. Facilitating communication for students at a distance from campus, however, requires additional mechanisms. These include setting up in-bound, toll-free WATS lines for students' use, encouraging faculty members to have regular telephone office hours, supporting faculty travel to off-campus sites for group and individual advising sessions, and supporting the use of communications technologies for student-faculty communication (for example, audio- and video-teleconferencing for group meetings and computer conferencing for individual and group communications).

Program Promotion. Many effective methods of promotion have been developed for continuing education offerings. However, a few comments about some specialized methods of promoting degree and certificate programs are in order. Most credit programming units produce a direct-mail course catalog, which includes policy and procedural information and a list of course offerings for each academic term. The usefulness of these publications for degree and certificate programs can be vastly improved if they also contain information about programs offered and a tentative schedule of course offerings for future terms.

Specialized program brochures can also be used effectively as direct-mail items. These brochures should contain a program description, a tentative course schedule, an outline of program requirements, admission and enrollment criteria and procedures, information about advisement and instructional resources, and a form for potential participants to request additional information or application materials. Another effective means of promoting programs, especially in urban areas, is a newspaper advertisement announcing the availability of programs and containing a coupon the potential students can mail in to request additional information. Promotion of this sort not only provides broad exposure for programs, but it also helps develop mailing lists of potential participants.

Developing relationships with professional and trade associations and with employers of potential clients is another critical ingredient in program promotion. These relationships allow the programming unit to use in-house communication vehicles to announce course and program offerings. They may also result in invitations to meetings, trade shows, and other public events where programs can be described, questions answered, and participants recruited.

SUMMARY

This chapter has considered two dimensions internal to the credit programming unit—the organization and work of staff, and the systems and procedures employed by the unit in its work. Three factors associated with staffing were reviewed, as were three principles of staff organization. Implications for staffing associated with the introduction of distance education technologies to a unit's course and program delivery mechanisms were also reviewed to illustrate the effect that this form of program differentiation has on staffing and the organization of work. Finally, some of the major programmatic factors unique to organizing and administering credit programs were reviewed. The next chapter turns our attention outside the credit programming unit by focusing upon developing and maintaining relationships with others external to the unit.

Chapter 3
Developing and Strengthening Relationships

The administration of credit course offerings and programs involves the continuous process of building and maintaining relationships with others outside the unit. The process is critical for several reasons. The quality of the relationships directly affects the amount of influence that programming unit administrators will have in working with others. Building bridges to those outside the unit also opens channels of communication through which information vital to unit functioning can flow. Information, in the form of feedback about programs, services, and unit operation, is necessary for identifying and correcting problems. A good flow of information is also critical to environmental scanning. Information about the unit's parent organization and service area environment is needed so that the unit can adapt to environmental changes, as well as initiate strategic changes in the environment that benefit the unit.

This chapter deals with ways that relationships can be built and maintained with three external groups—colleges and departments, campus leadership, and client groups. Practical means to foster the process are suggested. Yet each means is based upon the principles for working with others outlined in chapter 1. The principles of reciprocity, goal compatibility and complementarity, openness, and ownership, in particular, are keys to success.

COLLEGES AND DEPARTMENTS

Maintain Frequent Contact with Academic Unit Leaders and Faculty

Frequent contact with others is prerequisite to the development of relationships. This contact, however, must go beyond meetings and other work-related activities. Informal means of contact are also critical. Striking up conversations with faculty members who come into the office on other business is a very useful approach. And the importance of setting aside some time to wander the halls of campus buildings to chat informally with others should not be underestimated. In short, administrators should take advantage of and create opportunities to be in contact with faculty and the leaders of colleges and departments.

Listen and Understand

Although mentioned in chapter 1, the principle of listening and understanding the perspectives, problems, and agendas of colleges and departments bears repeating. To achieve this requires openness. It also requires setting aside individual and programming unit perspectives, problems, and agendas so that what others say can be placed within their framework or view of the situation. This assists in obtaining a kaleidoscope of views useful in identifying and framing problems and contributes much to the quality of information critical to operational fine-tuning and strategic adaptation and change.

Assist in Problem Solving and Goal Achievement

When possible (and especially when goals are compatible and resources are available), colleges and departments should be assisted in solving their problems and achieving their goals. The principle of reciprocity is important here. Assistance to others will pay dividends to the programming unit in a multitude of ways. Failure to assist colleges and departments, especially when their problems and goals are directly related to the unit's total program, can either preclude developing a relationship or can do serious damage to existing ones.

Serve in Ways That Go Beyond Programming Unit Goals and Agendas

Unit administrators, to the extent that time and other resources permit, should serve on campuswide, college, and departmental committees when asked, show support through appropriate attendance at functions that may be unrelated or only peripherally related to the programming unit's work, and provide financial support for academic units' other activities (for example, a contribution of a few hundred dollars to support an activity of special interest to a department). Personal, "moral," and minor financial support that goes beyond the call of duty will do much to solidify relationships with colleges and departments. It shows that the unit administrator understands their agendas and problems. It also shows that the programming unit cares.

Share Information

Because credit programming units work with others across the campus, they have information that may not be readily available to others. Appropriate and timely sharing of this information opens channels of communication, cultivates other sources of information, and helps the programming unit administrator become an important part of informal campus communications networks. Sharing information not only contributes to the development and maintenance of relationships, but it also aids in gathering new information critical to the unit.

Communicate Pertinent Program Related Information

If relationships with colleges and departments are to be good, there should be no surprises in the unit's working relationship with them. If problems are foreseen in any aspect of the programming unit's work with academic units, the college or department should be alerted to these. Failure to communicate this information in a timely fashion will have negative consequences for the relationship. It will also require time and attention to crisis management when problems unfold and become known to the college or department.

Actively Serve on Programming Unit-Related Committees

It is important that programming unit administrators join and even lead committees related to the unit's total program. Campuswide committees with such a focus may be found in the institution's faculty senate, in campus offices of undergraduate education, and in the graduate college. These committees are most commonly charged with policy and program evaluation responsibilities, areas of critical importance to the credit programming unit. Colleges and departments with significant continuing education credit programming may also have committees that deal with programmatic issues, policies and procedures, and program evaluation specific to the college or department. Service on all such committees in either a membership or *ex officio* capacity is important for information transfer and for participation in decisions that directly affect the programming unit.

If committees do not exist as part of campus, colleges', or departments' governance structures, unit administrators should work to establish them. They provide useful forums for building relationships, joint planning and scheduling, curriculum articulation, policy setting, evaluation, and identifying and addressing problems of mutual concern. If academic units have no committees of this type, they can be jointly established and sponsored by both the credit programming unit and a college or department. They can be co-chaired by an academic unit administrator or faculty member and a programming unit staff member. In evaluating the establishment of new committees in support of continuing education, unit administrators should assure that the committees are appointed by individuals in significant roles on the campus. Their own credibility will add a degree of credibility to the continuing education advisory or administrative committee.

Irrespective of how committees are established and organized, the importance of positioning oneself for service on them should not be underestimated. Participation gives the unit administrator a role in making many of the decisions that directly affect the unit. Failure to participate results in the unit administrator being at the margins of decisionmaking, with little or no input or control over decisions that have implications for the unit. Committees also serve a legitimizing function. By being part of the formal structure, credit programming unit activities gain legitimacy. Committees play this legitimizing role even if the committee is only a formality (the actual work and decision making is done informally and outside the committee structure).

Be Candid

In building and maintaining good relationships with others, programming unit administrators should be candid and forthright. Mistakes and errors should be admitted, problems shared, and program limitations should be communicated. Covering up mistakes and letting problems lurk in the background form the seeds for credibility crises that can seriously damage relationships with others.

Be Flexible in Providing Support

Different colleges and departments require varying types and sources of support to enable them to work with the credit programming unit. Many will want overload compensation for faculty. Others will want credit for the instructional hours generated through participation in the unit's courses and programs. Some will want graduate assistants and other forms of in-kind support. Several may want a share of indirect income generated through contract credit courses and programs. Still others may require funding of faculty positions to enable them to offer continuing education credit courses and programs. And combinations of these and other forms of support may be required. To the extent that campus and other applicable policies permit, the programming unit should be flexible enough to provide different, but appropriate, forms of support to solidify relationships and enable colleges and departments to participate in its programming.

"Go To Bat for Them"

When issues and problems arise that intersect with the goals of a college or department and the programming unit, administrators should assume a leadership role in working with superiors and other campus leaders. Doing so will require informing others about the issue or problem, advocating attention to it, and suggesting solutions. This form of leadership communicates to others that the administrator cares; failure to act communicates the opposite.

Use Evidence and Logical Arguments as Armament in Persuasion

When fostering relationships with colleges, departments, and faculty members, programming unit administrators must keep in mind that the academy, by the very nature of its work, responds best to persuasion built upon solid evidence. Thus programming unit administrators should be fully aware of existing research related to the types of programs offered and to those being proposed. They should also be proficient in research design, data collection, and interpretation of findings. Proficiency in these areas and knowledge of research contribute much to others' perceptions of an administrator's expertise, facilitate persuasion, and help strengthen relationships by virtue of working relationships built in part upon the programming unit administrator's understanding and respect for evidence and logical argument.

Don't Question Motivations

As noted earlier, faculty members, colleges, and departments have varying motivations for working with the credit programming unit. Given continuing educators' dedication to serving adult learners, credit programming unit administrators may be tempted to be skeptical or even contemptuous of motivations that fall short of altruism. This is a temptation to be avoided. Rather, people should be met on their own terms. Judging the motives of colleges and departments often occurs because unit administrators are so intent on "getting the job done." As a result, they only hear what is being said on the surface instead of really listening and understanding the perspectives of others, which is critical to developing good working relationships. When unit administrators feel the temptation to judge the motives of others, this should be a warning to stop, think, and ask, "Am I really listening to what is being communicated?"

This is not meant to imply that no effort should be made to build a faculty member's, college's, or department's commitment to serving adult learners. But if this commitment is an *a priori* condition for developing a working relationship, very little programming probably will result. Others' motivations are starting points, not barriers, for relationship and commitment building.

Support and Assist College Continuing Education Units

As alluded to in the "Introduction," at some institutions centralized continuing education offices coexist with decentralized and often parallel continuing education offices in selected academic colleges. These college offices may also have responsibility for continuing education credit course and degree programming. It is often tempting to view these units as competitors that should either be fought or, at best, ignored. This too is a temptation to be avoided. Instead, the credit programming unit should support, assist, and share expertise with college continuing education units and the individuals who administer them.

This approach is not only essential to building good working relationships across the campus (with the particular college and other colleges, as well as with campus leadership), but it also supports the mutual sharing of information and expertise among all the units concerned with extending credit course and degree program opportunities to adult learners, something which is integral to creatively and effectively serving different adult client groups. It is important to recognize that these college programming units also control resources, in the form of additional course offerings, which may be needed by the adult learners who are served by the credit programming unit. Therefore, rather than seeing these college offices as competitors, programming unit administrators should view them as units worthy of support and assistance, as units that also have experiences, information, and expertise of value to the credit programming unit, and as units that have valuable resources for the adult learners the credit programming unit serves.

CAMPUS LEADERSHIP

Developing and maintaining relationships with campus leaders requires many of the same things required in working with faculty members, colleges, and departments. Listening, understanding, and being candid, for example, are equally applicable to working with this group. But there are other strategies that must be employed in working with campus leaders, and these are reviewed here.

Be Responsive

Programming unit administrators should be responsive to campus leaders' requests, interests, and agendas. Although these may at times appear to be disruptions to the unit, failure to be responsive can seriously damage good working relationships. If requests and agendas place undue burdens on the programming unit, their effect should be communicated, and ways of modifying the expectations should be explored within the context of responsiveness.

Represent the Institution Well

The programming unit's work and programs are a reflection on and of the entire institution. The unit therefore needs to work within the context of the institution's mission, to carry out responsibilities in a professional manner, and to project the appropriate institutional image in programming and publicity. Success in these areas will communicate to campus leaders that credit programming unit administrators not only understand the institution and their vision of it, but that the unit is also contributing to the realization of that vision.

Assist in Problem Solving and Strengthening the Institution

Instead of creating problems for campus leaders, assist them in solving their problems and those of the institution. Letting programming unit problems come to the attention of leaders in search of a solution only interferes with good relationships. It is critical that the unit solve its own problems, while ensuring that its programming contributes to institutional vitality. It is also important for unit administrators to position the unit to be a solver of problems for campus leaders rather than a requester of assistance from them. For example, supplying current, accurate, and relevant research data about particular legislative districts to university presidents when they appear before legislative committees is a type of service that credit programming units can often provide. This form of assistance builds relationships as well as internal support for the unit (Votruba, 1987).

Use Formal Communication Channels Well

Because credit programming unit administrators are not close to campus leadership on the institution's organizational chart, direct lines of communication are seldom available for frequent use. However, times do arise when information is requested either directly or through superiors, when meetings are called where face-to-face communications with campus leaders can occur, and when situations arise that require communications with campus leaders through formal channels. When these infrequent opportunities do arise, it is important to use them well. Information about the unit's total program of offerings can be shared so that those in leadership positions can become more informed about the work of the unit and its contributions to the institution. These occasions may also provide opportunities to bring the unit's special needs and problems to the attention of the campus leadership.

Use Informal Channels of Communication

At times, informal channels of communication (or at least the lines of communication open to a unit administrator) should be employed to communicate with campus leaders. This is especially effective when the problems the unit faces are also those of others who have more direct access to campus leaders. As in many other cases, networking is again the key.

Provide Pertinent Information Succinctly

It is important that campus leaders be provided relevant and pertinent information. Campus leaders are barraged with demands on their time and with requests for their attention to a variety of problems and needs. When communication opportunities do arise, programming unit administrators must ensure that the information provided is on-target and succinct. Extraneous and poorly formulated information only clouds the issues and detracts from the messages being sent. It may also reduce the limited number of communication opportunities if unit administrators are perceived as not using leaders' time appropriately and well.

CLIENT GROUPS

Again, many of the strategies already outlined are equally applicable for building and maintaining relationships with client groups. However, one strategy already covered bears repeating and an additional strategy needs to be introduced.

Be Candid

In working with client groups, programming unit administrators must be candid about the limitations of what the programming unit and the institution can do for them. While responding to requests and meeting needs is important, neither the institution nor the programming unit can be all things to all people. Therefore, unit administrators should be up front about limitations. Promising more than can be delivered is not only ethically questionable, it is also administratively imprudent.

Get to Know Client Group Representatives Well

When clients are represented by an individual, it is important to get to know the representative well. Although neither the programming unit administrator nor the client group representative has formal power over the other in an interorganizational, cooperative relationship, personal power and expert power can be at unit administrators' disposal if they take the time to develop the foundations for them. This requires frequent contact with representatives, sharing information with them, listening to and understanding the clients' problems and concerns, and dealing with these if possible.

Changes in policies and procedures must be communicated well in advance so that appropriate adjustments can be made within the other organization in timely fashion. Site visits to the other organization should be made. These extra efforts show concern for them. Finally, unit administrators should work with the representative in a team environment to solve mutual problems and to improve the efficiency, effectiveness, and quality of programming.

SUMMARY

This chapter has outlined some practical means for developing and maintaining effective working relationships with faculty members, colleges, departments, campus leadership, and client groups. Strengthening these relationships requires the constant attention and effort of credit programming unit administrators. In the process, they often have to do a balancing act in order to manage the needs and interests of everyone concerned. However, by positioning oneself as a "nerve-center" of information and by dealing with others in a candid, forthright, and understanding way, an administrator can develop and maintain effective working relationships. These relationships are crucial to effective day-to-day unit operation and to development of the unit's overall strategic planning.

Chapter 4
Working With Faculty

Faculty members are one of the most important institutional resources for the continuing education credit programming unit. Yet, as anyone who has ever worked in continuing higher education knows, faculty members are also a limited, and very often hesitant, resource. They have many other demands placed upon their time. And the rewards for continuing education and public service activities are seldom as great as those for research and publication. As a result, their participation in credit courses and programs does not come easily.

When they do participate, however, faculty members have the major responsibility for designing educational experiences and for teaching adults. By virtue of this responsibility, they have more direct contact with individual members of client groups than programming unit administrators can ever hope to achieve. Their success in working with adult learners will therefore have a direct impact upon the success and quality of the continuing education credit unit's programs.

This chapter considers three important aspects of working with faculty members: (1) developing rewards for campus faculty participation in credit courses and programs, (2) working with non-university instructors, and (3) orienting faculty to work with adult learners.

REWARDS FOR PARTICIPATING IN CREDIT COURSES AND PROGRAMS: A MULTIFACETED AND INTEGRATED APPROACH

Developing faculty rewards for participation in continuing education credit courses and programs is a complex topic. It requires focusing on three institutional levels: campus policies and procedures; college and departmental policies, procedures, and needs; and the motivation of individual faculty members. It also requires an understanding of (1) role theory, especially when faculty members are assigned to participate as part of their normal responsibilities; (2) intrinsic and extrinsic patterns of motivation, and (3) the need to maintain a relative balance between role expectations, intrinsic rewards, and extrinsic incentives (Katz & Kahn, 1978). And it requires a focus upon work satisfaction factors and the need to eliminate disincentives that can have a negative impact upon faculty participation. In short, supporting faculty involvement in continuing education credit programming requires an integrated and multifaceted approach. To be effective in this area, programming unit administrators must be armed with an understanding of the dynamics involved in this aspect of programming, as well as with the ability and resources to support faculty involvement along several dimensions.

Institutional Policies and Perspectives

The work that has been done on institutional policies and procedures for developing faculty rewards for continuing education activities has focused on integrating continuing education into the primary reward system of the institution. This work suggests that four issues must be addressed: obtaining support of campus leadership, defining faculty participation in continuing education credit programming as instruction, developing supportive policies and procedures, and gaining support of individual colleges and departments and their leaders. Each issue is discussed below.

Obtaining Support of Campus Leadership. The most fundamental of these issues is to obtain the support of campus leaders for faculty participation in credit programming. Without support from the top, much of what else is done becomes unoperationalized rhetoric. Faculty participation may be mentioned in policy documents and referred to in speeches. But as long as campus leaders do not operationalize policy statements in reviewing tenure and promotion papers, another message is sent to faculty, colleges, and departments: "Continuing education simply does not count toward tenure or promotion."

Defining the Activity as Instruction. Faculty participation in continuing education credit courses and programs should be defined and viewed as instruction and not as continuing education or public service (Votruba, 1978). This perspective permits several things to occur. Instruction is a more clearly defined activity in the minds of faculty members than are either continuing education or public service. Viewing credit courses and programs as instruction grounds the activity in one of the major two activities and value systems of higher education. It helps the continuing education credit programming unit achieve at least partial parity within the value structure of the institution (Clark, 1956; Donaldson, 1988a). (Full parity could be achieved at many institutions only if participation in courses and programs were on a par with research and publication.) It permits faculty members to be evaluated for their participation in a manner similar to (if not the same as) the way they are evaluated for resident instruction.

To the extent that continuing education credit instruction is done as part of faculty members' regular loads, data can also be collected to report on faculty, departmental, and college instructional activities. These reports, in turn, can be used in resource allocation decisions made by campus leadership (Hanna, 1981a). Continuing education credit instruction done as part of faculty members' regular loads can therefore serve either to maintain or to increase a college's or department's resources. Part-of-load instruction can also serve to better integrate continuing education instruction into the fabric of college and department programming and thereby contribute to the quality of offerings.

Developing Supportive Campus Policies. Appropriate policies and procedures must be developed and accepted at the campus level. These policies should address not only the importance in the tenure and promotion process of faculty participation in continuing education credit programming, but also the ways in which this participation will be documented and evaluated (Votruba, 1978; Elman & Smock, 1985). In a study done at the University of Illinois at Urbana–Champaign, it was found that most faculty members simply listed their involvement in continuing education activities in their tenure and promotion papers, failing to provide evidence of either the quality of their involvement or its impact on or beyond the campus. As a result, tenure and promotion committees summarily dismissed these activities in their tenure and promotion decisions (Hanna, 1981a, 1981b).

To rectify this situation, faculty members were encouraged to collect evidence of the quality and impact of their involvement in continuing education activities. "A Faculty Guide for Relating Continuing Education and Public Service to the Promotion and Tenure Review Process" (University of Illinois at Urbana–Champaign, 1981) was developed to assist faculty members (1) in understanding the importance of emphasizing continuing education and public service activities that made contributions to their field and (2) in planning the collection of data that demonstrated the quality and impact of their efforts.

Gaining College and Departmental Support. Obtaining the support of campus leadership for faculty participation in credit programming, defining participation as instruction, and developing supportive policies and procedures are necessary preconditions to faculty participation, but they are insufficient unless colleges, departments, and their leaders are also supportive. Programming unit administrators must work with each college and department to ensure that campus policies are implemented in ways that meet college and departmental needs. One need that all academic units have is to see junior faculty members, in whom they have invested much, receive tenure. Programming unit administrators should work with colleges and departments in communicating and interpreting campus policies and assisting academic units and individual faculty members in gathering data that support faculty members' cases for tenure and promotion.

As noted earlier, however, each college and department also has different needs that the unit administrator must attend to. This is no less true when faculty rewards are considered. For example, some units in which enrollments are declining may see continuing education as a means to bolster enrollments. In this situation, part-of-load instruction *coupled* with generation of reports that provide evidence of instructional activity will be necessary for the college and department to support its faculty members' participation.

In other instances, enrollment pressures on colleges and departments may be great, and other mechanisms must be used to support faculty participation within the context of faculty rewards. Two means of giving this support are using distance education delivery methods and providing additional faculty positions for the colleges and departments. Distance education delivery methods can be used to extend faculty members' student loads without increasing their course loads. Courses can be taught on the campus while they are being delivered or taped for later distribution to off-campus locations. These modes of delivery can reduce the time that faculty members would otherwise spend in continuing education credit instruction while also increasing the instructional productivity of faculty members, colleges and departments.

Another mechanism that needs to be explored is providing faculty positions to colleges and departments, with the understanding that these additional resources will be used to facilitate academic unit participation in continuing education credit programming. Although this means of support is generally more costly than overload payments to faculty members, it has the advantages of ensuring part-of-load instruction, obtaining program commitment from colleges and departments, and integrating continuing education credit programming into the day-to-day instructional activities of academic units.

The Individual Dimension

Although much can be done at the organizational level to support faculty involvement in continuing education, programming unit administrators must also attend to the motivations of individual faculty members and how individual incentives interrelate with the organizational dimensions of participation.

The Part-of-load Dilemma and Balancing Motivational Rewards

Much can be gained through faculty participation in credit programming on a part-of-load basis. However, an inherent tension may crop up in these assignments. Faculty members who teach adults on an overload basis can choose to participate or not. In contrast, faculty members who teach in a continuing education credit program on a part-of-load basis either have no choice or a limited range of choice about their participation. If they do not also have an intrinsic commitment to teaching adults or do not receive some extrinsic payoffs for participating, they might rebel (Katz & Kahn, 1978) and the quality of instruction might decrease (Donaldson, 1988b).

The dilemma of part-of-load instruction points out the need for programming unit administrators to heed the advice of Katz and Kahn (1978) to have an integrated and multifaceted reward system that also maintains a relative balance among intrinsic rewards, extrinsic motivators, and the assignment of duties. Some means of providing an integrated approach at the individual level are outlined below.

Attending to the Faculty Members' Resources

For faculty members, one of the most valuable resources is time. For many, no amount of extra compensation for participation in continuing education activities is worth the time they would lose to conduct additional research, publish, or consult. Since most continuing education credit activities require more time of faculty than residence instruction does, it is important whenever possible to reduce the time commitment of faculty and to compensate them through some form of differential pay.

As mentioned earlier, resident and off-campus teaching can be integrated through the use of distance education technologies to increase student loads instead of course loads. Yet increased student loads also demand additional time of instructors. Providing of grading stipends or grading assistance are ways to recognize and compensate faculty members for taking on an increased student load. Traveling to off-campus teaching locations takes much more time than simply walking down the hall from office to classroom. At the University of Illinois at Urbana–Champaign, a travel dislocation allowance is given to faculty, whether they teach on a part-of-load or on an overload basis. Payment is based on miles traveled during a semester to teach an off-campus course (Hanna, 1981b).

Recognizing and Rewarding Excellence. Faculty members can be recognized and rewarded for their participation in continuing education activities through an award program that acknowledges excellence in teaching adults (Donaldson, 1988a, 1988b). Such a program provides an extrinsic reward in the form of praise and recognition. A monetary component to the award provides yet another extrinsic motivator. Although an award program can be operated by the continuing education unit, it is better to integrate the program with campuswide instructional award programs that most institutions sponsor. This integration helps to further define participation in the continuing education credit courses and programs as instruction, thereby increasing its value to the campus community and to those faculty members who participate. And integration of the award program into a campus ritual, such as a teaching awards banquet where the value of excellent teaching is celebrated, provides an important symbol in the management of meaning—the meaning of the credit programming unit's activities for the institution as a whole.

One should not overlook the national and regional awards provided by professional associations and other groups as means to recognize and reward faculty members for their participation. For example, several divisions and regions of the National University Continuing Education Association provide awards for the contributions that faculty members make in different types of programming. These awards also provide extrinsic rewards for faculty members, but because of their regional and national character the awards also add to the status of faculty members on their campuses.

It is not enough, however, to be aware of these national and regional awards and communicate their availability to faculty members. Rather, credit programming unit staff should actively encourage faculty members to apply (in itself a form of recognition) and help them develop their applications for the awards. This assistance can be provided by accumulating relevant data and other information, suggesting how the application should be developed, reviewing the application and recommending improvements, and providing clerical and other in-kind support in preparing the application.

Encouraging, Supporting, and Participating in Faculty Research. Defining faculty participation in credit programming as instruction and building an integrated reward system around this reconceptualization is a potent strategy. But programming unit administrators must not forget that research and publication remain the chief criteria by which faculty are evaluated at most universities. Therefore, encouraging, supporting, and participating in faculty research is a critical component in any integrated reward system. Participation of faculty in continuing education credit programming provides a fertile area for two major forms of research: that related to continuing education credit programming itself and that related to research in faculty members' own fields.

Research can be encouraged by giving faculty members some examples of ways they might conduct research related to their participation in the unit's programs. For example, research can address (1) the teaching of adults, (2) the circumstances different groups of part-time learners face in their studies, (3) models of course and program development for different groups of part-time learners, and (4) the use and instructional effectiveness of different distance education technologies. These are all research areas that faculty members have addressed and can still address through their participation in continuing education credit courses and programs.

It is important to emphasize that these and other areas can be researched from faculty members' unique professional and disciplinary perspectives. Research on continuing education credit programming does not necessarily have to be grounded in adult and continuing education literature. In fact, cross-disciplinary or multidisciplinary perspectives on the field add richness and depth of insight that can benefit the whole of continuing education. Finally, encouraging research on continuing education credit programming must be coupled with giving faculty members information about publication vehicles other than the publication outlets of their own fields.

Research can also be encouraged by highlighting ways in which faculty members can use their participation to facilitate research in their own fields. By working with adults who may be practicing professionals associated with business, industry, school districts, and social service agencies, faculty can (1) be made aware of current problems in need of research and (2) develop relationships with students and organizations that can lead to consulting, research support, or joint research projects. When faculty members travel off-campus to teach, they can also take advantage of being in the field setting without bearing the cost of travel.

Although encouraging of research by faculty members is necessary, it is insufficient. Whenever possible, means must be found to support their research. This can be done in several ways. In-kind support of faculty research can be given, for example, through mailing survey questionnaires, by providing institutional data related to a faculty member's research topic, by providing secretarial and clerical support, and by having office graduate assistants and undergraduate help assist in literature searches. Direct support of research can also be provided. A minimum of additional travel funding can be provided, for example, to permit faculty members to stay overnight in an off-campus location to collect data. The credit programming unit can also set aside some discretionary funding to be distributed to participating faculty on a competitive basis to support their research agendas. Review of proposals should be a shared responsibility of colleges or departments and credit programming unit staff. To the extent that academic units can be encouraged to provide matching funds, the research activities, as well as faculty participation in credit programming, become better recognized and more fully integrated into college and departmental activities.

Finally, programming unit administrators can join in team research efforts with faculty members. By participating in research with faculty members, administrators can support projects through their contributions of time and expertise. The unit will benefit through improved professional practice that can come from research findings. An administrator's participation in the most valued academic activity also helps develop strong professional ties between faculty and unit administrators. It also contributes in no small measure to others' perceptions of programming unit administrators as experts.

Eliminating and Controlling Disincentives and Negative Motivators. Programming unit administrators also need to focus on maintenance factors (Herzberg, 1966). Although the elimination and control of disincentives are insufficient for fostering faculty participation, the failure to eliminate or control them can interfere with the motivating factors outlined above (Donaldson & Walker, 1986). The credit programming office must try to make faculty participation as "hassle-free" as possible; for example:

1. Information about the unit's policies and procedures has to be fully communicated and explained to faculty.

2. Travel to off-campus locations must be well orchestrated.

3. Information should be provided about the communities where faculty members will be teaching.

4. Distance education technologies must be made as user friendly as possible.

5. Classrooms must be accessible, open, and comfortable.

6. Administrative details such as student registrations, class cancellations, and reimbursement for travel expenses must be handled smoothly.

7. Staff members must be readily available to provide support services and local contact, especially for faculty members who teach at a distance from campus. Failure to attend to these important details will serve only to negate the benefits of developing a comprehensive reward system for faculty participation in the unit's programs.

This section has provided several examples and suggestions for developing a reward system for faculty participation in continuing education credit programming. The unique context of each credit programming unit will determine in part what specific rewards can be made available to faculty. Whatever rewards are developed, however, they must fit into an integrated and multifaceted reward system if they are to contribute effectively to faculty participation.

WORKING WITH NON-UNIVERSITY INSTRUCTORS

So far in this chapter we have focused exclusively on campus-based faculty. But credit programming units have another source of instructors that they must not overlook—non-university faculty. The use of

non–university individuals to teach credit courses varies among institutions. Some rely almost exclusively on non-university instructors; others
rely almost exclusively on campus-based instructors. The nature of the use
of non-university individuals also varies within institutions. Strother and
Klus (1982), for example, distinguish between ad hoc faculty, who are paid
on a course-by-course basis, and adjunct faculty, who are appointed by the
university on the basis of a continuing part-time commitment to teach in a
particular department's program. The extent to which non-university individuals are used as course instructors, as well as the mixture of ad hoc and
adjunct faculty in a unit's overall program, will affect the nature of the credit
programming unit's work in two ways: in its internal systems and procedures for obtaining non-university instructors and managing their employment, and in its working relationships with colleges, departments, and
campus-based faculty.

The University—Non-University Instructor Connection

The connection between university and non-university instructors is
based on a combination of motivations: those of the university for seeking
out non-university persons, and those of non-university persons for pursuing teaching opportunities in continuing education programs. Credit programming units usually employ non-university people for at least three
reasons. The first is a university policy and strategic decision to use non-
university instructors as the primary instructional resource. Several of the
more nontraditional degree programs have been developed along this
particular model. The second reason is a shortage of faculty resources on the
campus, which occurs from a lack of (1) enough faculty members to teach
in the credit unit's programs, (2) necessary interest or motivation of full-
time faculty, or (3) requisite expertise and experience among campus-based
faculty to teach certain courses. In this last case, non-university persons, by
virtue of their experience and expertise, can provide an invaluable resource
to the credit programming unit's instructional programs. The third reason is
that using non-university instructors provides yet another means of developing and building relationships with outside organizations and groups. For
example, employing instructors from business, industry, and school districts, strengthens the links with potential pools of participants. Likewise,
relationships between academic units and their external stakeholders (for
example, between an academic department and a professional association)
can be enhanced (Donaldson, 1989a).

Universities seek out well-qualified non-university people for instructors, but these people also look for opportunities to teach for universities for
a variety of reasons. First, teaching in a continuing education credit unit's
courses and programs gives them an additional source of income. Second,

for some, association with a university gives them added status that assists them in their jobs or meets a particular psychological need they have. Third, working for a university gives individuals, and the organizations for which they work, a means to develop relationships with the university, and especially with certain academic departments and faculty members. Finally, some individuals want to teach in a credit unit's courses and programs simply for the love of teaching and working with adult learners.

These motivations refocus our attention on the importance of role expectations, intrinsic rewards, and extrinsic incentives in working with faculty. These principles are no less important for non-university instructors, and they should be taken into account when recruiting, selecting, and developing this particular instructional resource.

Recruiting and Selecting Non-University Instructors

The recruitment of non-university instructors can range from the simple to the complex. For credit programming units that rely heavily upon this instructional resource, recruitment of a cadre of qualified instructors is a critical process. A great deal of time and effort is expended to develop promotional procedures, including advertising, to attract a sufficient pool of individuals from which the most highly qualified instructors can be selected. When non-university instructors provide only a small proportion of instruction, recruitment procedures are much more informal. Instructors are recruited on an "as-needed" basis by credit programming unit administrators working through heads of departments to identify qualified instructors; they are recruited by campus-based faculty members as they work with outside organizations and groups; and applications to teach on a part-time basis are simply received by academic departments and credit programming units from individuals who, for whatever reason, wish to teach for the unit.

Although recruitment is important, even more critical are the criteria and procedures used to select individuals to become non-university instructors. The procedures again range from the simple to the complex, depending upon the level of a unit's use of non-university instructors and the nature of the relationship (whether ad hoc or adjunct) between the institution and the non-university person. Irrespective of their level of complexity, however, the procedures must ensure three things: (1) that the person has the requisite expertise, content mastery, and academic preparation to teach in the program, (2) that the individual has the ability and skills to teach adults effectively, and (3) that the credit programming unit staff recognizes and values the expertise and authority of the college or department in assessing the non-university faculty member's credentials. This last element helps to establish mutual respect.

Making the decision about a person's academic preparation should be the sole responsibility of the academic unit that sponsors the course to be taught. Usually this decision is based on a review of the person's resume and perhaps an interview. Although academic preparation and content mastery are essential credentials for an instructor, they are insufficient. The person must also be a good teacher of adults.

Making a decision about the person's ability and skills in teaching adults is the more difficult part of the overall decision about whether to hire a person as an instructor. First, it requires the attention of the sponsoring academic unit, since in most cases employing instructors is its prerogative. Again, good working relationships with academic units are critical. Without them, the importance of instructional skills cannot be adequately communicated to, understood by, and acted on by the academic unit. Second, it requires at least two other components in the selection procedure. The first is an interview. The interview should explore an applicant's experience with and approach to the teaching of adults. It is preferable (although not always possible) for credit programming unit administrators to participate in this process. If administrators are unable to participate, those conducting the interview should clearly understand the importance of exploring these dimensions with the applicant. The second component is a thorough check of the applicant's references. It is important to determine how applicants relate to other adults with whom they work and to learn about their track record (if they have one) in teaching adults. Although neither of these two additional components in the selection process guarantees that the person will be a successful instructor of adults, each does provide additional information upon which judgments can be made.

Individuals who administer credit programs that rely heavily upon non-university instructors may wish to consider using more sophisticated selection procedures like the assessment center approach of Regis College in Colorado (Paprock, 1988). This approach includes five activities:

1. An interview in which the interviewer assesses applicants' attitudes towards teaching, learning, adult education and nontraditional teaching techniques

2. An in-basket exercise which assesses applicants' evaluation skills and the type and quality of feedback they are able to give learners

3. An oral presentation in which applicants' abilities and skills in teaching and relating to an adult audience are assessed

4. An essay that is used to assess applicants' writing ability and the congruence of their philosophy with that of the institution and the sponsoring academic unit

5. A group discussion surrounding a group consensus problem that is used to assess applicants' ability to work with others and facilitate the group process.

Research has suggested that people who do well in the assessment process also do well in the adult classroom, thereby making up for the weaknesses in relying only upon interviews and references (Paprock, 1988). The sophistication and complexity of this process require many more resources than perhaps can be justified for the employment of ad hoc instructors or for units who rely little on the use of non-university instructors. However, the assessment center procedures do suggest some other means that might be considered in building more sophistication and predictability into the selection process.

Even the most sophisticated process does not guarantee complete success. There are times when non-university instructors perform poorly in the classroom, and steps must be taken to prevent future poor performance. Sometimes the difficulty can be addressed through faculty development activities. But more often the programming unit will want to dismiss the person from instructional responsibilities. Dismissal requires working closely with sponsoring academic units. They must be made to understand the difficulty that poor performance creates not only for the programming unit, but for the institution and the academic unit as well. And they must be assisted in devising strategies to deal with the situation.

For ad hoc instructors, this process may be as simple as not asking the person in question to teach again and focusing upon finding another person to teach the course. For adjunct instructors who teach with the understanding of a continuing part-time commitment to the credit programming unit's and academic department's program, the process required is more complex. It may be possible in such cases to reassign these people to other duties, while permitting them to maintain their association with the institution and academic unit. But it may also require sensitivity, good human relations skills, use of due process procedures, confirming memos noting discussions with them about their inadequate performance, and following the same institutional policies and procedures required in severing the relationship of employees with the institution. Although credit programming unit administrators seldom have primary responsibility for dismissing an instructor, they have to work closely with academic units to carry out this responsibility with sensitivity so that the incident does not damage the credit programming unit's relationship with the academic unit.

Four Principles for Working with Non-University Instructors

Carefully attending to the procedures and criteria for selecting non-university instructors can reduce the probability of their dismissal. Attending to four other principles will also reduce this probability and will assist in the dismissal process if it becomes necessary.

Clearly Communicate Expectations. The credit programming unit must clearly communicate what it expects of non-university instructors. This must include communications about university and unit policies and procedures such as those on course scheduling, required contact hours, and grading. Likewise, non-university instructors should be told what support will be routinely given them by the credit programming unit, as well as what types of support are generally unavailable. The credit programming unit must also be clear about what pay the instructor will receive for teaching, what expenses will be covered, and how payment and reimbursements are to be handled.

Academic departments also have a responsibility to communicate to the instructor what content is to be covered in a course and at what level. They should also be responsible for communicating their expectations about the quality of instruction that is envisioned. The credit programming unit may need to work with academic units to ensure that these expectations have been communicated.

If these expectations are not clearly communicated, instructors may not adequately fulfill their instructional obligations as expected, with the added consequence of poor evaluations of their performance. Because of poor communication, instructors may expend funds that the unit cannot reimburse, or they may not understand the basis for their pay. The repercussions of not communicating expectations can also go beyond poor performance and lead to bad feelings all around—feelings that can seriously interfere with the good working relations necessary in this situation.

Involve Non-University Instructors in the Life of the Academic Department. Non-university instructors are being asked to represent the institution and a particular academic department in their dealings with adult learners. The more they know about the policies of a department, its curriculum, and its expectations about instruction, the better they will be able to represent the institution and perform well. Although communication of expectations through contracts and distribution of materials will help in this process, whenever possible non-university instructors should be included in the life of the academic department. They should be invited to faculty meetings and social events with faculty and students so that they can get to know other faculty members, learn how the courses they teach fit into the department's curriculum, and begin to understand some of the academic issues in the department. They should also routinely receive departmental communications that deal with curricular and instructional issues. If involved properly, non-university instructors can also provide valuable perspectives and information in departmental deliberations about continuing education credit activities.

Credit programming units must often take responsibility for facilitating this form of involvement by encouraging departments to reach out to non-university instructors. The programming unit, when necessary and possible, may also have to support non-university instructors' travel to attend faculty meetings. Although not routinely a component of the development of non-university instructors, quality involvement in the life of the academic unit contributes much to the effective use of this important instructional resource.

Non-University Instructors Should Not Teach Persons Who Report to Them. As noted earlier, one of the motivations for universities and credit programming units to seek out non-university instructors is to foster relationships with outside organizations and groups. In this situation, the path of least resistance is often to assign these individuals to teach learners who are also their subordinates. This practice should be avoided at all costs. Seldom can supervisors and subordinates cast aside their work roles when they enter the classroom. As a result, the academic freedom the instructor requires in grading is compromised, role relationships conducive to a good work environment may actually interfere with the development of an environment conducive to learning, and what goes on in the classroom may have a negative effect within the work environment of instructor and students alike. The potential compromises and harm inherent in this situation are often not understood by academic departments and non-university instructors. Consequently, credit programming unit administrators have not only a role in establishing this principle as policy, but also in explaining its rationale to all affected parties.

Non-University Faculty Members Should Be Viewed as Resources to Be Developed. Non-university instructors should be viewed as resources worthy of further growth and development as instructors of adults. Significant time, energy, and resources are expended in recruiting and selecting non-university instructors and in administering the instruction for which they are responsible. If this investment is to have a payoff, non-university instructors must be as effective as they can be in teaching the programming unit's clients. Therefore, their professional development in this area must be fostered. It is to this topic that we now turn our attention.

ORIENTING FACULTY MEMBERS TO TEACHING ADULTS

A major responsibility of credit programming unit administrators is to help faculty members, whether campus-based faculty or non-university instructors, prepare to teach adults and to contribute to continued faculty development. But unit administrators must be sensitive to faculty member, college, and departmental prerogatives about instruction. Administrators cannot simply represent themselves as unabashed experts in this area without inviting negative responses. Rather, their approach should incorporate accurate, practical and up-to-date information, sensitivity to faculty prerogatives, and multiple and politically sensitive methods of communicating information.

Distribute Relevant and Practical Literature

Distributing practice-oriented literature written by recognized experts for all participating faculty members' information is one effective means of assisting faculty in their teaching of adults. For example, an especially useful guide for non-university instructors is *Enjoying the Challenge: A Guide for Part-Time Instructors* (Hofstrand & Kozoll, 1986). This material can be handed out as it becomes available, or it can be included in packets of material the unit distributes at the beginning of each term to inform faculty of unit policies and procedures.

Include the Topic of Teaching Adults in Faculty Orientation Programs

Most credit programming units offer orientation programs for participating faculty members at the beginning of each academic year or more frequently. These programs provide an excellent opportunity for the topic of teaching adults to be considered. Non-university instructors should be encouraged to attend these sessions, especially if they live in the same community or, if few in number, their travel expenses to attend the orientation can be reimbursed. If large numbers of adjunct instructors who live a distance from campus are employed, then it may be best to offer orientation sessions for them in their communities. It is important in this case to take campus-based faculty members or faculty program coordinators to this off-campus orientation session. Doing so fosters communications between non-university and campus-based instructors, and it also allows campus-based faculty to talk about the specifics of teaching their particular subject matter to adults.

One effective technique for dealing with this topic in an orientation program is to invite a faculty member who is respected by other faculty for his or her expertise in this area to make a presentation. (This can be a non-university instructor if the orientation is primarily for non-university instructors.) Having "one of their own" speak on how to teach adults will be accepted more readily and have a more significant impact than will presentations made by administrators, irrespective of how much expertise the administrators might have in this area. A second effective technique is having a panel of experienced instructors share their experiences with others. If chaired by a faculty member and facilitated in an open and supportive way, the panel discussion can serve as a springboard for information sharing and problem solving among peers.

These two techniques can be combined, and other techniques are also possible. The point is simply this: Considering the topic of teaching adults in orientation programs will be more effective if it is grounded in the sharing of experiences and expertise among faculty peers.

Work through Academic Unit Leadership to Support Faculty Instructional Development

Department heads and college deans have administrative responsibility for the instructional effectiveness of their faculty. Therefore, they are natural allies of programming unit administrators in this area. This mutual interest has become reinforced during the past several years as adults have continued to return to campus in increasing numbers. The ability to work effectively with adult students has become as critical an ingredient in resident instruction as it has traditionally been in continuing education.

Working with the leadership of academic units permits programming unit administrators to pursue their own agendas while integrating their efforts with those of department heads and deans and avoiding interfering in a faculty prerogative. It also provides a mechanism by which unit administrators can deal with problematic situations without becoming directly involved in a personnel matter that belongs within the domain of college and departmental leadership. Finally, academic unit leaders or their delegates often have experience in working with adults. Therefore, letting leadership intercede on behalf of the programming unit can result in peer tutoring of any faculty member (whether campus-based or non-university) in need of assistance.

Give Faculty Members Information and Advice When They Request It

The previous section is not meant to imply that programming unit administrators have no expertise in the teaching of adults. Rather, it is meant to highlight the tensions that arise, because of academic prerogatives, when administrators attempt to facilitate the development of faculty members as teachers. Suggestions have been made about techniques that can be used to facilitate faculty development without pointed forays into this domain. But occasions do arise when campus-based and non-university instructors request help and advice from programming unit administrators. In these instances, the administrators should respond in a sensitive and supportive manner, offering resources, information, and advice as the situation demands. Failure to act upon such requests communicates lack of expertise and interest to the very faculty members upon which the unit depends for the maintenance and growth of its total program.

SUMMARY

Faculty members are one of the most important resources for a continuing education credit programming unit. This chapter has reviewed ways to develop a multifaceted and integrated reward system to support this resource's participation in credit programming. It has also dealt with ways to recruit, select, and work with non-university instructors. The responsibility of programming unit administrators for faculty instructional development has been highlighted, as have ways that unit administrators can fulfill this obligation without treading upon academic prerogatives.

The manner in which programming unit administrators approach their work with faculty members is central to developing effective influence throughout the whole institution. For it is in and from the perceptions of the faculty that one's expertise, interpersonal skills, and position within the continuing education and campus organization are not only defined but also communicated to others. Good and supportive working relationships with faculty are as important to administrative effectiveness as is one's understanding of and work with colleges, departments, campus leaders, external organizations, and adult client groups.

Chapter 5
Evaluating Credit Courses and Programs

The issue of assuring high quality courses and programs cuts across all the activities in which the credit programming unit becomes involved. Central to the assurance of high quality programming is evaluation. But a unit's ability to conduct evaluations well can have other payoffs. It can do much to foster unit expertise, which will in turn strengthen the influence of unit administrators across the campus. Also, if the ownership of evaluations is shared, it can foster good working relationships with all the unit's stakeholders.

This chapter will briefly review some principles of program evaluation that have particular relevance to credit programming, highlight a few approaches to evaluating continuing education credit courses and programs, and describe three additional approaches that have not been commonly employed by programming units. Although not always made explicit, many of the concepts introduced earlier (especially in the chapter on developing and strengthening relationships) are applicable to the design and implementation of course and program evaluations.

EVALUATION PRINCIPLES IN CONTINUING EDUCATION CREDIT PROGRAMMING

Focus on the Purposes of Evaluation

How will evaluation results be used? This is a question that needs to be asked early in the planning of evaluations. The answer will determine in large measure the information collected, the data sources tapped, and the individuals and groups with whom results will be shared. Evaluation results can be used for accountability, for decision making, for policy development, and for strengthening internal support. If the evaluation has been effectively planned and conducted, the results can be used for all four purposes.

Accountability is important because credit courses and programs are so jealously guarded by the academic community. Evaluation must be employed as a means by which the credit programming unit, as well as colleges, departments, campus leaders, and client groups can judge the quality of the unit's operations and programs.

Evaluation results can also contribute to decision making about programs, procedures, and policies. In this case, evaluations should be designed so that the information obtained can contribute not only to the unit's decision making, but to that of academic departments and client groups as well. Academic departments can use evaluation results to identify improvements needed in their program planning, advising, and communications with students. Where courses and programs are offered on a contractual basis (for example, to businesses, school districts, or governmental units), the employing organization can use the evaluation results to improve the support provided adult learners.

The results can also be used in policy development. In many respects, this application is a blend of the decision making and accountability uses. Results can be provide evidence that supports the development of policies favorable to continuing education credit programming. Evaluation should also be included as a component of any program innovation. Given the skepticism and concern with which academic communities embark on changes in traditional programming, evaluation often becomes a necessary precondition to program experimentation. The academic community's acceptance of each successful innovation contributes in subtle and incremental ways to shifts in a campus's perspective on credit programming. As a result, innovations that are accompanied by high quality evaluations have the potential to influence policy and procedural decisions, which can reduce the constraints on the credit programming unit and its operation.

Finally, an evaluation and its results can be used to gain internal support, as well as external support (for example, from state legislators and local advisory boards). Well-developed evaluation procedures serve the symbolic purpose of communicating that the credit programming unit is not taking the quality of programming for granted and is concerned about program improvement. Also, results showing that the unit's programs are comparable in quality to residence programs (and most studies have shown this to be the case) provide information that can be communicated to influential others throughout the campus. Having a reputation for high quality programming and for understanding the importance of constantly monitoring course and program quality does much to strengthen the academic community's and external stakeholders' support for the programming unit.

However, in order to effectively use evaluation results for the purposes outlined above, evaluations must be conducted well. Faculty members will expect the same level of rigor and rationality in evaluations that they expect in their own and others' research. Otherwise, results will be considered invalid and will have only negative consequences for the unit, its total program, and others' perceptions of programming unit administrators' expertise.

Evaluate through Both Formal and Informal Means

Although formal evaluation provides results that can be used for accountability and decision making, programming unit administrators should not overlook the usefulness of obtaining evaluation information informally. Positioning themselves at a nerve center of information, administrators can gather information from campus leaders, colleges, departments, faculty members, and client groups. Information obtained informally through contacts with others often has as much or more value than information obtained through formal evaluation methods. This information can seldom be used for accountability, but it can be used by the programming unit to make corrections in its operations, and to improve its programming. It can also be passed along to others as input to their decision making and programming.

Be Open to Negative Feedback

It is critically important that programming unit administrators be open to negative feedback. Positive feedback obtained from evaluations and through other means confirms that what is being done is being done well, and such feedback is gratifying. But it provides no basis upon which to make adjustments and corrections in courses and programs or in the operation of the credit programming unit. Negative feedback is required to enable the programming unit to make continual adjustments and improvements.

Although negative feedback is often hard to take, it should actually be more highly valued because it, unlike positive feedback, provides the basis for action. To obtain this kind of feedback, however, requires an openness to it. It requires the willingness to include questions in evaluation instruments that might point out weaknesses, and it requires a sincere openness in relationships with faculty members, academic units, and client groups so that they will feel comfortable in providing negative feedback. It also requires helping others with whom the credit unit works to understand the value of negative feedback.

Look Beyond the Surface of Evaluation Results

In the press of day-to-day activities, unit administrators often find it difficult to make the time to look beyond the face value of evaluation results. To use the results effectively for course and program improvement and as a basis for rational argument for change, however, administrators must look beyond the surface level of results. Relying upon frequency counts and descriptive statistics is simply not enough (Schroeder & Donaldson, 1986). First, additional data analysis will generate insights and further questions that would otherwise remain unnoticed in descriptive statistics. For example, correlational analysis of evaluation data for an off-campus program of a large midwestern university resulted in finding that students' evaluation of quality was negatively correlated to the length of time the students spent in the program (Schroeder & Donaldson, 1986). Reliance upon descriptive statistics would not have uncovered this relationship and would not have raised the question of why some students took so long to complete it.

Second, additional data analysis also lends credibility to the validity and reliability of evaluation methods. Evaluation results are being reported to faculty members who are also scholars and researchers. Therefore, evaluation that goes beyond description will do much to improve the credibility and acceptability of results by the academy (Schroeder & Donaldson, 1986).

Be Involved in Establishing Evaluation Policy, Procedures and Criteria

Remember Dr. Stone in the first vignette of the "Introduction"? The negative interpretations he gave evaluation data resulted from his lack of understanding about continuing education credit programming and adult instruction. The probability of this occurrence would have been reduced had evaluation policy, procedures, and criteria included consideration of some special characteristics of credit programming. This is not meant to say that evaluations should not include criteria similar to those used to evaluate residence programs. Rather, it is meant to point out that the continuing education credit programming context differs from residence programming and instruction.

These differences must be taken into account if evaluations are to be valid. Continuing education credit programs can be comparable in quality to residence programs, but they cannot and should not be equivalent. Therefore, it is incumbent upon programming unit administrators to be actively involved in developing policies, procedures, and criteria for the evaluation of continuing education credit courses and programs to ensure that evaluations will provide appropriate and valid results.

Legitimize the Interpretation of Results

To legitimize interpretation of evaluation results, programming unit administrators must involve faculty members, college and department administrators, and campus leaders in the interpretation process. Representatives from various segments of the institution, including the credit programming unit and the sponsoring academic department, should be involved. This approach provides yet another way to avoid the difficulties described in the Dr. Stone vignette. It precludes unilateral interpretation by any one person or group. It also provides an opportunity for unit administrators to have input to data interpretation and to educate others about the different perspectives that should be taken into account when evaluating continuing education credit programs.

Include Procedures for Evaluation in Planning

Evaluation procedures should not be developed after the fact. Rather, they should be developed as part of planning. This is especially important when an academic department begins to develop plans for a certificate or degree program. Having the academic department consider evaluation as program plans are unfolding has several benefits. It draws attention to the fact that the program will be evaluated, thereby highlighting the need for careful planning. It requires a focus on the different components of a program (for example, courses, curriculum, advising, information provision) that will be evaluated. This fosters more careful consideration of each component during planning, and it helps communicate to academic departments what is needed to offer a high quality program. Finally, it helps identify and address problems before they occur. Including evaluation as part of planning highlights the need for a well-developed plan that anticipates various contingencies that may arise during program implementation.

These seven principles of evaluating continuing education credit courses and programs are applicable irrespective of the specific evaluation approach adopted by a credit programming unit. They not only ensure a focus upon high quality programming and course and program improvement, but they also help build internal support and strengthen working relationships across the institution.

A COMPREHENSIVE APPROACH TO EVALUATION

Since continuing education credit programs can range from isolated course offerings to certificate and degree programs, the full range of offerings should be taken into account in developing evaluation procedures. The unit of evaluation with which one must begin, however, is the course.

Course Evaluation

Course Instruction. Course evaluation may take one of three forms or some combination of these. The first is student evaluation of course instruction. These evaluations usually focus upon a number of instructional and course dimensions and are similar to or the same as evaluations of resident instruction. Course organization, instructor knowledge and preparation, and overall course and instructional quality are examples of dimensions covered in this form of course evaluation. To the extent that credit programming unit and college and department administrators receive results of these evaluations, information is gained about the quality of instruction in continuing education credit courses. This information can assist in planning faculty development efforts and in identifying faculty members whose instruction is either exemplary or in need of improvement.

Instructional Resources. The second form of course evaluation focuses upon resources needed if the quality of a course is to be comparable to that of resident courses. The focus upon resource requirements is especially crucial when courses are offered off campus, or on campus at times when the full array of campus instructional resources are unavailable. This form of evaluation requires obtaining information about resources needed for quality instruction before a course begins, as well as about faculty members' judgments of the quantity and quality of resources provided for their instruction. It also calls for recognizing that each individual faculty member will teach the same course in a unique way and will therefore need different instructional resources.

One example of this form of course evaluation has been developed at the University of Illinois at Urbana–Champaign. Before an academic term begins, instructors are sent a "Resources and Facilities Request Form." This form asks them to identify their particular needs for classroom facilities, duplication of materials, audio-visual equipment, and library and other instructional resources so that they can teach the course in a comparable fashion to the way they teach it on campus. This form is shared with those responsible for making the various instructional support arrangements. Instructors' requests are either met or modified to their satisfaction well before the courses begin.

At the end of the academic term, a "Resources and Facilities Follow-Up Form" is sent to instructors asking them to evaluate the provision of instructional resources for the course they have just taught. Items related to the quality of assistance provided by the credit programming unit and requesting suggestions for improvement are also included in this questionnaire. Thus the form is not only used to obtain feedback about the quality of instructional support, but is also used to obtain information about the unit's overall support of instructors' participation in courses and programs sponsored by the unit. The form therefore serves also as a tool through which information can be obtained for improving the credit unit's operation.

Impact. The first two types of evaluation focus, respectively, on process and inputs. What is missing is a focus upon outcomes. Although often more difficult to design and justify financially, evaluation that asks what impact a course has had on learners' personal and professional lives is also important. As will be noted later, this type of information can be obtained as part of program evaluation. However, mechanisms should also be in place to collect this information about the outcomes of isolated courses. Single course offerings are usually taken by nondegree students who enroll to achieve some specific personal or occupational goal. Therefore, information about how well courses are helping this group of learners to achieve their objectives is important.

Such evaluation provides information necessary for the design and instruction of these courses and communicates to nondegree students that the institution also values them, even though they are not pursuing a degree. If follow-up evaluations of this type cannot be justified for each course (because of logistical, financial, or other limitations), the programming unit might consider conducting a periodic evaluation of a random sample of nondegree students to determine how courses are meeting their needs. Such an evaluation can also be integrated with needs assessments for various groups of nondegree students and evaluations of marketing strategies.

Program Evaluation

If certificate or degree programs are offered, these must also be evaluated. Although course evaluations provide the foundation for program evaluation, they alone are insufficient. Program evaluation requires collecting data from many sources across a number of dimensions not addressed by course evaluation. Sources of data include students who have graduated or who are currently enrolled in the program, faculty members who teach and advise in the program, and the sponsoring department or college. The kind of information that can be collected from each source will differ somewhat. These are outlined below.

Students. Information that can be collected from students includes:

1. Socio-demographic information that will permit analysis of data based upon different learner characteristics

2. Students' perception of course quality

3. Judgments about the contributions a program has made to individual learning objectives

4. Students' perceptions of the helpfulness of support services

5. Students' perceptions about the quality of program advisement, including provision of information about the program, admissions, course planning, and personal concerns

6. Students' judgments about the impact a program has had upon their personal and professional lives

Information can also be collected about learners' motivations for continuing their education, their reasons for selecting the institution's program, and how they learned about the program. Although this information does not relate directly to program quality, collecting it as part of program evaluation provides a cost-effective means of gathering additional and vital data about program clientele and marketing.

Faculty Members. Information collected from faculty members can include:

1. Information about faculty members, such as academic rank, number of courses taught, and role (instructor, advisor, faculty program coordinator) in the program

2. Assessment of the adequacy of facilities and instructional resources

3. Their judgment about the quantity and quality of program information provided to them

4. The comparability of residence and continuing education credit courses with respect to subject matter, amount of material covered, assignments and examinations, student performance, and course quality

5. The comparability of residence and continuing education students with respect to student traits, such as academic abilities, motivation, and maturity

6. Their perceptions of the quality of program advisement

7. Their judgment of the overall quality of the program.

Information collected about faculty members permits analysis of data based upon faculty members' different levels of experience and roles in a program. Such detailed analysis can provide important insights about factors that contribute to faculty perceptions of quality. Gathering data about a variety of program specifics allows a focus upon different program components, so that the sources of any problems can be readily identified. Asking faculty members to assess program components also requires them to think through the quality of each component before making an overall judgment of program quality. This exercise increases the validity of the overall evaluation and serves to remind faculty members of the elements necessary in offering high quality continuing education credit programs.

Information about the comparability of courses and students must be collected with great care. The concept of comparability (in contrast to equivalence) must be emphasized. In addition, the use of nontraditional methods of course delivery and of awarding credit must be understood by faculty members before their judgments can be considered valid.

Sponsoring Department or College. The third source of data is the sponsoring college or department. The type of information collected at this level focuses on more global dimensions, such as:

1. Program description and history

2. Quantity and quality of faculty involvement in all aspects of the program

3. Program rationale and purpose(s)

4. Program coordination

5. Extent to which the program has complemented and supported the unit's teaching, research and service missions

6. Current program status and future plans

7. Current enrollment and graduates by year

8. Courses offered and enrollment by term and year

9. Course delivery and scheduling

10. Student progress

11. Criteria and standards for admission.

Evaluation data collected from students and faculty members focus upon each group's perceptions of quality. Information collected from the sponsoring college or department focuses, in contrast, upon some organizational dimensions related to the program—the academic unit's support and coordination of the program, the unit's rationale for offering it, and the program's fit with the unit's overall mission. Other information collected from the academic unit is related to global curricular dimensions such as student progress, adequacy and coherence of course offerings, and course scheduling and delivery. This information complements data obtained from students and faculty, thereby providing a more complete picture of the program than would otherwise be available.

Interpretation and Reporting

Once collected and assembled, the data must be interpreted and results reported through appropriate channels to the sponsoring college or department and the credit programming unit. As noted earlier, to obtain both legitimacy and objectivity in data interpretation it is important to involve a variety of persons in the interpretation process. Once reported, the results of the evaluation should serve as a means for the sponsoring department and the credit programming unit to correct any problems that have been identified and to highlight other areas upon which to focus in an effort to continually improve the program.

OTHER EVALUATION TOOLS

So far the procedures described in this chapter have concentrated on traditional evaluation methods. However, there are three infrequently used tools that can be profitably used by programming unit administrators to gain valuable insights about programs. These are transcript analysis, student tracking systems, and follow-up studies.

Transcript Analysis

Student transcripts can be an important source of institutional data about programming. Transcripts usually include (1) the age, gender, and previous educational accomplishments of students; (2) dates of program entry and completion; (3) a chronological listing of courses and credits earned; (4) information about students' academic performance; and (5) information about course completion and transfer credits. The information in transcripts can be used to answer a host of questions about a program. These fall into three major categories: student progress, curricular coherence, and curricular choice.

In the student progress category, one can determine the number of years and semesters it takes students to complete a program, the number of semesters students "stopped out" and took no courses, and the number of times students withdrew from courses. In the curricular coherence category, course-taking patterns can be analyzed, the extent of adherence to predetermined course sequences can be ascertained, and students' movement from one form of registration to another (for example, between on- and off-campus registration) can be established. In the curricular choice category, one can assess students' curricular efficiency (ratio of credits taken to credits required), the number of transfer credits in students' programs, and the makeup of their curriculum with respect to course level, electives and required courses, independent study courses, and integrating experiences (for example, internships and practica). By comparing courses taken by students with courses offered at a location by the institution, students' curricular choice and flexibility in taking a variety of courses can also be determined (Donaldson & LeGrand, 1988).

The value of transcript analysis lies in the richness of transcript data, the longitudinal perspective that transcripts provide, and the opportunity they offer for analyzing data along a number of student characteristics, including age, gender, program, and previous degree. To the extent that other data have been collected from students (for example, their perceptions of different dimensions of program quality), the data compiled from transcripts can be analyzed in relation to these other data. This gives yet another basis for obtaining valuable information about a program. For example, one can determine if there is a relationship between the curricular choice offered students and their perceptions of program quality (Donaldson & LeGrand, 1988).

Transcript analysis is very labor intensive, however. The analysis takes much time and can seldom be fully computerized. Programming unit administrators must therefore determine whether the information obtained from this technique is worth the investment of resources needed to undertake it. In addition, before analyzing students' transcripts, administrators must determine whether doing so is permitted by institutional policies and whether the analysis of transcripts conforms with state and federal regulations about informed consent and privacy.

Student Tracking Systems

Rich, longitudinal data can be obtained through student tracking systems. A student tracking system offers many of the same strengths as transcript analysis. But it has the added advantage of control by unit administrators. It uses a predetermined plan for data collection instead of relying upon retrospective analysis of data accumulated at the discretion of the registrar. Also, because the system is under control of the programming unit, problems with programs or problems that students are experiencing can be identified at the time instead of after they occur. A tracking system is also especially useful in reviewing issues related to student recruitment and retention.

Developing and operating a student tracking system has some of the same weaknesses as transcript analysis. It too is labor intensive. Data about students must be entered each term. And unless a computer program that fits all or most of a credit programming unit's specifications can be readily obtained, the cost of developing a student tracking computer program must also be borne. Again, costs must be weighed against benefits. An excellent source about student tracking systems and their design is *Establishing a Longitudinal Student Tracking System: An Implementation Handbook*, which was prepared by the National Center for Higher Education Management Systems (Ewell, Parker, & Jones, 1988).

Follow-Up Studies

Follow-up studies focus upon the impact that a program has had on the personal and professional lives of program graduates. These studies can be conducted on a one-time basis (cross-sectional design) or can follow graduates for several years (longitudinal design). The particular approach taken will depend upon the specific questions one wants to answer. Follow-up studies can consider the impact that programs have had on (1) students' employment (for example, full-time, part-time, and whether employed in the field trained for), (2) students' earning power, (3) job performance, (4) job satisfaction, (5) performance in students' personal lives, (6) general life satisfaction, and (7) a combination of these and other factors. But here, too, these studies are costly and labor intensive. They require identification of all graduates, careful design of questionnaires or interview guides, mail or telephone surveys, and data analysis that may be quite complex, perhaps requiring statistical consultation.

The three evaluation tools just suggested have two things in common. They provide rich information about programs that is unavailable through traditional methods. But they also are costly. Costs must therefore be weighed against benefits when considering any of these tools. One must keep in mind, however, that institutions of higher education are increasingly being held accountable for the impact of their programs. The same is true of continuing education credit programming units. The additional information obtained through transcript analysis, student tracking systems, and follow-up studies has much potential for contributing to the quality of local decision making and for providing rich insights into the impact that programs have on the personal and professional lives of adult learners.

SUMMARY

In this chapter several evaluation principles in continuing education credit programming have been detailed, some approaches to the evaluation of courses and programs have been suggested, and three special evaluation tools have been briefly reviewed. Offering high quality credit courses and programs is basic to a credit programming unit's acceptance and credibility. Well-developed evaluation policies and procedures contribute much to high quality programming. When conducted well and when ownership is shared, evaluation also builds support and strengthens relationships.

Conclusion
The Challenges of Credit Programming

Several themes have emerged throughout this discussion of continuing education credit programming units and the courses and programs they sponsor.

THE IMPORTANCE OF INFLUENCE

The first theme is that unit administrators must rely upon leverage, or influence, to effectively coordinate programs and to gain the institution's acceptance of policies and procedures that support the credit programming unit and the adult learners it serves. A programming unit administrator's ability to exercise influence is contingent upon a continuous process of building and maintaining good working relationships with a variety of programming unit stakeholders and upon the recognition of the administrator's managerial and educational expertise. Although leadership has always been required of deans of continuing education, today it is also being demanded of credit programming unit administrators.

During the past few decades higher education institutions have become more complex and their component parts have grown increasingly interdependent. As a result, the power once wielded by a few over an entire institution has been reduced, and leadership has been increasingly required of persons at lower organizational levels. Therefore, credit programming unit administrators can no longer limit their activities to program coordination. They must also take up the challenge of leadership.

THE COMPLEXITY OF CREDIT PROGRAMMING

A second theme is the comprehensive nature of organizing and administering credit courses and programs. As noted in the "Introduction," the administration of credit courses and programs requires most of the functions needed to run many small colleges. Administrators must simultaneously juggle needs assessment, budgeting, marketing, student recruitment and retention, program development, program coordination, faculty participation and development, budgeting and financing, various modes of course and program delivery, student support services, and course and program evaluation, while also attending to the demands and constraints imposed by external agencies and by the parent institution. Administrators must also contend with being caught in a constant tug-of-war between, on the one hand, serving the educational needs of client groups and, on the other, honoring the expectations of internal stakeholders and opinion leaders that

79

the credit programming unit and its programs in no way deviate from the institution's vision of quality.

Consequently, administering credit courses and programs requires much energy, a capacity to deal with plenty of ambiguity, flexibility in approach, a willingness to live vicariously, and the ability not to take oneself too seriously. It requires programming unit administrators to know their strengths and weaknesses and to schedule free time and personal time to avoid having the job become all-consuming.

OPPORTUNITIES AND LEADERSHIP

The third theme is opportunity. Continuing education credit programming has reached a stage of maturity during the past decade. The recognition of its importance is intensifying in continuing education and higher education alike. Credit programming is becoming more differentiated in form, level, and mode of delivery, thereby creating more opportunity for administrators to work with a variety of people across the campus and with a diversity of client groups.

The potential for stimulation and personal and professional growth through such opportunities is boundless. By being at the margins, administrators must also deal with the tension of having to be closely associated with the values and workings of the parent institution while also having to be innovative and represent the educational needs of adults. But from this tension arise opportunities for leadership. To take advantage of these opportunities, however, unit administrators must be willing to participate fully and proficiently in leading higher education into a new era of educational service to adults.

References

American Society for Training and Development (1983). *Models for excellence,* Baltimore: American Society for Training and Development Press.

Bennis, W. (1984). The 4 competencies of leadership. *Training and Development Journal, 38* (8), 14-19.

Clark, B. R. (1956). Organizational adaptation and precarious values: A case study. *American Sociological Review, 21,* 327-336.

Deal, T. E. (1987). Building an effective organizational culture: How to be community-oriented in a traditional institution. In R. Simerly & Associates, *Strategic planning and leadership in continuing education* (pp. 87-102). San Francisco: Jossey-Bass.

Donaldson, J. F. (1988a). Exemplary instruction of adults: The case of an excellence in off-campus teaching award, part I. *The Journal of Continuing Higher Education, 36* (1), 10-14.

Donaldson, J. F. (1988b). Exemplary instruction of adults: The case of an excellence in off-campus teaching award, part II. *The Journal of Continuing Higher Education, 36* (2), 11-18.

Donaldson, J. F. (1989a). Recruiting and retaining adult students in continuing higher education. In P. S. Cookson (Ed.), *Recruiting and retaining adult students.* New Directions for Continuing Education, no. 41 (pp. 63-78). San Francisco: Jossey-Bass.

Donaldson, J. F. (1989b). The many faces of leadership in continuing education. *National University Continuing Education Association Division of Continuing Education for the Professions Newsletter, 4*(3), 3-4.

Donaldson, J. F., & LeGrand, B. F. (1988, November). *Off-campus graduate degree continuing professional education: Issues of curricular choice and job performance.* Paper presented at the annual conference of the American Association of Adult and Continuing Education, Tulsa, OK.

Donaldson, J. F., & Walker, M. B. (1986). Faculty selection and compensation for continuing engineering education. In L. P. Grayson & J. M. Biedenbach (Eds.), *Proceedings of the 1986 World Conference on Continuing Engineering Education* (pp. 317-320). Lake Buena Vista, FL.

Elman, S. E., & Smock, S. M. (1985). *Professional service and faculty rewards: Toward an integrated structure.* Washington, DC: National Association of State Universities and Land Grant Colleges.

Ewell, P. T., Parker, R., & Jones, D. P. (1988). *Establishing a longitudinal student tracking system: An implementation handbook*. Boulder, CO: National Center for Higher Education Management Systems.

Handy, C. B. (1985). *Understanding organizations* (3rd ed.). New York: Penguin.

Hanna, D. E. (1981a). Securing faculty involvement in continuing education. *Continuum*, *45*(4), 51-56

Hanna, D. E. (1981b). Strengthening collegiate faculty rewards for continuing education. In J. C. Votruba (Ed.), *Strengthening internal support for continuing education*. New Directions for Continuing Education, no. 9 (pp. 43-50). San Francisco: Jossey-Bass.

Hanniford, B., & Basil A. (1988). *Credit programming in continuing education: A survey conducted by the National University Continuing Education Association's Division of Summer, Evening, and Off-Campus Credit Programs*. Washington, DC: National University Continuing Education Association.

Herzberg, F. (1966). *Work and the nature of man*. Cleveland: World.

Hofstrand, R. K., & Kozoll, C. E. (1986). *Enjoying the challenge: A guide for part-time instructors*. Urbana: University of Illinois at Urbana–Champaign.

Katz, D., & Kahn, R. L. (1978). *The social psychology of organizations* (2nd ed.). New York: Wiley.

Knox, A. B. (1979). *Enhancing proficiencies of continuing educators*. New Directions for Continuing Education, no. 1. San Francisco: Jossey-Bass.

Knox, A. B. (1981). The continuing education agency and its parent organization. In J. C. Votruba (Ed.), *Strengthening internal support for continuing education*. New Directions for Continuing Education, no. 9, (pp. 1-11). San Francisco: Jossey-Bass.

Knox, A. B. (1987). Leadership challenges to continuing higher education. *Journal of Higher Education Management*, *2*(2), 1-14.

NUCEA (1988). *Self assessment inventory*. Washington, DC: National University Continuing Education Association.

Paprock, K. E. (1988). An exploratory study of the assessment center process used to select faculty for an adult degree-granting program. *Adult Education Quarterly*, *39*(1), 11-18.

Patchner, M. A., Gullerud, E. N., Downing, R., Donaldson, J., & Leuenberger, P. (1987). Socialization to the profession of social work: A comparison of off-campus and on-campus MSW students. *Journal of Continuing Social Work Education, 4*(2), 15-19.

Peters, T. J., & Waterman, R. H., Jr. (1982). *In search of excellence: Lessons from America's best-run companies.* New York: Harper & Row.

Quinn, J. B. (1980). *Strategies for change.* Homewood, IL: Irwin.

Schroeder, E. H., & Donaldson, J. F. (1986, October). *Evaluating credit programs in the university setting: Tools for administrators.* Paper presented at the Region IV National University Continuing Education Association conference, Minneapolis.

Sonntag, S. (1986, January 5). Fitting graduate programs to working-adult problems. *The New York Times,* section 12, p. 17.

Stewart, R. (1982). *Choices for the manager.* Englewood Cliffs, NJ: Prentice-Hall.

Strother, G. B., & Klus, J. P. (1982). *Administration of continuing education.* Belmont, CA: Wadsworth.

University of Illinois at Urbana–Champaign (1981). *A faculty guide for relating continuing education and public service to the promotion and tenure review process.* Urbana: University of Illinois at Urbana–Champaign.

Votruba, J. C. (1978). Faculty rewards for university outreach: An integrative approach. *Journal of Higher Education, 49*(6), 639-648.

Votruba, J. C. (1987). From marginality to mainstream: Strategies for increasing internal support for continuing education. In R. Simerly (Ed.), *Strategic planning and leadership in continuing education* (pp.185-201). San Francisco: Jossey-Bass.

About the Author

Joe F. Donaldson, associate professor of adult education, received his Ph.D. in continuing education in 1980 from the University of Wisconsin–Madison. He has had more than thirteen years of experience in continuing higher education. From 1974 to 1979 he served as administrative assistant to the provost for University Outreach in the University of Wisconsin System. From 1979 until he joined The Pennsylvania State University adult education program in the fall of 1987, he was assistant head, then head (1983 to 1987) of the Division of Extramural Courses at the University of Illinois at Urbana–Champaign—a unit in the Office of Continuing Education and Public Service, which is responsible for administering the university's off-campus credit course and noncredit course programs.

His research interests are in continuing higher education and continuing professional education. He has written on strategic planning, noncredit course development and planning, faculty incentives for continuing education, continuing engineering education, continuing social work education, and the exemplary instruction of adults. He is currently conducting studies (1) on the curricular design and implemenatation of off-campus graduate degree programs, and (2) on the working roles of continuing higher education program administrators.

amerasia
journal

The national interdisciplinary

journal of independent scholarship,

criticism, and literature on Asian and

Pacific Americans. Published by the

Asian American Studies Center Press,

University of California, Los Angeles, since 1971.

subscription rates
$35.00 annually for individuals; $55.00 for libraries
and other institutions. Amerasia is published three
times a year: winter, spring and fall.

single and back issues
Available at $13.00 per issue plus $3.00 handling.
(See order form on last page for a list of back issues.)

indexed and/or abstracted in
*America: History and Life; Bibliography of Asian Studies;
Writings on American History;
Arts and Humanities Citations Index;
Sage Race Relations Abstracts;*
and *The Western Quarterly.*

mailings and communications

Articles for publication, books for review, and
subscription matters should be addressed to:
Amerasia Journal
UCLA Asian American Studies Center
3230 Campbell Hall, Box 951546
Los Angeles, CA 90095-1546
Phone: (310) 825-2968; FAX (310) 206-9844
email: ku@ucla.edu

www.sscnet.ucla.edu/aasc

COVER IMAGE:
"Peace Sunday—Los Angeles 1969."
(Yuji Ichioka speaking at rally against the war in Vietnam).
Gidra photographer. Courtesy of the UCLA Asian American
Studies Center Movement Archives.

histories and historians in the making

Volume 26 Number 1 2000

GUEST EDITOR—
Valerie J. Matsumoto

Table of Contents

i

iii.

intersections is authentic self representation

intersections links history and culture to the articulation of self
and to the diversity of community in the twenty-first century

intersections crosses scholarly disciplines and generates inquiries
that are transcultural and transnational

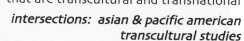

intersections: *asian & pacific american transcultural studies*

intersections is a collaborative series of university of hawai`i press in
conjunction with the ucla asian american studies center

general editor: russell c. leong

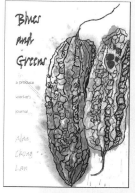

Blues and Greens:
A Produce Worker's Journal
Alan Chong Lau

Alan Chong Lau's poetic memoir of his days as a produce
worker in Seattle's Chinatown reveals a microcosm of
grassroots, working-class Asian America—a world where
customers, workers, and fruit and vegetables intersect in
exchanges that crackle with energy and brim over with
humor.

July 2000, 136 pp., illustrations
CLOTH ISBN 0-8248-2210-2 $36.00
PAPER ISBN 0-8248-2323-0 $17.95

Music through the Dark:
A Tale of Survival in Cambodia
Bree Lafreniere

The extraordinary story of one man's experience during the
1970s Cambodian holocaust—Daran Kravanh takes readers
into the heart of a horrifying tragedy. The lives of his
parents and seven siblings and as many as three million other
Cambodians were claimed by the holocaust. It was the
exquisite grace of music—in the unlikely form of an
accordian—that saved him.

April 2000, 168 pp., illustrations
CLOTH ISBN 0-8248-2227-7 $36.00
PAPER ISBN 0-8248-2266-8 $17.95

To Order:

University of Hawai`i Press
2840 Kolowalu Street
Honolulu, Hawai` 96822-1888

www.uhpress.hawaii.edu
phone: 888-UHPress, (808) 956-8255
fax: (800) 650-7811, (808) 988-6052
email: **uhpbooks@hawaii.edu**

2000, Year of the Dragon. Scratchboard drawing by Valerie J. Matsumoto.

Histories and Historians in the Making

Valerie J. Matsumoto and Russell C. Leong

> The basic building blocks of historical explanation are socially-shared experience. These also are the building blocks of ideological construction. Historical explanation and ideological construction are closely related. One seeks to comprehend the present by reconstructing the past; the other to shape the future by constructing foresights of history in the making.
>
> —Alexander Saxton

What the following *Amerasia Journal* essays challenge us to do is to expand our preconceived notions of what Asian and Pacific Islander American (APIA) histories are and can be, how they are researched and written, and why divergent historical approaches to interpreting APIA experiences can yield insights into the past and into the future, our "histories in the making."

I. Pluralities

We begin with plural histories colored and contoured by generation, gender, race, ethnicity, and training. We asked historians at different stages of their careers to write essays that linked their own lives with the lives, the moments, and the movements they studied. We hoped these accounts of individual historians would shed light on the role of Asian Americans as active agents in the shaping of their histories. At the same time, these essays show how larger ideological, economic, political, and cultural forces derived from nineteenth- and twentieth-century U.S. imperialism in Asia

VALERIE J. MATSUMOTO is professor of history at University of California, Los Angeles, and author of *Farming the Home Place: A Japanese American Community in California, 1919-1982* (Cornell University Press, 1994) and co-editor with Blake Allmendinger, *Over the Edge: Remapping the American West* (University of California Press, 1999).

as well as anti-Asian xenophobia and class struggles in America today have coalesced to influence current interpretations of the APIA experience. Moreover, the essays themselves serve to illuminate the intellectual and social construction of twentieth-century historians—as women and men who have chosen to study Asian and Pacific Islander Americans. This *Amerasia* volume is the first time these interrelated themes have been explored within Asian American Studies or within U.S. history.

The research of these contributing historians illuminates the experiences of Asian and Pacific Islander Americans through the nineteenth and twentieth centuries. Though not entirely representative of those doing work on Asian and Pacific Islander Americans or in history, the essays included here do represent historians at various points in their research and in their scholarship, spanning the past fifty years. At the same time, these essays suggest the new ways historians have approached methodology during the last three decades, namely, by incorporating new approaches suggested by women's and gender studies, cultural studies, post-colonial and postmodernist studies, social and labor history, comparative ethnic and racial relations, and studies of transnational migration. These new perspectives have enriched the ways in which Asian and Pacific Islander Americans can understand their roles domestically and internationally. Further, these approaches complicate the ways in which twenty-first-century Asian and Pacific Islander Americans need to see themselves as affecting the course of their history within and outside the United States.

II. Transformations

As these essays show, APIA history retains deep roots in the social transformation and political activism of the 1960s and 70s, and the related burgeoning of social history. Scholars of racial-ethnic history and women's history sought to create a more inclusive, more complete picture of U.S. history, warts and all. This effort has engaged the energies of undergraduate and graduate students, academics, members of historical societies, cultural institutions, and museums, as well as independent community historians, documentary filmmakers, ethnographers, writers, and journalists. Pioneering researchers focused on issues of immigration, community formation, labor, and anti-Asian activity from the passage of discriminatory laws to the internment of Japanese Americans during World War II. This work of claiming a place for Asian Pacific

Islander Americans in the story of the American past has involved the painstaking collection and interpretation of fragmentary documents, winnowing through multiple versions of family stories, and imaginatively using both conventional and less-tapped sources to track individuals and groups through the years. In the past decade, historians have extended the boundaries of APIA history in time and space, exploring new ways of conceptualizing the past and new avenues of inquiry that are enriching our understanding of APIA communities, cultural practices, gender roles, and interethnic relations.[1]

The development of APIA history has, since the 1960s, also mirrored demographic patterns in the APIA population. The majority of the early literature examined the experiences of Chinese Americans and Japanese Americans, then the largest and oldest communities, with a focus on the West Coast, the region of initial concentration. Some APIA groups—especially those who swelled the waves of newcomers following the Immigration Act of 1965—have yet received little attention from historians. There is particular need for specific ethnic-group studies of immigrants and refugees from the Philippines, Korea, India, Pakistan, Sri Lanka, Vietnam, Cambodia, Laos, Taiwan, Thailand, and the Pacific Islands. Scrutinizing the experiences of Asian and Pacific Islander Americans "east of California" and comparative study of Hawaii will add an important dimension.

Because of shifts in community composition and classroom constituencies as well as developments in scholarship, the way APIA history has been taught has begun to chafe at the seams of old timelines and frameworks. As we move into a new century, the changes in the demographic and political landscape necessitate rethinking the focus and format of survey courses in APIA history. This is a daunting challenge: how to develop a coherent structure, acknowledging new perspectives, and trying to shoehorn in an increasing number of ethnic groups, while integrating gender and class. The essays in this issue of *Amerasia*, while they do not directly address teaching, shed light on the enormity and timeliness of the task.

III. Designers of Change

The histories of the contributing historians reveal some of the foundations of Asian American Studies, now little seen beneath the elaborate edifices and bustling activity that have grown from them. The essays of Him Mark Lai, Yuji Ichioka, and Alexander

Saxton convey a sense of the ways in which national and international events have shaped scholars' perspectives on themselves, their roles, and the past.

Him Mark Lai created a tradition of Chinese American scholarship where none had existed before. Growing up during the Japanese invasion of China in the 1930s, Him Mark Lai felt and developed acute nationalist sentiments about building a new and stronger China. Subsequently World War II and the U.S. foreign policy toward the People's Republic of China and Taiwan forced Chinese Americans, in his words, "to conclude that the future for themselves and their posterity would be in America." Yet, as a progressive member of the Chinatown community, Him Mark Lai, together with his wife Laura, laid the foundations for interpreting the history of Chinese Americans within both a domestic and international perspective. As the foremost historian on Chinese Americans, Lai doggedly pursued Chinese language materials related to the Chinese in America, wrote dozens of articles and books, established the research journal on Chinese Americans, taught classes and mentored two generations of younger scholars, including Judy Yung, Ruthanne Lum McCunn, Genny Lim, Joe Chung Fong, and many others. His book *Cong Huaquiao dao Huaren* (From overseas Chinese to Chinese American) was published in 1992 as a 544-page work with 380,000 characters. It remains the first and only general history of the Chinese in America in the Chinese language written from the perspective of an American-born Chinese.

Like Him Mark Lai, Yuji Ichioka did not become a historian by "long-term, personal design." Rather, he was propelled "through force of circumstances within the context of the Civil Rights and anti-Vietnam War movements" to link his politics with his teaching and research. Ichioka, in fact, founded the Asian American Political Alliance at UC Berkeley in 1968 and taught the first APIA class at UCLA in 1969 under the title, "Orientals in America." Utilizing his bilingual and bicultural skills during the past thirty years, he continues to be firmly rooted in interpreting American history and society. Ichioka, in his essay, makes important distinctions between the research approaches of Japanese scholars who study Nikkei within an ethnocentric "Japan" framework, and the approaches of Japanese American scholars like himself who address the question of "what is an American?"

In his essay, Alexander Saxton weaves his own journey of social consciousness together with a meditation on how scholars of U.S. history have grappled with ideological construction and thus with shaping the future. Radicalized by the Great Depression and driven by a desire to experience and write about industrial America, Saxton for twenty-five years worked on railroads, in factories, in steel mills, and as a carpenter. In 1962 he turned to history, beginning a doctorate at UC Berkeley and seeking a dissertation topic that would illuminate the relationship between racial prejudice and class consciousness. His works of history and his novels—both infused by a social vision of moral responsibility—have explored the power relations of class and race in American culture. In this vein, Saxton contemplates the changing socioeconomic context of Ethnic Studies and affirms the importance of maintaining dynamic ties between intellectuals and ethnic communities.

The essays of Eileen Tamura and Chris Friday survey the landscapes of their areas of research, assessing gaps and unrealized potential as well as recent trends in development. Their work particularly addresses the need for scholars to study the dynamics of interethnic and interracial relations, in the home, neighborhood, workplace, and larger society.

Eileen Tamura calls attention to Hawai`i as an ideal site at which to heed the pressing call in Asian American Studies to move beyond a biracial paradigm and to examine the interethnic interactions of multiple groups. In Hawai`i scholars have a unique opportunity to examine a history that has given rise to a strong sense of panethnic "local" identity that overshadows an Asian American identity. Two generations of scholars have laid the groundwork for this through single-ethnic-group studies of native Hawaiians and succeeding waves of Asian immigrants. An emerging third generation of researchers is beginning to investigate Hawai`i's "local" identity as well as the identity formation of multiracial APIA individuals. Tamura urges a more complex view of the unequal power dynamics and cultural adaptation beneath the popular image of tropical harmony.

Asian American labor history, as Chris Friday demonstrates, also offers a critical site for the exploration of interethnic and interracial relations and power dynamics. In his essay, Friday reflects on the uneasy relationship—or lack thereof—between the fields of Asian American Studies and U.S. labor history. His analysis of the development of both fields provides insights into the difficulties of bridging the gulf between them. In the rise of Cultural Studies and its impact on both fields, Friday sees opportunities to transform the larger prevailing narratives of U.S. history. He asserts that acknowledging transnational influences in workers' lives, past and present, adds needed dimension and complexity to a labor history that has grown increasingly focused on the assimilative power of U.S. capitalism and consumer culture.

While most historians have presented their findings via the avenue of scholarly publication, Ruthanne Lum McCunn has turned to biographical and historical fiction. Her experiences as an elementary and junior high school teacher prompted her to address the need for works on Chinese American history. Undaunted by the lack of interest by mainstream publishers in the late 1970s and 80s, McCunn and her husband Don for years pursued the challenging route of self-publication. Her farflung research forays and love of variety introduced her to a host of Chinese—including a nineteenth-century mining-camp heroine, a leading horticulturalist, and the world's foremost ocean survivor—whose vivid lives and exploits counter persistent stereotypes of Asians. In tracing the pathways of her projects, McCunn lays bare the realities of the commercial literary marketplace, as well as revealing the unexpected rewards of excavating and reinterpreting the past.

The next essays particularly reflect the ways in which the analytical tools that historians can bring to their study of the past have multiplied, under the influence of new currents of humanities and social science inquiry. Alice Yang Murray discusses the ambivalence some social historians feel about postmodern theory, while pointing out the exciting potential of bridging the scholarly divide between the two fields. As she states in her essay, she began as "a staunch social historian dismissive of cultural theorists." In the course of her research, she established relationships with political activists and participated in community events that reinforced her notion of the value of doing social history based on grassroots and traditional archival research. At the same time, her deepening research on the Japanese American internment and the redress movement led her to reconsider her own assumptions about oral history and revealed the multiplicity of interpretations of an event. In postmodern theory, Murray found critical insights into the process of memory, the situation of gender and generation, and the relationship between the ethnographer and subject.

Henry Yu utilizes similar conceptual tools to examine the linkages between the history of "Orientals" as an intellectual problem for white scholars, and the marginalization of Asian Americans within academia. He studied the first generation of Asian American intellectuals at the University of Chicago, influenced by Robert

Park. It was not until Asian Americans themselves linked their scholarship with their political representation in the university—and fought for both in the 1960s—that the doors nudged open, grudgingly. Yu argues for a departure from the past world "in which the most interesting qualities we have are defined by the points of view of whiteness." Instead, Yu calls upon Asian Americans to produce knowledge from new regional and ideological vantage points.

Catherine Ceniza Choy is one of an emerging wave of historians who are tackling this challenge. Her two-shores research illuminates the experiences of one of the most high-profile professional groups of the post-1965 influx from Asia while drawing attention to how this labor migration is rooted in early twentieth-century U.S. colonialism. Choy's study of Filipino nurses underscores the importance of a multidirectional perspective in migration studies in addition to the critical significance of gender as a category of analysis. Her experiences and frustrations in fieldwork parallel those of an earlier generation of APIA historians, especially with regard to the need to build archives of primary materials. This essay reflects the ways in which creatively rethinking the past can shed light on contemporary communities and the shifting tides of transnational relations.

IV. Futures Foreseen

These nine historians provide a "cook's tour" of the process of making history, giving an inside view of how they think about, grapple with, construct, revise, and present their understandings of the past. Their essays make clear the importance of communities of all kinds to historical inquiry, showing how their work draws from and speaks to that of others. And their accounts of their own experiences, perceptions, reference points, and choices reveal them as subjects of history, working within the framework of their times, as well as shapers of the past. Historians, their assessments of where we have come from and the tasks that lie before us, thus help us to foresee where we may be headed.

Utilizing the ideological base developed by Alexander Saxton, historian Scott Kurashige explores the relationship between urban community formation and anti-Asian violence in his essay. Kurashige, by extending the study of racist ideology into the latter part of the twentieth century, asks us to consider the conflicted future of Asian Americans in relation to race and class in a multiracial society. His essay, "Beyond Random Acts of Hatred: Analyzing Urban Patterns of Anti-Asian Violence," received the Alexander Saxton History Award for 1999-2000.

We hope this special issue of *Amerasia Journal* will serve to encourage others to explore their own histories, to imagine alternative futures, and to develop new languages that ask new, braver questions of social reality.

Forbidden City, San Francisco 1950.

Him Mark Lai's practice sheet.

The Lai family, 1940 (Him Mark Lai is standing, center).

Amerasia Journal 26:1 (2000): 2-30

Musings of a Chinese American Historian

Him Mark Lai

No Tradition of Scholarship

Among my forebearers, there was no tradition of scholarship. Thus, my deep involvement in Chinese American historical research was largely due to fortuitous decisions made at important junctures of my life.

My father Bing was the eldest son in a poor peasant family surnamed Maak (anglicized Mark) in rural Nanhai, part of Sam Yup, west of Guangzhou (Canton). He came to America through the generosity of his maternal aunt who had retired to Guangzhou after sojourning in San Francisco Chinatown as a hairdresser and maid at the turn of the century. She not only provided financial aid but also persuaded her cousin, a merchant with the surname Lai, to bring my father along as his son. Hence my father embarked on the *S.S. Siberia* and arrived at San Francisco during the beginning of 1910 as Bing Lai, a merchant's paper son. He was among the Chinese immigrants transferred from the dilapidated shed at the Pacific Mail Steamship Company wharf to become the first tenants of the newly opened Angel Island Immigration Detention Barracks. I am doubtful whether my father was in any mood to savor this historic occasion.

After entering the country and working a few years, my father saved enough to return to China after the First World War to marry his aunt's foster daughter, Dong Hing Mui, who was raised in Guangzhou. In 1923 the young couple left for Hong Kong to arrange for passage to America just before a warlord's army was

---

Hɪᴍ Mᴀʀᴋ Lᴀɪ is an active member of the Chinese Historical Society of America and the Chinese Culture Foundation of San Francisco.

Bing Lai and Dong Hing Mui, 1923.

threatening to invade Guangzhou and communications between Guangzhou and Hong Kong were severed for several weeks. They could not even return to Guangzhou to pick up wedding gifts stored there, and my father's aunt had to bring the lot when she took the ferry to Hong Kong to see them off. This experience appeared to have so traumatized my parents that it may have contributed to their lack of desire to return to China again even though they continued to maintain contacts with relatives in China. Neither did they ever encourage their own children to go back.

Bing Lai and his bride landed in San Francisco about a year before enactment of the 1924 Immigration Act that imposed more restrictions on Asian immigration. I came into this world in San Francisco Chinatown in 1925 as the first-born of five children. We were similar to many other Chinese immigrant families of that era in that we were at the lower end of the economic scale. During the first eleven years of my youth our family lived on Grant Avenue at the north end of San Francisco Chinatown where there were Sam Yup organizations, businesses, and other Sam Yup people. In fact we lived about half a block from Philip Choy, whom I later met in the Chinese Historical Society of America; however, we did not know each other during this period. Our family lived in the former clubrooms of the notorious Wah Ting San Fong, a secret society (tong) with a Sam Yup membership.[1] I remembered the numerous artifacts and documents left by the society as well as a council chamber with teakwood furniture and an altar to Guan Di, the god of war. Regrettably, I was too young then to appreciate the historic value of these artifacts. By a strange coincidence, after World War II the same site housed the Chinatown branch of Federal Savings and Loan Association from which manager J. K. Choy launched in 1965 the founding of the Chinese Culture Foundation, which I was destined to serve as a member of the board of directors for more than two decades starting in the mid-1970s.

In spite of my father's merchant status, both my parents were sewing machine operators at Chinatown factories manufacturing workers' clothes and overalls during their entire working careers. They were both very intelligent individuals, but my father had only the equivalent

Lai family portrait, 1937.

of an elementary school education in the village and did not learn much more than the rudiments of English; my mother could read some Chinese but her knowledge of English was even less than that of my father. Although my parents always followed Chinese traditions, they were fairly lenient about enforcing them on their children. Being working class, my parents did not feel comfortable mixing with the merchant leaders of our district associations and rarely did so. Thus I did not have much contact with traditional Chinatown society during my youth. On the other hand, neither did they encourage me, nor did I have the inclination, to participate in the YMCA, the Christian church, or similar institutions. Like many San Francisco Chinese children of the period, I attended Chinese school until I entered high school in the public school system. Since my mother spoke and taught us the city dialect, which was standard in the Chinese schools, it probably facilitated my learning the Chinese language, and I became proficient in the fundamentals of the language and culture.

I enrolled in public school a semester after I started Chinese school. The school was 100 percent Chinese except for the teachers. I did not have non-Chinese classmates until I attended junior and senior high school, but even then there were high percentages of Chinese Americans in the schools.

The environments of the Chinese school and of the public school were worlds apart. My attendance in Chinese school coincided with the period when Japan was invading China. The curriculum was colored by Chinese nationalist sentiments. Besides advocating resistance to Japanese aggression, the teachers also and often touched upon injustices afflicted upon China by the imperialist powers during the past century. In public school the major effort was to guide the Chinese American students toward assimilation. By the third grade the teacher had convinced most of the students with Chinese personal names to change to western names, but somehow I escaped the teacher's attention and my name remained unchanged. Usage of Chinese was discouraged in the schools and Chinese Americans were often made to feel, sometimes in not so subtle ways, that China was a weak nation and that the Chinese language and culture were not as acceptable as western languages and institutions.

During this period, due to the numerous immigrants entering America by illegal means, fear of discovery by immigration authorities was constantly hanging like a sword of Damocles over the Chinese community. My father's status as a paper son brought this feeling to a personal level. My siblings and I all carried Mark as middle names in order to remind us of our origins and we always went by our Chinese surname in Chinese school. But, even as I began public school, my father taught me a concocted story explaining the discrepancy in surnames in case a curious teacher should ask. This bifurcated world with conflicting signals and behaviors was not at all unusual for San Francisco Chinese Americans of that period.

When I entered high school, I began working twenty hours per week as a helper in a Chinatown garment factory, which did not leave me much opportunity to participate in school activities. But I did well in class, especially in literary subjects and social sciences, and even won first prize in a citywide history competition during my senior year. However, a career in the social sciences never entered my mind since during those days the object of an education for members of families such as ours was to learn some marketable skill that could ensure making a living. Thus, I turned to engineering even though typically I was all thumbs when it came to working with my hands. In 1947 I graduated from University of California College of Engineering and worked in the field for more than three decades until my retirement from Bechtel Corporation in 1984.

Chinese American Consciousness

Although I was unaware of it at the time, World War II was a divide for minorities in America. Due to the labor shortage during the war, many Chinese Americans found skilled and technical jobs from which they had been barred during the exclusion era.

In 1943 Congress repealed the Chinese exclusion laws and granted Chinese the right of naturalization. After the war, an increasing number of Chinese Americans continued to find employment in professional, technical and clerical fields as racial bars relaxed in face of the need for such skills during the post-war prosperity. A Chinese American middle class grew in numbers and strength. As their interests became increasingly firmly rooted in this country, they overcame their feelings of alienation and their sense of identity with America grew. This was sped along by international developments when the United States engaged in hostilities with the People's Republic of China that had ousted the Kuomintang regime from the Chinese mainland; the U.S. imposed an embargo that in effect cut off Chinese in America from relatives in China. These developments forced Chinese Americans to reassess their situation and conclude that the future for themselves and their posterity would be in America.

During this period of great changes in the international and domestic scenes, I was among those who entertained great hopes for the New China in its struggle to overthrow foreign domination and feudal rule. These expectations had since been greatly tempered by the unfolding of subsequent events but I remained interested in developments in China. In the fifties I was active in Mun Ching, a progressive Chinese American youth club, and became its president. It was there that I met Laura Jung whom I married in 1953. Since most club members were immigrants who were more comfortable using the Chinese language, my Chinese that I had seldom used since my high school days now became more fluent due to constant practice. During this period I also acquired a better understanding of Chinese history as interpreted by progressive historians, as well as became acquaninted with the writings of progressive writers such

Him Mark Lai and Laura Jung's wedding party at Mun Ching, 1953.

Mun Ching was a progressive Chinese American youth group.
Above, a Mun Ching chorus is performing at the Chinese Workers
Mutual Aid Association, 1951. Laura is right of conductor, Him Mark Lai
is rear right.
Below, vernacular drama at Mun Ching. Laura is center stage.

as Lu Xun and performance arts of the New China such as the *Yellow River Cantata*. I also learned to use simplified characters and Hanyu pinyin after they had been introduced in China. This basic knowledge greatly facilitated my historical research and community cultural activities at a future date, but it also came at a price, for this period was at the height of the Cold War anti-Communist hysteria, and many club members and I came under FBI surveillance. In my case this continued at least until 1980 when I asked for and received a two-and-one-half inch thick, heavily censored copy of my files under provisions of the Freedom of Information-Privacy Act. Surely the tens of thousands of dollars spent to observe and record my personal life for three decades could have been better used on more worthwhile projects! The experience taught me that government was willing to wield its enormous powers to root out, intimidate and discourage what it considered to be political heresies in American society. It sensitized me to civil liberties issues, especially those concerning Chinese Americans.

In the meanwhile, ethnic minorities who had been asked to give their all to "defend democracy" during World War II returned to America expecting better treatment. By the late 1950s their persistent efforts demanding equal rights led to the emergence of the African American-led civil rights movement. The study of race relations and the ethnic minority communities became a topic of interest to the academic community. In 1957, Stanford Lyman, then a sociology doctoral candidate at the University of California, Berkeley, initiated a class, "The Oriental in North America," at the University of California Extension in San Francisco based on his research for his doctoral dissertation. This was the first semester-length course on Asian American studies taught at a major university.[2] Around 1960 I enrolled in the course and received my first exposure to the historical experiences of the Chinese, Japanese and Filipinos in America.

Soon afterward the Chinese Historical Society of America (CHSA) was founded in San Francisco in 1963 as an expression of the growing Chinese American consciousness. Although I did not join until 1965, within a short time I became an active member committed to researching the history of the Chinese in America. I soon found that my knowledge of Chinese was a great advantage in research.

By the mid-1960s, the demand for change in American society expressed by the civil rights movement had spread to the Chinese American community where activists from the post-war generation spearheaded it. They urged increased involvement and equal participation in mainstream American society. Within the Chinese community they pushed for changes to improve the quality of life and sought a share in the process of making decisions affecting the community. The bilingual *East/West, the Chinese American Weekly*, founded by Gordon Lew in San Francisco in 1967, became the first community newspaper to provide coverage expressing some of the concerns of these activists. At the end of 1967, the paper's editor, Maurice Chuck, invited me to help with the proofreading as a volunteer and also to write a series of articles on Chinese American history. Although I had never fancied my writing as having very high literary quality, the articles found a readership among the increasing number of Chinese Americans anxious to learn more about their historical heritage.

In the meantime, CHSA, in response to the growing interest in the history of ethnic minorities, had scheduled a seminar on Chinese American history in April 1969 at the Chinese Americans Citizens Alliance Hall targeting California school district educators. Early in 1969 Thomas Chinn, who led the effort, called upon Philip Choy and me to work with him to compile some reference materials to be distributed to seminar attendees. Actually the committee had only a vague idea of the desired end result when it was first convened. Taking the bull by the horns, I used my *East/ West* articles, did additional research, added citations, and submitted them for inclusion as part of the reference materials. Within three months, the committee had compiled and published an 81-page syllabus, *A History of the Chinese in California* (San Francisco: Chinese Historical Society, 1969). This compilation has remained a basic reference work on Chinese American history even today, particularly on the role of Chinese labor in California during the nineteenth century.

Teaching Chinese American History

After the CHSA seminar Professor Chester Cheng of San Francisco State College (known as San Francisco State University today) invited Philip Choy and me to teach an evening pilot course in Chinese American history. This was the first college level course in America on the history of the Chinese in America. The students in that first class were somewhat older than average college students of the day and included a number who had participated in the prolonged students' strike that had just ended with the establishment of a School of Ethnic Studies. More so than younger students, they were interested in contemporary issues and one of the criticisms of our course at the end of the semester was that there were insufficient materials given on the contemporary Chinese community. Of course, the truth is that not much research had been done at that time on the subject, and even today, three decades afterward, there remain great gaps in our knowledge of that sector. But the pilot course was evidently substantial enough to satisfy the history department's criteria, whatever they were, for it was transferred to the Asian American Studies Department in the School of Ethnic Studies the succeeding semester and became a regular course offered by the department.

Since the relaxed immigration policy instituted in 1965 had not yet made an impact on the Chinese community at the time, most Chinese students were derived from the earlier Cantonese families. Philip Choy and I prepared an ambitious course outline starting with the history of Guangdong and the Cantonese people before launching into the history of the Chinese in continental America from 1785 to the 1960s, and then ending the course with lectures comparing the Chinese community of the continental United States with that of Canada and Hawai`i. However, we soon found that we had crammed too much material into the one-semester course. Thus, in subsequent teaching stints I limited the lecture material on Chinese history to cover only the period after the Opium War, which was relevant to any discussions on Chinese emigration abroad. I also deleted the sections on the Chinese communities in Hawai`i and Canada. This last deletion was unfortunate in view of the fact that many valuable insights could be gained by comparisons of the historical experiences of Chinese in the continental United States with that of these communities.

I had never considered taking up teaching for a permanent career and taught only when requested to fill a need. Subsequently, I taught at San Francisco State University from 1972 to 1975 and then at the University of California, Berkeley in 1978, 1979, and 1984, where I substituted for Professor Ling-chi Wang. The challenge of teaching had been of great benefit to me personally in that it pushed me to think through historical issues to reach conclusions that seemed rational and logical to me that I could present to the class. It is my firm belief that this is the only way to leave a lasting impression on the students' minds rather than presenting them a plethora of rhetoric and academic jargon and mumbo-jumbo.

Since I was already in my early forties, some fifteen to twenty years older than faculty members then running Asian American Studies, and also was only occasionally teaching, I never was an integral part of the discipline, although I was supportive and continued to maintain contacts with many faculty members and students. My situation precluded my being in any position to exert any direct influence on the course of development of Asian American Studies; however, it also freed me from involvement in the internal politics, intrigues and power struggles that seem to arise inevitably in organizations when strong and ambitious personalities interact. Not having academic status, however, also meant that I was free to undertake research without having to worry about academic guidelines to justify funding, tenure and promotion requirements.

Juggling Career, Community and Research

Writing projects and preparation of lecture notes forced me on a sustained search for resources. Since much of the materials relating to Chinese American history were scattered throughout numerous publications, I spent many weekends in various collections in the San Francisco Bay Area perusing books and periodicals. Continuing this single-minded quest doggedly through the 1970s, I did not let up even when I was on vacation trips. Sometimes such fishing expeditions led to unexpected finds. For example, a visit to the Library of Congress in 1972 resulted in the discovery of four declassified volumes listing all villages and hamlets, together with associated clan names, for Taishan (Toishan), Kaiping (Hoiping), Xinhui (Sunwui), and Zhongshan (Chungshan) counties. These had been compiled by the U.S. Consul General in Hong Kong during the 1960s to help detect immigration fraud.

However, I sometimes found it difficult to give a straight answer to curious friends who asked what project I was doing this for, since I did not have any specific objective except to gather as much materials on Chinese American history as possible. But, gradually, I built up an extensive and useful information file.

During this period I had the benefit of counseling from Yuk Ow, a history buff who since the 1950s had been quietly researching the Chinese American historical experience in California. Ow stressed the importance of bibliographic work, particularly on Chinese language materials. I soon added East Asian collections to the itinerary of my library visits. I also came to realize that Chinese newspapers provide far more information on the Chinese community than English newspapers and began reading them regularly. Chinese newspaper clippings in my information files soon exceeded English language items for certain categories. The obvious truth began to sink in that since foreign-born Chinese outnumbered American-born for almost the entire history of the community, it was natural that much of the documentation would be in Chinese and I began to appreciate the importance of these sources for Chinese American historical research.

During the early 1970s Victor and Brett Nee came to San Francisco to do research and oral history interviews for *Longtime Californ'* (New York: Pantheon Books, 1973), a history on San Francisco Chinatown. Also entrusted with the duty of editing an Asian American issue for *Bulletin of Concerned Asian Scholars*, they invited me to submit an essay for the publication. After some consideration, I picked a subject in which I had long been interested, the Chinese American Left, for I had been an active member in a progressive Chinese American youth organization in San Francisco Chinatown for a decade during the 1950s. My first attempt at a scholarly essay "A Historical Survey of Organizations of the Left among the Chinese in America" was published in the publication in fall 1972. The subject aroused some interest, especially among activists, and UCLA's Asian American Studies Center included a revised version in its anthology, *Counterpoint: Perspectives on Asian America* (Los Angeles: UCLA Asian American Studies Center, 1976). This was the beginning of my association with the Center.

Due to the scarcity of documentation on the subject, my essay had to depend in part on information gleaned from oral interviews. When citing such sources in this and subsequent essays I always tried to assess their reliability since the memory of individuals is not perfect and their accounts of events occurring many years ago often confuse details or embellish the facts. Also, accounts are usually affected by the individual's own bias. However, I feel that such sources are no worse than published accounts that are prejudicial. Certainly, for certain areas of Chinese American historical research they are the only sources available.

The following year the president of Sam Yup Association invited me to join a committee to compile the association's history. Yuk Ow became the chief editor and Philip Choy and I assisted. Yuk Ow played a key role as he contributed the fruits of his years of meticulous research on the subject, which, adding to information from the association's existing records dating back to 1881, oral interviews, and research materials founded by the committee, resulted in the publication of *A History of the Sam Yup Benevolent Association in the United States, 1850-1974* (San Francisco: Fook Chong Hong Sam Yup Association, 1975). It is up to the present the only documented, detailed history of any of the *huiguan* in San Francisco. In 1998 I became involved again in the revision of this history which will probably be published in 2000. A striking fact was that this time, unlike the 1970s, there was practically no one left who could offer much useful historical information on the pre-World War II era, demonstrating the importance of timely action to record the experiences and thoughts of individuals that can add to the understanding of historical events and make available additional materials for researchers. This was particularly important for Chinese American history where much was undocumented, or where documented, was distorted or even falsified.

As I became more immersed in Chinese American historical research from the late 1960s on, life became hectic as I juggled my limited time between an engineering career, community activities and historical writing. Around 1971 the Chinese Media Committee under the civil rights group Chinese for Affirmative Action negotiated free air time for Chinese American radio programming and put the weekly Hon Sing Chinese Community Hour on the air. This Cantonese language program included news analysis free from the Cold War anti-Communist rhetoric as well as news of community activities. It also introduced to the radio audience for the first time Chinese folk, classical and operatic music that had been composed or rearranged in China since 1949. The activist who was the program coordinator soon retired from the scene and by fall 1971 I found myself shouldering the responsibility of supervising the weekly tape recording of the program as well as compiling the program notes for the musical selections. This chore as volunteer producer lasted thirteen years until the mid-1980s.

The Chinese Media Committee also successfully lobbied Channel Four television station to agree to produce the first television series on Chinese American history. In 1972 Philip Choy and I became volunteer consultants for the production of the six-part *Gam Saan Haak*. During the development of the script Philip and I met with the program producer almost weekly after my workday at Bechtel. The program premiered on the air in 1974; however, the original scheduled date had to be postponed due to preemption by a live broadcast of the police shootout with the Symbionese Liberation Army, a radical group that had earlier kidnapped newspaper magnate William Randolph Hearst, Jr.'s daughter Patricia. Eventually the program was aired, but soon after it had been broadcast several times, the station erased the program without even the courtesy of notifying us or making us a copy. In subsequent years I also acted as consultant for other film and television productions on Chinese American history such as Felicia Lowe's *Carved in Silence* (1981-87) and *San Francisco Chinatown* (1995), Loni Ding's *Ancestors in America* (1989-1998), Jennie Lew's *Separate Lives, Broken Dreams* (1993).

My community activities sometimes also opened new areas for research. In 1974 I became member of a California State Legislature appointed advisory committee to make recommendations on the preservation and restoration of the Angel Island Immigration Station detention barracks. The interest stimulated by this activity prompted poet Genny Lim to ask writer Judy Yung and me in 1976 to join her to publish a translation of the poems carved by Chinese immigrants on the barracks walls, together with a history of Chinese immigrants detained on Angel Island. Subsequently the scope was expanded to include interviews of detainees. *Island: Poetry and History of Chinese Immigrants on Angel Island, 1910-1940* (San Francisco: Hoc Doi, 1980) was finally published in 1980. The effort, which I had joined mainly to provide a technical service in translation, appears to have withstood the test of time, for it is still on the market today two decades later. It was fortunate that the team decided to undertake the extra work of interviewing the detainees to preserve their experiences on record, for by the end of the 1990s many had passed away and their experiences would have been lost to posterity.

Even while I was busy with community activities, I never ceased my never-ending search for historical materials. During the 1970s, I had corresponded with university libraries to seek information on their Chinese American newspaper holdings. Karl Lo, head of the East Asian Collection at the University of Washington who was collecting the same information, contacted me and suggested that we collaborate to compile a bibliography. This resulted in the publication of *Chinese Newspapers Published in North America, 1854-1975* (Washington, D.C.: Center for Chinese Research Materials, 1977) which included an historical introduction that in 1987 was revised and published as "The Chinese American Press" in Sally Miller's *The Ethnic Press in the United States* (New York: Greenwood Press, 1987). By coincidence, the chapter "The Japanese American Press" in the same book, was written by Professor

Harry Kitano of UCLA, who was my classmate in Galileo High School in 1941!

In 1977 my association with UCLA's Asian American Studies Center became closer when Russell Leong, editor of its *Amerasia Journal*, invited me to join its editorial board. In 1978, he asked me to compile *A History Reclaimed: An Annotated Bibliography of Chinese Language Materials on the Chinese of America* (Los Angeles: UCLA Asian American Studies Center, 1986), based primarily on collections in the San Francisco Bay Area. This, together with the work on newspapers, filled a gap in Chinese American bibliographic literature. Although both bibliographies contained obvious gaps and much more material is now available in collections all over the country, the bibliographies can still function as starting points for researchers. As for myself, I benefited greatly by becoming more familiar with the availability of Chinese language source materials. That may have been one of the reasons that led the Asian American Studies Library, University of California at Berkeley to invite me in 1979 to join an advisory committee for starting a Chinese archival collection. I continued to work closely with the librarian and periodically would donate books, directories, newspapers, periodicals and other documentary materials to the collection, which had become one of the leading collections of Chinese American materials in America.

Trans-Pacific Links

Even while Chinese American historical research was taking root in America during the 1970s, diplomatic relations between the United States and the People's Republic of China (PRC) were also improving. Chinese Americans were once again allowed to travel to the PRC. In July 1976, toward the end of the Cultural Revolution in China, I led a delegation that included volunteers from the Hon Sing Chinese Community Hour to visit China. On this trip my wife and I reestablished contacts with relatives that we had lost contact with for several decades. Soon after our group left China, Communist Party Chairman Mao Zedong passed away; a *coup d'état* overthrew the "Gang of Four" who had ruled the nation with a fanatical reign of terror. This opened the way to a policy of economic reform and ending of China's isolation in the international community. One of the changes was the reactivation of the Overseas Chinese Affairs Office (OCAO) and the Federation of Returned Overseas Chinese (FROC) and implementation of a policy to win the support of Chinese abroad.

In 1979 UCLA became the first American university to collaborate with a Chinese institution of higher learning on a scholarly project when Professor Lucie Cheng of the Asian American Studies Center signed an agreement with Zhongshan University of Guangzhou to interview emigrant families in two villages in Taishan County. She invited me to be one of the participants on the American team, probably because there were at the time not many in Asian American Studies who were fluent in both Chinese and English. Although I had just been on another visit to Guangzhou the previous year and had not thought of going again so soon, I decided to join this groundbreaking project. Using accumulated vacation time, I spent a week researching pertinent materials at the Zhongshan University library, another week in Taishan examining its archival material and spending a night with the project team at one of the target villages. Also I visited several of the *qiaoxiang,* or emigrant areas, with the help of the provincial and local OCAO and FROC.

During the next two decades, contacts in both OCAO and FROC facilitated numerous visits to emigrant areas in China as well as meeting with returned overseas Chinese. My understanding of Chinese emigration and its effects on China broadened considerably. I also gathered additional materials relating to the Chinese in America. For example, on one trip during the mid-1980s I bought a book that included drafts of reports that San Francisco Chinese Consul-General Huang Zunxian made during 1882 to Chinese envoy Zheng Zaoru in Washington DC, discussing efforts to found the Chinese Consolidated Benevolent Association in San Francisco.

The Taishan project tapered off after the principals departed for greener pastures. One essay was published in *Amerasia Journal* (Spring/Summer 1982); however, most of the data and information collected in Taishan are still awaiting further analysis. The project was followed in 1981 by another agreement among Zhongshan University, Hong Kong University, and UCLA for a joint five-year project to research Chinese American history. In the same year Zhongshan University published a bibliography *A Reference Guide to Overseas Chinese History* (Guangzhou: Zhongshan University, 1981), listing articles in publications in the Guangzhou area, but the other two parties never did publish corresponding bibliographies for Hong Kong and California per the agreement. The project, however, did convene two conferences, one in 1984 hosted by Hong Kong University and a second in 1985 hosted by

Zhongshan University. At these conferences I began to establish useful contacts with scholars from China doing research on Chinese overseas.

Full-time on Research

The years ending the 1970s were busy and productive. In 1976 and 1977, I became president of the Chinese Historical Society of America (CHSA) and on behalf of the society applied for and received successive grants to design a traveling exhibit *Journeys Made and Yet to Come* that was completed in 1987, followed by a permanent exhibit *The Promise of Gold Mountain* for the CHSA museum that was unveiled in 1979. As the project approached completion, the Chinese Culture Foundation of San Francisco (CCF) board of directors appointed me to supervise the completion of the large-scale exhibit *Chinese of America, 1785-1980,* and the planning of the second conference on Chinese American studies to accompany the opening of the exhibit in 1980. I collaborated with Joe Huang and Don Wong to write the illustrated history and catalog for the exhibition; project coordinator Jack Chen, in a parallel effort based largely on the research for the exhibition, also published *The Chinese of America, from the Beginnings to the Present* (San Francisco: Harper and Row, 1980).

After the *Chinese of America* exhibit had toured several American cities, CCF as a gesture of friendship gave the exhibit to the All-China Returned Chinese Association for its proposed museum of overseas Chinese. In 1985 I accompanied this first large-scale depiction of the Chinese American experience to be sent to China and spent two weeks in Shanghai translating the captions into Chinese for its premiere showing. The next year I returned to help curate its opening in Beijing. Subsequently the exhibit traveled to Guangzhou, Taishan, Zhongshan, and Hong Kong.

As mentioned previously, 1980 saw the publication of *Island.* In addition my long essay on the Chinese in the continental United States was published in *Harvard Encyclopedia of American Ethnic Groups* (Cambridge: Belnap Press of Harvard University Press, 1980). Shortly afterward, Maurice Chuck worked with me on a Chinese translation of the essay for publication in *San Francisco Journal.* I soon concluded that the article was too skeletal to have sufficient details to satisfy the Chinese reader and decided to expand the essay using materials from accumulated lecture notes and file documents. I soon found that these too were often inadequate and needed additional research. By the time I realized this, I was well into the weekly series and could not extricate myself gracefully. All I could do was to continue to forge ahead doing research on the fly to meet the weekly deadline. I had optimistically entitled the series "A Brief History of the Chinese in America," but the series dragged on for four years and ran some 200,000 characters. One benefit of this entanglement was that my Chinese composition writing showed great improvement!

I was leaving for a visit to China in 1984 when Teo Ng, manager of Eastwind Books and Arts in San Francisco, suggested that I submit the manuscript to Joint Publishing Company, the leading book dealer and publisher in Hong Kong. I did as he suggested, but without any high expectations. To my surprise, after reading the manuscript, the company not only agreed to publish the work, but also offered a contract. I decided then and there that I had given enough of my life to Bechtel Corporation and took early retirement in order to devote more time to prepare the manuscript for publication. At that time I was not quite fifty-nine years old. After making revisions and additions that almost doubled the word-count, *Cong Huaqiao dao Huaren* (From overseas Chinese to Chinese American) (Hong Kong: Joint Publishing Company, 1992) was finally published in 1992 as a 544-page work with 380,000 characters. It was the first general history of the Chinese in America in the Chinese language written from the perspective of an American-born Chinese.

In 1987 CHSA decided to begin publishing a scholarly journal and appointed me to serve on the editorial committee. When the publication was about to go to press, committee members racked their brains to find a suitable name. I suggested *Chinese America: History and Perspectives* since it appeared to be broad enough to cover a wide variety of writings. To my surprise the suggestion was adopted. *Chinese America* was not the first non-academic scholarly journal on Chinese American history and society, but in the 1990s it was the only one still being published. In order to draw upon the expertise of Asian American studies, CHSA invited the Asian American Studies Department of San Francisco State University to become a cosponsor of the journal in 1989. This has proven to be a mutually beneficial arrangement that enhanced the image of the publication.

In 1991 Albert Cheng and I became co-coordinators of the CCF and CHSA-sponsored "In Search of Roots" program that had been set up in the aftermath of a family history/genealogical seminar sponsored by the same groups in 1989. In that annual program, ten Chinese American youth interns under guidance researched their family histories, visited their ancestral villages in the Pearl River Delta as guests of the Guangdong Provincial Overseas Chinese Affairs Office, and then displayed their findings and family histories in an exhibition at the Chinese Culture Center. The program was geared toward encouraging the interns to relate their family histories to the historical experience of the Chinese in America. Information and materials I had picked up in visits to the Pearl River Delta during the 1980s proved to be of great help for planning the group's travel itinerary. I also rewrote my 1969 lecture notes on Guangdong history, expanding them to cover the geography and histories of the Guangzhou (Sam Yup), Zhong-shan, and Jiangmen (Sze Yup) regions.

Most participants in the program did not come from Chinatown families and were highly assimilated and English-speaking. A common thread among them was a search for their identity in American society. It is gratifying to note the progam had been of assistance providing some guidance in this quest, and many interns have exhibited an increased awareness of Chinese American and Asian American issues.

During the last half of the 1980s, the convening of a number of conferences on the Chinese overseas indicated that scholars worldwide were increasingly interested in the subject, and conditions were ripe for the appearance of an international coordinating group. In 1992 I joined a committee headed by Professor Ling-chi Wang of the University of California at Berkeley to make plans for a *Luodi Shenggen* international conference in San Francisco on the Chinese diaspora. After the successful conclusion of the conference the International Society for the Study of Chinese Overseas (ISSCO) was established to serve as a liaison among scholars in the field. The network has facilitated the staging of subsequent international conferences at Shantou (1993), Hong Kong (1994), Xiamen (1996), Manila (1998) and Havana (1999). Attending some of these conferences enabled me to have useful exchanges with scholars from other countries and to keep abreast of developments in the field. Understanding more of the experiences of Chinese in other countries has been particularly helpful in developing a broader perspective. I personally feel also that by comparing the experiences of Chinese in other countries with that of Chinese in the United States, one can gain insights that are helpful for more in-depth interpretations of certain phenomena and issues in Chinese American history. However, so far conferences of this nature have attracted only a few scholars from Asian American Studies.

In 1992 I also became consultant and contributor to a proposed *Asian American Encyclopedia* (New York: Marshall Cavendish, 1995). Involvement in that project really exposed to me the fact there were only a limited number of scholars versed in Chinese American history and society despite the three decades that had elapsed since Asian American Studies began. A number of proposed articles, particularly ones on biographies and institutions that should have been included, had to be dropped for lack of knowledgeable writers. Apparently many Chinese-Americanists, in spite of their protestations of working to advance the interests of the Chinese (or Asian) American community, meant it only in the abstract. The reality is that many Chinese Americans, particularly the American-born and even immigrants who arrived at a tender age, had become familiar and comfortable with only the English-speaking and westernized sectors of the Chinese community due to the effectiveness of the assimilation process. Most felt out of place in the immigrant-dominated Chinese-speaking community and hence had only limited understanding of its history, personalities and institutions.

After this project, I was engaged to write a long essay on Chinese in the United States for *Encyclopedia of Chinese Overseas* (Singapore: Archipelago, 1998), a work published in three different editions—English, traditional Chinese, and simplified Chinese characters. During the same period, I also was asked to submit several dozen articles on Chinese schools and Chinese American scholarly organizations for *Shijie Huaqiao Huaren baike quanshu* (Encyclopedia of Chinese and people of Chinese descent overseas) (Beijing: Overseas Publishing Company, 1999).

While all these activities were of great help to me personally for gathering and organizing my understanding of Chinese America, they took up time that could have been used to make headway in an English-language version of *From Overseas Chinese to Chinese American* that I had initiated earlier. Of course, it may be that since I had already done the book once in Chinese, there was a subconscious reluctance to revisit the subject matter. However, completion of such a work still remains on the agenda.

Pages Yet to Be Written

A major factor in American society that defined the course of the long and complex development of the Chinese community in

America was racism. Thus it was not surprising that many researchers focused on race relations between Chinese and the dominant white society. As Chinese Americans strove to attain equal status in American society, they in turn stressed areas that demonstrate that their community had been and is an integral part of American society. On the one hand, they concentrated on "accurate" and positive accounts of the Chinese role contributing to American society and, on the other, made strenuous efforts to combat and dispel stereotypical images of Chinese Americans current in mainstream America. However, since the Chinese American community is complex and diverse, its complete historical experience covers much more than the aforementioned phenomena. During the three decades since 1970, some researchers have plowed some new ground delving into such topics as Chinese in California agriculture; Chinese in different regions such as the South, New York, Monterey Peninsula, Stockton; Chinese American women; Chinese Americans in World War II. Others probed contemporary communities such as Sacramento, Flushing and Monterey Park.

As for myself, publication of my initial research paper in 1972 helped crystallize my thinking as to the direction I should take in Chinese American historical research. I decided to focus on the twentieth century, which to me was the principal arena where many Chinese institutions and attitudes evolved that are essential to any understanding of the community. I had written essays on social history covering such topics as Chinese newspapers, Chinese language schools, political and social organizations, regional and dialect groups, China politics in the community, as well as some biographies. But in spite of all the new areas that had been probed, there are still too many blank pages, and even more that are incomplete or poorly defined, that await further delineation. Some of these are described below:

❖ Immigration

Chinese emigration was a phenomenon that arose out of the intersection of a number of local and international factors—economic, political, and geographical. Beginning with mid-nineteenth century a large part of the emigration from the Pearl River Delta was directed toward the Americas and Hawai`i. However, not all counties in the region contributed equally to the flow, and the flow to different destinations differed in composition with respect to their geographical origins. Thus, immigrants from Sze Yup, mostly from Taishan, predominated on the American continent, while the great majority of emigrants to Hawai`i came from Zhongshan. What factors led to these differences? What effect did this difference have on the subsequent development of the local Chinese community? Why didn't other areas along the China coast become major sources of emigrants to the New World during this same period? Chinese immigration is an interlinking global phenomenon. Economic and political developments in the host countries were factors that led to adjustments in the emigration flow to various destination. One such major development was the anti-Chinese Movement and Chinese exclusion in the U.S. that caused part of the emigration flow to be diverted to southeast Asia, Canada, Mexico, and the Hawaiian Kingdom. What were the magnitudes of these diversions? What was its effect on the development of the new host countries?

❖   Race Relations

Much has been written on race relations between Chinese and the dominant white society. How were the relations of Chinese with other ethnic groups? With Native Americans? With Mexicans? With African-Americans? With Jews? With other European immigrants? With other Asians? Did they influence one another's culture and society?

❖   Organizations

For many years historians had not done much research on organizations in the Chinese American community and had often used sources of limited reliability. A case in point is the well-known Chinese Six Companies or Chinese Consolidated Benevolent Association (CCBA) in San Francisco. For many years and even today the most widely quoted source had been William Hoy's *The Chinese Six Companies* (San Francisco: Chinese Consolidated Benevolent Association, 1942), a pamphlet that was commissioned and published by the organization to project a better public image during World War II. Gunther Barth in his *Bitter Strength* (Cambridge: Harvard University Press, 1964) was first to work out the history of the district associations, or *huiguan*, up to 1870 based on documentation. During the late 1960s, Yuk Ow pointed out to me the numerous errors in Hoy's work. After collecting pertinent documents for almost two decades, I finally published "The Historical Development of the Chinese Consolidated Benevolent Association/*Huiguan* System" in 1987 to settle many of the questions concerning the founding of the Chinese Consolidated Benevolent Association in San Francisco.[3]   However, the origins and history of Chinese Consolidated Benevolent Associations and district associations in most other Chinese communities as well as other important Chinatown organizations such as clan associations, secret societies, labor guilds, chambers of commerce, and political, civic and religious groups are still sketchily explored, if at all. How did these organizations begin? What roles did they play in the Chinese community? How did they change over time? Why was there such a proliferation of secret societies and internecine conflicts in the continental United States in contrast to the relatively less violent environment in Canada and Hawai`i? Since the activities of these organizations played important roles in shaping the Chinese community, more knowledge is essential to better understand some of the dynamics driving the development of the community.

❖ Businesses

Many early Chinese business firms in America were engaged in merchandising and labor contracting. Later there was an increasing number of small industrial firms, followed by major modern commercial, industrial, and financial enterprises although the bulk of Chinese businesses remained small scale. What was the historical process followed by Chinese businesses as they developed through the various stages? How did these changes affect the Chinese community and its relations to mainstream American society? How were regional solidarities and inter-regional rivalries expressed in the business sphere? Major Chinese merchandising firms in America established networks of associated firms in East Asia as well as in the Americas. These networks still exist today even though the firms involved may be different. How were these networks formed? How did they function?

❖ Paper Sons

It is a known fact that during the exclusion era many immigrants assumed exempt class, or "paper son" identities, in order to skirt the exclusion laws and enter America. The *gamsaanjong* had been the principal vehicle facilitating such transactions between would-be immigrants and the "owner" of such identity documents. How did the *gamsaanjong* system originate? How did they become involved in immigration to the United States? How did the system function? What caused this system to decline and disappear? What was the role played by the embargo placed by America on the PRC? There was a confession program during the mid-1950s to adjust the status of Chinese who had immigrated using fraudulent identities. How did this program affect the Chinese community?

❖ American-born Chinese

The exclusion period saw the emergence of a growing group, mostly American-born, who were influenced strongly by western institutions and partially or wholly assimilated into the American cultural tradition. Studying the historical experience of this group would shed more light on the dynamics of the assimilation of the Chinese into American culture. What is the historical experience of the American-born group and what was its place in the Chinese community? What are the differences in the timing and pace of development between the American-born group in Hawai'i and on the mainland, and on the mainland between San Francisco and other communities? The social needs of members of this group led them to set up their own institutions and organizations, many of which were modeled after and were parallel to corresponding groups in mainstream America. What is the history and function of organizations and institutions of the American-born? How were they different from traditional Chinese organizations and institutions?

❖   Nationalism

During the first half of the twentieth century, Chinese nationalist sentiments attracted many Chinese in America alienated by lack of opportunities for Chinese in America. How were nationalist feelings manifested in the Chinese community? How did they function as a causative factor spurring modernization of the community infrastructure, or as a divisive factor leading to intra-community strife? Some Chinese Americans, influenced at least partially by nationalist feelings, traveled to China for a Chinese education and to seek career opportunities. Many studied in universities such as Lingnan in Guangzhou, St. John's in Shanghai, and Yen Ching in Beijing. Some carved out careers in China, but many eventually returned to America, where their bilingualism often helped to win them entry into community leadership circles. Who were some of these leaders? How influential were members of this group in the community leadership? Similarly, nationalism also was a driving force inducing more affluent Chinese to invest at least some of their capital in China and Hong Kong enterprises. What effect did this outflow have on the growth of the Chinese enterprises in America?

❖   Extraterritoriality

Extraterritorial political influence from China has long been a factor affecting developments in the community. How was this influence exhibited during different periods in history? As part of the monarchist-republican rivalry? As part of China's fight against imperialist domination? As part of the Sino-Japanese War? As part of the conflict between the PRC and Taiwan? What was the effect on the Chinese American community? On mainstream society?

❖ Labor

A large percentage of the Chinese in this country belonged to the working class, but little research has been done on Chinese American labor history. How did workers protect their interests? How were labor-management disputes resolved? How were workers organized? What was the relation of Chinese worker organizations to labor organizations in mainstream America? When did Chinese first join labor unions in the American mainstream?

❖ Overseas Students

Students had come from China to study in America since the latter part of the nineteenth century. During the exclusion era they had their own organizations and institutions that interacted with the mainstream and Chinese immigrant communities. Some also participated in Chinese community activities. Most returned to China upon completion of their studies. After World War II, another wave of students arrived, mostly coming from Taiwan and Hong Kong. A third wave came with the opening of the PRC in the 1980s. Each of these groups in turn formed its own organizations and institutions. Due to a more relaxed immigration policy in America, many post-war students were able to stay for extended periods in America; many successfully acquired permanent resident status and became part of the Chinese American community. What were the historical experiences of the three waves of students? What were their organizations and institutions? How were they affected by events in China and in the United States? What were their relations to the Chinese American community? To mainstream American society?

❖ Chinese American Consciousness

The improved social and economic status of Chinese Americans during the post-World War II decades led to a change in psychology among many immigrants from an orientation toward China to an attitude that America is the permanent home for themselves and their posterity. What was the historical experience of Chinese Americans as they underwent this change? This change coincided with the rise of the Peoples Republic of China (PRC) and development of tense relations with the United States. What role did U.S.-China hostility play in this change of attitude? How did this change in attitude affect existing community traditions and institutions? How was this change expressed in the relations of the Chinese community with mainstream society?

❖ Middle Classes

During the quarter century after the end of World War II, a middle class with interests rooted in America increased in numbers and influence when many Chinese were able to enter occupations in the professions, sciences, and technology, fields where entry had hitherto been severely restricted; others became successful entrepreneurs in modern businesses. What had been the historical experience of Chinese in academia? In engineering and the professions? What was the history of development of Chinese American scientific and technological enterprises in America? How was this reflected in American politics? In international relations and the global economy?

❖ Ethnic Chinese Diversity

The rapid influx of immigrants since the 1970s was accompanied by a phenomenal growth and diversification of the Chinese population in America into several major groupings as follows: 1) Cantonese-speaking immigrants arriving before the 1960s together with later arrivals from Hong Kong and from the PRC, many of whom were connected to the Chinatowns; 2) Immigrants, mostly from Taiwan, many of whom arrived as students after the late 1950s and subsequently stayed as professionals, scientists and engineers in new concentrations such as the San Gabriel Valley in Southern California, Flushing in New York, and Bellaire in Houston; 3) Refugees belonging to several Chinese-dialect groups who arrived after the end of the war in the IndoChina Peninsula and Vietnam's persecution of ethnic Chinese with many settling in the existing Chinatowns or new concentrations such as in Westminster and Sacramento; 4) Immigrants from the Fuzhou area, many of whom were smuggled into the country during the 1980s and settled on the east coast; 5) Mandarin-speaking students and intellectuals from other regions of China who decided to stay when the PRC was founded and ex-officials and other Nationalist supporters who arrived after the Communist triumph in China, mostly via Taiwan and Hong Kong; 6) Mandarin-speaking students, intellectuals and business representatives from the PRC, who began arriving after the PRC relaxed emigration restrictions at the end of the 1970s. There are also smaller sub-communities of Chinese from Cuba, Latin America, Burma, countries of Southeast Asia, and other regions. In addition there are the English-speaking Chinese, who are descended from earlier immigrants, mostly Cantonese. However, increasingly their numbers are being augmented by the second and third generations of the other more recent groups. Except for the Cantonese group on which much of the attention of scholars has focused up to now, little research has been done on the society and history of the other groups.

❖ Ethnic Enclaves

For many decades, San Francisco has been considered the political, cultural, and political center for the Chinese in America. Thus, more documentation is available from this location than any other, and many Chinese American historians tend to focus much of their research on developments in San Francisco to the neglect of communities in other areas. However, in a way, the San Francisco community is rather atypical in that the large concentration of Chinese exerted a conservative influence that tended to help the population to preserve its Chinese language and culture and to slow their assimilation into mainstream culture. Also, the pervasive oppressive discrimination against Chinese resulting in *de facto* segregation of the community during the Exclusion era also had a significant impact in shaping psychological attitudes somewhat different from those among Chinese in other communities. Thus, even though the San Francisco community no doubt plays an important role among Chinese in America, there is a definite need to examine in more detail the historical development of Chinese Americans in other communities, such as New York, and Los Angeles, as well as smaller towns, to reach a fuller understanding of the dynamics of development of Chinese American society. During the decades after World War II Hawai`i had not seen as large an influx of immigrants as the mainland. How did this affect the post-war development of the Chinese community in Hawai`i? What role is being played by Chinese in Hawaiian society?

❖ Biographies and Life Histories

A characteristic of many current Chinese American histories in the English language has been the fact that the Chinese appeared to be faceless and nameless. Surely such personalities as Norman Assing, Tong K. Achik, Li Po Tai, Wong Ching Foo, Ng Poon Chew, Look Tin Eli, Tan Foon Chew, Lew Hing, K. C. Li, Kathryn Cheung, Louise Leung Larson, Walter U. Lum, Lue Gim Gong, Chun Quon and others have contributed to the building of America and merit mention in historical chronicles. There is a definite need to develop more Chinese American biographical materials for historical research.

❖ A Comprehensive History

Lastly, there is a need for a comprehensive work tying together the many threads of the Chinese American historical experience. Such works have been available in the Chinese language for some time; however, existing works in the English language are either too uneven in coverage, with emphasis on nineteenth century Chinese labor but scant attention paid to developments in the twentieth century, or are so abbreviated that many details on events and personalities are omitted and Chinese come across as faceless and nameless.

One problem faced by the field is that many scholars in Asian American Studies have appeared to favor literature, identity and other issues as research topics in recent years. While there is no question as to the value of such studies, the result is that only a limited number of scholars are engaged in Chinese American historical research. Another problem is that most researchers do not use, or underutilize Chinese-language sources. Since the Chinese American community has had a predominantly immigrant population during practically all of the historical period, most documentation was necessarily in Chinese; hence, Chinese-language materials are essential for in-depth investigations of many facets of the Chinese American historical experience, especially those connected with the community's internal dynamics. Asian American graduate programs up to now have resisted making knowledge of the Asian languages a requirement. Since nature abhors a vacuum and Chinese American historical research is not a private preserve, scholars proficient in Chinese have entered the field. Some of these have also come up with some fresh interpretations of Chinese American history.

The Chinese in America are a major Asian group with a long history in this country whose experiences played an important role in the development of America. Studying Chinese American history will provide valuable insights into the complex process whereby a non-European, non-Caucasian, ethnic-minority community survived and developed to eventually become an integral part of American society. Given the need for a comprehensive record, surely there must be scholars who will rise to the challenge and publish such work in the foreseeable future, thus building a new tradition of Chinese American scholarship.

Notes

1. The Wah Ting San Fong was still active in 1913 when it was one of the 27 secret societies in San Francisco signing a compact agreeing to the formation of the Peace Society to mediate disputes by peaceful means. But by the mid-1920s when our family moved in, the group was no longer active and only a few old members were living in the clubrooms. Sam Yup means "three counties" and refers to three counties adjacent to Guangzhou—Nanhai, Panyu, and Shunde.

2. "Acknowledgments," in Stanford M. Lyman, *The Asian in North America* (Santa Barbara: American Bibliographical Center-Clio Press, 1977), ix-xii. The interest in race relations and ethnic minorities continued to be evidenced by publication of several academic works on the Chinese in America during the early 1960s: Rose Hum Lee, *The Chinese in the United States of America* (Hong Kong: Hong Kong University Press, 1960); S. W. Kung, *Chinese in American Life* (Seattle: University of Washington Press, 1962); Ping Chiu, *Chinese Labor in California* (Madison: State Historical Society of Wisconsin, 1963), and Gunther Barth, *Bitter Strength* (Cambridge: Harvard University Press, 1964). Soon afterward came Betty Lee Sung, *Mountain of Gold* (New York: MacMillan Company, 1967), targeted at the general reading public.

3. *Chinese America: History and Perspectives, 1987* (San Francisco: Chinese Historical Society of America, 1987), 13-51.

"Peace Sunday," Los Angeles Little Tokyo, 1969.
Gidra Photographer. Courtesy of the UCLA Asian American
Studies Center Movement Archives.

Yuji Ichioka, Tokyo, December 1999, being interviewed by
Akahata, official organ of the Japanese Communist Party.
Photograph by Akahata. © Akahata.

Amerasia Journal 26:1 (2000): 32-53

A Historian by Happenstance

Yuji Ichioka

I shy away from describing myself as a professional historian. The reason is quite simple. Unlike most professional historians, I did not become a historian through the conventional process of completing a Ph.D. program in history at an established university. True, at one time, I had aspired to be a historian of modern China, but I quickly divested myself of this idea when I dropped out of Columbia University in 1963 after less than a year in graduate school. My brief exposure to graduate studies persuaded me that a doctoral program was not my cup of tea. Nor did I become a historian by long-term, personal design. My public school education did everything but instill in me an interest in history. Indeed, it is not too far-fetched to say that I was a veritable embodiment of ignorance in all matters relating to history upon my graduation from Berkeley High School in 1954. I came upon my interest in Asian-American history much later in life through force of circumstances within the context of the Civil Rights and anti-Vietnam War movements.

Circumstantial Beginning

Thirty-one years ago, in the spring of 1969 at UCLA, I taught the first class in what we now call Asian American Studies under the title "Orientals in America." I was invited to teach this class by UCLA student activists who were spearheading the push for Asian American Studies on their campus. They had heard of my political activities in northern California. In the spring of 1968, I had founded the Asian American Political Alliance, a political action group in Berkeley. The students contacted me and asked if I would

YUJI ICHIOKA is a research associate and adjunct associate professor of history, Asian American Studies Center, University of California, Los Angeles.

consent to have them submit my name as a potential instructor. I gave them the go ahead, and once I was approved as the instructor, I accepted a part-time, one-quarter lectureship that marked the beginning of my personal involvement with Asian American Studies. Thus my entrance into the academy was different from that of my colleagues. I began my career under these special circumstances without standard academic credentials.

The atmosphere at UCLA was politically charged from the outset. The San Francisco State Third World Strike had erupted in November, 1968, followed by the Berkeley Third World Strike in January, 1969. Both strikes had a profound impact on racial minorities on the campus. Charles E. Young, the youngest chancellor in the history of the University of California system, assumed his post at UCLA on July 1, 1968, and he immediately found himself under great political pressure. Black, Latino, and Asian students were clamoring for the appointment of Third World faculty and classes in Ethnic Studies. Angela Davis, then a young professor in the Philosophy Department and a self-proclaimed member of the American Communist Party, was one of the most popular lecturers on the UCLA campus. Once the Board of Regents learned of her communist background, however, it decided to dismiss her, forcing Young to defend her in the name of academic freedom. In January 1969 a shoot out occurred on the campus between members of the Black Panther Party and US, Ron Karenga's African nationalist group. Two Black Panthers were killed. Some have charged that this incident was instigated by FBI provocateurs. Whether true or not, a pervasive sense of crisis enveloped the campus.

The UCLA students who invited me had decided on the class outline in advance of my appointment. In this sense, I was the nominal rather than the actual instructor (although I did make a few changes once the class got underway). Approximately 150 students enrolled for the class. The class format mainly featured small sections, led by the student organizers, in which weekly discussions of politics and identity dominated. At the time, many, if not most, of the enrolled students were wrestling with their own identity problems revolving around the question of what it meant to be an Asian in American society. Inasmuch as I had never faced a class in my life, this class became my baptism into teaching.

With scant knowledge of the history of Asians in the United States, I realized that I had to educate myself to prepare for the class. I quickly read the "classics" in Asian American Studies for the first time: Mary Coolidge, *Chinese Immigration* (1909); Bruno

Lasker, *Filipino Immigration to the Continental United States and to Hawaii* (1931); Yamato Ichihashi, *The Japanese in the United States* (1932); Hilary Conroy, *The Japanese Frontier in Hawaii, 1868-1898* (1953); and Rose Hum Lee, *The Chinese in the United States* (1960). I also examined the two standard works on the anti-Chinese and anti-Japanese exclusion movements: Elmer C. Sandmeyer, *The Anti-Chinese Movement in California* (1939) and Roger Daniels, *The Politics of Prejudice* (1962); as well as the standard work on California labor history: Ira A. Cross, *A History of the Labor Movement in California* (1935). And I set about reviewing the then already voluminous literature on the wartime internment of Japanese-Americans.

My interest in Japanese-American history was reinforced by the Japanese American Research Project (JARP). Sponsored by the Japanese American Citizens League, JARP had been launched in 1962 as a socio-historical study of Japanese immigrants and their descendants. In 1969 it was still an ongoing research project based on the UCLA campus. One of its research assistants was Yasuo Sakata, a former classmate of mine and a doctoral candidate in the UCLA History Department. In 1962 we had graduated together as history majors from UCLA, I as a young Nisei and he as a foreign student from Japan. From him I learned that JARP had collected a sizable body of primary sources in the Japanese language on Japanese immigration history. I also learned (and much to my dismay I might add) that the collection was in an unorganized state with the material still stored in dusty carton boxes. Yet I didn't have to look at everything in order to arrive at a reasonable judgement as to the worth of the collection. A cursory inspection sufficed to confirm Sakata's view that it indeed contained many primary sources of immense historical value relating to Japanese immigration history.

The Asian American Studies Center at UCLA was established on July 1, 1969. Those of us who were involved in the first class in Asian American Studies had drafted the proposal for the establishment of the Center. I served as the Associate Director in the first year. From its inception, the Center had, among its multiple purposes, the goal of doing research on Asians in American society in the past and present. At the time the Director of JARP had no plans to organize the JARP collection. I consulted with Yasuo Sakata. Because he and I both agreed on its historical value, we decided to undertake the accession work of organizing and annotating the Japanese language material in the collection. So in 1971, with the support of the Asian American Studies Center, we commenced the tedious and dirty work of going through the dusty carton boxes in which the material had been stored. Our labor bore fruit three years later with the publication of *A Buried Past: An Annotated Bibliography of the Japanese American Research Project Collection* (1974).

My work on the bibliography laid the foundation for my research work. A reading of the secondary literature on Japanese-American history convinced me of the accuracy of Roger Daniels' observation, made in 1966, that Asians had been studied only because they had been objects of exclusion. Studies of prewar Japanese-American history almost exclusively concentrated on what had happened to the Issei generation. They focused on the anti-Japanese exclusion movement and the exclusionists, but rarely, if ever, touched upon how the excluded, the Issei, felt, thought, and reacted to being excluded. In general, researchers assumed that Japanese immigrants left no records of their American experience; and even when they assumed otherwise, they failed to look into the records, often using the difficulty of reading the Japanese language as a convenient excuse. What resulted was an askew view of the Issei as mere objects of exclusion. That is why I selected the title *A Buried Past* for our bibliography. In my opinion, Issei history remained an unexhumed past.

The accession work opened my eyes to the existence of Japanese language sources by and about the Issei. The JARP Collection included the microfilm records of the Japanese Foreign Ministry on overseas Japanese immigration and the Japanese exclusion movement; Japanese immigrant newspapers and periodicals; Japanese Association records; numerous general, regional, and local histories as well as histories of religious institutions and other community organizations; biographies, memoirs, and autobiographies; published works of fiction and poetry; rich personal papers of prominent Issei; and photographic albums and other material. Taken together, these Japanese language sources constituted a rich treasure trove never before tapped by past historians.

Today, it is no longer a question of the availability of Japanese language sources. Rather, it is the question of the ability of researchers to use such sources, now even more abundantly available than when we annotated the JARP Collection. In the introduction to the JARP bibliography, I wrote that the interest in the history of racial minorities should entail "the debunking of old distortions and myths, the uncovering of hitherto neglected or unknown facts, and the construction of a new interpretation of that past." I came away from the accession work with the firm conviction that research in the Japanese language sources in the JARP Collection offered the best possibility of accomplishing all three tasks as far as Japanese-American history was concerned. This conviction became the cornerstone of my research work and later efforts to collect additional sources to enhance the JARP Collection.

Fits and Starts

In 1969 my knowledge of Japanese was not good enough to do in-depth historical research. I was a typical postwar Nisei who grew up ignorant of the Japanese language. I never attended a Japanese language school, and I only spoke broken Japanese at home. When I graduated from high school, my speaking ability was, at best, at a kindergarten level. It goes without saying that I had absolutely no reading or writing ability. My introduction to Chinese characters took place in Chinese language classes I took in connection with my early aspiration to become a historian of modern China, which ended abruptly when I dropped out of graduate school. Subsequently, I took a job as far removed from East Asian Studies as possible. I became a Youth Parole Worker with the New York State Training School for Boys, a social service agency working with so-called delinquent youth. I worked a year in an institutional setting in Warwick, New York and another year as a parole worker in New York City.

While working as a parole worker, I began to study Japanese in preparation for a trip to Japan. I studied on my own for the most part, but had some help from a few Japanese friends. One couple had come to New York City from Tokyo to do a book on Malcolm X. Unable to understand the colloquial expressions in the speeches and writings of Malcolm X, they sought help from me. In exchange for my assistance, they offered to give me private Japanese lessons. I accepted their offer and studied with them for about six months. In the winter of 1966 I sailed to Yokohama aboard the *Argentina-maru*, an old Osaka Steamship Company vessel that had transported many Japanese immigrants to Latin America. Since I booked steerage passage, I shared quarters with many people, many of whom were Japanese immigrants returning to their homeland after long sojourns in Brazil.   For the first time in my life, I found myself in an all-Japanese speaking environment. What little Japanese I had studied until that time proved to be woefully wanting. I still could not adequately communicate my thoughts and feelings in the language. I often felt like an imbecile among my shipmates with whom I shared crammed quarters during the 11-

day trans-Pacific passage. This experience, at once disappointing and exasperating, motivated me to continue learning Japanese during my subsequent three-month stay in Japan.

Upon my return to the States, I worked as a warehouseman until the winter of 1967 when I entered the East Asian Studies M.A. program at the University of California at Berkeley. I enrolled in a few classes in Japanese literature and culture, but most of my classes were in history, especially modern Japanese history. Under the guidance of Professor Yamaguchi Kôsaku, a visiting professor of history from Japan, I did my M.A. thesis on Takayama Chogyû, a Meiji writer and conservative political thinker. While studying toward my M.A. degree, I went out of the way to socialize with native Japanese speakers with the goal of improving my spoken Japanese. I also served as an occasional, unofficial interpreter for members of the Japanese Council Against the A- and H-Bomb (Gensuikin) who came to participate in anti-Vietnam War rallies and activities in the San Francisco Bay Area. The Council was an official organ of the Japanese Socialist Party

In this way, I improved my Japanese proficiency, but it still was not good enough to do research in Japanese immigration history. I was unable to easily read or fully comprehend Japanese written in late Meiji times, not to mention hand transcriptions of Japanese diplomatic cables and reports. Nor could I read with facility early Japanese immigrant newspapers and periodicals. Fortunately, I had Yasuo Sakata as my mentor. As we worked together on the accession work of organizing and annotating the JARP Collection, he taught me about the characteristics of Meiji-style writing, the meaning of old idiomatic expressions, and the secret of deciphering difficult passages. The accession work was my on-the-job training, so to speak. At it I learned a new grammar, a new vocabulary, and new idioms, all related, directly or indirectly, to Japanese immigration history which prepared me for my future research work. Through these circumstances, I became keenly interested in Japanese-American history, to the extent indeed that I began to entertain the idea of doing research on the topic myself.

The field of Japanese-American Studies was wide open. Except for studies of the prewar Japanese exclusion movement and the wartime internment of Japanese-Americans, there were no historical studies of any merit. During the early 1970s, under the influence of the Civil Rights Movement, most Japanese-Americans were self-absorbed in reassessing their wartime internment experience. While this was perfectly understandable, it had the unintended effect of promoting a myopic view of Japanese-American history, at least as I saw it at the time. With so much attention paid to the internment years, it was as if Japanese-American history had begun with the Second World War, consigning the half century or more of prewar history to a state of almost complete oblivion. If I decided to do historical research, I promised myself that I would stay clear of the wartime years. I would take advantage of the opportunity afforded by the JARP Collection and study the prewar years, especially the Issei generation during the late nineteenth and early twentieth century.

Research and Related Work

I commenced research in earnest after the publication of our annotated bibliography. I published my first essay, on Issei socialists and anarchists, in 1971 in the second issue of *Amerasia Journal*. The research and writing for this piece predated my work on the JARP annotation project and originated in my first encounter with the late Karl Yoneda, the long-time Japanese-American leftist. Although I had heard of Karl prior to 1967, I never had had the privilege of meeting him. I met him for the first time in the summer of 1967. Almost immediately after, I read his Japanese book on the history of Japanese workers in the United States. From my reading, I learned, much to my surprise and joy, that there had been Issei socialists and anarchists at the turn of the century in the San Francisco Bay Area. I felt an immediate kinship with them because they, too, had struggled against racism, political oppression, and economic exploitation. I felt an even greater kinship as I learned that one of the anarchists, Ueyama Jitarō, was the father of Dr. Hajime Ueyama. Dr. Ueyama was our family doctor who lived and practiced medicine a block from our home in Berkeley. Despite the fact that I grew up with Dr. Ueyama's son, I had been unaware that his grandfather had been a member of the Social Revolutionary Party, the Issei anarchist organization formed in Oakland in 1906. With my curiosity whetted, I decided to do my piece on the Issei socialists and anarchists. In retrospect, I think I selected this topic because it enabled me to link the Japanese-American past, in a very personal way, to what I was doing politically in Berkeley at the time.

My subsequent writings consisted of essays on other topics in Japanese-American history. In doing the research for them, I used the Japanese language sources in the JARP Collection, sometimes supplementing them with other sources. With no clear book in mind, I moved from one topic to another with each essay standing on its own. My initial focus was on Issei laborers. I worked on such topics as the Japanese labor contracting system and American railroads and the United Mine Workers of America and Japanese coal miners in Rock Springs, Wyoming. Working as I was in new research terrain, I always faced the challenge of having to start more or less from scratch in writing my essays. For example, when I began research on the landmark 1922 Takao Ozawa naturalization test case, I discovered that no one had bothered to examine the Japanese immigrant background to the case. The extant secondary works only covered the legal issues it raised. So I reconstructed the Japanese immigrant background from my reading of the Japanese immigrant press, Japanese Foreign Ministry cables and reports, and other Japanese language sources. Similarly, when I started asking myself questions about the adverse effects of the California alien land laws, I discovered that very little had been produced on how the Japanese immigrants themselves perceived and reacted to the laws. Some researchers, without examining Japanese language sources, maintained that the laws had no real negative effects. To refute this unfounded claim, I wrote about the effects as evidenced by how Japanese immigrants actually reacted to the enactment and enforcement of the alien land laws. Eventually, I put all of my essays into a coherent narrative in book form as *The Issei: The World of the First-Generation Japanese Immigrants, 1885-1924* (1988).

Alongside my research work, I did other related things. For one, I suggested to Karl Yoneda that he should write an autobiography, believing that it was important for people to read the story of his life of struggle as a trade-unionist, communist, writer, and political activist. Karl hesitated at first because he thought his English was inadequate to the task. Though born in the United States, he had been educated—except for a year in an elementary school in Glendale, California—entirely in Japan. Understandably, Japanese was his first language. Once he agreed to my suggestion, however, he approached the job of writing in English with characteristic dogged determination. Using his index fingers in a hunt-and-peck manner, he knocked out a draft on an old typewriter. I assumed the job of editing. As much as possible, I retained the flavor of his original English, but made deletions and recommended additions wherever I thought they would improve the draft. In 1983, after considerable give-and-take, the Asian American Studies Center published the autobiography under the title *Ganbatte: Sixty-Year Struggle of a Kibei Worker*. Attracting a wide readership, the book sold out in a very short time.

I also worked to expand the JARP Collection. Convinced that some Japanese American families still had personal records of their Issei parents or grandparents, I sought out such families. Many of these families, unable to read Japanese, were not aware of the historical value of what they possessed. The JARP Project officially had ended in 1972. I persuaded families with personal papers to donate them to UCLA through the Asian American Studies Center. Among the most significant ones are the Sakai Yoneo Papers, Karl Yoneda Papers, Abiko Family Papers, Fujita Akira Papers, Togawa Akira Papers, and Fujii Ryōichi Papers, all rich in Japanese language manuscript material. Sakai Yoneo (1900-1978) was an Issei newspaperman affiliated with the *Rafu Shimpō* before the Second World War; Fujita Akira (1920-1988) was a Kibei writer who was a prominent figure in the Nanka Bungei, a postwar literary group in Southern California; Togawa Akira (1903-1980) was an Issei poet and member of the Nanka Bungei as well; and Fujii Ryōichi (1905-1983) was an Issei newspaperman and founder of the *Chicago Shimpo*. The Abiko Family Papers primarily consist of the papers of Abiko Yonako (1880-1944), the Issei wife of Abiko Kyūtarō, founder and publisher of the *Nichibei Shimbun* of San Francisco. I have already identified Karl Yoneda (1906-1999). Besides the foregoing papers, we also acquired the Edison Uno Papers, Charles Kikuchi Papers, and T. Scott Miyagawa Papers, papers of three prominent Nisei.

Both the registries of each of the papers and the papers themselves are available at the Department of Special Collections in the UCLA Charles E. Young Research Library where the entire JARP Collection is deposited. *Fading Footsteps of the Issei: An Annotated Check List of the Manuscript Holdings of the Japanese American Research Project Collection* (1992), compiled by Yasuo Sakata, is an annotated bibliography of the manuscript holdings of the original JARP Collection. *A Buried Past II: A Sequel to the Annotated Bibliography of the Japanese American Research Project Collection* (1999), which I most recently compiled with Eiichiro Azuma, is an annotated bibliography of all the new Japanese language material added to the JARP Collection since 1973, including numerous new studies on Japanese immigration history published in Japan. Combined with the original collection, this new material makes the JARP Collection unrivaled. It is without a doubt the finest collection of primary and secondary sources in the United States in the Japanese language on Japanese immigrants and their descendants.

Finally, I presented many public lectures. From the beginning, the staff of the Asian American Studies Center committed itself to forging ties with the Asian American communities of southern California and making some kind of contributions to them. Accordingly, I taught community classes on Japanese-American history over an eight-year period. These classes were held in the evenings at churches, temples, and other community institutions and were attended, for the most part, by Japanese-Americans. Many were Sansei and Yonsei who were probing into their own family roots and therefore especially eager to learn about the Japanese-American past. Older Nisei attendees often shared their knowledge and life experiences with class members, providing unanticipated but important personal lessons in history from which everyone in the classes benefited. No instructor could have asked for a better group of motivated, engaged, and attentive students.

Japanese Academic Studies

During the last twenty-five years, I have followed closely Japanese researchers and their writings on Japanese-Americans. From about the late 1970s, an interest in overseas Japanese arose in academic and other circles in Japan. This interest was stimulated, in part, by the 1978 commemorative events marking the seventieth anniversary of Japanese immigration to Brazil. In Sao Paulo, the President of Brazil and the Crown Prince of Japan participated in the week-long events carried out with great fanfare. The Japanese news media gave wide coverage to all of the events, the effect of which was to generate a popular interest in Japanese-Brazilians and other Nikkei living outside of Brazil. At the beginning there were only a handful of researchers who studied overseas Japanese, but the number of such people increased dramatically during the 1980s, so much so that, in 1991, the Nihon Imin Gakkai or Japanese Association for Migration Studies was established. From its inception, the membership of this new academic association, now exceeding three hundred members, was comprised of people in the social sciences and humanities conducting research on Japanese emigration abroad, particularly to North America. The official organ of the association, the *Imin Kenkyū Nenpō* ["The Annual Review of Migration Studies"], has been published since 1995.

Throughout the years, I have met many Japanese researchers. My relationship to them has not been always cordial. On the one hand, I have met researchers who have a sincere interest in Nikkei and have produced admirable studies. These persons have my respect and gratitude. On the other hand, I have come across others whom I have found, to put it bluntly, rather hard to stomach. My first research trip to Japan occurred in 1974. After seeing *A Buried Past* through publication, I decided to go to Tokyo to search for more Japanese language sources. On this my second trip to Japan, I met Itō Kazuo, a well-known Japanese writer on Japanese-American history. In 1969 he had published *Hokubei Hyakunen Zakura*, an edited collection of Issei reminiscences about prewar life and labor in the Pacific Northwest, on which his reputation rested. Itô impressed me as an arrogant, conceited Japanese male. Draping himself in a mantle of authority, he was a self-anointed "expert" on Japanese-American history.

Apart from dislikable personalities, I am critical of Japanese researchers for other reasons. I have long advocated that sources in Japanese-American history should be deposited in public institutions accessible to all bona fide researchers. This belief has served as my guiding principle in my work of expanding the JARP Collection. Hence I have opposed sources going into private hands, especially into Japanese hands for exclusive usage in Japan. After all, the Issei made history in the United States and the records of that history should remain in this country as a part of our historical heritage. Nonetheless, some Japanese researchers have managed to get their hands on sources, sometimes by methods bordering on thievery, and then have carted them off to Japan.

The *Utah Nippō* of Salt Lake City once had valuable source material accumulated since the day it was launched back in 1914. When I paid a call on the newspaper office, I was shocked to find that the office shelves had been picked clean of books and other material. The Nisei daughter of the deceased publisher informed me that Japanese visitors, who visited the office periodically, had taken everything away. In my opinion, these visitors took advantage of the fact that this daughter did not know what the office shelves held because she could not read Japanese. Then there is the case of the personal library of Reverend Tamai Yoshitaka, the longtime Buddhist minister of the Tri-State Buddhist Church of Denver. When he passed away, Nakagaki Masami of Ryūkoku University, an onetime Buddhist minister himself, obtained the library and took it to Kyoto. Today, this library is not accessible to outside researchers. This is why I appealed to the family of Asano Shichinosuke not to donate his personal papers to Japan as soon as I learned that he, too, had passed away. Asano was an Issei newspaperman affiliated with the prewar *Nichibei Shimbun* and the postwar *Nichibei Jiji*. Like the Tamai library, I feared that his personal papers would be irretrievably lost to us if they fell into Japanese hands.

Members of the Japanese Association for Migration Studies are drawn to the study of overseas Japanese primarily because it is a new field offering more research opportunities than older established fields of study. Many members have had no personal contacts with or experience living among overseas Japanese. With little empathy for their subjects, they study the Nikkei as mere "objects" of investigation, at times with paternalistic condescension, sometimes with thinly disguised contempt. Tamura Norio of Tokyo Keizai University is an example. He heads a research group which has studied Japanese immigrant newspapers over the years. He is a founding member of the Japanese Association for Migration Studies and onetime past president. He invited me to join his research team in 1984 after he received a Toyota Foundation grant. The grant required American participation because his research project had been funded as a joint international undertaking. While I was a member, I took part in two symposia. In fact, I organized the second symposium, held in Los Angeles in 1985, with partial support from the Times-Mirror Foundation. I also contributed an essay to an anthology.

In 1987 I withdrew from Tamura's research group. I reached the conclusion that Tamura had little respect for Nikkei people as a whole. On the surface he voices concern for the past and present welfare of Japanese-Americans, but his attitude and behavior invariably belie such sentiments. Like many insular Japanese, Tamura cannot accept and embrace the fact that, by definition, Nikkei are not Japanese. Nor can he acknowledge that we have our own *raison d'etre* equally as valid as being Japanese. Consequently, he looks down upon us, often in a patronizing manner, at other times in amused contempt, but always with a presumption of superiority. To him, Japanese immigrant newspapers are "objects" of academic research. In this sense, Japanese-Americans are means to an end—research fodder as it were—with the end being the professional advancement of Tamura and the members of his research team. His group has also collected sources in Canada and the United States, but he does not permit outsiders to see or use them, an objectionable practice rooted in Japanese academic insularity.

In some cases, different research approaches make disputes between Japanese researchers and me all but a foregone conclusion. Some Japanese researchers study overseas Japanese emigration as an integral aspect of modern Japanese history and overseas Japanese immigrant communities as extensions of Japanese society. In direct contrast, I anchor Japanese-American history and communities firmly within the boundaries of American history and society. Other Japanese researchers, explicitly or implicitly, study overseas Japanese within the framework of the question, What is a Japanese? This question is rooted in contemporary Japanese society and its obsession with the meaning of "Japanese." Again, in direct contrast, I place Japanese-Americans within the framework of the question, What is an American? Given these and other contrasting approaches, setting aside my stated objections to Japanese researchers, I bear in mind that there are unavoidable disagreements over interpretations of Japanese-American history between Japanese historians in Japan and someone like myself in the United States.

Present and Future Status

Looking back over the last three decades, no one can deny that there has been progress in the writing of Asian-American history. We now know much more about our past than we did thirty years ago, validating the adage that historical knowledge is cumulative. And we should not forget that we would not know what we know today had it not been for the emergence and development of Asian American Studies. In recent years, many scholars have made noteworthy contributions to Japanese-American history. Among these scholars, however, only a handful have researched Japanese language sources to produce their studies. To correct the past and present imbalance in writings on Japanese-American history, based as it is almost exclusively on English-language sources, many more monographs using Japanese-language sources are needed.

There is no question that further research into Japanese language sources can enhance our understanding of Japanese-American history. We still lack a study of the small but vocal Japanese-American left in the 1920s and 1930s. The Karl Yoneda Papers, with an almost complete set of leftist publications in Japanese, provide ample sources. We also lack studies of Japanese-Americans in Japan and Asia during the 1930s and 1940s. As an initial foray into this topic, I edited and contributed to "Beyond National Boundaries: The Complexity of Japanese-American History," a special issue of *Amerasia Journal* 23:3 (1997-98). Future studies should examine in much greater detail the role of the Issei and Nisei in the service of the Japanese government and military before and during the Second World War.

We know virtually nothing about Issei and Kibei literary writings, except for a few anthologies of Issei poetry translated into English. This sad state of affairs is not due to a dearth of sources. The Togawa Akira Papers in the JARP Collection lend themselves to the writing of several doctoral dissertations on this topic. These papers include Togawa's complete writings and his 57-volume diary spanning the years 1921-1978; many albums of Japanese immigrant newspaper clippings on art and literature from 1925 to 1978; the best collection of Issei poetry anthologies and literary writings; and almost complete sets of the *Shūkaku*, *Tessaku*, *Dotō*, *Posuton Bungei*, *Nanka Bungei*, and other literary journals. Combined with the Fujita Akira Papers, these sources can be the basis of indepth studies of Issei and Kibei poets and writers. Their writings, now preserved in the JARP Collection, only await a competent literary historian to give them their rightful voice and place in Japanese-American literature and history.

Studies of the wartime internment can also profit from the use of Japanese language sources. In my reading of the existing literature, one thing has always struck me: the conspicuous slighting of the Issei, equally so of those interned in Justice Department internment camps as well as those interned in so-called WRA Relocation Camps.[1] This slighting has taken many different forms. To cite but one example, autobiographical and biographical accounts of internment in Japanese by and about Issei (and Kibei for that matter) have never been incorporated into the wartime internment studies. This glaring omission and others must be corrected by future researchers. To give readers some idea of such accounts, I list some of them below with brief annotations.[2]

Beyond more research into Japanese language sources, we need to broaden our research focus. One possible area of fruitful inquiry is that of interethnic relationships. Japanese immigrants and their descendants interfaced and interacted, not just with white Americans, but with other racial and ethnic minorities as well. Depending on the locale, they lived, and often worked, alongside Chinese, Koreans, Filipinos, Asian Indians, Mexicans, Armenians, Afro-Americans, Jews, and other people. Their relationships to these groups were often competitive and hostile, but sometimes amicable. Past studies of race-relations, commencing with the Race Relations Survey by Robert E. Park in the 1920s, have stressed the centrality of Japanese-white relations, ignoring

Photograph by Akahata. © Akahata.

the relationships Japanese immigrants and their descendants had with other racial and ethnic minorities. The recent prize-winning essay by Eiichiro Azuma on Japanese-Filipino relations in the San Joaquin River Delta during the 1930s is an excellent example of what can be done on this neglected topic.[3]

The histories of the Issei in Hawai`i and on the mainland warrant reconsideration. So far the two have been treated apart from each other under the assumption that geographical separation led to distinctive histories. This assumption has precluded the examination of connections between the Issei in Hawai`i and their counterparts on the mainland, not to mention shared experiences in their presumed separate histories. I can think of many linkages yet to be explored. In 1928 a sensational racial incident occurred on the islands. Myles Yutaka Fukunaga, a poor, working-class Hawai`i-born Nisei, kidnapped and murdered the ten-year-old son of a prominent white Honolulu banker.[4] According to his confession, racial resentment and revenge played a role in his premeditated crime. Fukunaga's trial and execution had a dramatic impact, not only on the Japanese in Hawai`i, but on the mainland as well. The mainland Japanese immigrant press covered the case closely. Mainland Issei leaders were stunned by what they called this "heinous" crime, and they asked themselves the logical question, could such a crime be repeated on the Pacific Coast? This question was not an idle one, for the first signs of juvenile delinquency and youth gangs had already surfaced on the mainland. The news of the Fukunaga Incident forced the leaders to pay closer attention to the looming problems of the second-generation and rededicate themselves to imparting Japanese moral values to Nisei youngsters to avert a similar happening on the Pacific Coast. Their reactions illustrate how the histories of the Issei in Hawai`i and the mainland are closely interrelated.

Comparison of the Nikkei experience in North and South America should also be considered as a new line of research. Japanese immigration to Latin America began with Mexico in 1897, Peru in 1898, Brazil in 1908, and in later years to other countries. Today, there are significant Nikkei populations in Brazil, Peru, Argentina, Bolivia, Peru, and Mexico. Brazil has the largest population of approximately 1.2 million, far outnumbering the combined Japanese-American population of Hawai`i and the continental United States. In my view, one broad question should be addressed in any comparative historical research, and that is: What was the historical process through which Japanese immigrants (including Okinawans) became Nikkei in North and South America? Regardless of whether Japanese immigrants left Japan during the Meiji, Taisho, or early Showa periods, they generally shared a common Japanese identity and culture and adhered to a common set of Japanese values. Today, as descendants of Japanese immigrants, we are all no longer Japanese, but we differ considerably as Nisei, Sansei, and Yonsei (and even Gosei in the case of Hawai`i) living in different countries in the Western Hemisphere. The explanation for the differences lies in the historical process through which Japanese immigrants became Nikkei.

Comparative historical studies will add to our storehouse of knowledge about the Nikkei by highlighting what we in North and South America share in common and what we do not. The International Nikkei Research Project, recently launched by the Japanese American National Museum of Los Angeles, marks a small but significant beginning. Funded by the Nippon Foundation, this three-year project is an initial attempt at comparative research of Nikkei in the Western hemisphere. Comparative historical studies will require research in English, Japanese, Portuguese, and Spanish language sources, no small challenge for future researchers.

Final Thoughts

In a recent essay, Arif Dirlik reexamines the purposes and scope of Asian American Studies in the light of the changes brought about by the post-1965 Asian immigration and transnational capital.[5] Rightfully, he places me among the founders of Asian American Studies dedicated to claiming our legitimate place in American history and society. Asian American Studies has undergone many changes in its short thirty-one-year history. I have welcomed most of them, but I find it difficult to go along with the present shift to cultural studies dressed up in so-called postmodern and postcolonial language. Most of us who established the initial programs in Asian American Studies began with the political agenda of critiquing American society and of promoting and advancing the welfare of Asian-Americans within it. I fail to see how postmodern cultural studies relate to these purposes. Try as I might, I find myself unable to comprehend most of the studies because they are written in such arcane language. I ask myself, if I cannot understand them, how can the vast majority of ordinary educated people who live outside of university circles understand them? It seems to me Asian American Studies is now producing cultural studies decipherable to only a handful of ivory tower academics. In this sense, our field has gone astray.

Although bilingual and bicultural, I identify myself as an American committed to politically changing our country for the better. At the same time, I believe in the oldtime practice of doing narrative history, of telling a story in ordinary language based on substantive research in primary sources. Such are the views of this Asian American historian who entered the historical profession by happenstance and who still insists on practicing the craft in his "old-fashioned" way.

Notes

1. Admittedly, there are some exceptions to this generalization. The recent publication of Gordon Chang, ed., *Morning Glory, Evening Shadow: Yamato Ichihashi and His Internment Writings, 1942-1945* (Stanford: Stanford University Press, 1997), is a major contribution to the wartime internment literature, but it is based on the original English writings of Professor Yamato Ichihashi. Similarly, Lane Ryo Hirabayashi, ed., *Inside an American Concentration Camp: Japanese American Resistance at Poston* (Tucson: University of Arizona Press, 1995), presents the English writings on camp life by Richard S. Nishimoto, an Issei. Louis Fiset, ed., *Imprisoned Apart: The World War II Correspondence of an Issei Couple* (Seattle: University of Washington Press, 1997), reprints the wartime correspondence (some originally in Japanese) of Matsushita Iwao with his wife, Hanaye. Teruko Imai Kumei, "'Skeleton in the Closet': The Japanese American Hokoku Seinen-dan and Their 'Disloyal' Activities at the Tule Lake Segregation Center During World War II," *Japanese Journal of American Studies* 7 (1996), 67-102, is an outstanding recent example of the use of Japanese language sources. Patsy Sumie Saiki, *Ganbare: An Example of the Japanese Spirit* (Honolulu: Kisaku Inc., 1982), takes a look specifically at those Issei in Hawai`i who were classified as so-called dangerous enemy aliens and interned in Justice Department camps. Other studies of Justice Department internees include: Paul F. Clark, "Those Other Camps: An Oral History Analysis of Japanese Alien Enemy Internment During World War II," MA Thesis, California State University, Fullerton, 1980; Tetsu-den Kashima, "American Mistreatment of Internees During World War II: Enemy Alien Japanese,"

in Roger Daniels et al., *Japanese Americans: From Relocation to Redress* (Salt Lake City: University of Utah Press, 1986), 52-56; John J. Culley, "The Santa Fe Internment Camp and the Justice Department Program for Enemy Aliens, in *ibid.*, 57-71; John J. Culley, "Trouble at the Lordsburg Internment Camp," *New Mexico Historical Review* 60 (1985), 225-248; and Carol Van Valkenburg, *An Alien Place: The Fort Missoula, Montana Detention Camp, 1941-1944* (Missoula: Pictorial Histories Publishing Company, 1995). Violet Kazue De Cristoforo, ed., *May Sky: There Is Always Tomorrow, An Anthology of Japanese American Concentration Kaiko Haiku* (Los Angeles: Sun & Moon Press, 1997), an anthology of haiku poems composed by Issei during the war, is an excellent example of what we can learn from Issei poetry in translation. Bunyu Fujimura, *Though I Be Crushed* (Los Angeles: Nembutsu Press, 1985), and Claire Gorfinkel, ed., *The Evacuation Diary of Hatsuye Egami* (Pasadena: Intentional Productions, 1995), are two brief autobiographical accounts of internment in English. There are a few English translations of other autobiographies: Fukuda Yoshiaki, *My Six Years of Internment: An Issei's Struggle for Justice* (San Francisco: Konko Church, 1990), an autobiography by the Bishop of the Konkōkyō Mission, originally published as *Yokuryū Seikatsu Rokunen* (San Francisco: Konkōkyō San Furanshiko Kyōkai, 1957); Minoru Kiyota, *Beyond Loyalty: The Story of a Kibei* (Honolulu: University of Hawai`i Press, 1997), originally published in the third person as *Nikkei Hangyakuji* (Tokyo: Nihon Hanbai Kabushiki Kaisha, 1990); James Oda, *Heroic Struggles of Japanese Americans: Partisan Fighters From America's Concentration Camps* (Los Angeles: Privately printed, 1981), originally published as *Aru Nikkei Beihei no Shuki* (Los Angeles: Privately printed, 1973); and Seiichi Higashide, *Adios to Tears: The Memoirs of a Japanese-Peruvian Internee in U.S. Concentration Camps* (Honolulu: E & E Kudo, 1993), originally published as *Namida no Adeiosu: Nikkei Perū Imin, Beikoku Kyōsei Shūyōjo no Ki* (Tokyo: Sairyūsha, 1981). Howard Schonberger, "Dilemmas of Loyalty: Japanese Americans and the Psychological Warfare Campaigns of the Office of Strategic Services, 1943-45," *Amerasia Journal* 16:1 (1990), 20-38, discusses the wartime service of Issei in the O.S.S. A few earlier works round out this short list of English language material on the Issei: Eleanor Hull, *Suddenly the Sun: A Biography of Shizuko Takahashi* (New York: Friendship Press, 1957); Takeo Kaneshiro, comp., *Internees: War Relocation Center Memoirs and Diaries* (New York: Vantage Press, 1976); Daisuke Kitagawa, *Issei and Nisei: The Internment Years* (New York: Seabury Press, 1967); and Zuigaku Kodachi et al., eds., "Portland Assembly Center: Diary of Saku Tomita," *Oregon Historical Quarterly* 81 (1980), 149-171.

2.   Some Issei and Kibei autobiographies and biographies:
Akiya Kāru, *Jiyū e no Michi: Taiheiyō wo Koete—Aru Kibei Nisei no Jiden* (Kyoto: Korosha, 1996). An autobiography of a Kibei. Includes his internment at Tanforan and Topaz and wartime service with the O.S.S.;
Aoki Hisa, *Dai-Niji Kōkansen Teia-Maru no Hōkoku* (Tokyo: Maeda Shobo, 1944). An account of internment and return to Japan aboard

the second exchange ship by a Japanese language school teacher and prewar columnist for the *Kashū Mainichi*;

Asano Shichinosuke, *Zaibei Yonjūnen: Watakushi no Kiroku* (Tokyo: Yuki Shobo, 1962). An autobiography of an Issei newspaperman which includes his internment at Tanforan and Topaz;

Ebina Kazuo, *Karifuonia to Nihonjin* (Tokyo: Taiheiyō Kyōkai, 1943). A wartime propaganda account of wartime internment by an Issei newspaperman who had returned to Japan before Pearl Harbor;

Fujioka Shiro, *Ayumi no Ato* (Los Angeles: Ayumi no Ato Kankō Kōenkai, 1957). A comprehensive history of the Japanese in the United States by an Issei newspaperman which includes an account of the author's arrest and interrogation by FBI agents and internment at Ft. Missoula;

Furuya Kumaji (Suikei), *Haisho Tenten* (Honolulu: Hawai Taimususha, 1964). A Hawai`i Issei's account of internment at Ft. Missoula and Santa Fe;

Hashimoto Masaharu, *Nankin Rokunen* (Tenrikyō-shi: Hashimoto Kiyoshi, 1953-1954), 2 vols. A Tenrikyō minister's diary of internment at Lordsburg and Santa Fe;

Ikeda Kandō, *Senjika Nikkeijin to Beikoku no Jitsujō—Nikkeijin no Ketsurui Jitsushi to Dai-Ni Taisen Rimenshi* (Oakland: Daireikyō Kenkyūjo, 1950-1951), 2 vols. An Issei conservative's interpretation of the wartime internment of Japanese-Americans;

Itō Kazuo, *Nakagawa Yoriaki no Sokuseki* (Tokyo: Nichibō Shuppansha, 1974). A biography of an Issei Japanese language school teacher in Seattle. Includes his arrest and internment at Ft. Missoula and Minidoka;

Koide Jō, *Aru Zaibei Nihonjin no Kiroku* (Tokyo: Yūshindo, 1967, 1970), 2 vols. An autobiography of an Issei communist. Volume two covers his internment at Santa Anita and Heart Mountain and wartime service with the O.S.S;

Nakamura Kenta, *Kōkansen* (Tokyo: Shinwasha, 1966). An Issei account of internment at Santa Fe and Lordsburg and repatriation to Japan aboard the second exchange ship;

Nakazawa Ken, *Amerika Gokuchū Yori Dōhō ni Tsugu* (Tokyo: Sonshobo, 1943). A propagandistic account of internment and repatriation aboard the first exchange ship by a prewar staff member of the Los Angeles Japanese Consulate;

Nishi Shigeki (pseud.), *Kenedei Shūyōjo* (New York: Privately printed, 1983). A Peruvian Issei's account of internment at Kennedy, Texas. The author's real name is Nishioka Shigeyuki;

Noda Kasen, *Posuton Tenjūki* (Los Angeles: Nippon Shoten, 1968). An Issei account of internment at Poston;

Noda Nobuo, ed., *Hokujin, Nagumo Seiji no Ikō* (Tokyo: Takagi Reiko, 1978). Autobiographical essays by Nagumo Seiji, an Issei leader of the Southern California Gardeners Federation. Includes internment at Pomona and Heart Mountain;

Noda Nobuo, *Manzanā no Arashi* (Los Angeles: Privately printed, 1971). An Issei account of the so-called Manzanar Incident of December 6, 1942;

Oka Naoki et al., ed., "Sokoku wo Teki to Shite," *in Nihon Heiwaron Taikei* (Tokyo: Nihon Tosho Sentā, 1994), vol. 17, 273-478. A reprint of a biography of Oka Shigeki, a longtime Issei socialist, printer, and newspaper publisher. Includes an account of his internment at Heart Mountain and wartime service with the British government in India;

Sasaki Shūichi (Sasabune), *Yokuryūsho Seikatsu* (Los Angeles: Rafu Shoten, 1950). An Issei newspaperman's account of internment primarily at Ft. Missoula;

Shirai Noboru, *Karifuorunia Nikkeijin Kyōsei Shūyōjo* (Tokyo: Kawade Shobo Shinsha, 1981). An account of internment at Tule Lake;

Soga Yasutarō (Keiho), *Tessaku Seikatsu* (Honolulu: Hawaii Times, 1948). The Nippu Jiji Issei editor's account of internment at Lordsburg and Santa Fe;

Sugimachi Yaemitsu, *Amerika ni Okeru Nihongo Kyōiku* (Pasadena: Sugimachi Mitsue,1968). An autobiography of a Japanese language school teacher in Southern California. Includes his wartime arrest and internment at Lordsburg and Seagoville;

Susuki Sakae, *Zuiri Kaikō Gojūnen* (Los Angeles: W.M. Hawley, 1959). An autobiography with illustrations by an Issei physician commonly known as Dr. P.M. Suski. Includes his wartime internment at Santa Anita and Heart Mountain;

Tana Daishō, *Santa Fē Rōzubāgu Yokuryūsho Nikki* (Tokyo: Tana Tomoe, 1976, 1978, 1980, 1985), 4 vols. A Buddhist minister's internment diary at Santa Fe and Lordsburg;

Yamamoto Asako (pseud.), *Ibara Aru Hakudō* (n.p.: Privately printed, 1952). A diary of internment at Santa Anita and Gila covering the period from December 7, 1941 to July 31, 1943. The diarist returned to Japan aboard the second exchange ship. Her real name is Aoki Hisa. See above;

Yamashiro Masao, *Toi Taigan* (Tokyo: Gurobyūsha, 1984). Autobiographical essays by a Kibei writer. Includes his internment at the Tule Lake Segregation Camp and his assessment of the Kibei there;

Yoneda Kāru, *Manzanā Kyōsei Shūyōjo Nikki* (Tokyo: PMC Shuppan, 1988). A diary of a Kibei communist interned at Manzanar covering the period from December 7, 1941 to December 17, 1942.

A few non-immigrant Japanese, who returned to Japan aboard the first exchange ship, also published noteworthy accounts of their own arrest and internment: See Taguchi Shūji, *Senjika Amerika ni Kokyū Suru* (Tokyo: Shōwa Tosho Kabushiki Gaisha, 1942); Hoshino Jigorō, *Amerika Seikanki* (Tokyo: Kōkoku Seinen Kyōiku Kyōkai, 1942); Katō Masuo, *Beikoku Tokuhain Kichō Hōkoku—Tekikoku Amerika* (Tokyo: Dōmei Tsūshinsha, 1942); Nakano Gorō, *Sokoku ni Kaeru* (Tokyo: Shin Kigensha, 1943); Akasaka Seisaku, *Amerika Kankin Seikatsuki* (Tokyo: Nippon Shuppansha, 1943).

3. Eiichiro Azuma, "Racial Struggle, Immigrant Nationalism, and Ethnic Identity: Japanese and Filipinos in the California Delta, 1930-1941," *Pacific Historical Review* 67:2 (1998), 163-199.

4. For this incident, see Miwa Haruie, *Tensaiji Fukunaga Yutaka* (Honolulu: Matsuzakaya Shoten, 1929); Kihara Ryūkichi, *Hawai Nihonjin*

Shi (Tokyo: Bunseisha, 1935), 770-75; Sōga Yasutarō, *Gojūnenkan no Hawai Kaikō* (Honolulu: Gojūnenkan no Hawai`i Kaikō Kankōkai, 1953), 431-38; Makino Kinzaburō Den Hensan Iinkai, *Makino Kinzaburō Den* (Honolulu: Makino Michie, 1965), 65-67; Ozawa Gijō, ed., *Hawai Nihongo Gakkō Kyōiku Shi* (Honolulu: Hawai Kyōiku Kai, 1972), 153-54; Ogawa, Dennis M., *JAN KEN PO: The World of Hawaii's Japanese Americans* (Honolulu: Japanese American Research Center, 1973), 112-49; Kotani, Roland, *The Japanese in Hawaii: A Century of Struggle* (Honolulu: Hawaii Hochi, 1985), 71-76; and Tamura, Eileen, *Americanization, Acculturation, and Ethnic Identity: The Nisei Generation in Hawaii* (Urbana: University of Illinois Press, 1994), 81-84, 168.

5. Arif Dirlik, "Asians on the Rim: Transnational Capital and Local Community in the Making of Contemporary Asian America," *Amerasia Journal* 22:3 (1996), 1-24.

Amerasia Journal 26:1 (2000): 55-85

Using the Past to Inform the Future:
An Historiography of Hawai`i's Asian and Pacific Islander Americans

Eileen H. Tamura

The Hawai`i experience might inform us as we look to the future of history. This essay[1] thus traces the historical literature on Asian and Pacific Islander Americans (APIAs) in Hawai`i, touching also on some social science publications of interest to historians.[2] I have chosen to include both Pacific Islander Americans and Asian Americans in my discussion because both are central to Hawai`i's panethnic concept of "local" and integral to people of mixed ancestry, subjects of importance in this essay. Moreover, as I explain later, including both groups can help point to possibilities for future historical studies.

The origins of the APIA grouping go back to the aftermath of the 1964 Civil Rights Act. Although by this time federal bureaucrats recognized the artificiality of racial categories and were aware of the presence of a large proportion of the population who could trace their "racial" ancestry to more than one group, the need to check compliance with the law necessitated information on race and ethnicity. As a result, the 1970 and succeeding decennial censuses continued to include questions on racial identity. But the need for compliance data made the process of ethnic enumeration highly political. In response, in 1976 the Office of Management and Budget, whose role is to determine federal data collection standards, directed all federal agencies, including the Bureau of the Census, to provide reports using the four categories of White, Black, American Indian or Alaskan Native, and Asian or Pacific Islander. Previously three groupings had been commonly used: White, Ne-

EILEEN H. TAMURA is associate professor at the Curriculum Research and Development Group, University of Hawai`i.

gro, and Other Races.[3] Native Hawaiians, who have been designated as Pacific Islanders in the 1980, 1990, and 2000 censuses, have attempted to be included instead with the "American Indian or Alaskan Native" group because of their status as an indigenous people.[4]

Since the 1970s, not only federal agencies but also many health and social service groups as well as advocacy, legal, and academic organizations have grouped Pacific Islanders with Asian Americans, as, for example, the Pacific/Asian Coalition, the Asian Pacific American Legal Corporation, the Asian Pacific American Labor Alliance, LEAP Asian Pacific American Public Policy Institute, Asian Pacific Americans in Higher Education, and National Association for Asian Pacific American Education. (The Association for Asian American Studies does not include Pacific Islanders in its name but includes Pacific Islander American scholars among its members and conference presenters.) Combining the two groups was largely a political decision, taken to increase the organizations' visibility and political clout.[5]

In the 1970s and 80s some scholars believed that grouping Asian Americans with Pacific Islanders would lead to a panethnic unity, but this expected development failed to materialize, mainly because of the artificiality of the construct and the rejection by Pacific Islanders of their marginal status within the APIA grouping. By the end of the twentieth century, efforts had begun to forge a pan-Pacific Islander American identity.[6] Meanwhile, the U.S. Census Bureau has decided to separate the Pacific Islander and Asian American categories in the 2000 census.

This separation was a natural consequence of the forced grouping of widely disparate peoples having a diversity of languages, belief systems, cultural traditions, and histories. Yet, while recognizing that "Asians and Pacific Islanders have been peoples apart,"[7] this essay suggests that the very diversity of these peoples and the act of bringing them together can serve to point us to fruitful areas of historical study. The APIA construct can direct our attention away from single-ethnic-group histories to an historical landscape that foregrounds panethnicity, mixed-ethnicity, and interethnic and multiethnic interactions. In this regard, Hawai`i's past, not necessarily as it has been written but as it could be written, might serve as a point of departure.

The Hawai`i Landscape

Asian and Pacific Islander Americans have always constituted the majority of Hawai`i's population. The first inhabitants of the islands were Native Hawaiians, and in the years since the arrival of other peoples, some combination of APIAs has predominated numerically. Today, in a population of well over one million, more than 76 percent are APIAs, the largest numbers of which are Native Hawaiians, Japanese, Filipinos, Chinese, and Koreans. To be sure, these single ethnic-group distinctions are misleading, since intermarriage, occurring ever since newcomers began arriving and rising dramatically during the twentieth century, has made people of mixed ancestry the islands' fastest growing group.

Because APIAs have predominated in Hawai`i and have been integral to every aspect of island life—economic, political, social, and cultural—ethnicity and ethnic relations are dominant themes in Hawai`i's history. All histories of Hawai`i, if not centered on one or more APIAs, invariably touch on some aspect of their lives. Such is the case with general histories of Hawai`i.[8] It is also the case with more specific historical studies that focus on particular subjects, such as land, statehood, and labor.[9]

If we turn to ethnic-group histories, we can discern two long-standing and overlapping generations and the possible emergence of a third.[10] Broadly speaking, the first generation, written from the 1920s through the 60s, was dominated by European American social scientists who were concerned largely with issues of assimilation of single ethnic groups. A second generation emerged beginning in the early 1970s—born from the Vietnam War protest movement, Black Power and Black Studies movements, and the rise of social history—and lasting through the 1990s. No longer were only outsiders looking in, but now insiders, too, were writing the histories of their own ethnic groups. As with mainland studies, the emphasis moved from the assimilation paradigm of the first generation to an emphasis in the second generation on oppression and later on ordinary people as active agents in their own lives. What these two generations had in common was their focus on the experiences of particular ethnic groups as distinctive entities within what might be called a cultural vacuum. Aside from a group's relationship with the more powerful Whites, these histories gave little regard to intersections with other less powerful ethnic groups. Moreover, their focus of attention was on the interior history of an ethnic group—on its old-world background, its problems, its culture and communities, and the persistence of its ethnic identity within the larger community. While these histories will continue to be written and will continue to contribute to our historical understanding, the 1990s produced seeds of a new generation of historical scholarship.

The First Generation

The pioneer researcher of Hawai`i's ethnic groups was not an historian but the sociologist Romanzo Adams. Receiving his Ph.D. from the University of Chicago, Adams arrived in Hawai`i in January 1920, just as the College of Hawaii was in transit to become a university. Adams established what later became known as the Romanzo Adams Social Research Laboratory, which produced sociological studies on Hawai`i's multiethnic population. Andrew Lind, also a graduate of the University of Chicago, joined Adams in 1927. Inspired by Robert E. Park, doyen of the Chicago School of Sociology, Adams and Lind produced numerous studies on ethnicity and ethnic relations and encouraged others to do the same.[11] Among Adams' works are *The Peoples of Hawaii* and "The Education of the Boys of Hawaii," and Lind's classic, *Hawaii's People*, remains an important reference for researchers today.[12] Some later scholars have criticized Adams and Lind for glossing over inequities, discrimination, and other problems in ethnic relations.[13] Yet no one can deny their pioneering work in amassing volumes of demographic and sociological data that have been of inestimable value to later scholars.

Robert Park's mark on studies of Hawai`i's multiethnic population extended even further than his influence on Adams and Lind when his Survey of Race Relations on the Pacific Coast came to the islands in 1927 with the sociologist William Carlson Smith, who had participated in the Survey on the West Coast. Over a period of three years, Smith collected hundreds of life histories written anonymously by students attending public and private secondary schools on the various islands, the Territorial Normal School, and the University of Hawai`i. These essays, which discuss the youths' early life experiences, aspirations, accommodations, and relationships with other groups, provide a wealth of source material for historians. Smith's publications used the life histories collected in Hawai`i and on the West Coast.[14]

Another effort to study the islands' ethnic groups came from the University of Hawai`i's Sociology Club. In 1935, under guidance from Lind, it began publishing *Social Process in Hawaii*, an annual journal conceived as a venue for essays written primarily by the University's students and faculty. After three productive decades, it stopped publication temporarily, continuing in 1979 when the University's Department of Sociology assumed responsibility. The volumes provide a rich resource for historians seeking to understand aspects of Hawai`i's Asian and Pacific Islander Americans in past decades.

As on the mainland United States, social scientists dominated the study of ethnic groups in this early period.[15] One publication by the psychologists Stanley Porteus and Marjorie Babcock, *Temperament and Race*, received considerable notoriety a half-century later. In 1974 when the University's Board of Regents decided to name the Social Science Building after Porteus, who had died in 1972 and had been a professor at the University from 1922 to 1948, a coalition of students and faculty vigorously protested the action and attempted to remove Porteus' name from the building. They were unsuccessful then, but after students revived the issue in 1998, the Board of Regents voted in favor of removing Porteus' name from the building.[16]

Porteus and Babcock's work reflected the popular thinking of the early decades of the twentieth century, the idea that there were inherent psychological and mental differences between individuals of different "races."[17] According to the authors, "When a man has stated his race, he has stated one of the most significant and important facts about himself, important in its bearing on his physical makeup, his personality, and his spiritual and mental outlook." This premise and the book's faulty methodology resulted in a work that has failed to hold muster with scholars. Written at a time when negative stereotypes about ethnic groups were still prevalent, the later controversy over *Temperament and Race* illustrates the extent to which popular and scholarly thinking has changed since the early twentieth century.[18] Adams and Lind, though rightly criticized today for glossing over discrimination and inequities in territorial Hawai`i, did not fall prey to such unexamined stereotypes.

The controversy *Temperament and Race* generated decades after its publication suggests an avenue for historical inquiry: an analysis of views on the academic, occupational, and social achievements of APIAs. What values and beliefs have been prevalent in different periods of history? How have scholars and the popular press treated these issues over time? What continuities and changes have occurred in the methodologies and conclusions of scholars? While there have been a number of studies on APIA academic achievement, there is a need to include occupational and social achievement, and to provide historical perspective.

As the foregoing indicates, the first generation of studies of ethnic groups in Hawai`i often included more than one ethnic group, but each group was discussed by itself, with little or no regard to the others.[19] Also during this period, historical publications were largely absent, with the exception of Bruno Lasker's study of Filipino immigration to Hawai`i and the mainland, Ernest Wakukawa's *A History of the Japanese People in Hawaii*, and well over a decade later, Hilary Conroy's study of Japanese immigration to Hawai`i.[20]

The Second Generation

In the second generation of studies, beginning in the 1970s and extending through the 1990s, the proliferation of publications focusing on single ethnic groups continued, and the people most written about were Native Hawaiians. Now categorized as Pacific Islander Americans, Native Hawaiians hold the distinction of being an indigenous colonized people, in contrast to other Pacific Islanders who arrived in Hawai`i during the 1800s and thereafter. Samoans and then Tongans follow Native Hawaiians in population size, but together in 1996 they constituted only 0.7 percent of the state's population, in contrast to the larger percentage (20.6) of Native Hawaiians, most of whom are Part-Hawaiian.[21]

With the exception of Native Hawaiians, there have been relatively few studies on Hawai`i's Pacific Islanders. Most studies have been sociological and anthropological in nature, most often discussing kinship and family patterns, and adaptation and adjustment.[22] To encourage further research, faculty and students at Brigham Young University-Hawai`i, which serves a large number of Pacific Islander students, established in 1991 the Pacific Islander Americans Research Project.[23] Several years later *Social Process in Hawaii* published a special issue devoted to Pacific Islander Americans in Hawai`i. While none of the essays in this issue provides an historical analysis, the subjects examined, such as family dynamics and images of other ethnic groups, will provide fertile ground for future historians.[24]

Although for over a century Pacific Islanders have left their home islands to settle elsewhere, it has been only since World War II that they have migrated with greater frequency and in large numbers, mainly to Hawai`i and the West Coast. Harry Kitano and Roger Daniels, Paul Spickard, and Fay Alailima have written brief but useful historical sketches, while Andrew Lind and J. Bennett offer essays on the early history of Pacific Islanders to Hawai`i.[25]

In contrast to the dearth of studies on non-Hawaiian Pacific Islander Americans, and in contrast to the lack of historical studies before the 1970s on Asian Americans in Hawai`i, there have been many books and articles over the past century on the history of Native Hawaiians. Several reasons account for this proliferation: their status as an indigenous people, the existence of a kingdom, unique among lands that later became part of the United States, and the unresolved issues resulting from the overthrow of the monarchy and the subsequent annexation.[26] In this essay I focus on sovereignty, the dominant Native Hawaiian issue of the past two decades.

Some basic facts relevant to sovereignty are these: the Hawaiian kingdom was overthrown in 1893, a provisional government and then a republic were formed, and the republic was annexed in 1898 by the United States. Since the 1980s, these seemingly simple facts have become the center of much discussion and debate. A proliferation of books and articles have appeared, some more cogently argued than others. Among them are historical analyses of the loss of Native Hawaiian land, the overthrow of the Hawaiian monarchy, and the annexation of the islands to the United States. These three issues have formed the basis for the sovereignty movement.[27]

Understanding land issues is crucial to understanding the push for sovereignty. In "Land Tenure in Hawaii," Marion Kelly discusses the destruction of the Hawaiian communal land tenure system during the decades after the arrival of Westerners. Other works analyze the Great Māhele, the historic land division of the mid-nineteenth century that left Native Hawaiians landless, and the state's mismanagement of ceded lands—lands formerly ceded to the United States upon annexation and subsequently entrusted to the state government for the benefit of Native Hawaiians.[28] Still other lands, Hawaiian Homelands, have been a bone of contention because of the generally poor quality of the soil, and the issues of breach of trust, misuse of lands, and mismanagement.[29]

Numerous works focus on the overthrow of the monarchy and the annexation of Hawai`i to the United States. Accounts sympathetic to the architects of the overthrow and annexation include Albertine Loomis' *For Whom Are the Stars?* and two of William

Adams Russ's works, *The Hawaiian Revolution* and *The Hawaiian Republic and Its Struggle to Win Annexation*. In *Hawaiian Sovereignty* Thurston Twigg-Smith, grandson of Lorrin A. Thurston, one of the masterminds of the overthrow and annexation, argues a more recent defense. In *Unconquerable Rebel,* ostensibly a biography of controversial figure Robert Wilcox, Ernest Andrade challenges the claim of sovereignty activists that U.S. minister John Stevens conspired with annexationists to overthrow the monarchy.[30]

Works critical of the overthrow and annexation include Thomas Osborne's *Annexation Hawaii*, Tom Coffman's well-written but meagerly documented *Nation Within* (also in video format), Merze Tate's *The United States and the Hawaiian Kingdom*, Rich Budnick's *Stolen Kingdom,* Jennifer Chock's "One Hundred Years of Illegitimacy," and Noenoe Silva's studies on Native Hawaiian resistance to annexation. In *Hawaii's Story by Hawaii's Queen*, the last monarch Queen Lili`uokalani gives her view of events, while Lorrin Thurston and Sanford B. Dole, key figures in the overthrow, authored memoirs that present their perspectives.[31]

The Hawaiian political activism that emerged in the 1970s, and the Hawaiian Renaissance—a revival of Hawaiian chant and hula, language, and religious and cultural practices that began during the 1960s—were the seeds from which the sovereignty movement emerged in the 1980s. Davianna McGregor-Alegado and Haunani-Kay Trask have provided historical accounts on the political activism of the 70s. George Kanahele explains the Hawaiian Renaissance, while Albert Schutz, in *Voices of Eden*, provides an analysis of the history of Hawaiian language studies.[32] The political advocacy of Native Hawaiian water rights and gathering rights, increasing during the 1990s, will undoubtedly be fertile soil for historians in coming decades.

With the emergence of self-determination as a key issue among Native Hawaiians, numerous works advocating sovereignty have been published.[33] Native Hawaiians have also organized sovereignty groups, several of which opposed efforts by the state government to sponsor the convening of a Native Hawaiian convention that would decide on a form of self-government. Opposition groups argued that Hawaiians themselves, not the state, need to direct and control the process toward self-determination. Not until the twenty-first century will these efforts toward sovereignty and the rifts among sovereignty advocates be suitable for historical analysis.

While Native Hawaiians have been what John Ogbu calls "involuntary minorities" who carry a sense of loss and dislocation, Asian Americans have been "voluntary minorities" who themselves decided to live and work in Hawai`i to improve their lives.[34] This fundamental difference and the particular ways in which this difference has played out highlight the need for scholars inquiring into interethnic and multiethnic relations, an area ripe for historical study, to be well-grounded in the particular histories of the groups involved before they can expect to understand the dynamics between and among groups.

The earliest Asians to reach the islands were the Chinese, the first of whom arrived in 1789 on trading ships. Their numbers were minimal until sugar industrialists began recruiting contract laborers in the mid-nineteenth century. By 1884 the Chinese constituted as much as 22.6 percent of Hawai`i's population. At the turn of the twentieth century, however, their proportion began to decline, and since the 1930s it has ranged between 4 to 7 percent.[35]

Prior to the 1970s, there were a few studies on the Chinese in Hawai`i, and most of them were by social scientists.[36] Historical essays of note began appearing in the 70s, and were published primarily in *The Hawaiian Journal of History*.[37] Noteworthy books also began appearing in the 70s. Tin-Yuke Char's *Sandalwood Mountains* focuses on the Chinese immigrants who arrived in the nineteenth and early twentieth centuries. Clarence Glick's *Sojourners and Settlers* is a comprehensive study of the Chinese who immigrated to Hawai`i before World War II, detailing their transformation from birds-of-passage to permanent settlers. Among the historical works on the Chinese, a significant proportion have been biographies, autobiographies, and family histories, of which the more noteworthy include Violet L. Lai's *He Was a Ram: Wong Aloiau of Hawaii*, which details the struggles and successes of a nineteenth century immigrant; and Bob Dye's *Merchant Prince of the Sandalwood Mountains*, which weaves historical and contextual background to provide a lively account of an amazing nineteenth-century figure.[38]

The Japanese were the second group and the most numerous of the Asians to work on the sugar plantations. By 1900 they had become the largest single ethnic group in Hawai`i, and for the next four decades they constituted between 37 and 43 percent of the territory's population. Since 1950 their proportion has decreased steadily so that by the end of the 1990s it was 20 percent.[39]

Because of the near century-long numerical dominance of the Nikkei—people of Japanese ancestry—in the islands, until 1970 more numerous in Hawai`i than on the West Coast, the scholarly literature on Hawai`i's Nikkei is abundant.[40]   In the 1970s historical scholarship began in earnest with Louise Hunter's *Buddhism in Hawaii*, an analysis of the controversy over this religion during Hawai`i's territorial days; John Reinecke's *Feigned Necessity*, a well-crafted analysis of anti-Japanese efforts in the early 1920s; and Dennis Ogawa's *Kodomo No Tame Ni*, an anthology of primary and secondary sources.   Important publications in the 80s and 90s include *Uchinanchu*, a collection of essays on the history of Okinawans in Hawai`i; Yukiko Kimura's *Issei*, a study of the immigrants in Hawai`i; Alan Moriyama's *Imingaisha: Japanese Emigration Companies and Hawaii*, a major contribution to an understanding of the early period of Japanese emigration; Gary Okihiro's *Cane Fires*, which argues that there was an identity of interests among planters, government officials, and military officers that led anti-Japanese efforts in this "mythical racial paradise"; and Eileen Tamura's *Americanization, Acculturation, and Ethnic Identity*, which analyzes the ways in which the Nisei (children of Japanese immigrants) interacted with their multifaceted environment to shape their lives during the decades before World War II.[41]

As with other ethnic groups, biographies of Hawai`i's Nikkei abound, including Daniel Inouye's *Journey to Washington*, H. S. Kawakami's *Japan to Hawaii*, and a series begun by Dennis Ogawa on the Nisei in Hawai`i.   Numerous books have also been published on the experiences of the Nisei veterans of World War II. Among the more notable are Thomas Murphy's pioneering *Ambassadors in Arms*; Masayo Duus's *Unlikely Liberators*; and Lyn Crost's *Honor by Fire*.   In contrast to mainland studies, scholarship on the World War II incarceration of Nikkei in Hawai`i is minimal.   Of the 157,000 Nikkei residing in the islands, only about 1,500, primarily immigrants, were detained in camps, compared to the 120,000 West Coast Nikkei, immigrants and American citizens, who were confined.   A thought-provoking essay on the homefront, "Bayonets in Paradise" by Harry Scheiber and Jane Scheiber, explains why Hawai`i's Nikkei chose not to file suit during martial law, while German-born naturalized Americans did.[42]

Recent historical studies of Hawai`i's Nikkei women suggest promising possibilities.   Barbara Kawakami's *Japanese Immigrant Clothing*, in examining the ways in which women redesigned traditional Japanese clothing for the Hawai`i setting, masterfully uses material culture to understand issues of adaptation and change. A later like effort is Shiho Nunes and Sara Nunes-Atabaki's *The Shishu Ladies of Hilo*, which provides a glimpse into the everyday lives of a community of women who adapt a Japanese art form to a new environment. Another work that adds to our understanding of the rich tapestry of Nikkei women's lives is Laurie Mengel's "Issei Women and Divorce in Hawai`i," which helps to break stereotypical images of immigrant Japanese women as passive and subservient.[43]

In contrast to the numerous ethnic Japanese in Hawai`i, ethnic Koreans have constituted only 1 to 2 percent of the population since the time of their first arrival in 1903.[44] If few published historical studies exist on Chinese in Hawai`i, fewer still are available on Koreans.[45] The standard scholarly work on their pre-1924 immigration is Wayne Patterson's *Korean Frontier in America: Immigration to Hawaii*, an analysis of this early influx of workers within the context of Hawai`i's labor needs, the declining Yi dynasty, American-Korean relations, Japanese-Korean relations, and Japanese-American relations. Another study of the same period is Linda Pomerantz's "The Background of Korean Emigration." On a later historical period, Michael Macmillan's "Unwanted Allies" discusses an ironic twist of fate during World War II when Hawai`i's Korean immigrants, as subjects of Japan, found themselves branded as enemy aliens despite their deep animosity toward Japan for its aggressions in their homeland.[46] What is lacking is an historical analysis of the post-1965 Korean settlement in the islands.

Arriving after the Koreans were the Filipinos, who first migrated to the islands in 1906 to labor in the sugar cane fields.[47] Since 1965 a steady stream has arrived annually so that by the closing decade of the twentieth century, Filipinos were the third largest and fastest-growing ethnic group in Hawai`i.[48]

Despite some pioneering studies made in the 1930s, published scholarship on Filipinos in Hawai`i remained minimal until the 1980s. With the exception of Sister Mary Dorita's account of Filipino immigration to the islands,[49] the few studies produced between 1940 and 1980 focused on contemporary social and economic conditions, and cultural aspects. While such works continued to appear in the 1980s, there were also an increasing number of historical studies, which became even more noticeable during the 1990s, a trend that will likely continue in the twenty-first century.

The histories written in the 1980s focused on the plantation experience: Miriam Sharma's "Pinoy in Paradise, " John Reinecke's *The Filipino Piecemeal Sugar Strike*, Ruben Alcantara's *Sakada*, and Luis Teodoro's *Out of this Struggle*.[50] To compensate for the relative dearth of studies on Filipinos in Hawai`i, *Social Process in Hawaii* published two special issues in the 1990s, the second of which included a strong historical dimension. While the plantation experience has continued to interest historians, they have also begun to examine other subjects: an exploration by Linda Revilla of the situational ethnic identities of second-generation Filipinos who served in the U.S. Army during World War II, and an examination by Steffi San Buenaventura of a Filipino American social and religious movement that became an important acculturating influence at the same time that it advocated Philippine nationalism.[51]

Seeds of a Third Generation

When compared with social scientists, historians are latecomers to studies of Hawai`i's Asian and Pacific Islander Americans. This is to be expected, since history is a discipline that is reflective of the past. Histories have been best when they have waited for the passage of time, since temporal distance helps to provide needed context and perspective in the attempt to explain why things happened the way they did. In this light historians have in recent decades made substantial contributions to our understanding of Hawai`i's APIAs.

While the chief feature of past historical scholarship on Hawai`i's ethnic groups treated each group singularly and with little, if any, regard to other non-White groups, the 1990s witnessed the beginning of what can become the next generation of ethnic histories.

One fruitful area of historical inquiry is the panethnic "local" identity that has derived from Hawai`i's century-long ethnically-diverse society. Jonathan Okamura argues that this local identity in Hawai`i has contributed to the absence of an Asian American identity, in contrast to the situation on the mainland.[52] The concept of a panethnic local identity overlaps with Asian American panethnicity on the mainland as conceptualized by Yen Le Espiritu: panethnicity as the basis for political resistance, panethnicity being "the result of political and social processes, rather than cultural bonds," the subsequent development of a panethnic culture, and the maintenance of separate single ethnic identities within the panethnic phenomenon.[53]   Yet the development of the Hawai`i panethnic local identity that transcends an Asian American panethnicity has been unique, due to historical circumstances, a small geographic space, and frequent opportunities for interethnic mixing.

Emerging in the 1930s and 40s as a way merely to distinguish between Hawai`i's people and mainlanders, the word "local" later took on a special meaning. In the mid-1960s "local" began to refer to "a blending and sharing of ethnic cultures," "a community value-orientation," and a "reaction to an oppressive dominant culture."[54]   The underlying basis for this special meaning was the "ethclass" structure dominant during Hawai`i's plantation days, when Native Hawaiians and immigrant groups were economically and socially subordinate to a white elite. Continuing to hold emotional and cultural significance and prevalent in the islands, the term "local"—though somewhat fluid—has commonly referred to people born and raised in the islands. Often implied is a lifestyle that is casual, family-oriented, humble, generous, open to others, and appreciative of Hawai`i's land, peoples, and cultures.  Portuguese are considered "local" because they came as plantation workers, but other whites, even those born and raised in Hawai`i, often are not. This exclusionary aspect of the term, while decidedly negative, is understandable in light of the concept's genesis: the once-prevalent economic and political domination of the White elite.[55]

One badge of "localness" is the ability to speak Hawai`i Creole English, commonly referred to in the islands as "pidgin English." The scholarly literature on this subject has been dominated by linguists, but a couple of historical studies exist: John Reinecke's seminal work, completed in the 1930s; and Eileen Tamura's examination of the ways in which residents have grappled with this language during most of the twentieth century.[56]

Despite the insider-outsider mentality of the local identity as well as other interethnic problems, there is a widespread notion of Hawai`i as a relatively harmonious multiethnic society.[57]   Some social scientists who have attempted to explain this harmony have pointed to the development of a local culture and identity as one of several elements that have helped people cross ethnic group divisions.[58]   Other scholars see problems within and emerging from the local identity and challenge the notion of Hawai`i as a model of harmonious ethnic relations.  In "The Illusion of Paradise," Jonathan Okamura argues that mainstream multiculturalists in Hawai`i, whom Okamura describes as conservatives who promote the status quo, feel threatened by the Hawaiian sovereignty movement because it distinguishes Native Hawaiians from all other ethnic minorities and calls for special rights and privileges for *Na Kanaka Maoli*, the true people of Hawai`i. In *Institutional Racism*, Michael Haas points to inequities resulting from discriminatory hiring practices. In a similar vein Jeff Chang exposes the rifts among Asian Americans, pointing to the refusal of "locals" to hire immigrant Filipinos as public school teachers.[59]

Studies of interethnic intolerance among and by APIAs are not recent avenues of inquiry. In 1947 Phyllis Kon Cooke discussed negative sentiments among APIAs toward African Americans, demonstrating then that Hawai`i was not a racial paradise. Editors of *Social Process in Hawaii* devoted their 1954 volume to issues in race relations, with essays on race prejudice, residential segregation, and minorities within minorities.[60] As the foregoing illustrates, social scientists have taken the lead in exploring interethnic and multiethnic relations in Hawai`i, suggesting possibilities for future historical studies. Archival and other collections await historians who will mine them in new ways in order to understand how APIA groups have interacted with each other and with others.

Eiichiro Azuma's historical studies of California, "Racial Struggle, Immigrant Nationalism, and Ethnic Identity," and "Interethnic Conflict under Racial Subordination," demonstrate what can be done for the first half of the twentieth century. Possibilities expand for the succeeding half century when the country became increasingly diverse with people of color constituting an ever larger proportion of the population. With a solid foundation of single-ethnic-group studies available, with a base of social science studies on interethnic relations undertaken in recent years, and with the complexity of issues related to sovereignty and indigenous peoples' traditional gathering rights in Hawai`i and on the mainland, historians can more seriously take heed of Shirley Hune's admonition to move beyond the Black-White paradigm, to bring history to bear in examining the multiple dynamics involved when minorities competed, clashed, marginalized, discriminated, dominated, formed alliances, and otherwise interacted among themselves.[61]

Another major byproduct of Hawai`i's ethnic diversity has been the prevalence of mixed marriages, common well before World War II, and becoming increasingly so since the 1960s. Social scientists have studied Hawai`i's mixed-marriages since Romanzo Adams' 1937 study, and later publications have inquired into the relationship between interracial marriage and adjustment problems, divorce, and occupational status. Paul Spickard's *Mixed Blood*, which integrates Hawai`i and mainland experiences and compares the experiences of three groups—Nikkei, Jews, and African Americans—is one of the few historical treatments of the subject.[62]

A natural consequence of mixed-marriages are ethnically-mixed offspring. At the threshold of the twenty-first century, people of mixed ethnicity constituted over 40 percent of the islands' population. Ronald C. Johnson, who has studied intermarriage and mixed-group people in Hawai`i, predicts "an almost totally mixed population in a few generations."[63] Nationwide a significant proportion of the population are bi- or multi-ethnic. Large proportions of Hispanics, African Americans, Filipinos, American Indians, Alaskan Natives, and Native Hawaiians are multiethnic, as are many European Americans and Asian Americans. The practice by the U. S. Bureau of the Census of enumerating according to monoracial and monoethnic categories continues to frustrate many. Philip Tajitsu Nash and others suggest a remedy, that of allowing people to check a "multiracial" category as well as a "primary group affiliation."[64]

There have been some important publications in recent years about ethnically-mixed APIAs with a few focusing on Hawai`i—one by Paul Spickard and Rowena Fong, and another by Ronald Johnson. Like those on the mainland, studies of Hawai`i's ethnically-mixed people have focused mainly on sociological and psychological aspects. Except for Spickard's "Injustice Compounded," which discusses multiracial individuals in World War II American concentration camps, and a section in his *Mixed Blood*, historical studies on mixed-ethnic APIAs have been largely absent.[65]

Future historical studies might inquire into the ways in which people of mixed ethnicities have identified themselves, and the role that ethnicity has played in their identities. As Li'ana Petranek explains, the concept of ethnic identity can only go so far, particularly but not only for people of mixed ethnicities.[66] How does a person, for example, of German, Portuguese, Native Hawaiian, Chinese, and Filipino ancestry self-identify? What about a person who is not a Native Hawaiian but who grew up among Native Hawaiians and identifies strongly with Native Hawaiian culture? How much of our understanding of ethnic identity assumes biological inheritance and how much cultural practices? And what about those in Hawai`i who identify themselves as "local," in which case cultural identity takes precedence over ethnic identity? For mixed-ethnics and for people of the fourth, fifth and more generations of an ethnic group, has ethnic identity been central or even important in defining themselves?

The 1990s have also seen Asian history and Asian American history become progressively intertwined. Moreover, the late twentieth-century phenomenon of transnational families commuting across the Pacific has become more widespread and is expected to continue in the next century. This particular development, as well as the recognition of transnational ties of earlier decades, creates an increasing demand for bilingual and multilingual scholarship. Already a number of exemplary historical works like John Stephan's *Call of Ancestry* have demonstrated the value of such studies. In a recent issue of *Amerasia Journal*, Yuji Ichioka brought together essays by historians of both Japanese and Japanese American history. Exciting developments are taking place as planning proceeds for a working conference that will bring scholars to the University of Hawai`i from Japan and the United States to engage in discussions on internationalist efforts among Japanese and Americans during the years between the two world wars.[67]

The lack of historical studies comparing Hawai`i with the mainland provides another challenge for historians. There have been sociological studies published in the 1930s that encompass both mainland and Hawai`i experiences, and historical studies like Sucheng Chan's *Asian Americans*, Paul Spickard's *Mixed Blood*, Roger Daniels' *Asian America*, and Ronald Takaki's *Strangers from a Different Shore* have offered some comparisons between Hawai`i and mainland experiences, but at the time that these studies were made, adequate groundwork had not yet been laid for an extensive comparative historical examination.[68] In the new millennium, with the increase of studies on APIAs in Hawai`i and on the mainland available, the time will be ripe for in-depth comparative histories. Possible fruitful avenues include agricultural labor history; the labor movement and unionization; the development of Chinatowns, Little Manilas, and other urban enclaves; Asian American servicemen in the Vietnam war; and post-1965 immigration history.

The foregoing does not rule out the importance of continuing to produce histories of particular ethnic groups, especially of those previously neglected, among them Pacific Islanders, Koreans, and Filipinos. Historians of these and other groups should continue to explore the multi-dimensional complexities of ethnic, cultural, and national identities, highlighting the ways in which APIA females and males of different socioeconomic classes, adults and youths, shaped their lives. In this respect, studies of how these groups acted upon, interacted with, and reacted to other APIAs and other nonwhite people would be most fruitful.

There is a need for further explorations in using material culture to illuminate cultural changes and adaptations; for increased historical scholarship on APIA women; for studies of class differences within ethnic groups; for the history of APIA gays, lesbians, and bisexuals; for the underside of APIA family history, including spouse and child abuse; and for historical analyses of the scholarly and popular thinking about the academic and social achievements of APIAs. Franklin Ng recently completed a multi-volume collection of articles on Asian Americans, written mainly by social scientists, that includes many of the above-mentioned issues—pointing to possible avenues for historical study.[69]

Historians can look to a future of challenges in the next millennium as we attempt to contribute to the effort to provide fuller accounts of the multi-dimensional pasts of APIAs. Without falling into the trap of an essentialism that reduces the diversities within and among ethnic groups by overstating patterns and themes, we will continue to seek to portray people in their full humanity. In so doing, we will dismantle old myths and reveal failings and shortcomings as well as efforts and aspirations. As we continue to craft our understanding of our histories, our portraits will become more complex and less heroic. In this way we can contribute substantially in providing "a denser, more layered portrait" of Asian and Pacific Islander American life.[70]

Notes

1. I would like to thank Roger Daniels, Dwight Hoover, Idus Newby, Franklin Ng, Jonathan Okamura, and Paul Spickard for their help on earlier drafts of this essay.

2. Previous Asian American historiographies include Roger Daniels, "No Lamps Were Lit for Them: Angel Island and the Historiography of Asian American Immigration," *Journal of American Ethnic History* 17 (Fall 1997), 3-18; Sucheng Chan, "Asian American Historiography," *Pacific Historical Review* 65 (August 1996); Shirley Hune, *Pacific Migration to the United States: Trends and Themes in Historical and Sociological Literature* (Washington, DC: Smithsonian Institution, 1977); Daniels, "American Historians and East Asian Immigrants, *Pacific Historical Review* 43 (1974), 449-72; Daniels, "Westerners from

the East: Oriental Immigrants Appraised," *Pacific Historical Review*
35 (1966), 373-83.

3. Yen Le Espiritu, *Asian American Panethnicity: Bridging Institutions and Identities* (Philadelphia: Temple University Press, 1992), 120, 122, 186 n.11; Philip Tajitsu Nash, "Will the Census Go Multiracial?" *Amerasia Journal* 23:1 (1997), 21.

4. Juanita T. Lott, *Asian Americans: From Racial Category to Multiple Identities* (Walnut Creek, California: AltaMira Press, 1998), 96.

5. Lott, *Asian Americans*, 95-96; Sucheng Chan, *Asian American-Pacific American Relations: the Asian American Perspective* (Seattle: Association for Asian/Pacific American Studies, 1982).

6. Debbie Hippolite Wright and Paul Spickard, "Pacific Islander Americans and Asian American Identity," in *Intersections and Divergences: Contemporary Asian Pacific American Communities*, ed. by Linda Trinh Vo and Enrique Bonus (Philadephia: Temple University Press, in press); Antoinette C. McDaniel, "An Accidental Asian *Pacific* American: Reflections on Asian Pacific American Studies at Oberlin College," forthcoming.

7. Quote is from Paul R. Spickard et. al., *Pacific Islander Americans: An Annotated Bibliography in the Social Sciences* (Laie, Hawai`i: Institute for Polynesian Studies, Brigham Young University Hawai`i, 1995), vi.

8. General histories include Ralph S. Kuykendall, *The Hawaiian Kingdom*, 3 vols. (Honolulu: University of Hawai`i Press, 1938-1967; Lawrence H. Fuchs, *Hawaii Pono: A Social History* (New York: Harcourt, Brace, and World, 1961); Gavan Daws, *Shoal of Time: A History of the Hawaiian Islands* (Honolulu: University of Hawai`i Press, 1968); Edward Joesting, *Hawaii: An Uncommon History* (Honolulu: University of Hawai`i Press, 1972); Edward Joesting, *Kauai: The Separate Kingdom* (Honolulu: University of Hawai`i Press, 1984); and Noel Kent, *Hawai`i: Islands under the Influence* (New York: Monthly Review Press, 1983).

9. George Cooper and Gavan Daws, *Land and Power in Hawaii* (Honolulu: Benchmark Books, 1985); Roger J. Bell, *Last among Equals: Hawaiian Statehood and American Politics* (Honolulu: University of Hawai`i Press, 1984); Edward D. Beechert, *Working in Hawaii: A Labor History* (Honolulu: University of Hawai`i Press, 1985); Ronald Takaki, *Pau Hana: Plantation Life and Labor in Hawaii, 1835-1920* (Honolulu: University of Hawai`i Press, 1983); Chad Taniguchi, "The First Time: 1979 Hawaii United Public Workers Strike," *Amerasia Journal* 7:2 (1980), 1-28; Baron Goto, "Ethnic Groups and the Coffee Industry in Hawaii," *The Hawaiian Journal of History* 16 (1982), 112-24.

10. Ethnic historians have been fortunate to have at their disposal the numerous volumes of transcripts produced by the Center for Oral History. For a list of the volumes, see <http://www2.soc.hawaii.edu/css/oral_hist>.

11. *Social Process in Hawaii* 19 (1955) pays tribute to the work of Romanzo Adams. Adams was at the University of Hawai`i from 1920 to 1942;

Lind was there from 1927 to 1955. Clarence Glick, who in 1938 received his doctorate also from the University of Chicago, began teaching at the University of Hawai`i's sociology department in 1935.

12. Romanzo Adams, *The Peoples of Hawaii* (Honolulu: Institute of Pacific Relations, 1933); Romanzo Adams and Dan Kane-zo Kai, "The Education of the Boys of Hawaii and Their Economic Outlook," *University of Hawaii Research Publications* 4 (January 1928), 1-59; Andrew W. Lind, *Hawaii's People*, 4th ed. (Honolulu: University of Hawai`i Press, 1980). See also Romanzo Adams, T. M. Livesay, and E. H. VanWinkle, "A Statistical Study of the Races in Hawaii, 1925," Special Collections, Hamilton Library, University of Hawai`i Manoa, Honolulu; Andrew W. Lind, "Immigration to Hawaii," *Social Process in Hawaii* 29 (1982), 9-20; Andrew W. Lind, "Occupational Trends among Immigrant Groups in Hawaii," *Social Forces* 7 (December 1928), 290-99; Andrew W. Lind, "Occupational Attitudes of Orientals in Hawaii," *Sociology and Social Research* 12 (Jan.-Feb. 1929), 245-55; and Andrew W. Lind, *An Island Community* (Chicago: University of Chicago Press, 1938).

13. See, for example, Gary Okihiro, *Cane Fires: The Anti-Japanese Movement in Hawaii, 1865-1945* (Philadelphia: Temple University Press, 1991), x; and Jeff Chang, "Local Knowledge(s): Notes on Race Relations, Panethnicity and History in Hawai`i," *Amerasia Journal* 22:2 (1996), 4-7.

14. The materials produced by the Survey of Race Relations team, including life histories, are located at Stanford University's Hoover Institution. The Hawai`i collection of life histories is housed at the University of Oregon Library and is on microfilm at the University of Hawai`i Manoa: William Carlson Smith Papers, "Life Histories of Students," 1926-27, Hamilton Library, University of Hawai`i, Honolulu. For information on Smith's study, see William Carlson Smith, "The Second Generation Oriental in America," Preliminary Paper Prepared for the Second General Session of the Institute of Pacific Relations, July 15-27, 1927, Special Collections, Hamilton Library, University of Hawai`i, Honolulu. William Carlson Smith's publications include "Changing Personality Traits of Second Generation Orientals in America," *American Journal of Sociology* 33 (1928), 922-29, and *Americans in Process: A Study of Our Citizens of Oriental Ancestry* (Ann Arbor: Edwards Brothers, 1937).

15. Some examples of studies by social scientists include John W. Coulter and Alfred G. Serrao, "Manoa Valley, Honolulu: A Study in Economic and Social Geography," *Bulletin of the Geographical Society of Philadelphia*, April 30, 1932, 109-30; Edwin G. Burrows, *Chinese and Japanese in Hawaii during the Sino-Japanese Conflict* (Honolulu: Institute of Pacific Relations, 1939); Thayne M. Livesay, *A Study of Public Education in Hawaii* No. 7 (Honolulu: University of Hawaii Research Publications, 1937); George K. Yamamoto, "Political Participation among Orientals in Hawaii," *Social and Social Research* 43 (May-June 1959), 359-64; Harry V. Ball and Douglas S. Yamamura, "Ethnic Discrimination and the Marketplace: A Study of Landlords' Pref-

erences in a Polyethnic Community," *American Sociological Review* 25 (October 1960), 687-94; Walter D. Fenz and Abe Arkoff, "Comparative Need Patterns of Five Ancestry Groups in Hawaii," *Journal of Social Psychology* 58 (1962), 67-89. Demographic studies include Romanzo Adams, *The Peoples of Hawaii* (Honolulu: Institute of Pacific Relations, 1933); Andrew W. Lind, *Hawaii's People*, 4th ed. (Honolulu: University of Hawai`i Press, 1980); Robert C. Schmitt, *Demographic Statistics of Hawaii: 1778-1965* (Honolulu: University of Hawai`i Press, 1968); Eleanor C. Nordyke, *The Peopling of Hawai`i*, 2nd ed. (Honolulu: University of Hawai`i Press, 1989).

16.   Stanley D. Porteus and Marjorie E. Babcock, *Temperament and Race* (Boston: R. G. Badger, 1926). See David E. Stannard, "Honoring Racism: The Professional Life and Reputation of Stanley D. Porteus," *Social Process in Hawai`i* 39 (1999), 85-125. Newspaper articles that appeared on the controversy include *Honolulu Star Bulletin* December 12, 1974, December 14, 1974, March 28, 1975, April 5, 1983, December 12, 1997, December 13, 1997, January 17, 1998, April 17, 1998, April 18, 1998; *Honolulu Advertiser* April 25, 1975, May 7, 1975, April 9, 1983, April 21, 1983, January 11, 1998, February 1, 1998, February 24, 1998, April 20, 1998, April 22, 1998.

17.   Communication with Dwight W. Hoover and Idus A. Newby. See also Dwight W. Hoover, *The Red and the Black* (Chicago: Rand McNally, 1976).

18.   Porteus and Babcock, p. v. In Part II, Porteus is guilty of faulty methodology when he uses without question the descriptions of different APIAs written in immigration and labor reports. In Part III, he uses, again without question, his respondents' ratings of others to depict APIAs with characteristics related to social success. The idea of inherent mental differences among groups continues to resonate, as shown by the controversial bestseller by Richard J. Herrnstein and Charles Murray, *The Bell Curve: Intelligence and Class Structure in American Life* (New York: Free Press, 1994). Book reviews of *Temperament and Race* ranged from neutral to negative. See *Social Forces* 5 (1927), 540; *American Journal of Sociology* 32 (1926-27), 300-302; *Social Science* 2 (1927), 456; *Journal of Applied Sociology* (later *Sociology and Social Research*) 10 (1926), 595; *Social Forces* 5 (1927), 656-61; *Psychological Bulletin* 24 (1927), 249-50; *American Journal of Psychology* 24 (1927), 249-50. An example of negative ethnic stereotypes in the popular press is Edward P. Irwin, "Ed Irwin More Than Suggests That We Should Not Try to 'Americanize' Orientals in Hawaii, Even if We Can," *Paradise of the Pacific* 37 (December 1924), 54-56.

19.   A "first-generation" scholar who focused solely on one group was Roman R. Cariaga, recognized as the founder of Filipino American studies in Hawai`i. Jonathan Y. Okamura, "Writing the Filipino Diaspora: Roman R. Cariaga's *The Filipinos in Hawai`i*," *Social Process in Hawaii* 37 (1996), 36-37. Cariaga's published works include Roman R. Cariaga, *The Filipinos in Hawaii: Economic and Social Conditions, 1906-1936* (Honolulu: Filipino Public Relations Bureau, 1937), which is based on his Masters thesis; "Filipinos in Honolulu," *So-*

cial Science 10 (1935), 39-46; "Some Filipino Traits Transplanted," *Social Process in Hawaii* 2 (1936), 20-23.

A larger set of single-ethnic-group studies by social scientists focused on Japanese Americans, many appearing in *Social Process in Hawaii*. Other important early studies include John F. Embree, *Acculturation among the Japanese of Kona, Hawaii* (Menasha, Wisconsin: American Anthropological Association, 1941); Romanzo Adams, *Japanese in Hawaii* (New York: National Committee on American Japanese Relations, 1942); Andrew W. Lind, *The Japanese in Hawaii under War Conditions* (Honolulu: American Council, Institute of Pacific Relations, 1943); Gerald M. Meredith, "Acculturation and Personality among Japanese-American College Students in Hawaii," *Journal of Social Psychology* 68 (1966), 175-82; Frederick Samuels, *The Japanese and the Haoles of Honolulu* (New Haven: College and University Press, 1970).

20. Bruno Lasker, *Filipino Immigration to Continental United States and to Hawaii* (Chicago: Institute of Pacific Relations, 1931); Ernest K. Wakukawa, *A History of the Japanese People in Hawaii* (Honolulu: Toyo Shoin, 1938); Hilary Conroy, *The Japanese Frontier in Hawaii, 1868-1898* (Berkeley: University of California Press, 1953).

21. Hawai`i State, Department of Business, Economic Development, and Tourism, *State of Hawaii Databook 1997* (Honolulu: DBEDT, 1998), table 1.29, n.p.

22. Two useful bibliographies are Paul R. Spickard et al., *Pacific Islander Americans: An Annotated Bibliography in the Social Sciences* (Laie, Hawai`i: Institute for Polynesian Studies, Brigham Young University-Hawai`i, 1995); and *Samoans in Hawaii: A Bibliography* (Honolulu: Hawai`i State Library, 1991).

23. Paul Spickard, "Introduction," *Social Process in Hawaii: Pacific Island Peoples in Hawaii* 36 (1994), 1.

24. *Ibid.*

25. Harry H. L. Kitano and Roger Daniels, *Asian Americans: Emerging Minorities*, 2nd ed. (Englewood Cliffs, New Jersey: Prentice Hall, 1995), 129-43; Paul R. Spickard et. al., *Pacific Islander American*, v-ix; Fay C. Alailima, "The Samoans of Hawaii," *Social Process in Hawaii* 29 (1982): 88-94; Andrew W. Lind, "The Immigration of South-Sea Islanders," *Social Process in Hawaii* 29 (1982), 45-49; J. A. Bennett, "Immigration, 'Blackbirding,' Labor Recruiting? The Hawaiian Experience 1877-1887," *Journal of Pacific History* 11:1 (1976), 3-27.

26. The historical literature on Native Hawaiians is abundant. See David J. Kittelson, *The Hawaiians: An Annotated Bibliography* (Honolulu: Social Science Research Institute, University of Hawai`i, 1985); Chieko Tachihata, "The Hawaiians, Supplement, 1983-87," typescript, Hamilton Library, University of Hawai`i, 1998; Chieko Tachihata, "Sovereignty Movement in Hawaii: Bibliography," *Contemporary Pacific* 6 (Spring 1994), 201-210; Chieko Tachihata, *Library Resources about Native Hawaiians* (Honolulu: School of Library and Information Science, University of Hawai`i, 1994); Pauline Delamarter, "Bibliography of Biographies

of Native Hawaiians," typescript, 1987, Special Collections, Hamilton Library, University of Hawai`i; *Overthrow and Annexation, A Bibliography* (Honolulu: Hawai`i State Library, 1993). Also available is David W. Forbes, *Hawaiian National Bibliography, 1780-1830*, vol. 1 (Honolulu: University of Hawai`i Press, 1999), an annotated bibliography of printed works, including books, newspaper articles, circulars, and playbills.

27. I would like to thank Sharyn Funamura for sharing her unpublished essay on the sovereignty movement with me.

28. Marion Kelly, "Land Tenure in Hawaii," *Amerasia Journal* 7:2 (1980), 57-73; Jocelyn Linnekin, "Statistical Analysis of the Great Mahele," *Journal of Pacific History* 22 (1987), 15-33; Lilikalā Kame`eleihiwa, *Native Land and Foreign Desires: Pehea Lā E Pono Ai?* (Honolulu: Bishop Museum Press, 1992); Riley M. Moffat and Gary L. Fitzpatrick, *Surveying the Mahele: Mapping the Hawaiian Land Revolution* (Honolulu: Editions Limited, 1995); Dorothy B. Barrere, *The King's Mahele: The Awardees and Their Lands* [Honolulu: D. B. Barrere, 1994]; Jon Chinen, *The Great Mahele: Hawaii's Land Division of 1848* (Honolulu: University of Hawai`i Press, 1958); Mitsuo Uyehara, *The Hawaii Ceded Land Trusts: Their Use and Misuse* (Honolulu: Hawaiiana Almanac Publishing, 1977).

29. Allan Spitz, "Democratic Transplantation: The Case of Land Policy in Hawaii," *Land Economics* 42 (November 1966), 473-84; Allan Spitz, "The Transplantation of American Democratic Institutions: The Case of Hawaii," *Political Science Quarterly* 82 (September 1967), 386-98; Davianna Pōmaika`i McGregor, "`Āina Ho`opulapula: Hawaiian Homesteading," *Hawaiian Journal of History* 24 (1990), 1-38; Mark A. Inciong, "The Lost Trust: Native Hawaiian Beneficiaries under the Hawaiian Homes Commission Act," *Arizona Journal of International and Comparative Law* 8:2 (1991), 171-85. See also U. S. Commission on Civil Rights, Hawaii Advisory Committee, *A Broken Trust: The Hawaiian Homelands Program* (Honolulu: The Committee, 1991); U. S. Commission on Civil Rights, *Breach of Trust? Native Hawaiian Homelands, A Summary of the Proceedings of a Public Forum* (Washington, D.C.: The Commission, 1980).

30. Albertine Loomis, *For Whom Are the Stars?* (Honolulu: University of Hawai`i Press, 1976); William Adams Russ's *The Hawaiian Revolution, 1893-1894* (Selinsgrove, Pennsylvania: Susquehana University Press, 1992 [1959]); William Adams Russ, *The Hawaiian Republic and Its Struggle to Win Annexation* (Selinsgrove, Pennsylvania: Susquehana University Press, 1992 [1961]); Thurston Twigg-Smith, *Hawaiian Sovereignty: Do the Facts Matter?* (Honolulu: Goodale Publishing, 1998); Ernest Andrade, Jr., *Unconquerable Rebel: Robert W. Wilcox and Hawaiian Politics, 1880-1903* (Niwot: University Press of Colorado, 1996). See also Ernest Andrade, Jr., "Great Britain and the Hawaiian Revolution and Republic, 1893-1898," *Hawaiian Journal of History* 24 (1990), 91-116.

31. Thomas J. Osborne, *Annexation Hawaii: Fighting American Imperialism* (originally *"Empire Can Wait": American Opposition to Hawaiian*

Annexation), (Waimanalo, Hawaii: Island Style Press, 1998); Tom Coffman, *Nation Within* (Kāne'ohe, Hawaii: Epicenter, 1998); Merze Tate, *The United States and the Hawaiian Kingdom: A Political History* (Westport, Connecticut: Greenwood Press, 1965); Rich Budnick, *Stolen Kingdom: An American Conspiracy* (Honolulu: Aloha Press, 1992); Jennifer M. L. Chock, "One Hundred Years of Illegitimacy: International Legal Analysis of the Illegal Overthrow of the Hawaiian Monarchy, Hawaii'i's Annexation, and Possible Reparations," *University of Hawaii Law Review* 17 (Fall 1995), 463-512; Noenoe K. Silva, "Kū'ē! Hawaiian Women's Resistance to the Annexation," *Social Process in Hawaii* 38 (1997), 4-15; Noenoe K. Silva, "Kanaka Maoli Resistance to Annexation," *Oiwi: An Native Hawaiian Journal* 1 (December 1998), 40-75; Queen Lili'uokalani, *Hawai'i's Story by Hawai'i's Queen* (Rutland, Vermont: Charles Tuttle, 1964 [1898]); Lorrin A. Thurston, *Memoirs of the Hawaiian Revolution* (Honolulu: Advertiser, 1936); Sanford B. Dole, *Memoirs of the Hawaiian Revolution* (Honolulu: Advertiser, 1936). John S. Whitehead's, "The Anti-Statehood Movement and the Legacy of Alice Kamokila Campbell," *Hawaiian Journal of History* 27 (1993), 43-64, supports studies on opposition to annexation. Other works include Helena G. Allen, *The Betrayal of Liliuokalani: Last Queen of Hawaii, 1838-1917* (Glendale, California: Arthur H. Clark, 1982); and Michael Doughtery, *To Steal a Kingdom* (Waimanalo, Hawai'i: Island Style Press, 1992). An important set of primary documents, including President Grover Cleveland's message and the report of James Blount, whom Cleveland sent to investigate the overthrow, are compiled in U. S. Congress (53rd, 3rd session: 1894-1895), House, *Affairs in Hawaii*, 2 vols. (Washington, D.C.: GPO, 1895).

32. Davianna McGregor-Alegado, "Hawaiians: Organizing in the 70s," *Amerasia Journal* 7 (1980), 29-55; Haunani-Kay Trask, "The Birth of the Modern Hawaiian Movement: Kalama Valley, Oahu," *Hawaiian Journal of History* 21 (1987), 126-53; George S. Kanahele, *Hawaiian Renaissance* (Honolulu: Project Waiaha, 1982); Albert J. Schutz, *Voices of Eden: A History of Hawaiian Language Studies* (Honolulu: University of Hawai'i Press, 1994).

33. American Friends Service Committee, ed. *He Alo a he Alo—Face to Face: Voices on Hawaiian Sovereignty* (Honolulu: American Friends Service Committee, 1983); Haunani-Kay Trask, "Hawaiians, American Colonization, and the Quest for Independence," *Social Process in Hawaii* 31 (1984): 101-136; Michael Kinoni Dudley and Keoni Agard, *A Call for Hawaiian Sovereignty* (Honolulu: Nā Kāne o ka Malo Press, 1990); Mililani Trask, "Historical and Contemporary Hawaiian Self-Determination: A Native Hawaiian Perspective," *Arizona Journal of International and Comparative Law* 8 (1991), 77-91; Peter Akwi, "Hawaiian Sovereignty," *Whole Earth Review* 72 (Fall 1991), 70-80; Leslie K. Freidman, "Native Hawaiians, Self-Determination, and the Inadequacy of the State Land Trusts," *University of Hawaii Law Review* 14 (Fall 1992), 519-38; Haunani-Kay Trask, *From a Native Daughter: Colonialism and Sovereignty in Hawai'i* (Monroe, Maine: Common Courage Press, 1993); Poka Laenui, "The Rediscovery of

Hawaiian Sovereignty," *American Indian Culture and Research Journal* 17 (1993), 79-86; Noelle M. Kahanu and Jon. M. Van Dyke, "Native Hawaiian Entitlement Sovereignty: An Overview," *University of Hawaii Law Review* 17 (Fall 1995), 427-42; Robert H. Mast and Anne B. Mast, *Autobiography of Protest in Hawaii* (Honolulu: University of Hawai`i Press, 1996); Serena Nanda, "Trouble in Paradise: Native Hawaiians v. The United States of America," *Journal of Criminal Justice Education* 7 (Spring 1996):, 155-68; William H. Rodgers Jr., "The Sense of Justice and the Justice of Sense: Native Hawaiian Sovereignty and the Second 'Trial of the Century,'" *Washinton Law Review* 71 (April 1996), 379-98; Norman Meller and Anne Feder Lee, "Hawaiian Sovereignty," *Publius* 27 (Spring 1997), 167-83. Related to sovereignty is Native Hawaiians Study Commission, *Report on the Culture, Needs and Concerns of Native Hawaiians Pursuant to Public Law 96-565, Title III*, 2 vols. (Washington, D.C.: GPO, 1983).

34. John U. Ogbu and Margaret A. Gibson, eds. *Minority Status and Schooling: A Comparative Study of Immigrant and Involuntary Minorities* (New York: Garland, 1991); John U. Ogbu, "Minority Coping Responses and School Experience," *Journal of Psychohistory* 18 (Spring 1991), 433-55; John U. Ogbu, "Cultural Diversity and Human Development," *New Directions for Child Development* 42 (Winter 1988), 11-28.

35. Clarence E. Glick, *Sojourners and Settlers: Chinese Migrants in Hawaii* (Honolulu: University of Hawai`i Press, 1980), x-xi, 12, 18, 23; Andrew W. Lind, *Hawaii's People*, 4th ed. (Honolulu: University of Hawai`i Press, 1980), 28.

36. Two useful bibliographies are Nancy Foon Young, *The Chinese in Hawaii: An Annotated Bibliography* (Honolulu: SSRI, University of Hawai`i, 1973); and *Chinese in Hawaii: A Bibliography* (Honolulu: Hawai`i State Library, 1996).

37. Tin-Yuke Char, "Chinese Merchants: Adventurers and Sugar Masters in Honolulu: 1802-1852," *Hawaiian Journal of History* 8 (1974), 3-9; Tin-Yuke Char and Wai-Jane Char, "The First Chinese Contract Laborers in Hawaii, 1852," *Hawaiian Journal of History* 9 (1975), 128-34; Clarence E. Glick, "The Voyage of the 'Thetis' and The First Chinese Contract Laborers Brought to Hawaii," *Hawaiian Journal of History* 9 (1975), 135-39; Richard A. Greer, " 'Sweet and Clean': The Chinatown Fire of 1886," *Hawaiian Journal of History* 10 (1976), 33-51; William Hillebrand, "Chinese Immigration: A Letter to the Board of Immigration, 1865," *Hawaiian Journal of History* 6 (1972), 142-55; Dennis A. Kastens, "Nineteenth Century Chinese Christian Missions in Hawaii *Hawaiian Journal of History* 12 (1978), 61-67; Peggy Kai, "Chinese Settlers in the Village of Hilo before 1852," *Hawaiian Journal of History* 8 (1974), 39-75; Steven B. Zuckerman, "Pake in Paradise: A Synthetic Study of Chinese Immigration to Hawaii," *Bulletin of the Institute of Ethnology* 45 (Spring 1978), 39-80.

38. Tin-Yuke Char, *The Sandalwood Mountains: Readings and Stories of the Early Chinese in Hawaii* (Honolulu: University of Hawai`i Press, 1975); Clarence E. Glick, *Sojourners and Settlers: Chinese Migrants in*

Hawaii (Honolulu: Hawai`i Chinese History Center and University of Hawai`i Press, 1980); Violet L. Lai, *He Was a Ram: Wong Aloiau of Hawaii* (Honolulu: University of Hawai`i Press, 1985); Bob Dye, *Merchant Prince of the Sandalwood Mountains: Afong and the Chinese in Hawai`i* (Honolulu: University of Hawai`i Press, 1997). Other historical works include Edward C. Lyndon, *The Anti-Chinese Movement in the Hawaiian Kingdom, 1852-1886* (San Francisco: R and E Research Associates, 1975); Tin-Yuke Char and Wai-Jane Char, eds., *Chinese Historic Sites and Pioneer Families of the Island of Hawaii* (Honolulu: Hawai`i Chinese History Center, 1983); James H. Chun, *The Early Chinese in Punaluu* (Honolulu: Yin Sit Sha, 1983); Arlene Lum, ed., *Sailing for the Sun: The Chinese in Hawaii, 1789-1989* (Honolulu: Three Heroes, 1988); Eleanor C. Nordyke and Richard K. C. Lee, "The Chinese in Hawai`i: A Historical and Demographic Perspective," The *Hawaiian Journal of History* 23 (1989), 196-216; Diane M. L. Mark, *Seasons of Light: The History of Chinese Christian Churches in Hawaii* (Honolulu: Chinese Christian Association of Hawai`i, 1989); Bob Dye, "The Great Chinese Merchants' Ball of 1856," *The Hawaiian Journal of History* 28 (1994), 69-78.

39. Andrew W. Lind, *Hawaii's People*, 28; Hawai`i State, Department of Business, Economic Development, and Tourism, *State of Hawaii Databook 1997* (Honolulu: DBEDT, 1998), table 1.29, n.p.

40. For comparative population figures in the United States, see Paul R. Spickard, *Japanese Americans: The Formation and Transformations of an Ethnic Group* (New York: Twayne, 1996), 47, 162-63. Two important bibliographies are Mitsugu Matsuda, rev. by Dennis M. Ogawa, *The Japanese in Hawaii: An Annotated Bibliography of Japanese Americans* (Honolulu: University of Hawai`i, 1975); and Joan Hori, "The Japanese in Hawaii: A Bibliography of Publications, Audiovisual Media, and Archival Collections, Supplementing the Bibliography by Mitsugu Matsuda and Revised by Dennis Ogawa," typescript, University of Hawai`i, Hamilton Library, Special Collections, 1988.

41. Louise H. Hunter, *Buddhism in Hawaii: Its Impact on a Yankee Community* (Honolulu: University of Hawai`i Press, 1971); John E. Reinecke, *Feigned Necessity: Hawaii's Attempt to Obtain Chinese Contract Labor, 1921-1923* (San Francisco: Chinese Materials Center, 1979); Dennis M. Ogawa, *Kodomo No Tame Ni, For the Sake of the Children: The Japanese Experience in Hawaii* (Honolulu: University of Hawai`i Press, 1978); Ethnic Studies Oral History Project, ed., *Uchinanchu* (Honolulu: ESOHP, University of Hawai`i, 1981); Yukiko Kimura, *Issei: Japanese Immigrants in Hawaii* (Honolulu: University of Hawaii Press, 1988); Alan T. Moriyama, *Imingaisha: Japanese Emigration Companies and Hawaii, 1894-1908* (Honolulu: University of Hawai`i Press, 1985); Gary Y. Okihiro, *Cane Fires: The Anti-Japanese Movement in Hawaii, 1865-1945* (Philadelphia: Temple University Press, 1991); Eileen H. Tamura, *Americanization, Acculturation, and Ethnic Identity: The Nisei Generation in Hawaii* (Urbana and Chicago: University of Illinois Press, 1994). Other important publications include James H.

Okahata, ed. *A History of Japanese in Hawaii* (Honolulu: United Japanese Society of Hawaii, 1971); Yukiko Irwin and Hilary Conroy, "Robert Walker Irwin and Systematic Immigration to Hawaii," 40-55, in Hilary Conroy and T. Scott Miyakawa, eds., *East across the Pacific: Historical and Sociological Studies of Japanese Immigration and Assimilation* (Santa Barbara: ABC Clio Press, 1972); John N. Hawkins, "Politics, Education, and Language Policy: The Case of Japanese Language Schools in Hawaii," *Amerasia* 5:1 (1978), 39-56; Joan Hori, "Japanese Prostitution in Hawaii during the Immigration Period," *Hawaiian Journal of History* 15 (1981), 113-24; John J. Stephan, *Hawaii under the Rising Sun: Japan's Plans for Conquest after Pearl Harbor* (Honolulu: University of Hawai`i Press, 1984); B. K. Hyams, "School Teachers as Agents of Cultural Imperialism in Territorial Hawaii," *Journal of Pacific History* 20 (October 1985), 202-19; Roland Kotani, *The Japanese in Hawaii: A Century of Struggle* (Honolulu: Hawaii Hochi, 1985); Franklin Odo and Kazuko Sinoto, *A Pictorial History of the Japanese in Hawaii, 1885-1924* (Honolulu: Bishop Museum Press, 1985); Dorothy O. Hazama, and Jane O. Komeiji, *Okage Sama De: The Japanese in Hawaii, 1885-1985* (Honolulu: Bess Press, 1986); Noel J. Kent, "Myth of the Golden Men: Ethnic Elites and Dependent Development in the 50th State," in Michael C. Howard, *Ethnicity and Nationbuilding in the Pacific*, 98-117 (Tokyo: United Nations University, 1989); Nobuhiro Adachi, *Linguistic Americanization of Japanese-Americans in Hawaii* (Osaka: Osaka Kyoiku Tosho, 1996); Eileen H. Tamura, "Gender, Schooling and Teaching, and the Nisei in Hawai`i: An Episode in American Immigration History, 1900-1940," *Journal of American Ethnic History* 14 (Summer 1995), 3-26; Eileen H. Tamura, "The English-Only Effort, the Anti-Japanese Campaign, and Language Acquisition in the Education of Japanese Americans in Hawaii, 1915-40," *History of Education Quarterly* 33 (Spring 1993), 37-58.

42. Daniel K. Inouye, and Lawrence Elliott. *Journey to Washington* (Englewood Cliffs, New Jersey: Prentice-Hall, 1967); H. S. Kawakami, *From Japan to Hawaii: My Journey* (Honolulu: H. S. Kawakami, 1976). The first publication in the Nisei in Hawai`i series is Matsuo Takabuki, *An Unlikely Revolutionary: Matsuo Takabuki and the Making of Modern Hawai`i* (Honolulu: University of Hawai`i Press, 1998). Publications on the World War II experiences of the Nikkei include Thomas D. Murphy, *Ambassadors in Arms: The Story of Hawaii's 100th Battalion* (Honolulu: University of Hawai`i Press, 1954); Masayo Duus, *Unlikely Liberators: The Men of the 100th and 442nd* (Honolulu: University of Hawai`i Press, 1987); Lyn Crost, *Honor by Fire: Japanese Americans at War in Europe and the Pacific* (Novato, California: Presidio, 1994); Harry N. Scheiber and Jane L. Scheiber, "Bayonets in Paradise: A Half-Century Retrospect on Martial Law in Hawai`i, 1941-1946," *University of Hawai`i Law Review* 19 (Fall 1997), 477-648.

43. Barbara F. Kawakami, *Japanese Immigrant Clothing in Hawaii: 1885-1941* (Honolulu: University of Hawai`i Press, 1993); Shiho S. Nunes and Sara Nunes-Atabaki, *The Shishu Ladies of Hilo: Japanese Embroidery in Hawai`i* (Honolulu: University of Hawai`i Press, 1999); Laurie

M. Mengel, "Issei Women and Divorce in Hawai`i, 1885-1908," *Social Process in Hawaii* 38 (1997), 18-39.

44. Lind, *Hawaii's People*, 28; Hawai`i State, Department of Business, Economic Development, and Tourism, *State of Hawaii Data Book 1997* (Honolulu: DBEDT, 1998), table 1.29, n.p.

45. Two bibliographies on Koreans in Hawai`i are Arthur I. Gardner, *The Koreans in Hawaii: An Annotated Bibliography* (Honolulu: Social Science Research Institute, University of Hawai`i, 1970); and *Koreans in Hawaii: A Bibliography* (Honolulu: Hawai`i State Library, 1990).

46. Wayne Patterson, *The Korean Frontier in America: Immigration to Hawaii, 1896-1910* (Honolulu: University of Hawai`i Press, 1988); Linda Pomerantz, "The Background of Korean Emigration," 277-315, in Lucie Cheng and Edna Bonacich, eds., *Labor Immigration under Capitalism: Asian Workers in the United States before World War II* (Berkeley: University of California Press, 1984); Michael E. Macmillan, "Unwanted Allies: Koreans as Enemy Aliens in World War II," *Hawaiian Journal of History* 19 (1985), 179-203. Other works include Sarah Lee Yang, "Koreans in Hawai`i," *Social Process in Hawaii* 29 (1982), 89-94; Myongsup Shin and Daniel B. Lee, eds., *Korean Immigrants in Hawaii: A Symposium on Their Background History, Acculturation and Public Policy Issues* (Honolulu: Korean Immigrant Welfare Association of Hawaii and Operation Manong, 1978); Samuel S. O. Lee, ed., *Their Footsteps: A Pictorial History of Koreans in Hawaii since 1903* (Honolulu: Committee on the 90th Anniversary Celebration of Korean Immigration to Hawaii, 1993); Samuel S. O. Lee, ed., *75th Anniversary of Korean Immigration to Hawaii, 1903-1978* (Honolulu: 75th Anniversary Committee, 1978); U.S. Army, Hawaiian Dept., Office of the Assistant Chief of Staff for Military Intelligence, *A Survey of the Korean in the Territory of Hawaii* (Honolulu: Military Intelligence, 1930); Alice Y. Chai, "Picture Bride from Korea: The Life History of a Korean American Woman in Hawaii," *Bridge: An Asian Perspective* 6:4 (Winter 1978/79), 37-42; Margaret K. Pai, *The Dreams of Two Yi-min* (Honolulu: University of Hawai`i Press, 1989).

47. Useful bibliographies include Shiro Saito, *The Overseas Filipinos: A Working Bibliography* (Honolulu: East-West Center Population Institute, 1974); Ruben R. Alcantara, et al, *The Filipinos in Hawaii: An Annotated Bibliography* (Honolulu: Social Sciences and Linguistics Institute, University of Hawai`i, 1977); Alice W. Mak, "Filipinos in Hawaii: A Bibliography," *Social Process in Hawaii* 33 (1991), 211-30; *Filipinos in Hawaii: A Bibliography* (Honolulu: Hawai`i State Library, 1993).

48. Eleanor Nordyke, *The Peopling of Hawaii,* 2nd ed. (Honolulu: University of Hawai`i Press, 1989), 80, 253; Pauline Agbayani-Siewert and Linda Revilla, "Filipino Americans," 142, in Pyong Gap Min, ed., *Asian Americans: Contemporary Trends and Issues* (Thousand Oaks, California: SAGE, 1995); Hawai`i State, Department of Business, Economic Development, and Tourism, *State of Hawaii Databook 1997* (Honolulu: DBEDT, 1998), table 1.29, n.p.

49.   Sister Mary Dorita, *Filipino Immigration to Hawaii* (San Francisco: R and E Research Associates, 1975).

50.   Miriam Sharma, "Pinoy in Paradise: Environment and Adaptation in Pilipinos in Hawaii, 1906-1945," *Amerasia Journal* 7:2 (1980), 91-117; John E. Reinecke, *The Filipino Piecemeal Sugar Strike of 1924-1925*, eds. Edward Beechert and Alice Beechert (Honolulu: Social Science Research Institute, University of Hawai`i, 1996); Ruben Alcantara, *Sakada: Filipino Adaptation in Hawaii* (Washington, DC: University Press of America, 1981); Luis V. Teodoro, ed., *Out of This Struggle: The Filipinos in Hawaii* (Honolulu: Filipino 75th Anniversary Commemoration Commission, 1981). See also Robert N. Anderson et al, *Filipinos in Rural Hawaii* (Honolulu: University of Hawai`i Press, 1984); Jonathan Okamura, "A History of Filipino Federated Organizations in Hawai`i," 73-77, in J. C. Dionisio, ed., *The Filipinos in Hawai`i: The First 75 Years* (Honolulu: Hawai`i Filipino News, 1981).

51.   The two issues of *Social Process in Hawaii* devoted to Filipinos in Hawai`i are vols. 33 (1991) and 37 (1996). Plantation histories published in the 1990s include Melinda Tria Kerkvliet, "Pablo Manlapit's Fight for Justice," *Social Process in Hawaii* 33 (1991), 153-68; Dean T. Alegado, "Carl Damasco: A Champion of Hawaii's Working People," *Social Process in Hawaii* 37 (1996), 26-35; Steffi San Buenaventura, "Hawaii's '1946 Sakada,'" *Social Process in Hawaii* 37 (1996), 74-90; and Melinda Tria Kerkvliet, *For Justice and a Square Deal: Biography of Pablo Manlapit, Filipino Labor Leader in Hawaii* (Honolulu: Filipino American Historical Society of Hawaii, forthcoming). Non-plantation histories include Linda A. Revilla, " 'Pineapples,' 'Hawayanos,' and 'Local Americans': Local Boys in the First Filipino Infantry Regiment, U.S. Army," *Social Process in Hawaii* 37 (1996), 57-73; Steffi San Buenaventura, "The Master and the Federation: A Filipino-American Social Movement in California and Hawaii," *Social Process in Hawaii* 33 (1991), 169-93; and Steffi San Buenaventura, *Nativism, Ethnicity, and Empowerment: A Filipino American Socio-Religious Movement, 1925-1975* (Stanford: Stanford University Press, 1999).

52.   Jonathan Okamura, "Why There Are No Asian Americans in Hawai`i: The Continuing Significance of Local Identity," *Social Process in Hawaii* 35 (1994), 161-178.

53.   Yen Le Espiritu, *Asian American Panethnicity*, 5-7, 13, 164.

54.   Eric Yamamoto, "The Significance of Local," *Social Process in Hawaii* 27 (1979), 102, 105.

55.   Jonathan Okamura, "Aloha Kanaka Me Ke Aloha `Aina: Local Culture and Society in Hawaii," *Amerasia Journal* 7:2 (1980), 126-31. Okamura disputes the notion of a blended culture and instead emphasizes the history of the plantation ethclass structure as the basis for the local identity. See Okamura, "Why There Are No Asian Americans in Hawai`i," 162-63.

56.   John E. Reinecke and Stanley M. Tsuzaki, *Language and Dialect in Hawaii: A Sociological History to 1933* (Honolulu: University of Hawai`i Press, 1969); Eileen H. Tamura, "Power, Status, and Hawai`i

Creole English: An Example of Linguistic Intolerance in American History," *Pacific Historical Review* 65: 3 (August 1996), 431-54.

57.   Glen Grant and Dennis Ogawa, "Living Proof: Is Hawai`i the Answer?" *Annals of the American Academy of Political and Social Sciences* 530 (November 1993), 137-54; Michael Haas, "Explaining Ethnic Harmony: Hawai`i's Multicultural Ethos," *Nationalism and Ethnic Politics* 2:2 (Summer 1996), 169-90; and Michael Haas, ed., *Multi-cultural Hawaii: The Fabric of a Multiethnic Society* (New York: Garland Publishers, 1998).

58.   See, for example, Noel Jacob Kent, "When Multiethnic Societies Work: Notes on an Ethnic Relations Model in Balance," 131-39, in Franklin Ng, Judy Yung, Stephen S. Fujita, and Elaine H. Kim, *New Visions in Asian American Studies: Diversity, Community, Power* (Pullman: Washington State University Press, 1994).

59.   Jonathan Y. Okamura, "The Illusion of Paradise: Privileging Multiculturalism in Hawai`i," 264-84 in Dru C. Gladney, ed., *Making Majorities: Constituting the Nation in Japan, Korea, China, Malaysia, Fiji, Turkey, And The United States* (Stanford: Stanford University Press, 1998); Michael Haas, *Institutional Racism: The Case of Hawai`i* (Westport, Connecticut: Praeger, 1992); Jeff Chang, "Local Knowledge(s): Notes on Race Relations, Panethnicity and History in Hawai`i," *Amerasia Journal* 22:2 (1996), 1-29; Jeff Chang, "Lessons of Tolerance: Americanism and the Filipino Affirmative Action Movement in Hawai`i," *Social Process in Hawaii* 37 (1996), 112-146.

60.   Phyllis Kon Cooke, "Post-war Trends in the Island Attitude toward the Negro," *Social Process in Hawaii* 7 (1947), 100-106; *Race Relations in Hawaii: Social Process in Hawaii* 18 (1954).

61.   Eiichiro Azuma, "Racial Struggle, Immigrant Nationalism, and Ethnic Identity: Japanese and Filipinos in the California Delta," *Pacific Historical Review* 67 (May 1998), 163-99; Eiichiro Azuma, "Interethnic Conflict under Racial Subordination: Japanese Immigrants and Their Asian Neighbors in Walnut Grove, California, 1908-1941," *Amerasia Journal* 20: 2 (1994), 27-56; Shirley Hune, "Rethinking Race: Paradigms and Policy Formation," *Amerasia Journal* 21:1, 2 (1995), 29-40. Recent social science studies include Leland Saito, *Race and Politics: Asian Americans, Latinos and Whites in a Los Angeles Suburb* (Urbana: University of Illinois Press, 1998); Pyong Gap Min, *Caught in the Middle: Korean Merchants in America's Multiethnic Cities* (Berkeley: University of California Press, 1996); Edward T. Chang, ed., *Los Angeles—Struggles toward Multiethnic Community: Amerasia Journal* 19:2 (1993). Ulla Hasager's "Indigenous Rights, Praxis, and Social Institutions," *Social Process in Hawai`i* 39 (1999), 155-80, provides a helpful explanation of recent developments in Native Hawaiian access rights.

62.   Romanzo Adams, *Interracial Marriage in Hawaii: A Study of the Mutually Conditioned Processes of Acculturation and Amalgamation* (New York: Macmillan, 1937); Ch'eng K'un Cheng and Douglas S. Yamamura, "Interracial Marriage and Divorce in Hawaii," *Social Forces* 36 (Oc-

tober 1957), 77-84; Andrew W. Lind, "Interracial Marriage as Affecting Divorce in Hawaii," *Sociology and Social Research* 49: 1 (October 1964), 17-26; Clarence E. Glick, "Interracial Marriage and Admixture in Hawaii," *Social Biology* 17:4 (1970), 278-91; Wen-Shing Tseng, John McDermott, and Thomas W. Maretzki, *Adjustment in Intercultural Marriages* (Honolulu: Dept. of Psychiatry, School of Medicine, University of Hawai`i, 1977); Margaret M. Schwertfeger, "Interethnic Marriage and Divorce in Hawaii: A Panel Study of 1968 First Marriages," *Marriage and Family Review* 5 (Spring 1982), 49-59; *Interracial Marriage and Offspring in Hawaii, 1896-1989* (Honolulu: Center for Research on Ethnic Relations, SSRI, University of Hawaii, 1995); Xuanning Fu and Tim B. Heaton, *Interracial Marriage in Hawaii, 1983-1994* (Lewiston, New York: Edwin Mellen Press, 1997); Paul R. Spickard, *Mixed Blood: Intermarriage and Ethnic Identity in Twentieth-Century America* (Madison: University of Wisconsin Press, 1989).

63. Hawai`i State, Department of Business, Economic Development, and Tourism, *State of Hawai`i Databook 1997* (Honolulu: DBEDT, 1998), table 1.29, n.p.; Ronald C. Johnson, "Offspring of Cross-Race and Cross-Ethnic Marriages in Hawaii," 244, in Maria P. P. Root, ed., *Racially Mixed People in America* (Newbury Park, California: Sage Publications, 1992).

64. Nash, "Will the Census Go Multiracial?" 24; Lott, *Asian Americans*, 97-99. The 2000 Census allows people to check multiple boxes for ethnicity.

65. Paul R. Spickard and Rowena Fong, "Pacific Islander Americans and Multiethnicity: A Vision of America's Future?" *Social Forces* 73: 4 (June 1995), 1365-1383; Johnson, "Offspring of Cross-Race and Cross-Ethnic Marriages in Hawaii," 240; Paul R. Spickard,"Injustice Compounded: Amerasians and Non-Japanese Americans in World War II Concentration Camps," *Journal of American Ethnic History* 5 (Spring 1986), 5-22; Spickard, *Mixed Blood*. Publications on multi-ethnic APIAs include Maria P. P. Root, ed., *Racially Mixed People in America* (Newbury Park, California: Sage Publications, 1992); Velina Hasu Houston and Teresa K. Williams, eds., *Amerasia Journal* 23:1 (1997); and Cindy Nakashima and Teresa Williams, *Reconfiguring Race, Redefining Ethnicity* (Philadelphia: Temple University Press, 1999).

66. Li'ana M. Petranek, "Ethnic Identity, Identity Politics and the Trouble One Will Have in Constituting an Identity," *Social Process in Hawai`i* 39 (1999): 256-74.

67. John Stephan, *Call of Ancestry: American Nikkei in Imperial Japan, 1895-1945* (forthcoming); Yuji Ichioka, *The Issei: The World of the First Generation Japanese Immigrants, 1885-1924* (New York: The Free Press, 1988); Patterson, *The Korean Frontier in America*; Moriyama, *Imingaisha: Japanese Emigration Companies and Hawaii*; Stephan, *Hawaii under the Rising Sun*; Brian Hayashi, 'For the Sake of Our Japanese Brethren': Assimilation, Nationalism, and Protestantism Among the Japanese of Los Angeles, 1895-1942* (Stanford: Stanford University Press, 1995). Essays in *Amerasia Journal* 23:3 (Winter 1997-98), edited by Yuji Ichioka, in-

clude John Stephan, "Hijacked by Utopia: American Nikkei in Manchuria," 1-44; Yuji Ichioka, "The Meaning of Loyalty: The Case of Kazumaro Buddy Uno," 45-72; Eriko Yamamoto, "Miya Sannomiya Kikuchi: A Pioneer Nisei woman's Life and Identity," 73-102; and Igor R. Saveliev, "Japanese across the Sea: Features of Japanese Emigration to the Russian Far East, 1875 and 1916." University of Hawai`i scholars have formed a planning committee for a working conference scheduled for spring 2001 on Japan-U. S. internationalism.

68. Sucheng Chan, *Asian Americans: An Interpretive History* (Boston: Twayne Publishers, 1991); Paul R. Spickard, *Mixed Blood*; Roger Daniels, *Asian America: Chinese and Japanese in the United States since 1850* (Seattle: University of Washington Press, 1988); Ronald Takaki, *Strangers from a Different Shore: A History of Asian Americans* (Boston: Little, Brown, and Co., 1989). Sociological studies of the 1930s that discussed mainland and Hawai`i experiences include William C. Smith, *Americans in Process* (Ann Arbor: Edwards Brothers, 1937); Edward K. Strong and Regional Bell, *Vocational Aptitudes of Second-Generation Japanese in the United States* ([Palo Alto]: Stanford University Press, 1933); Edward K. Strong, *The Second Generation Japanese Problem* ([Palo Alto]: Stanford University Press, [1934] 1970.

69. There are social science studies on spouse and child abuse and non-historical works on APIA gays, lesbians, and bisexuals. For example, the entire issue of *Amerasia Journal* 20:1 (1994) is devoted to sexual orientation. Franklin Ng, ed., *Asian American Interethnic Relations and Politics* (New York: Garland Publishers, 1998); Franklin Ng, ed., *Asian American Women and Gender* (New York: Garland Publishers, 1998); and Franklin Ng, ed., *Adaptation, Acculturation, and Transnational Ties among Asian Americans* (New York: Garland Publishers, 1998).

70. For a discussion of the pitfalls of essentialism, see Keith Osajima, "Pedagogical Considerations in Asian American Studies," *Journal of Asian American Studies* 1:3 (October 1998), 274. Quote is from Hasia R. Diner, "Comment," *Journal of American Ethnic History* 11 (Summer 1992), 56.

Amerasia Journal

Photograph by Valerie Matsumoto.

"UCLA Colloquium, 1998. Professors Don Nakanishi and Bob Nakamura for Asian American Studies Center are giving me a historic blockprint originally in *Harpers Weekly*."

Amerasia Journal 26:1 (2000): 86-102

The Indispensable Enemy and Ideological Construction:
Reminiscences of an Octogenarian Radical

Alexander Saxton

I began writing *The Indispensable Enemy: Labor and the Anti-Chinese Movement in California* about thirty-five years ago. It was my doctoral dissertation in history. The circumstances leading to that subject were so close to me then that I took them for granted. Now, in order to place my book in historical context, it requires an effort of memory to bring them back. I will begin by recalling certain details of personal history and try then to relate those to the study of ideology in American culture. I will be struggling here with a problem that all scholars of human history must cope with: that of the relationship between particular facts and experiences on one hand, and generalized conclusions on the other.

Some scholars, perhaps even some historians, regard the effort to generalize from particulars as arrogant and self-serving because it permits escalating one's own particulars to universalizing status. I take the opposite view. To move from the particular to the general is an exercise in humility because it forces one to recognize that particulars—even those privileged details of one's own individual existence—remain meaningless and essentially useless to other people unless they can be shown to typify, or *illuminate*, larger streams of human experience. The basic building blocks of historical explanation are socially-shared experience.

Those also are the building blocks of ideological construction. Historical explanation and ideological construction are closely

ALEXANDER SAXTON is professor of history, UCLA, emeritus; author of *The Indispensable Enemy: Labor and the Anti-Chinese Movement in California* (University of California Press, 1995) and *The Rise and Fall of the White Republic: Class Politics and Mass Culture in Nineteenth Century America* (Verso, 1990).

related. One seeks to comprehend the present by reconstructing the past; the other to shape the future by constructing foresights of history in the making.

I

I was born in 1919. Mine was the generation that reached adolescence during the Great Depression. My own history, at the broadest scope, typifies the experience of that generation. More narrowly and more intensely, it typifies the experience of young Americans who were radicalized by the Great Depression. This was a group relatively small in numbers but impressively influential in its time. Some of us organized industrial unions among America's vast new labor force of second generation immigrants. Others tried (and largely failed) to unionize white and black tenant farmers and sharecroppers in the agricultural South. Many of my generation became activists in the left-wing of President Roosevelt's New Deal. Two or three won Oscars in Hollywood. Some volunteered to fight against fascism in Spain.

I am sorry to say I did none of those heroic things. But by sympathy and identification, I was part of the same generational cohort. And, at that point, I consciously entered history—on a miniscule scale, certainly—yet entered nonetheless, along with many others, as conscious participants in historical change. What particular experiences impelled such collective assumptions of responsibility?

Roosevelt—in his second inaugural in 1938—spoke of "one third of a nation, ill-housed, ill-clad, ill-nourished." I was lucky enough not to be born into that bottom third. My parents were middle-class professional people. I never went hungry nor suffered much by way of deprivation. Yet even adolescent boys are social animals, and I was not blind to what was going on around me. My family lived in New York City, in Manhattan, downtown, on the East Side. When my brother and I walked to school three blocks away, we passed at the corner of Third Avenue and Sixteenth Street the end of a breadline that looped all the way around the block. New York in winter can be cold, dismal, wet. People waited from before daybreak for a cup of soup and some slices of bread. They had fires smoldering in old oil drums spaced along the sidewalk, and they took turns crowding up close to warm their hands. Many of the older women were Italian immigrants. They wore black dresses and black shawls that hung down to their knees just as older women did in the old country at that time. I remember now exactly how the women's hands looked when they held them out to the fire—blue with gleaming white knuckles.

I said I would begin by talking about particulars. Not far away was Union Square where the New York City police grudgingly tolerated demonstrations of working class politics. Huge crowds converged there, especially on Labor Day and May Day. Coming home from school, we could see the crowds with placards and banners, hemmed in by mounted police, and surveyed by policemen from the roofs of buildings along the sides of Union Square. At first the mood of the Depression had been one of hopelessness, resignation, taking whatever came along as if it were punishment for some dereliction or failure. By the time I was in high school in 1933, the mood was changing to one of anger and self-assertion. With self-assertion came hope. All over the United States people began to organize. Farmers organized against mortgage foreclosures; city-dwellers against evictions; the unemployed organized for life-supporting standards of relief. Industrial workers organized unions in the great new mass-production industries like steel and automobile, farm equipment, textiles, meatpacking.

This vast amalgamation of people, upsurging from down under, provided the mass base for what historians now refer to as the New Deal coalition. What were the politics of that coalition? Its main thrust was to demand that the industrial apparatus be modified—humanized somehow—so as to yield to working people and their families some hope for the future; some protection against unemployment, injury-on-the-job, sickness, old age. It was in the signs and placards at Union Square I first heard about Social Security, sixty-five years ago; and Social Security remains today, at the turn of the century, a class-divisive, still bitterly-contested issue.

The 1930s was a period of populist nationalism. Among intellectuals, the expatriates came home from Paris. When I entered college in 1936, the books my classmates admired had titles like *Winesburg, Ohio, In the American Grain, USA, To Have and Have Not, Studs Lonigan, Tortilla Flat, Grapes of Wrath*. The American History survey at Harvard in 1937 assigned Charles and Mary Beard, Lincoln Steffens' *Autobiography*, the *Education of Henry Adams*. My parents, who had scrimped and saved to send my brother and myself to Harvard, were deeply distressed when I dropped out in 1938, and went west—WEST—to Chicago. For them, the Hudson River still marked the western boundary of American culture. I

"World War II, 1944, New York. The little girl is our oldest daughter, Catherine. I am home between Atlantic trips. With us, in U.S. Army uniform, is Tybor Blum, who escaped the Nazi takeover in Czechoslovakia, and his wife Eleanor. My wife, Trudy, was clicking the camera."

tried to make up for that by completing an undergraduate degree at the University of Chicago; but Chicago, to my parents at least, was never the same as Harvard.

II

For me, on the other hand, Chicago was Mecca. A romantic realist, I had read Carl Sandburg on Chicago: hog-butcher of the world, railroad center of the universe! I got a job as laborer in a roundhouse where railroad engines were serviced and repaired. I worked six days-a-week at twenty-five cents an hour. And by that time I had decided what I intended was to learn how people lived in the other America—the *real* America, as I thought, industrial America—and write about their lives. This too was a romantic decision; yet, as it turned out, a massively realistic one. For the next twenty years I worked at industrial jobs—railroads, factories, steel mills in Chicago; ammunition ships in the North Atlantic and Pacific during the Second World War; and afterwards, when my wife and I moved to California, I worked as construction carpenter in Marin County north of San Francisco. I give this job resumé in a single sentence because what I want mainly to focus on is writing history—and for me this came later.

But to get there, I must first say a few words about the first of three novels I published, long before I started writing history. The novel was titled *Grand Crossing*. I recall it with special fondness because it is the only book I ever wrote that earned any money—and the only one now totally out of print. I had started writing while I was still in college, before the war. By the time the novel was published—1943—I was trudging back and forth across the Atlantic on World War Two liberty ships. The title, however, had nothing to do with crossing the ocean. My brother suggested, facetiously, that the title referred to crossing the Hudson River.

My own thought was that it referred to the necessity—or aspiration—of crossing from an ethics of individual achievement, to one of moral responsibility for the social order one lived in. The novel was not cast in philosophical terms; nor had I then heard of Jean Paul Sartre, but the imperative was not dissimilar. Its narrative brought forward race and white racism, which, among novels written before the Second World War, made it somewhat unusual. Its *treatment* of race, however, was not unusual. This was the one-world treatment, already enunciated by Roosevelt; by Churchill even; and beaten into cliché during and immediately after the war. One thinks of Steinbeck's *Lifeboat*; or a whole genre of books and movies in which a Texan—along with a Jew from Brooklyn, an African American, or Mexican American, or American Indian—find themselves in a foxhole confronting the grim (and in this situation at least) non-discriminatory foe. I don't mean this was wrong. There were good reasons for suppporting the Allied cause in the Second World War; yet it added little to understanding white racism in American culture. What I now find significant about that first novel was its assertion of moral responsibility for the human condition: never mind whether God created the world *ex nihilo* or not; here it is, and I am responsible—you and I both—for what becomes of it.

III

Earlier, when I was recalling childhood memories of the Great Depression in New York, I was trying to convey two recollections that have stayed with me ever since. The first was of women waiting in the winter streets of the silent city. It symbolized what I perceived then (and still perceive) as an ultimate, unforgivable evil—an original sin, one might say—of the human condition. I mean the exploitation of humans by other human beings. The second image was of crowds at Union Square, with placards and banners, demonstrating for industrial unionism and Social Security under the hostile gaze of the police. This I took as symbol of a collective will to transform the human condition—from what it has been, or now is, to what it could be. Such a will, I imagined then (and still do), would be like a biological instinct, defining the human species. I can even give it a scholarly name—the *utopian impulse*—because I think it possesses both biological and cultural reality.

In Chicago I encountered a third image—that of black men working in gangs along the railroad tracks that laced in and out of the city. These were maintenance-of-the-way workers, called *gandy-dancers* for no reason I ever understood—the most miserable, exposed, hazardous, low-paid, despised occupation of the entire railroad hierar-

1953, California. I was working as a carpenter and we lived in Sausalito.

chy. Gandy-dancing belonged, in Chicago of the 1930s, to Americans who were African or Mexican. In New York, where I had grown up, and even more so at Harvard, there certainly had been racial segregation; yet to the eyes of a white, middle-class youth it remained scarcely visible. In Chicago, it dominated the social landscape. Cottage Grove Avenue sliced lengthways through the southern half of the city. The west side of that avenue was black, the east side white. There was no melding of the color line either on city streets or in the racial separation of jobs. And Cottage Grove Avenue, as I learned, did not end at city limits. It stretched from sea to shining sea, across the continent. Exploitation in the past was not always defined on racial lines, and perhaps may not be in the future. But that was then—and still is—the quintessential shape of human exploitation in our time.

These three remembered images converged for me into a kind of trinity—a triptych, an American Gothic of industrial America. And so, when as a college senior in 1939 I set about writing the Great American Novel, I knew these three images would have to form its major components. Yet they were not congruent. They clashed in absolute dissonance. To move beyond racial oppression would require a convergence of the human species; whereas exploitation itself, by fragmenting the human species, postpones any such convergence to astronomical distances. The set of problems conveyed by these images has been at the center of what I

1954-55, Sausalito, with Trudy and our two daughters, Catherine and Christine, in front of the house we built evenings and weekends.

have written during the past half century—not only novels and short stories of the first twenty years, but things I have written in history since then.

It seems I was a slow learner. It took me about two decades to learn I was not likely in the foreseeable future to earn a living writing short stories and novels. In 1962—I was then forty-three—I started work on a doctorate in United States history at Berkeley. As a historian I have published two books and the usual medley of journal articles and reviews. The first book, *The Indispensable Enemy*, as I noted at the outset, grew out of my dissertation. I have already summarized the particular experiences that preceded and led into my choice of topic. I need now to comment on certain ideological aspects and implications of that choice.

IV

When I switched from fiction to history, I had spent almost a quarter century as industrial worker, some of those years as activist and union organizer. I had been acutely aware that racial division was a major factor in the ongoing weakness of the American labor movement. I was looking for a topic centered on labor and race, hoping to illuminate—if only for myself—the relation of racial prejudice to class consciousness. What I had in mind, I remember, was something comparable to E.P. Thompson's *Making of the English Working Class,* which at that time was transforming the field of labor history both in England and the United States. Such a grand project, however, would have required being able to treat the Chinese segment of the labor force in California at the same level of intensity with which I could treat its European American segments. These latter had usually communicated and kept their records in English. But I did not know Chinese. And being past forty, with a wife and two children, that approach, for me, remained out of reach. Reluctantly I narrowed the problem.

So what was the problem? There was no question as to the actual behavior of white working people in California. Documentary evidence was abundant and already had been arranged by earlier historians into chronological sequences. I perhaps added something new by showing that anti-Chinese, anti-Asian hostilities had been systematically nourished and exploited for almost a century—by labor leaders, to construct racially exclusive craft unions; and by politicians to sustain a white supremacist political party—the Democratic party.

The real problem, however, as I think it must always be in historical study, was not *what* happened, but *why* it happened the way it did. European Americans, migrating to California after the Gold Rush, had never before encountered Chinese. Why did they so readily set aside their own voluminous ethnic and religious paranoias in favor of hating and despising Chinese? Several theories of racial conflict were available to me in the late 1960s. Most attractive of these was the economic argument from job competition. Many Chinese immigrants, coming out of desperate poverty, arrived in California as "coolie" laborers, that is, under indenture, a situation not very different from slavery. Since European Americans, acculturated to higher living standards, would be severely damaged by such job competition, they had no choice—so the argument runs—but to protect themselves *economically* by trying to

Passport photo, about 1963.

exclude Chinese from the labor market, or to bar them from entering the United States at all. This argument points out (correctly) that job competition could hardly be blamed on Euro-American working people, since it was entrepreneurial capitalists (such as the owners of the Central Pacific Railroad) who organized and financed the importation of Chinese; and they did so precisely for the purpose of reducing labor costs.

Apart from its presumed explanatory powers, the job competition argument offered the ideological advantage of exonerating white working people from accusations of racial prejudice—because it justified their actions as economically rational self-defense. Consequently it was often invoked by trade union leaders and held strong appeal for social scientists and historians sympathetic to organized labor. It appealed to me for the same reasons. Yet I quickly discovered that it could not meet my needs as an explanation of the anti-Chinese movement in California. Its timing was wrong. According to the competition argument, racial hostility results from job competition. California, however, from the Gold Rush in 1849 until the 1870s, exhibited a characteristic frontier economy in which labor was scarce and wages high. The actual effect of Chinese immigration during this period—by speeding up infrastructural development—was to *enhance* opportunities for European Americans to move up to self-employment, or into skilled trades and supervisory positions. Not until completion of the transcontinental railroad in 1869, and the Depression of 1873, did mass unemployment and job competition really hit the West Coast. Hostile actions against Chinese, by contrast, dated from their first arrival twenty years earlier.

Thus, while job competition might account for the intensification of racial hostilities after 1869, it said nothing as to the origin of those hostilities. What I needed was to explain why so many European American working people carried white racism with them on their journey to California. At that point I began assembling an argument which I thought of at first as simply political. It ran as follows: The Jacksonian Democratic party had dominated Amer-ican politics for thirty years prior to the Civil War. It governed California after the aquisition of California in 1848. Jacksonian Democracy functioned in national politics as a coalition of northern and western farmers and workingmen, on one hand, with slave-owning Southern planters on the other. Territorial expansion and defense of slavery headed the Jacksonian party's political agenda, while its moral catechism asserted racial inferiority of Africans and Indians—in contrast to the absolute fraternal equality of white men as members of the ruling race. The Jacksonian ethic was egalitarian for whites, hierarchical with respect to people of color.

This ideological baggage, I reasoned—absorbed in the eastern states—had traveled with European Americans, native and foreign-born, when they poured into California after the Gold Rush. Most European immigrants to California came by way of the Atlantic crossing and many of these had lingered for a generation or two on the East Coast before journeying West. From the work of other historians I was beginning to understand that Western Europe had been engaged almost as intensely as the United States in colonial exploitations and that newcomers from Europe would be carrying racial attitudes that needed only to be focused and lethalized to bring them into line with the Jacksonian persuasion they would encounter in California.

I actually used the phrase "ideological baggage" as title for the second and most important chapter of my dissertation. But I was then a long distance from anticipating the difficulties involved in the notion of ideological construction as a causal factor of historical change. To provide a foundation for the argument I was putting together about racial conflict in California, I would have needed to show—

(1) That belief in the inferiority of non-white people had been generated by slavery and the slave trade;

(2) That this same belief had been extended and reinforced by European wars of conquest worldwide, and especially against American Indians;

(3) That such white racist beliefs developed enormous retentive power—since they have lasted now for half a millennium;

(4) That white racism was socialized into the consciousness of generations of European American working people, most of whom had no direct contact with African slavery—nor with the slave trade, or wars against native Americans; and finally,

(5) That all this *ideological baggage* was brought to bear against Chinese immigrants in California.

The Indispensable Enemy, I am obliged to confess, touches base only at the last of these five points. The first four I simply took for granted; or remained unaware of any need for such explanatory sequences. Yet after I finished the book, these problems in their general form confronted me; and I can say I have been whittling away at them ever since. There is no need, here, to retrace all that step by step. One particular episode by way of illustration will serve to make my point. While scanning California newspapers of the 1850s, I had noted that blackface minstrel shows were popular in mining camps and that prominent minstrel companies from back East regularly visited San Francisco. I was then astonished to discover that one of the earliest on-stage caricatures of Chinese occurred at a minstrel performance, presumably in blackface. I set this nugget aside to follow up later when I could visit the New York Public Library's theatrical collection. The result was an essay, "Blackface Minstrelsy and Jacksonian Ideology," probably the most widely read historical piece I have written.

I won't claim I was first to observe the symbiosis of blackface minstrelsy—as mass entertainment—with the Democratic party program; but I think I am accurate in saying I was one of the first to treat this as significant information. In my own case, it has led me in pursuit of ideological construction as a major enterprise of human culture; and I mean not only at the low level, but the high; not only popular culture like blackface minstrelsy itself, or melodrama, or dime novels—but "elite" culture like *Moby Dick* or *Leaves of Grass*—or *Hamlet*, if you wish, or *Paradise Lost*.

V

This has the effect of placing the study of ideology on a wide screen. Such breadth is necessary, I think; but runs the risk of equating ideology with culture itself, or with *Weltanschauung*, worldview; in which case it becomes useless for analytical or explanatory purposes. On the other hand, narrowing the concept of ideology to mean only hypocrisy, or self-serving deceit, precludes its application—in whatever social order we may be studying—to the mainstream of intellectual and political behavior.

Lone Pine, California, 1985. Trudy and I with Robert Rydell, then a graduate student at UCLA, now professor of history at Montana State University, Bozeman.

In America, scholarly treatment of ideology has verged on the paranoid. I find it embarrassing, in the 1990s, to reread a work like Daniel Bell's *End of Ideology,* in which an otherwise intelligent writer shows himself totally unperceptive of the ideological baggage contained in his own status of social scientist in the Cold War establishment. During my working life as a historian, the two most influential treatments by American scholars have been Bernard Bailyn's *Ideological Origins of the American Revolution*, and Clifford Geertz' essay on "Ideology as a Cultural System." Both are serious works that contain illuminating insights. Both, however, deal with the concept of ideology by evading its cutting edge. Bailyn's *Ideological Origins* actually is a study not in *ideological* but *intellectual* history—in the history of ideas, almost as if ideas themselves were autonomous actors in historical change. Geertz' famous essay presents ideology as a particular *type* of sociopolitical discourse—one that makes use of *tropes*, symbolic figures of speech such as metaphor—to convey its meanings. Yet since all human discourse employs tropes and metaphors to convey meaning, the result is to equate ideology with culture-at-large; which, again (as I suggested above) is to render it useless for historical explanation.

Bailyn's book reduces historical explanation to the presumed self-propulsion of ideas. Geertz's essay tends to disparage the importance, or even possibility, of causal explanation.

Most written history is narrative. It recounts what happened, not why it happened. But if the crucial question always is *why*— then *why* mandates a search for causes. Causation in history has usually been conceived under three main headings: vast, impersonal determinisms; contingency (chance or accident); and doings of powerful individuals. The most frequently invoked determinisms are economic or geographic; but it is worth remembering that racism itself represents a deterministic theory of history; and that the most prevalent of all determinisms has been belief in Providential intervention—in the guidance, that is, of a divine but Invisible Hand, beyond human power to comprehend, yet somehow always benevolent. During our modern era of technology and science, we have learned to conceptualize Providential determinism as the Invisible Hand of the Free Market.

The value of ideology for causal explanation lies in its emphasis on *class* (or social group) as the dynamic component of socialization, therefore of individual and collective consciousness. Collective consciousness makes possible purposeful collective actions. Lacking a concept of ideology, we would be left with nothing, save sheer contingency between the historical determinisms on one hand, and acts by heroic or destructive individuals on the other. That is, we would be reduced in our accounts of historical causation either to arguments that exclude human purpose altogether, or to elitist arguments which locate effective purpose only in thoughts and actions of outstanding individuals. I think the reason American scholars encounter so much difficulty in coping with ideology is that American culture, during the past century at least, has been structured to obliterate any perception of class as a component of social consciousness. To explain this curious aspect of American exceptionalism historians have invoked both economic and geographic determinism as well as deeds and thoughts of great men, such as Adam Smith or Thomas Jefferson. For myself, I think it more helpful to construct an *ideological* explanation for the alleged end of ideology. This was what I attempted in *The Rise and Fall of the White Republic: Class Politics and Mass Culture in Nineteenth Century America* (1990), which I wrote more or less as an answer, or sequel, to *The Indispensable Enemy*.

If ideology expressed only class interest, it might serve to explain historical change but could offer no promise for amelioration of the human condition since all that could be expected would be an endless sequence of exploitive dominations by one class after another. Successful ideologies would then become ideologies of repression like white racism; yet we know there also are ideologies of the oppressed which often proclaim goals of universal liberation. My own concept is that while class interest sets the immediate goals of ideological behavior, its more distant goals derive from what I referred to earlier as utopian impulse. Such an impulse, I suggested, enters human consciousness as an almost-biological drive for direction and purposefulness. Ideology could then be seen as an ongoing effort to justify the short-range, self-serving demands of class or group interest by harnessing these to a broader sense of collective moral purpose. But what defines *collective moral purpose*? That group to which our most deeply-felt identification binds each one of us. If there is amelioration or progress in human history, it can reside only in a gradual expansion of this moral identification. In ancient times, moral identity was bounded by tribe or city-state; in our own era, by ethnic, or "racial," or national affiliations. Tomorrow, the world?

And that question brings me once again to the triptych of images inscribed in my own adolescent recollections of the Great Depression. One was an image of black gandy-dancers wielding their picks and shovels along the railroad embankments. Racial segregation was then (and still is) the quintessential shape of human exploitation in our time. To move beyond racial hatreds and separations would require an ideological convergence of the human species; yet exploitation itself fragments the human species, postponing any such convergence to astronomical distances. Will the Invisible Hand of our providential Free Market, extending its jurisdiction over a globalized economy, serve to reduce human exploitation? Visible evidence—thus far—points in the opposite direction.

VI

It is time now to bring this circle back to its starting point. *The Indispensable Enemy* has sometimes been cited as having contributed to the development of Asian American Studies in its early stages. I am proud of this association. Asian American Studies, we remember, developed as part of the broader Ethnic Studies movement which in turn stemmed out of the Civil Rights upsurge of the late 1950s and early '60s. Ethnic studies, like the Civil Rights Movement itself, challenged the dominance of white racism in

American culture and institutions. At this level, Ethnic Studies began as a cultural alliance of racial minorities—peoples of color—whose communities were enclaved within the overarching structure of the European American White Republic. On a deeper level, however, Ethnic Studies was also a class alliance. To confirm this point one need simply recall the economic goals targeted by affirmative action, such as equal access for Americans of all racial backgrounds to public and governmental services, housing, employment; and most important of all—through education—to an equitable share in the social and cultural creativity of American society. What held this alliance together (despite its cultural dissimilarities) was a shared awareness (*ideology*, if you please) of being similarly victimized by *class* exploitation. *Class* exploitation means economic exploitation, and all exploitation of humans by other humans is basically economic.

Affirmative action scored some signal victories. The cost of doing so was to unite powerful segments of the White Republic in opposition. This hampered affirmative action and prevented the filling out of its logical agenda. What affirmative action achieved is immensely valuable, but the achievements remain scattered and uneven. Their impact on the class status of different segments of the Ethnic Studies alliance has varied widely; and as the shared awareness of being similarly exploited fades into the background, cultural differences become more divisive. Moral identifications of class and ethnicity sometimes overlap and reinforce each other (as they did in the 1950s and '60s). More often, in American history at least, they have cut at right angles, impeding one another's progress (as they tended to do again in the 1990s). On college and university campuses, the Ethnic Studies movement proved extraordinarily successful; yet what was once a "movement" has now become a galaxy of discrete centers and departments each pursuing its own particular track of historical and cultural studies. Not only have Ethnic Studies moved apart because the racial minorities they represent stand in altered economic relations to one another; but class separation has penetrated each of these minorities more deeply than ever before. This structural change—resulting in part from the successes of affirmative action—alters the relationship of ethnic studies programs to working-class segments within their own constituencies.

I am not suggesting that the need for ethnic studies programs has diminished. On the contrary, I think the need will be greater than ever. But the socioeconomic context within which leaders of Ethnic Studies design and carry out their projects for research and teaching has changed profoundly. Leaders in Ethnic Studies will need to struggle to preserve whatever can be salvaged from the unity of the original coalition. They will need to shift from a retrospective view of particular immigrant minorities in American history to a contemporary view of those same minorities as related to the cultures in their lands of origin. Above all, I think, they will need to integrate working class components of their own ethnicities into the cultural (and political) projects proposed by the Ethnic Studies centers. Even in the United States, which sits rather crudely at the apex of the globalizing process, our social landscape also is being globalized. The providential Free Market hardly tolerates sanctuaries except those that may be privatized by wealth. So what will become of ideological construction and "utopian impulse" in our brave new world? Here I can best end these reminiscences by quoting from the final pages of my second—and perhaps last—work in history:

> . . .Yet in the long run the ancient wisdom seems likely to pre-vail: a camel will pass through the eye of a needle sooner than a rich man enter the kingdom of heaven. Wealth, privilege, power, tend to narrow the vision of ruling classes and their mercenary retainers. If this is true, far-reaching prospects of the human con-dition are more likely to be constructed in the ghettoes of great cities and third world barrios (or in the work of intellectuals whose socialization has contained "organic" links to such experience) than among the CEOs of global enterprize or within military-industrial complexes.

II.

"The Train Ride to the Topaz Camp in Utah."
Drawing by Sachi Fujii Matsumoto, 1942.

September 12, 1942

Barracks in Tanforan. Drawings by Sachi Fujii Matsumoto, 1942.

September 19, 1942

Amerasia Journal 26:1 (2000): 105-118

Oral History Research, Theory, and Asian American Studies

Alice Yang Murray

As I finish reading another batch of graduate school applications, I can't help but note the stark contrast in people's conceptions of historical research topics. Aspiring cultural theorists sprinkle their essays with terms like discourse, subjectivities, incommensurability, and indeterminacy. Future social historians, on the other hand, emphasize oppression, resistance, agency, and communal solidarity. Very few applicants mention both discourse and community in the same essay. Yet how can I be surprised when so few of us within Asian American Studies who call ourselves cultural theorists or social historians ever talk to each other? Occasionally, we'll even lob accusations at each other: theorists are pretentious elitists who lack any social commitment while social historians are naïve essentialists who fail to acknowledge their lack of objectivity. Most of the time, however, we simply ignore each other, read different articles, attend different conference panels, and almost never cite each other's research.

As an advocate of bridging this scholarly divide, I hope the students I advise won't take as long as I did to explore the benefits of cross-fertilization. I came out of graduate school a staunch social historian dismissive of cultural theorists and their study of "texts" as irrelevant to "real" historical research. They might talk about the process of doing history but I was out actually interviewing Japanese American redress activists about their experiences. While theorists spoke in a jargon few outside of academia could understand, I established relationships with political activ-

ALICE YANG MURRAY is an assistant professor in History at the University of California, Santa Cruz.

ists and participated in a growing number of Japanese American community events.

Ironically, however, it was this very contact with the Japanese American community that forced me to reconsider my assumptions about oral history and the value of postmodern theory. Over the years, as my relationships with activists changed, so did my interview questions and their responses. I became aware that redress activists had multiple and conflicting views of the meaning of the incarceration of Japanese Americans during World War II and the redress movement. This was not just a matter of comparing accounts among activists. A single individual could present different interpretations of history as the context of the interview changed. I could not help but become aware of how much the larger historical context and the dynamics of each interview affected the oral histories. I wasn't just recording each person's experience. I had a direct impact on how individuals represented their past. Consequently, I realized that I could not simply "tell what happened" during World War II or the redress movement. I also would have to analyze why individuals remembered and recounted the history of these periods to me in particular ways at particular times. Only then did I turn to postmodern theory for insight into the possible factors affecting the construction of these narratives of memory.

Recognizing oral history is a process and not a product makes both research and interpretation much more complicated. When I first began interviewing people in 1990, I never tried to "historicize" the interviews or consider the impact of my "positionality" on the process. In hindsight, however, I can trace how my selection of activists, the questions I developed, and my responses to their comments reflected certain scholarly and political agendas. Like many oral historians then and now, I was committed to "restoring" to history the perspectives of marginalized individuals. I wanted to challenge traditional political scholarship that privileged written sources and ignored the voices of people who experienced race, class, and gender oppression. I hoped to be a pioneer in the burgeoning field of Asian American history. Although my adviser and several faculty members in my graduate program supported this goal, I knew that many historians shared the views of two of my mentors who insisted Asian Americans were not an "important" enough group to study. Becoming a bit self-righteous, I vowed to prove to these well-meaning but poorly informed scholars that Asian American history was "real" history vital to the understanding of immigration, labor, citizenship, and civil rights.

Determined to study the concrete life experiences of individuals and communities, I assumed, like many social historians, that theory was preoccupied with "texts" and abstract concepts and was thus irrelevant to my research. Unfortunately my initial exposure to postmodern theory only reinforced this belief. The first few articles I tried to read deserved the criticism social historians often levy against theorists. Sentences in these articles never seemed to end or contain a verb other than variations of the verb "to be." The writers appeared to determine the value of a noun by the number of its syllables. Moreover, I couldn't understand why these articles contained so many adjectives, like Foucaultian, Derridean or Lacanian, that referred to theorists without explaining their concepts.

If I actually had read Foucault, instead of just a few individuals who invoked his name, I would not have dismissed all theorists. Instead I convinced myself on the basis of just a few articles that all theory was self-referential tripe that replicated the worst writing practices of the sciences. It was easy to rationalize not spending the time and effort to understand the esoteric terminology. For me, Foucault became a kind of "f" word. The presence of the dreaded "f" word in an article or book made me inclined to skip it.

I thus neglected to consider how theories of power, language, and meaning could affect my own research assumptions and methods. If I had, I might have recognized that my notions of "agency," "resistance," and "solidarity" were oversimplified and romanticized. Dismayed by a tendency in earlier scholarship to depict Asian Americans as "victims" of white oppression, I and many other social historians wanted to document a history of activism and protest against discrimination.[1] Given that there was so little scholarship on Asian Americans at all, it is perhaps not surprising so many of us wanted to promote stories of heroic individuals and communities. Such research not only could counter the common public image of Asian Americans as a "model minority" achieving "success" in America without a history of protest, but might even stimulate more current activism against oppression.

I still believe it was a necessary and logical development in the historiography to spend so much time refuting portrayals of Asian Americans as victims. Yet in our zeal to revise earlier victimization studies, too few of us contemplated alternative approaches or questions. Even as I questioned the conclusions of the paradigm of victimization, I still allowed it to dictate my research agenda. Instead of dismantling the paradigm, I simply refined it by adding the concept of "resistance." Substituting a homogenized depiction of resisters for a homogenized depiction of victims, I ignored the complexity and diversity of Asian American experiences.

After limiting my research radar to groups struggling against race, class, or gender oppression, it's no wonder most of my old graduate school papers contained the refrain ". . .but they were not passive or submissive victims." Given this research focus, a professor suggested I might enjoy an exhibit at the Oakland Museum entitled "Strength and Diversity: Three Generations of Japanese American Women." I thought a visit to the museum might help me develop a seminar paper on Japanese American redress activism. Instead I found a topic that had preoccupied me for the next ten years and forced me to rethink my assumptions about historical methodology and interpretation.

Initially, however, I had no idea that this research might change my views of postmodern theory and social history. At first, Japanese American redress seemed a clear "social history" subject. The role of racism in the government's forcible removal and confinement of Japanese Americans during World War II had been well documented. Although there was scholarship on how Japanese Americans responded to the incarceration during the war and a growing list of oral history anthologies and memoirs, there were few accounts of the long-term legacy of internment and almost nothing on the history of redress. In other words, I could still stake my claim that this was both an important and unexplored topic. Moreover, there was obvious appeal to studying a movement that had forced the national government to issue an apology and provide monetary compensation to surviving victims of racism. I could document both a history of oppression and a history of individual agency and communal solidarity triumphing over racial injustice.

I also was attracted to the prospect of talking to real people about their experiences. After a stint doing archival research for another seminar, I was eager for more human interaction. Reading archival material had been fascinating, but I had spent a lot of time wishing I could ask the people mentioned in these written sources how they felt about their experiences. Now I would get a chance to ask such questions of living historical sources.

I found it difficult to contain my excitement as I listened to four participants recount their lives during a museum panel entitled "Day of Remembrance: The Impact of the Detention Experience on Japanese American Women." One woman moved me to tears. Later I would learn that this was not the first time Kiku Hori Funabiki had spoken publicly about her experience in a World War II detention camp. In 1981 she had testified before a government commission investigating the causes of the incarceration and in 1984 she had lobbied Congress as part of the redress movement that won legislation providing government compensation for surviving detainees in 1988.[2] In all these presentations, Funabiki described the pain of watching her father being taken away in shackles by the FBI after the bombing of Pearl Harbor and the forty years of guilt she felt at being imprisoned behind barbed wire. But in 1990 she also wanted the audience to hear how sharing this painful personal history with the public had been cathartic and empowering. Remembering the war helped her to "reach down and purge repressed feelings about that dark chapter" and intensified her commitment to the struggle for redress. After recalling her own evolution from a silent victim to an outspoken critic of racism, Funabiki urged all the women in the audience who had been incarcerated to share their memories with their families, the ethnic community, and the nation.[3]

I doubt if there was a dry eye in the packed auditorium after Funabiki spoke. I could hear people around me sniffling even as I searched in vain for a tissue. As I listened to Funabiki and the other women, I rejoiced at "discovering" a history that needed to be told. I would interview these women and make sure that history recognized and celebrated their experiences. This attitude was not just a testimonial to the power of their inspirational stories. It also reflected my assumption that if they weren't mentioned in academic scholarship, they needed to be "reclaimed" and presented to the rest of the world. It didn't occur to me that they might be prominent within the Bay Area Japanese American community or appear often within the pages of the Japanese American press. I also never thought to examine their government testimony or the many stories that appeared about them in the mainstream press before I interviewed them. In retrospect, my attempt to "restore" them to history was ludicrous. Many of these women had been interviewed several times before and had conducted their own oral histories of other Japanese American women to prepare the text for the exhibit I had just viewed.

My ignorance, however, might have protected me from being intimidated by these extremely articulate women. It was difficult for me to listen to recordings of these early interviews without cringing at my obvious lack of knowledge about the community. At the time, I thought the interviews went well because the women gave such eloquent responses. But when I listen to many of these tapes, a common pattern appears: a poorly phrased question yields a half-hour story rich with detail and emotion. I just happened to be lucky that these women could draw on extensive experience speaking to interviewers and to the community about their experiences. They had told their stories before and they could do so again with great polish even if my questions were mundane or awkward. In other words, these oral histories were remarkable despite, rather than because of, me.

These oral histories also demonstrate the impact of changing relationships between ethnographers and informants that anthropologists have analyzed for more than a decade.[4] My unabashed admiration of these women and their desire to educate the public about the injustice of internment and inspire other activists clearly influenced the topics addressed in our oral history interviews. When I first showed up on these women's doorsteps with fruit basket in hand, I was greeted with varying degrees of appreciation and amusement. One woman thought bringing a present was a "very Nisei" (or second-generation Japanese American) thing to do and was surprised to learn that I had been raised to think of it as a Korean tradition. Most of these interviews, in fact, began long before the tape recorder was turned on as we "chatted" about why I was interested in interviewing them, what historical material I had read, who else I had talked to, and who I planned to approach in the future. Moreover, almost everyone expressed curiosity about how a second-generation Korean American became interested in Japanese American redress. In one case, I spent almost half an hour explaining my own family experiences and views of discrimination, patriarchy, ethnic identity, and history before I got a chance to ask my first question.

These interviews also illustrate how our agendas often converged. While I had designed questions to explore women's views of racism and sexism, it soon became evident that many of these women also wanted to emphasize the pernicious impact of these two forces on their responses to the incarceration. For example, Kiku Hori Funabiki told me that she never contemplated during the war "the injustice" of what happened or why she and her mother were put "behind barbed wire with watchtowers and armed guards." As a child, her parents tried to protect her from a racist society by urging her to "keep a low profile," "not make waves" and "defer to authority, particularly white authority." The incarceration only confirmed for her the second-class status of Japanese Americans. Desensitized and lacking a sense of self, she endured camp by "coping through denial."[5]

But while Funabiki and the other women I interviewed emphasized how much racism and sexism could silence women, they also wanted to convey to me a lesson in how community activism could empower women. After describing how painful it was for her to resurrect buried memories of her father's suffering during the war, Funabiki recounted how the process of sharing these memories with the public intensified her outrage at the injustice and her commitment to become an activist. Three years later she was shocked when she appeared before a congressional committee and a white male congressman tried to "ambush" her testimony by insinuating her father might have been a security risk during the war because he ran an employment agency.[6] As she recalled sending a letter to be included in the Congressional Record denouncing Congressman Thomas Kindness for trying to undermine her credibility, Funabiki clearly hoped I would learn from her experience:

> We have a right to stand toe to toe with these guys that are looking down on us trying to tell us what our rights are. I just came to realize that we were just being a little too timid about this. . .[7]

I was, of course, quite eager to help these activists spread their message. I might be a young and naive outsider but I could help the public remember the injustice of the incarceration, the struggle for redress, and the need for vigilance against racism. In recounting their transformation from silent victims to outspoken and successful activists, I might inspire others to emulate them. Consequently, these first oral history interviews and my analysis of their experiences emphasized the suffering caused by the incarceration, the onset of their activism, and their contributions to the passage of redress. It was an incredible history of individual empowerment, communal solidarity, and successful resistance to racism. I knew that I could devote the next several years to researching this history for my dissertation.

I would soon learn, however, that while this history was important, it was hardly complete. As I became friends with these women, conducted more research, and participated in various communal activities, my understanding of redress activism changed. Whereas earlier I had focused on the battle for redress, I began to learn more about conflicts within the activist community. What I had once thought was a simple story of an ethnic community coming together to win justice from the government became a much more complicated story of different groups fighting to represent the Japanese American community and to define the meaning of the incarceration and redress. Forced to acknowledge these different versions of history, I became aware of how much my relationships with activists affected the interviews I recorded. I also began to re-examine my views of historical memory and the ways historians and activists construct history before various audiences at different times.

I would not have learned as much about this history of factionalism among redress activists if I had not spent time with these women and other activists at community events. The women invited me to activities ranging from meetings of their Women's Concerns Committee and historical society programs to Mother's Day celebrations and picket-line demonstrations against the firing of Asian American female employees. I joined them at these events to learn more about their lives, to meet other members of the community, and to express my appreciation for their support of my research. I also, however, wanted to demonstrate to them that I too cared about community issues. Several recounted stories of researchers who promised to "give back" to the community and then were never seen again. I hoped that participating in an oral history workshop or volunteering my husband to fry fish for a fundraiser might assuage any fears they might have that I only cared about my own research.

But as I spent more time with the women and the line between researcher and friend blurred, I gained new insight into their experiences that changed my research agenda. Whereas my first interviews had focused on the impact of the incarceration and reasons for the success of the redress movement, casual conversations with these new friends exposed me to a history of communal disagreement about redress goals and strategies. In our formal interviews, some of the women had described differences between the three major redress organizations but in very general terms. As I became closer to the women, however, I began to hear a lot of "off the record" comments about problems within organizations, criticism of organizational leaders, and conflicts between organizations. Once they realized I was interested in this factionalism and would not use the information to try to discredit the concept of redress, they began regaling me with personal documents and lists of people within different organizations that illuminated these divisions.

Pursuing this line of investigation exposed me to other issues as well. It was soon apparent that much of the disagreement between redress organizations stemmed from different wartime experiences and different interpretations of the meaning of the incarceration that were shaped by postwar events. I couldn't understand redress activism without analyzing why people remembered the incarceration experience and legacy in such different ways at different times in their lives. Comparing accounts presented in interviews, government records, organizational newsletters, and ethnic newspapers also indicated that an individual activist or group representative might describe the history of the incarceration and redress in different ways before different audiences. Analyzing these depictions was important not so much to accuse someone of being inconsistent or manipulative but to shed light on how different contexts might affect both memories and representations. Once I became conscious of these various constructions of history, I also became interested in the role of other groups in promoting particular histories of the wartime incarceration and redress. My simple study of the passage of redress legislation developed into an exploration of why different groups of Japanese Americans, government officials, scholars, the media, and museum curators promoted multiple interpretations of the wartime incarceration and the significance of redress.

Understanding how particular contexts could impact memories and representations forced me to re-examine my views of oral history and the relevancy of postmodern theory. I no longer took it for granted that I could discover the "definitive facts" of someone's life from an interview. Instead I would need to analyze the constructions and interpretations of the past as influenced by the dynamics of our interview and the larger historical context. At the same time, however, I also realized that oral histories were no less "reliable" than other historical sources. All sources, whether newspapers, archival documents, personal letters, or oral histories, should be contextualized. All scholars, Bob Berkhofer notes in a useful analysis of the impact of postmodern theory on historical research and writing, need to examine the "relationships among a text, its author, and the social context of each" and how a "historian acts as a mediator between a postulated past and an experienced present through the medium of the text."[8] Many critics of oral history sources never consider how often supposedly more "legitimate" archival or newspaper accounts actually rely on oral sources. They almost seem to assume that the act of transmitting oral sources into written form suddenly endows these "texts" with greater credibility.

I, on the other hand, would argue that oral history sources should be used by more researchers because they can reveal a mediation process that can also be analyzed and incorporated into historical interpretation. I wholeheartedly agree with Michael Frisch when he asserts that oral history can be:

> a powerful tool for discovering, exploring, and evaluating the nature of the process of historical memory—how people make sense of their past, how they connect individual experience and its social context, how the past becomes part of the present, and how people use it to interpret their lives and the world around them.[9]

Oral historians have a special opportunity and responsibility to explore such issues. While researchers looking at archival or newspaper sources may have to guess the context for the creation of their sources, oral historians can design questions to analyze explicitly the creation and representation of particular memories. We can ask people and design questions to see if their views of the past may have changed. We can ask them about events and experiences that might have caused them to remember or forget certain experiences. We can even explore the possible meaning of silences, inconsistencies, revelations, and omissions in a way few archival scholars can even imagine.

The "interactive" and "collaborative" nature of oral history also can be seen as an asset rather than a liability. Anthropologists have made us aware that oral history is a "dialogue" shaped by such factors as the race, ethnicity, gender, class, age, and political identification of both the interviewer and narrator. We need to acknowledge how attitudes, demeanor, personality, expectations, and perceptions of intended audiences can affect research agendas, questions, responses, and interpretations.[10] Yet once we are conscious of these factors, we can also analyze how the evolution of our relationship with our informants affects their presentation of memories. Language choice, tone of voice, facial expression, body gestures, and narrative patterns can provide invaluable clues for analyzing the dynamics of the interview and the impact of particular contexts on how people remember and represent the past.

Self-reflexive scholars can and should design questions to shed light on how larger historical contexts and relationships between interviewers and informants might affect the agendas, assumptions, and responses of both parties. For example, after certain newspaper articles and books presented particular explanations of the passage of redress, I decided to ask some of my informants what they thought of these accounts. The immediate response was for some to give credit to the unsung, while others slung mud at the over-celebrated. I also asked them to analyze why they might agree or disagree with these different accounts and whether their attitude had ever or would ever change. I then asked them if they had any strong feelings about the role my book should play in challenging, confirming, or revising these accounts and if those views might affect our discussions.

Of course, there's a danger that preoccupation with the "process" of interviewing can overshadow our analysis of our informants' depictions of the past. I've heard some self-absorbed conference presentations on the dynamics of interviewing that only focus on the interviewer's dilemmas of "representation." Acknowledging our role in the construction of an oral history narrative should not become an excuse for navel-gazing.[11] It should only be the first step in a continuous process of both contextualizing and interpreting our oral history narratives. Obviously intertwined, context and interpretation must be analyzed when we present our research findings.

Based on my experience, I would assert that the real "dilemma" facing oral historians today is the problem of trying to choose from a seemingly inexhaustible supply of sources that might help contextualize our oral history narratives. At one time, I naively thought I could understand the history of redress by interviewing the leaders of the three different redress organizations. As I conducted more and more interviews, however, I realized that there was no "representative" account of one group or even one individual. I also discovered that there was a wealth of written material that could shed light on people's experiences, memories and representations. Anyone dealing with a twentieth-century topic has to face the possibility that there may be an enormous paper trail of sources that runs through government records, newspapers, organizations, courts, archives, and even people's garages. But how much written material should we consult before and after we interview people? How many times should we interview a single person? How many people should we interview when we know there are many who can shed light on the subject? Do we sacrifice quantity or quality? In other words, knowing that contextualization needs to be continuous can make it extraordinarily difficult to finally stop conducting research. There will always be another written and oral source one can consider. When is enough finally enough?

Lastly, if we acknowledge that both contextualization and interpretation are intertwined, how do we actually present these elements in our research findings? It's a lot easier to say that both must be included and analyzed than to do it without falling into the trap of navel-gazing. How much space should we devote to acknowledging how much we influenced the creation and interpretation of our sources? The idea of hearing a diary-like account of a historian's research and writing process has little appeal for me even if this provides the best way to contextualize one's historical sources. And if I have no tolerance for this, I can only imagine the derision such presentations would elicit from people within the Asian American community.

As Russell Leong has suggested, there are far too few attempts to "enhance and build linkages among community members, scholars, cultural workers and our youth." Researchers need to recognize that we are all guilty, to a certain extent, of "academic pimping" because we tend to utilize community sources for our articles and books for our own needs without considering the needs of the community.[12] But if we can never fully repay our debt to the community, we can give something back. We can at least try to revive the spirit of "serving the community" that was so vital to the creation of Asian American Studies. Only then can we challenge the increasingly common perception that academics care only about getting published, receiving tenure, and impressing other elitist colleagues.

Unfortunately, I know a few scholars who merit such criticism. I've heard academics say it doesn't matter if people within the Asian American community are "incapable" of understanding their research. The condescension is palpable and disgusting. I've also, however, heard well-meaning colleagues maintain that sophisticated new research requires the use of precise and complex terminology. I'll admit that "translating" theoretical terms into language non-specialists can understand may entail a loss of meaning and specificity. But isn't this true of all translations, whether the translation is of a different language or of scientific concepts? I'm sure that many scientists who find the articles in *Scientific American* to be simplistic are still glad that there's a forum where scientific ideas can reach a popular audience. If we really believe in the importance of our research, shouldn't we try to disseminate it as widely as possible? Can't we simultaneously publish the more "precise" scholarship in specialized journals and produce more accessible accounts for community journals, newspapers, and magazines?

As an oral historian, I have a vested interest in trying to improve relations between academics and community people. If the hostility gets much worse, oral historians may find doors slammed in our faces. But I also would argue that even self-proclaimed "theorists" could benefit from spending some time within the community. Ironically many theorists who write about the "politics of representation" miss the chance to explore the implications of their research for living people. I never would have anticipated that my contact with the Japanese American community as a "social historian" might make me more receptive to theory. I suspect that many theorists might also benefit from such cross-fertilization. To give just one possible example, I've heard many theorists discuss the concept of an "Asian American" identity as an essentialist construction necessary for political alliance. Couldn't oral history provide an ideal source to explore and compare how different individuals and groups have interpreted and represented the meaning of this concept not just during the late 1960s and 1970s but throughout the last three decades? Wouldn't such sources help theorists analyze the impact of race, ethnicity, class, gender, sexuality, and a variety of other factors on constructions and representations of memory, history, language, culture, and politics? In other words, couldn't oral history sources shed light on the multiple and complex contextualizations of language, power, and meaning relevant to both social historians and theorists? And perhaps by asking self-identified social historians, theorists, literary critics, activists, politicians, artists, and others to reflect on why they have categorized their "roles," the meaning of "Asian American," and the meaning of the "community" in particular ways, we can begin to understand and maybe even start to heal the rifts between these groups. Perhaps then we could begin to try to collaborate on mutually beneficial research and community projects.

Notes

1. For more on the "victim paradigm," see Shirley Hune, "Rethinking Race: Paradigms and Policy Formation," *Amerasia Journal* 21:1 & 2 (1995), 32.

2. "Testimony of Kiku Hori Funabiki," United States Congress, House of Representatives, Subcommittee on Administrative Law and Governmental Relations of the Committee on the Judiciary, *Hearings on H.R. 3387, H.R. 4110, and H.R. 4322, Japanese-American and Aleutian Wartime Relocation*, Ninety-Eighth Congress, Second Session, September 12, 1984 (Washington, D.C.: U.S. Government Printing Office, 1985), 767-768.

3. Kiku Hori Funabiki, "Day of Remembrance Presentation," Oakland Museum, Oakland, California, February 24, 1990.

4. James Clifford and George E. Marcus, eds. *Writing Culture: the Politics and Poetics of Ethnography* (Berkeley: University of California Press, 1986).

5. Interview with Kiku Hori Funabiki, San Francisco, California, May 10, 1990.

6. *Ibid.*

7. *Ibid.*

8. Robert F. Berkhofer, Jr., *Beyond the Great Story: History as Text and Discourse* (Cambridge, Massachusetts: Harvard University Press, 1995), 138.

9. Michael Frisch, *A Shared Authority: Essays on the Craft and Meaning of Oral and Public History* (Albany: State University of New York Press, 1990), 188.

10. Valerie Yow, "'Do I Like Them Too Much?': Effects of the Oral History Interview on the Interviewer and Vice-Versa," *Oral History Review* 24:1 (Summer 1997), 55-79.

11. For similar concerns, see Susan Armitage and Sherna Berger Gluck, "Reflections on Women's Oral History: An Exchange," *Frontiers: A Journal of Women's Studies*, 19:3 (1998), 2-3.

12. Russell Leong, "Lived Theory (*notes on the run*)," *Amerasia Journal* 21:1 & 2 (1995), ix.

Amerasia Journal 26:1 (2000): 119-140

Asian American History:
Reflections on Imperialism, Immigration, and "The Body"

Catherine Ceniza Choy

Speaking This Truth

May 1999. As my first academic year as an assistant professor comes to an end, I am filled with optimism about the state of Asian American Studies at the University of Minnesota, Twin Cities. University faculty with research interests in Asian American Studies formed an Asian American Studies Planning Group this year. Recently our group received two University grants to coordinate and strengthen our Asian American Studies research and course offerings.

However, while watching a recent local news program, my optimism is shaken. The newscaster reports that Minnesota Governor Jesse "The Body" Ventura has created an audio version of his autobiography, *I Ain't Got Time To Bleed.* More hype for our governor who claims that he speaks his mind and tells it like it is, I think. Then the news program plays an excerpt of the audiobook. Ventura goes on to say:

> I loved the Philippines. I was stationed at Subic, and I loved going into Olongapo. It was more like the Wild West than any other place on earth. In Olongapo, there's a one-mile stretch of road that has 350 bars and 10,000 girls on it every night. . . . To the kid I was then, it was paradise. [1]

I wonder: Am I listening to an advertisement for a sex tour in the islands? I immediately reject this soundbite as another example of Orientalist, colonial nostalgia in American popular culture, but then hesitate to dismiss it so quickly. Representations

CATHERINE CENIZA CHOY is an assistant professor of American Studies and history at the University of Minnesota.

of the Philippines on American television are so abysmally few that Ventura's excerpt (small as it is) has a potentially powerful impact. The power of Ventura's publicized memory of the Philippines is compounded by the fact that he is a national as well as local celebrity whose fame crosses the boundaries of politics, show business, and sports. He is currently known as the "refreshing" Independent Party governor who attributes his shocking political victory to his ability to "tell the truth."[2] Given his appearances on the *Today Show, Regis and Kathie Live, Late Night with David Letterman,* and the *Tonight Show with Jay Leno,* I cringe when fathoming the tens of thousands of people he has reached with his version of truth-telling.

I realize that by opening this essay with Ventura's Orientalist depiction of the Philippines I may be reinscribing the very stereotypes that I wish to reject. What has "The Body" got to do with my work on Filipino nurses, imperialism, and immigration anyway? However, Ventura's excerpt has inadvertently reminded me of an important agenda for the future of our discipline: analyzing the legacies of American imperialism and colonialism and their connection to contemporary U.S. immigration and labor. As George J. Sanchez argued at the 1998 American Historical Association annual meeting, "It is time for American scholars in general, and immigration historians in particular, to recognize the imperial origins of many of the racialized issues now confronting American immigration."[3]

What is equally important about Ventura's representation of the Philippines is what it excludes as well as includes. The use of Filipino women to em"body" a Philippine "paradise" for American men is a central part of this depiction. Invisible are the colonial and neocolonial relationships of inequality between the United States and the Philippines, and more specifically the history of U.S. military presence in the islands and its legacies of prostitution, disease, and environmental destruction. Erased once again is the history of American imperialism. As William Appleman Williams observed over forty years ago, "One of the central themes of American historiography is that there is no American Empire."[4]

Another salient interrelated theme of Ventura's excerpt is the privileged role of Ventura as an American adventurer. Ventura "goes into" Olongapo, which functions as an extension of the American West. In this familiar narrative, the movement of adventurers is unidirectional. Might we think of Filipino nurses, for example, migrating to the United States as adventurers? Probably not. In the celebratory narratives of Western expansion, invisible are the migrations of Filipinos east into the United States. Of these Filipinos, many thought of America as a paradise—yet another legacy of American colonial education in the Philippines—but ultimately became disillusioned by its exploitation, racism, and violence.

As we enter a new millennium, it is time for historians to vigorously engage with American imperialism and colonialism and its legacies. The future of Asian American history is to speak this truth.

The Personal and the Professional

One of the major arguments I make in my work on Filipino nurse migration to the United States is that this contemporary phenomenon is inextricably linked to early-twentieth-century American colonialism in the Philippines.[5] The establishment of Americanized nursing training in the Philippines during the U.S. colonial period laid the professional, social, and cultural groundwork for a feminized, highly-educated, and exportable labor force. And just as American colonialism in the archipelago needs to be understood in an international context of U.S. imperial power, so too does Filipino nurse migration. In the late twentieth century, the Philippines has been the *world's* top exporter of nurses, sending significant numbers of nurses to the Middle East and Canada as well as the United States. However, I did not originally approach my research with these perspectives. In this essay I chart the challenges I faced during this project and hope that this intellectual journey will reveal important insights for the future of our discipline.

My work has been and continues to be informed by personal experiences as well as diverse academic literatures. Growing up as a second-generation Filipino American in New York City in the 1970s and 1980s, I had observed that many of the Filipino women living in my apartment building were nurses. They worked in the cluster of hospitals that was within walking distance from my Lower East Side neighborhood: Beth Israel, Cabrini, New York Eye and Ear Infirmary, Bellevue. These women in their white uniforms were the most visible group of the growing Filipino-American immigrant community.

The scholarly literature on Filipino nurse migration to the United States confirmed my childhood observations. Beginning in the late 1960s, the increasing numbers of Filipino nurses ended decades of numerical domination by foreign-trained nurses from European countries and Canada. Paul Ong and Tania Azores estimated that at least 25,000 Filipino nurses migrated to the United States between 1966 and 1985.[6] They went so far as to suggest that in the United States "it could be argued that a discussion of immigrant Asian nurses, indeed of foreign-trained nurses in general, is predominantly about Filipino nurses."[7] Because foreign nurse graduates are more likely to be employed as staff nurses in critical care units of large metropolitan and public hospitals, the numbers of Filipino nurses are especially significant in urban areas. In New York City, Filipinos comprise 18 percent of RN (registered nurse) staff in the city's hospitals.[8]

I had entered a doctoral program in history with a commitment to documenting Filipino American experiences and specifically those of Filipino women. And I believed that further research on Filipino nurses would serve as an important window to view multiple historical phenomena, in particular the new highly-educated, professional, and female Filipino immigration to the United States.[9] I situate my study at the intersections of Asian American, migration, labor, and women's studies. My research participates in the project outlined by Asian American Studies scholars Paul Ong, Edna Bonacich, and Lucie Cheng who argued that new immigration and labor trends, in particular the shift toward higher-educated, professional immigrants from Asia, needed to be explained.[10] In a 1992 article, Paul Ong, Lucie Cheng, and Leslie Evans noted that between 1961 and 1972, approximately 300,000 scientific, technical, and professional workers from "developing" countries migrated to Western nations, and primarily to Australia, Canada, and the United States.[11] They observed that highly-educated laborers from Asian countries played a significant role in this form of migration. The nearly 30,000 Asians who settled in Canada during this time period comprised 52 percent of all "Third World" highly-educated labor, while the 65,000 Asians in the United States accounted for 72 percent.[12] While Ong, Cheng, and Evans included a number of Asian countries (India, South Korea, Philippines, China, Hong Kong, and Thailand) and occupations (math and computer scientists, natural scientists, social scientists, engineers, physicians, nurses, post-secondary teachers) in their study, their statistics revealed that the migration of Filipino nurses merited closer attention. For example, in their table of immigration of highly-educated Asians to the United States between 1972 and 1985, the number of Filipino nurses (20,482) surpassed those of other Asian (Indian,

South Korean, Philippine, and Chinese) highly-educated laborers in nine different occupations.[13]

My work also addresses one major area of feminist inquiry: the impact of work on women's lives, and specifically the lives of professional *and* migrant women of color. The ways in which race, nationality, gender, and class have shaped the experiences of this unique group of women have been virtually ignored in both ethnic and women's studies.[14] The study of professional migrant women workers is often subsumed under the categories of highly-educated laborers *or* migrant women workers in general. For example, while the Asian American and migration studies scholarship on Asian highly-educated labor migration has included women, it has not paid close attention to gender as a useful category of analysis.[15] In other words, this scholarship has tended to focus on the historical, economic, and demographic commonalities of all Asian professional migrant workers regardless of gender. And while the feminist scholarship on migrant women workers takes gender seriously in its analysis, the unique educational and socioeconomic backgrounds of professional migrant women workers are often lumped together with those of domestic workers and prostitutes.[16] I am not arguing that there is little value in grouping professional women workers with highly-educated male laborers or professional women workers with "unskilled" migrant women workers under specific circumstances. I am arguing that the experiences of professional migrant women workers need to be studied and understood on their own terms given the increasing significance of both highly-educated and female migrations in the late twentieth century.

Since most of the scholarly literature on Filipino nurses is sociological and statistical in nature, one of my major objectives as I embarked on this study was to document a history that took seriously the personal as well as professional aspects of Filipino nurses' lives.[17] My mother had befriended many of the Filipino nurses in our apartment complex. Thus I came to know these women in the context of my family's social relations, and not solely as an occupational immigrant group.

The stereotype of the Filipino-woman-as-nurse problematized this study. In the July 1969 issue of *Gidra*, an Asian American publication, a comic strip entitled "Stereotypes" featured several "controlling images" of Filipinos in America.[18] The first panel read, "One Filipino is a Ram quarterback," referring to former Los Angeles Ram Roman Gabriel. In the second panel, the strip contin-

Figure 1. "Stereotypes," *Gidra* (July 1969).

ued, "Two Filipinos is a nurses' shift." The accompanying illustration depicted two smiling Filipino women in white nurses' caps and uniforms.

Seeing this controlling image of the Filipino nurse as subservient, nurturing, exotic, and sensual made me reconsider my own study on Filipino nurses, as I feared that more attention to this racialized and gendered occupational group would only reinscribe a stereotype. I had personally encountered this stereotype of the Filipino-woman-as-nurse several times during the course of this project. For example, at a friend's wedding in New York, a woman whom I had just met asked me if I was a nurse. I unconsciously responded, "Oh, you must be thinking about my dissertation project on Filipino nurses," but then realized that she knew nothing about my project, and that she had made an assumption about my occupation based on my gender and ethnicity.[19]

From personal conversations, I learned that other Filipino/Filipino-American women had similar experiences. They expressed anger, frustration, and resentment at the conflation of their ethnic, gendered, and occupational identities. These conversations compelled me to question if this project on Filipino nurses would only compound this controlling image, especially given the dearth of historical studies about Filipino-American women.[20] However, I was reminded that there are multiple ways to challenge stereotypes.[21] One way is to focus on alternative images. Another way is to confront these controlling images directly.

"Re"-Viewing The Literature from an American Shore

My academic training in the United States as a U.S. historian and Asian American Studies specialist led me first to review the American literature on Filipino nurse migrants in the United States. On a practical level, the Philippine literature on this topic was not as accessible. More importantly, contemporary academic training is still very much divided by the borders of modern nation-states. For example, Rudolph J. Vecoli made this observation about immigration history:

> However, while the desirability—and indeed necessity—of multi-group, cross-national, and comparative studies of migration was extolled at the [1986 international conference on "A Century of Trans-Atlantic Migration, 1830-1930"], there were few examples of this genre on the program as there are in the literature. Most studies continue to be limited within a single country.[22]

Partly as a result of such observations, Jane C. Desmond and Virginia R. Domínguez have recently called for "a concerted effort throughout the American studies scholarly community to embrace actively a paradigm of critical internationalism as we move into the next century."[23]

Similar concerns have emerged in the field of Asian American Studies where conferences and symposia at Harvard University, University of Washington, and California State University have focused on "re-visioning" Asian American Studies. Until very recently, Asian American Studies scholarship has privileged the experiences of Asian Americans within a U.S.-nation-bound context. While scholars have done this in part to make the important point that Asian Americans have lived in the United States for over 150 years, contemporary demographics have compelled Asian American Studies scholars to re-think their methodological approaches.[24]

Contemporary Asian migration to the United States has shaped a very different, diverse, and complex Asian America. In the late twentieth century, Asian America has grown considerably from the influx of immigrants and refugees from Southeast and South Asia. By the late 1980s, the Philippines, Vietnam, and India were among the top ten sending-nations of immigrants to the United States. A majority of the contemporary Asian American population is foreign born. A significant percentage of this new immigration is highly-educated and female. Contemporary Asian American communities have been established beyond the West Coast, in New York, Massachusetts, Illinois, Minnesota, Texas, Virginia, and Georgia. Yet, despite these dramatic changes, most histories of the Filipino-American experience focus on the early-twentieth-century Filipino bachelor societies comprised of cannery, service, and agricultural male workers in Hawai`i, California, and the Pacific Northwest.[25]

Filipino nurse immigrants first appeared in American scholarly literature in the 1970s as part of a new wave of professional immigrants utilizing the newly-established occupational immigrant visas of the U.S. Immigration Act of 1965.[26] These pioneering studies laid the groundwork for the conceptualization of Filipino nurse migration to the United States as a post-1965 phenomenon, a chronological as well as thematic framework that has been adopted by Asian American historians. In the two major surveys of Asian American history, Ronald Takaki's *Strangers from a Different Shore* and Sucheng Chan's *Asian Americans: An Interpretative History*, Filipino nurses emerge in the "post-1965" chapters as a notable Filipino-American and professional sub-group.[27]

While this framework is useful in Asian American Studies (I myself have developed a "Post-1965 Asian America" course that I teach at the University of Minnesota), it also has a blinding effect for some Asian American historians. Yes, we believe that contemporary migration needs to be understood in an historical context. But we sometimes assume that post-1965 topics and themes are devoid of an earlier history, and that such research belongs in the disciplinary realm of sociology. On two separate occasions, I have had conversations with Filipino American historians who have quickly characterized my work as a "post-65 project" and expressed surprise when I told them that the first part of my study focused on the American colonial period in the Philippines.

I had previously made the same assumptions about my own study. These assumptions shaped my initial conceptualization of my methodology, and specifically the oral interviews I planned to do with Filipino nurses in New York City. I had originally tried to limit my interview pool by interviewing only those Filipino nurses who had immigrated through the occupational preferences of the 1965 Immigration Act because the academic literature on Filipino nurses often emphasizes the connection between the increase of professional immigrants and these preferences. However, as I tried to create a pool of interviewees, I quickly learned that Filipino nurses had entered the United States through a variety of avenues: tourism, family reunification preferences, and exchange programs. Furthermore, I learned that a Filipino nurse could (and often did) use multiple avenues to enter, re-enter, and/or remain in the United States. For example, when I interviewed Epifania Mercado, I asked her when she *im*migrated to the United States and she responded that she had arrived in 1971.[28] When I proceeded to ask her about her expectations about nursing in the United States, she then explained to me that she was *already* accustomed to working in this country. Epi (as she prefers to be called) first came to the United States in 1961 as an exchange nurse through the U.S. Exchange Visitor Program (EVP).[29]

Studies by Tomoji Ishi, Paul Ong, and Tania Azores have contributed to a more complex understanding of the macro-dimensions of Filipino nurse migration abroad.[30] Their findings helped me reconceptualize the spatial and chronological breadth of my project. These studies discussed several transnational links that facilitated this form of labor migration between the United States and the Philippines throughout the twentieth century: colonial nursing education in the early twentieth century, U.S. exchange programs in the 1940s and 1950s, and occupational immigrant preferences and temporary work programs in the 1960s and 1970s.

While Ishi, Ong, and Azores acknowledged the significance of the relationship among American colonialism, Philippine professional nursing training, and Filipino nurse international migration, their claim that Filipino nurse mass migration abroad was inextricably linked to an American and Philippine colonial past is undeveloped. In fairness to these authors, their article-length studies permit only an overview of the unequal political and economic relationship between the United States and the Philippines. However, their discussions of these transnational links between Philippine and American nursing inspired me to go beyond the unidirectional "Filipino nurse migration to and incorporation in the United States" approach that I had been pursuing in my research thus far, and to begin researching and conceptualizing Filipino nurse migration in an international and transnational context.

This different approach led me to other bodies of literature on the international dynamics of physician and nurse migration in general. After reading this literature, I emphasized an international context in my study because the migration of Filipino nurses is a phenomenon of global significance, and the United States is only one of their international destinations. For example, in 1979, the authors of a World Health Organization (WHO) report observed that the geographical distribution of the international migration of nurses was highly imbalanced.[31] Of an estimated 15,000 nurses moving each year, over 90 percent went to eight countries, mainly to the United States, the United Kingdom, and Canada. Among the nurse-sending countries, the largest outflow of nurses "by far" was from the Philippines. The authors noted with interest that, with the exception of the Philippines, five of the first six nurse-sending countries were "developed" countries. These puzzling WHO report findings led me to raise one of the major questions of my project: Why has the "developing" country of the Philippines emerged in the late twentieth century to provide professional nursing care for "developed" countries such as the United States?

I had begun legitimizing my research project with the premise that Filipino nurse migrants had made a significant impact on the nursing profession in the United States, but the knowledge that the Philippines was the *world*'s leading exporter of nurses pushed me in different scholarly directions. For example, this important point led me to read the literature on the Philippine's export-oriented economy, and to re-think this project with the Philippines (and not the United States) at the center of this study. Beginning in the early 1970s, the Philippine government under the dictatorship of Ferdinand Marcos institutionalized an export-oriented economy that included the export of female and male laborers as well as goods.[32]

The U.S.-based studies that focused on Filipino nurse migration to the United States emphasized the role of U.S. immigration and labor policies in facilitating this migration, and often marginalized was the equally important role of the Philippines' export-oriented economy and the nation's commodification of its own workers abroad. It seemed to me that, in order to answer the question I had posed above, engagement with both sides of this international story was necessary.

Transnational Spaces, Disciplinary Crossings

Although I approached my research as an historian, my work did not fall neatly into a traditional immigration historiography. Rather, my study has gained essential insights from the growing multidisciplinary body of scholarship on transnational frameworks and methodologies in migration, labor, ethnic, women's, and cultural studies. The work of Saskia Sassen was one of the primary influences on my study. In her 1988 work, *The Mobility of Labor and Capital*, Sassen explored the relationships among the transnational space for the circulation of capital, the formation of labor migrations, and the commodification of migrant laborers.[33] Although her work analyzed both male and female labor migrations within and across various countries, Sassen observed the large-scale migration of women and the commodification of migrant women's work. Particularly influential to my work was Sassen's analysis of the ways in which the presence of international/transnational institutions in certain countries, such as world market factories and plants in Export Processing Zones (EPZs) in the Philippines, was linked to domestic and eventually international migrations of women workers. Sassen argued that these domestic migrations of Filipino women workers overflow into international migrations given the widespread practice of firing these women after a few years of work. Sassen's work inspired my inquiries about the transnational space that enabled the production, recruitment, and export of Filipino nurses abroad. However, unlike chief executive officers who can transfer garment and microelectronics factories in EPZs, U.S. hospital administrators cannot relocate hospitals to the Philippines; they must recruit Filipino nurses to work in American hospitals. This type of transnational recruitment then shapes new social as well as spatial relationships between Filipino nurses overseas and their families and friends still in the Philippines.

Roger Rouse's analysis of Mexican migration to the United States and the ways in which Mexican migrants have re-shaped (as opposed to uprooted or transplanted) their ties with family and friends in Mexico informed my conceptualization of Filipino and Filipino-American communities in this study.[34] In the late twentieth century, access to airplane travel and long-distance phone calls has created what Rouse has called a geographically expansive "social space" which transcends national boundaries. These new social spaces have compelled researchers of contemporary urban, suburban, as well as rural Asian American communities to reconsider the ties that bind them together. They have challenged scholars to go beyond geographically-marked borders, such as ethnic enclaves, in their study of communities. Hsiang-Shui Chen responded to this challenge in his study of Taiwanese immigrants in contemporary New York entitled *Chinatown No More*.[35] Valerie Matsumoto confronted the newness and complexity of these social relations in her study of the Cortez Colony, a Japanese American rural community in California: "Previously unconnected lives are linked with stunning rapidity.... Shared meanings and relations may now span vast distances."[36] As Joseph Jinn observed about one part of the Chinese-American community in Southern California:

> Taiwan is so close. From Los Angeles to Taiwan, it's 15 hours....
> A lot of people still have family in Taiwan, they still have busi-

nesses in Taiwan. They buy and sell stocks in Taiwan, get rich and come to the United States and buy a house here and stay here, and then fly back to Taiwan and make some money and come back. It's a common practice. . . . In recent years the Chinese American community has become more complex than ever before.[37]

The work of Pierrette Hondagneu-Sotelo and Inderpal Grewal compelled me to take gender seriously as a category of analysis in transnational studies. Their work emphasized that the experiences of women were central to understanding contemporary forms of immigration and travel respectively. Hondagneu-Sotelo's 1994 *Gendered Transitions: Mexican Experiences of Immigration* focused on Mexican undocumented women and men who eventually settled in Northern California in the 1980s[38]; Inderpal Grewal's 1996 *Home and Harem: Nation, Gender, Empire, and the Cultures of Travel* analyzed the impact of the nineteenth-century European culture of travel on social divisions in England and India.[39] While these studies focused on different groups of women, time periods, and locations, and employed different methodological approaches (Hondagneu-Sotelo engaged in ethnographic research and conducted oral interviews; Grewal analyzed English and Indian women's travel narratives), they both effectively highlighted the theme of multiple gendered, racialized, and class-based subjectivities. Hondagneu-Sotelo's study featured the voices of Mexican immigrant husbands who migrated without their wives, the Mexican wives who stayed behind, and Mexican husbands and wives who immigrated together, among others. Grewal compared and contrasted the writings of English women who traveled to India, and Indian women and men who traveled to England and the United States. In my study I have tried to emulate the ways in which both works moved back and forth between broad political, ideological, and economic forces and individual perspectives, as well as within and across national boundaries. As Nina Glick Schiller, Linda Basch, and Cristina Blanc-Szanton astutely noted in their conceptualization of transnationalism, "transmigrants deal with and confront a number of hegemonic contexts, both global and national."[40]

Locating and analyzing Asian immigrant women's work in the context of global economies and cultures is a contemporary Asian American Studies project. In her chapter on "Work, Immigration, and Gender: Asian 'American' Women," Lisa Lowe challenged readers to imagine and rearticulate new forms of political subjectivity, collectivity, and practice when interpreting forms of Asian

immigrant women's cultural production such as oral testimony.[41] I
have attempted to respond to Lowe's challenges of imagination and
rearticulation by crossing the disciplinary boundaries of history,
anthropology, and sociology, and the geographical boundaries of
ethnic enclaves and nations. A study which illuminates the personal and professional significance of Filipino nurse migrants demanded these intellectual and national crossings.

A Two-Shores Approach

The methodology of this project presented me with the greatest
challenges and frustrations as well as rewards. The major source
of difficulty stemmed from the absence of a central archive of materials about Filipino nurses. As a result, I was compelled to cast a
wide net in my research, to find any materials I could about Filipino
nurses, and to engage in multidisciplinary methods: archival research, oral interviews, participant observation. I felt very much
like historian Kristin Hoganson who wrote in her book about
American masculinity and the Spanish-American and Philippine-
American Wars that "I sometimes had the sense of being in a kind
of interdisciplinary no-man's-land, far from familiar landmarks."[42]

My research required significant travel within the United
States to mine the American Nurses Association archives at Boston University, the Filipino American National History Society
(FANHS) archives in Seattle, Washington, the National Archives
in Chicago, and the newspaper collections of UCLA's Asian American Studies Reading Room. While the materials I found in these
places were eventually important in shaping my findings, during
the research stage they only provided clues to the questions I
was asking.

I built my own Filipino nurse archive primarily through ethnographic research, in particular the oral interviews. I conducted
forty-three oral interviews; forty of these interviews took place in
New York City, the remaining three in New Jersey and Washington. My observations during two months of volunteer work at
Bellevue Hospital in New York City, and attendance at a Philippine Nurses Association of Southern California meeting in Fuller-
ton, California and a Philippine Nurses Association of America
conference at Las Vegas, Nevada, as well as my reading informed
my interview questions.

Although I had collected a significant amount of materials in
the United States, I believed that a study that took seriously the
transnational dynamics of Filipino nurse migration required a two-

shores approach. My methodology included ethnographic and archival research in the Philippines as well as the United States. Being physically in the Philippines as well as reading Philippine Studies literature was invaluable to the reconceptualization of my study as a transnational project.

During a five-month research trip to the Philippines, I talked with nursing deans, faculty members, and students at several Philippine colleges and schools of nursing in Manila; directors of nursing and staff nurses at private and government hospitals in Manila; the current president and several members of the Philippine Nurses Association; government employees working in overseas-related agencies; and workers in non-governmental organizations focusing on the welfare of migrant and women workers. My participant-observation included observing a beginning nursing class at St. Luke's College of Nursing in Quezon City, Metro Manila (one of the oldest nursing schools in the country), participating in their community health projects and medical missions, and attending nursing and migration conferences.

I also conducted research in the libraries of Philippine government institutions, non-governmental institutions, the Philippine Nurses Association, colleges of nursing, and migration and women's studies centers. While these libraries contained a variety of materials about Filipino nurse international migration, among the most interesting were the advertisements in the *Philippine Journal of Nursing*, the official publication of the Philippine Nurses Association, that recruited Filipino nurses to work in the United States.

These advertisements illustrated the complex transnational dynamics of Filipino nurse recruitment. For example, by the late 1960s, individual U.S. hospitals actively recruited their Filipino exchange nurses who had returned to the Philippines to come back to them for permanent employment. A 1969 advertisement from a Chicago hospital featured the faces of Filipino nurses encircling the caption: "There's A Job Waiting for You at Michael Reese Hospital, Chicago, Illinois, U.S.A."[43] The advertisement targeted Filipino nurses who were former exchange visitors at Michael Reese Hospital and publicized bonuses such as "interest-free loans for travel expenses, continuous inservice education program, and tuition assistance at any recognized university." Furthermore, it highlighted the hospital's "beginning salaries for Philippine nurses with previous Reese experience."[44] They would earn $660 per month for day-shift work, $726 per month for nights, and $770 per month for evenings.

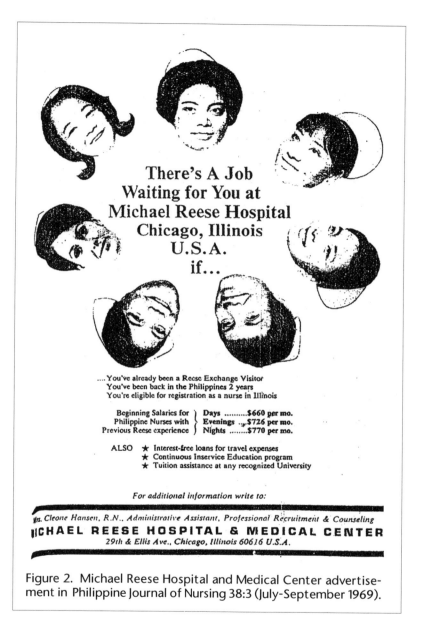

Figure 2. Michael Reese Hospital and Medical Center advertisement in Philippine Journal of Nursing 38:3 (July-September 1969).

Being physically in the Philippines allowed me to observe the interconnectedness as well as the inequality between the Philippine and United States economies in powerful ways that are difficult to translate in academic scholarship. For example, I ran into a St. Luke's nursing student at a McDonald's that was located a few blocks away from the school one afternoon. We were having a very pleasant conversation about my research; she told me that she really wanted to go to the United States, but that the waiting period for an immigrant visa was so long, and that travel costs were expensive. At that time, the Christmas holiday was soon approaching, and I was thinking that it would be difficult for me to be away from my immediate family that holiday season. But then this nursing student proceeded to tell me that her immediate family members were in different parts of the United States, and that it had been several years since they were able to celebrate Christmas all together.

As I reflected on this experience, I thought about how I might incorporate our conversation in my academic work. On one level, our presence in this McDonald's (that served Philippine-style spaghetti and rice as well as the usual Big Mac fare), the student's wait for a U.S. immigrant visa, the prohibitive Philippine-to-U.S. travel costs, and the presence of her family members in different areas abroad exemplified the intersection of the global, transnational, national, and individual forces that I hoped to document. On a personal level, this experience struck me because it caused me to reflect more seriously about the social and economic privileges that I have as a U.S.-based Filipino American scholar who is able to compete for lucrative grant money, travel to various places within the United States as well as to the Philippines for a limited research period, and then return to reunite with family and friends. I wondered how I would go about writing these intersections of imperial domination and individual agency.

An Internationally Dynamic History

After I had conducted research in the Philippines, I analyzed the ways in which the creation, expansion, and export of a Filipino nursing labor force had been transnational processes involving the collaboration of both Philippine and American nurses, professional nursing organizations, government officials, and hospital administrators. I emphasized the "transnational" nature of this phenomenon to highlight the significance of movements—of persons, capital, goods, images, and ideas—across U.S. and Philippine national boundaries. I wrote that these movements were multi-directional and interdependent. I emphasized this notion of multi-directionality because American immigration studies tend to focus on the unidirectional movement of immigrants from the sending country to the United States.

I also focused on the "collaboration" of Philippine and American nurses, nursing organizations, and governments to highlight the complex interaction between, and the historical agency of, the Filipino *and* American participants in this history.[45] For example, during the American colonial period in the Philippines, the agitation of elite Filipino women *and* American educators combined with the labor of American nurses *and* the first Filipino nurse trainees to make the development and growth of professional nursing training in the Philippines possible. In the second half of the twentieth century, the labor demands of U.S. hospital administrators intersected with the social and economic desires of Filipino nurses and nursing students to culminate in the mass migration of Filipino nurses to the United States.

Throughout my study, I have resisted subsuming Filipino nurses under the homogeneous and powerless category of "Third World women." As Chandra Talpade Mohanty observed, this homogeneity and powerlessness are the effects of Western scholarship, which—whether intentionally or inadvertently—stereotypes and silences women in the "Third World."[46] The creation of an international labor force of Filipino nurses was not a simple outcome of American conquest involving an almighty force of Americans controlling the minds and bodies of Filipinos. Rather, it is an internationally dynamic history that involves the interactions of numerous participants including the Filipino nurses themselves over time, across national borders, and in the context of unequal social, economic, and political forces.

Final Reflections

June 1999. I have often commented among friends that, after I had entered graduate school, I lost every creative bone in my body. In high school and college, I wrote poetry and short stories, and studied modern dance and choreography. And now it is so difficult for me to write without severely editing my thoughts. But the future of Asian American history demands our imagination and creativity. We will have to research, reflect, and write in different ways, to conceptualize alternative historiographies, and to build new archives as we study unchartered territory in history as it is currently written.

Can we imagine the United States as an extension of the Philippines? Such a picture might be fruitful for understanding Filipino migration overseas. In the late 1980s, the Philippines became the second top sending country of immigrants to the United States, second only to Mexico. Yet, even in the contemporary academic literature on U.S. immigration, the scholarship on Filipino immigrants is minimal. At the 1998 Conference of Social Science Research Council (SSRC) International Migration Fellows, sociologist Rubén Rumbaut shared his findings of an SSRC survey on immigration scholars and their areas of study. He observed that, despite the dramatic numerical significance of Filipino immigrants in the United States in the late twentieth century, very few immigration scholars chose to focus on Filipinos in their work. At that moment, I painfully realized that I was the only Filipino American Studies scholar in the room.

However, I'm not going to end on a note of pessimism here because, although change is slow, Asian American historians and our students are changing the academic landscape. I recently developed and taught a seminar on Asian Americans and the politics of labor at the University of Minnesota, and, as a result of my research, I was able to talk about professional Filipino nurse migration in more depth using the Michael Reese Hospital advertisement as a pedagogical handout. In my first year of teaching at the University, several students who have taken my Asian American Studies courses have approached me to mentor them as they have decided to embark on pioneering Asian American Studies research of their own. For example, this summer I am mentoring May yer Ly who is interviewing Hmong-American students about their undergraduate experiences, and Jennifer Nordin who is analyzing the creative writing of Korean adoptees in the United States.

I look forward to working with them. I look forward to reading the results of their research. I look forward to the future.

Notes

1. Jesse Ventura, *I Ain't Got Time to Bleed: Reworking the Body Politic from the Bottom Up* (New York: Villard, 1999), 78.

2. *Ibid.*, 4.

3. George J. Sanchez, "Race, Nation, and Culture in Recent Immigration Studies," paper presented at the 1998 American Historical Association annual meeting.

4. William Appleman Williams, "The Frontier Thesis and American Foreign Policy," *Pacific Historical Review* 24 (November 1955), 379-95.

5. See Catherine Ceniza Choy, "The Usual Subjects: Medicine, Nursing, and American Colonialism in the Philippines," *Critical Mass: A Journal of Asian American Cultural Criticism* 5:2 (Fall 1998), 1-28.

6. Paul Ong and Tania Azores, "The Migration and Incorporation of Filipino Nurses," in *The New Asian Immigration in Los Angeles and Global Restructuring*, ed. Paul Ong, Edna Bonacich, and Lucie Cheng (Philadelphia: Temple University Press, 1994), 164.

7. *Ibid.*, 165.

8. *Ibid.*, 182.

9. Not all Filipino nurses are women. However, the vast majority of them are. I agree with historian Barbara Melosh who, in her important work on the history of American nursing, wrote that "because most nurses have been women. . .I use 'nurse' as a feminine generic. . .As a feminist I eschew such usage in everyday life. But as a feminist historian I have chosen these markers to emphasize the sex-segregation of the work force in medicine and nursing and to underscore my arguments about the relationship of gender and work." Barbara Melosh, *"The Physician's Hand": Work Culture and Conflict in American Nursing* (Philadelphia: Temple University Press, 1982), 12.

10. Paul Ong, Edna Bonacich, and Lucie Cheng, "The Political Economy of Capitalist Restructuring and the New Asian Immigration," in *The New Asian Immigration in Los Angeles and Global Restructuring*, ed. Paul Ong, Edna Bonacich, and Lucie Cheng, 4.

11. Paul M. Ong, Lucie Cheng, and Leslie Evans, "Migration of Highly-educated Asians and Global Dynamics," *Asian and Pacific Migration Journal* 1:3-4 (1992), 543.

12. *Ibid.*, 543-544.

13. *Ibid.*, 545.

14. One notable exception is Agnes Calliste's article on the immigration of Caribbean nurses to Canada. Agnes Calliste, "Women of 'Exceptional Merit': Immigration of Caribbean Nurses to Canada," *Canadian Journal of Women and the Law* 6:1 (Winter/Spring 1993), 85-102.

15. Paul Ong and Tania Azores's article, "The Migration and Incorporation of Filipino Nurses," is a good example of this observation. See also Amara Bachu, "Indian Nurses in the United States," *International Nursing Review* 20:4 (1973), 114-116, 122.

16. Grace Chang, "The Global Trade in Filipina Workers," in *Dragon Ladies: Asian American Feminists Breathe Fire*, ed. Sonia Shah (Boston: South End Press, 1997), 132-152.

17. Only a few published oral history collections of Filipino Americans and hospital employees provided first-person accounts of Filipino nurses' lives in the Philippines and their work experiences in the United States. See Luz Latus, "My Dream Is to Be Able to Give Something Back to My Country and My People," in Yen Le Espiritu, *Filipino American Lives* (Philadelphia: Temple University Press, 1995),

81-91; the interview with Esther Villanueva in Sydney Lewis, *Hospital: An Oral History of Cook County Hospital* (New York: The New Press, 1994), 288-290; and interviews with Connie Chun, Maria Guerrero Llapitan, Perla Rabor Rigor, Irene Salugsugan, and Elizabeth Pucay Bagcal in Caridad Concepcion Vallangca, *The Second Wave: Pinay Pinoy* (San Francisco: Strawberry Hill Press, 1987), 86-91, 156-168.

18. "Stereotypes," *Gidra* (July 1969), 2. For an analysis of "controlling images" and their relationship to the economic exploitation and social oppression of subordinate groups, see Patricia Hill Collins, *Black Feminist Thought: Knowledge, Consciousness, and the Politics of Empowerment* (Boston: Unwin Hyman, 1990). For a comprehensive overview of "controlling images" of Asian Americans on television, see Darrell Y. Hamamoto, *Monitored Peril: Asian Americans and the Politics of TV Representation* (Minneapolis: University of Minnesota Press, 1994).

19. See Catherine Ceniza Choy, "The Export of Womanpower: A Transnational History of Filipino Nurse Migration to the United States" (Ph.D. diss., University of California, Los Angeles, 1998).

20. In Shirley Hune's bibliographic essay on teaching Asian American women's history, she writes under the heading of "Filipino American Women" that "Filipino Americans are an understudied community." She cites Fred Cordova's 1983 pictorial essay *Filipinos: Forgotten Asian Americans* and articles by Dorothy Cordova, Barbara M. Posadas, and Rebecca Villones in the 1989 edition of *Making Waves: An Anthology of Writings by and about Asian American Women* edited by Asian Women United of California as among the very few published studies about Filipino American women's history. Shirley Hune, *Teaching Asian American Women's History* (Washington, DC: American Historical Association, 1997), 47-48.

21. Historian Michael Salman reminded me of this significant point.

22. Rudolph J. Vecoli, "From *The Uprooted* to *The Transplanted*: The Writing of American Immigration History, 1951-1989" in *From Melting Pot to Multiculturalism: The Evolution of Ethnic Relations in the United States and Canada*, ed. Valerie Gennaro Lerda (Genova: Bulzoni, 1992), 35.

23. Jane C. Desmond and Virginia R. Domínguez, "Resituating American Studies in a Critical Internationalism," *American Quarterly* 48:3 (September 1996), 475.

24. For a critical analysis of these changes in the field of Asian American Studies, see Sau-Ling Wong, "Denationalization Reconsidered: Asian American Cultural Criticism at a Theoretical Crossroads," *Amerasia Journal* 21:1 & 2 (1995), 1-27.

25. The classic account of these Filipino male migrant workers' experiences is Carlos Bulosan's *America Is In The Heart* (Seattle: University of Washington Press, 1979). For a history of Asian American laborers in the Northwest canneries, see Chris Friday, *Organizing*

Asian American Labor: The Pacific Coast Canned-Salmon Industry, 1870-1942 (Philadelphia: Temple University Press, 1994). Chapter 6 of Friday's text focuses on Filipino cannery workers. For a history of Asian American laborers, including Filipino laborers, in Hawaiian plantations, see Ronald Takaki, *Pau Hana: Plantation Life and Labor in Hawaii* (Honolulu, 1983).

26. See James P. Allen, "Recent Immigration from the Philippines and Filipino Communities in the United States," *Geographical Review* 67:2 (April 1977), 195-208; Monica Boyd, "The Changing Nature of Central and Southeast Asian Immigration to the United States: 1961-1972," *International Migration Review* 8:4 (Winter 1974), 507-519; Charles B. Keely, "Philippine Migration: International Movement and Immigration to the United States," *International Migration Review* 7:2 (Summer 1973), 177-187; and Peter Smith, "The Social Demography of Filipino Migrations Abroad," *International Migration Review* 10:3 (Fall 1976), 307-353.

27. Ronald Takaki, *Strangers From A Different Shore: A History of Asian Americans* (New York: Little, Brown, and Company, Inc., 1989). Sucheng Chan, *Asian Americans: An Interpretive History* (Boston: Twayne Publishers, 1991).

28. Interview with Epifania O. Mercado, February 3, 1995, New York, New York.

29. In 1948, the American government through the U.S. Information and Educational Act established the Exchange Visitor Program. Exchange participants from abroad engaged in both work and study in their sponsoring American institutions for which they would receive a monthly stipend. Several thousand U.S. agencies and institutions were able to sponsor EVP participants, including the American Nurses Association and individual hospitals. The American government issued EVP visas for a maximum stay of two years. Upon the completion of the program, the American and the sending countries' governments expected the EVP participants to return to their countries of origin.

30. See Tomoji Ishi, "Class Conflict, the State, and Linkage: The International Migration of Nurses from the Philippines," *Berkeley Journal of Sociology* 32 (1987), 281-295.

31. Alfonso Mejía, Helena Pizorkí, and Erica Royston, *Physician and Nurse Migration: Analysis and Policy Implications* (Geneva: World Health Organization, 1979), 43-45.

32. See Manolo J. Abella, *Export of Filipino Manpower* (Manila: Institute of Labor and Manpower Studies, 1979).

33. Saskia Sassen, *The Mobility of Labor and Capital: A Study in International Investment and Labor Flow* (Cambridge: Cambridge University Press, 1988).

34. Roger Rouse, "Mexican Migration and the Social Space of Postmodernism," *Diaspora* 1 (Spring 1991), 8-23.

35. Hsiang-Shui Chen, *Chinatown No More: Taiwanese Immigrants in Contemporary New York* (Ithaca: Cornell University Press, 1992).

36. Valerie J. Matsumoto, *Farming the Home Place: A Japanese American Community in California, 1919-1982* (Ithaca: Cornell University Press, 1993), 4.

37. Joseph Jinn as told to Robert Scheer, "They Don't Think They Need to Change," *Los Angeles Times*, 14 February 1994.

38. Pierrette Hondagneu-Sotelo, *Gendered Transitions: Mexican Experiences of Immigration* (Berkeley: University of California Press, 1994).

39. Inderpal Grewal, *Home and Harem: Nation, Gender, Empire, and the Cultures of Travel* (Durham: Duke University Press, 1996).

40. Nina Glick Schiller, Linda Basch, Cristina Blanc-Szanton, "Transnationalism: A New Analytic Framework for Understanding Migration," in *Towards a Transnational Perspective on Migration: Race, Class, Ethnicity, and Nationalism Reconsidered*, ed. Nina Glick Schiller, Linda Basch, Cristina Blanc-Szanton (New York: The New York Academy of Science, 1992), 5.

41. Lisa Lowe, "Work, Immigration, and Gender: Asian 'American' Women," chap. in *Immigrant Acts: On Asian American Cultural Politics* (Durham: Duke University Press, 1996).

42. Kristin L. Hoganson, *Fighting for American Manhood: How Gender Politics Provoked the Spanish-American and Philippine-American Wars* (New Haven: Yale University Press, 1998), x.

43. Michael Reese Hospital & Medical Center advertisement, *Philippine Journal of Nursing* 38:3 (July-September 1969).

44. *Ibid.*

45. The theme of "collaboration" in Philippine historiography has been used to refer to the political collaboration among American and Japanese colonial officials and ambitious Philippines political elites. See Michael Cullinane, "Playing the Game: The Rise of Sergio Osmeña, 1898-1907," and Alfred W. McCoy, "Quezon's Commonwealth: The Emergence of Philippine Authoritarianism," in *Philippine Colonial Democracy*, ed. Ruby R. Paredes (New Haven: Yale University Southeast Asia Studies, 1988), 70-113, 114-160.

46. See Chandra Talpade Mohanty, "Under Western Eyes: Feminist Scholarship and Colonial Discourses," in *Third World Women and the Politics of Feminism*, ed. Chandra Talpade Mohanty, Ann Russo, and Lourdes Torres (Bloomington: Indiana University Press, 1991), 51-80.

Amerasia Journal 26:1 (2000): 141-161

On a Stage Built by Others:
Creating an Intellectual History of Asian Americans[1]

Henry Yu

During my dissertation research, I had the great pleasure of interviewing Beulah Ong Kwoh. During graduate school in the 1940s, Mrs. Kwoh had been a roommate at the University of Chicago of one of the most important Chinese American intellectuals of the time, social scientist Dr. Rose Hum Lee. Kwoh herself had studied sociology and written an important study on the career success of Chinese American college graduates. Since then, she and her family had become prominent in the Chinese American community of Los Angeles.

On this pleasant afternoon at their home in Silver Lake, we chatted about her years in graduate school nearly half a century ago, about what it was like to be one of the few Asian Americans in the social sciences, about the difficulties of raising a family and having an academic career, and finally how she had become a movie and television actress later on in her life. She had originally been brought in contact with the industry because actress Jennifer Jones had needed a dialogue coach to help her speak with a Chinese accent for the movie *Love Is A Many Splendored Thing* (1955). Unfortunately, since Kwoh had been raised in Stockton, California, she herself did not have an accent and had not been considered useful for the job. Kwoh did eventually find steady work in the small parts that Asian American actors were allowed, appearing, for instance, in an Elvis Presley movie and with Gregory Peck in *MacArthur* (1979), ending her career with a long run on the soap opera *General Hospital* as a street-wise housekeeper. She told me how difficult it had been finding roles

HENRY YU is professor of history and Asian American Studies, University of California, Los Angeles.

in such a discriminatory industry, and I grew to admire and respect all of Kwoh's accomplishments greatly. I left her company buoyed that I had been given the chance to meet such a wonderful person.

Several months later, I was watching *Chinatown* (1974), the Academy-Award-winning movie starring Jack Nicholson, Faye Dunaway, and John Huston. Kwoh had a minor part in the movie as Dunaway's maid, with only one spoken line. Near the climax of the movie, as Nicholson is frantically searching for Dunaway's character, he asks Kwoh for her employer. Kwoh, born and raised in California, an English literature major at Berkeley with a Masters degree in sociology from Chicago, answered in heavily accented English—"She no here."

This, for me, captured the difficult position of Asian Americans in American society, and illustrated the essential problem to be addressed in my research. How can we understand the intellectual and cultural life of Asian Americans in a nation that has long understood them first and foremost as "Orientals," representatives of an exotic, and by definition, non-American culture? My book, *Thinking "Orientals": A History of Knowledge Created About and by Asian Americans,* focussed on a group of Asian American sociologists (of whom Beulah Ong Kwoh was a member) who were recruited to study Chinese American and Japanese American communities in the U.S.[2] The possibilities and constraints that they encountered in conducting their research were indicative of how Asian Americans both have been known and have known themselves in the U.S.

Originally, my manuscript had been entitled "Thinking About Orientals," which suggested a focus on how Asian Americans have been made an object of curiousity, study, and ultimately desire for others. Following the advice of Russell Leong, the editor of *Amerasia Journal,* I changed the title to "Thinking Orientals." This seemed a good idea to me because it still captured the sense of how Asian Americans have been exoticized by other Americans. However, it increased the emphasis upon what I saw as the more important question—how have "Orientals" been forced by their subordinate position to understand themselves for much of U.S. history through the eyes of others. (Note: The term "Oriental" appears in this essay and in my book not because I condone its use as a label, but because it reflects a specific historic usage and conceptual category of earlier periods. Relatedly, I use the term "white" for that changing constellation of people who benefited from inclusion into the category of "whiteness" by being defined as different from Americans of "color.")[3]

"Orientals" or Asians have been understood within American social thought in two major ways—as a racial "problem" and as a racial "solution." From the time Chinese arrived in the mid-nineteenth century, migrants from Asia were considered a threat to white labor and American society. Categorized as "Oriental," these immigrants were demonized as exotic and non-American. From violent lynchings through the internment of Japanese Americans during WWII, Asian Americans were treated as a "problem." Since the 1960s, Asian Americans have seemingly become the opposite, sanctified as the "model minority" solution to racial and economic ills.

This new notion about Asians, however, still depends upon an exoticization of them as somehow not American, and it traces a theoretical lineage to early sociological studies of the "Oriental problem." In the early twentieth century, a number of American Protestant missionaries, along with scholars at the University of Chicago's sociology department, became interested in "Orientals" in America. Their interest led to Americans born of Chinese and Japanese ancestry being interested in the same questions, and the result was a series of scholarly texts produced by whites and Asian Americans about the "Oriental problem" in America. The history of this process of intellectual production was the subject of my dissertation research.

Intellectual history as a field has had a difficult reputation for many years. Intellectual history's traditional focus on elite, white, male thinkers has marginalized it on the whole from the political revolution that accompanied the rise in social history techniques. Because intellectual production and the structures of evaluation which validate ideas have been so racialized and gendered in U.S. history, the default standard existed that only a few white male thinkers who had been validated in their own time were serious intellectuals. Asian American studies on the whole has attacked this system of evaluation, yet in many ways left unchallenged the continuing production of scholarship by U.S. intellectual historians.

So much scholarship about race in the U.S. continues to ignore everything except the dichotomy between Black and White. Asians, Hispanics, and basically everybody else in the complex mix of U.S. society are evaluated as unimportant or uninteresting. I hoped that my study would show how crucial thinking about "Orientals" has been to the formulations of the most prominent theorists of race and culture in modern American intellectual life, and how a number of Asian American intellectuals were essential for producing those ideas.

What is it, in the end, to be an intellectual? Is it to be a person who thinks about things? If so, there might be no limit to who counts as an intellectual. Is it a person whose ideas about things are somehow important, coherent, provocative? That would cut down on the people who might fit the label, but begs the question of who might decide what are important or interesting ideas. In the end, the question of how one gets to be considered an intellectual is as interesting as who is one, for the two are connected with a larger story of institutional power.

In considering the history of "Orientals" as an intellectual "problem" in the U.S., and the number of Asian American intellectuals who became involved in researching this "problem," I wanted to trace how the success of these scholars was determined. How well did they do in academia? How were they evaluated in their careers? The question of who is an intellectual in America has come to be defined by academic institutions, and so part of the history of "Orientals" as a "problem" is a story of how a number of Chinese Americans and Japanese Americans entered a world where a "real" intellectual lies within the university system. Scholarly acceptance was equated with success as an intellectual.

Research into the "Oriental problem" validated certain kinds of knowledge as scholarship, taking information which Asian immigrants themselves might consider mundane or even trivial, and evaluating it as interesting and valuable. The scarcity of information about "Orientals" that made such knowledge so rare to the sociologists must be considered in light of the fact that much of this information was not scarce to the bulk of Chinese and Japanese in the United States. This evaluation of exotic information serves to highlight how academic interest in the "Oriental problem," by validating certain kinds of knowledge, structured for Asian Americans the very definition of what it meant to be an intellectual in America.

How did I come to study the intellectual history of Asian Americans? It is an interesting reflection of the historical constraints upon "Oriental" scholars that I came, like many historians of Asian America, to Asian American history from another academic field. Until recently (and still to a great degree), Asian American history has not been considered a serious subject for study by an academia dominated by the perspectives of whites. It was virtually impossible to enter into a Ph.D program in history if the stated purpose was to study Asian Americans. Either the subject was considered unimportant, or too narrow, or the program would decide that there were no professors with whom the student could work. And so the lack of professors who studied Asian Americans was perpetuated, since the only way such potential mentors could exist was if Ph.D's were trained in the first place.

Many of the first generation of academic Asian American historians in the 1960s and 1970s, therefore, were admitted to graduate school and trained in more "acceptable" fields such as East Asian history.[4] To these scholars, conducting research on Asian Americans was also a choice to try and build a difficult scholarly life on the margins of academic institutions. Research funding was hard to come by, and the peer evaluation of other scholars often missed the point. Having struggled to create research on Asian Americans in such a world, the survivors of that generation became the founders of Asian American studies.

As survivors, they have also vowed to make scholarly production easier for a younger generation. There was little scholarly and institutional support for them when they had embarked on studying Asian Americans, but they have changed the world for younger scholars. When I decided to research Asian American history after entering graduate school to study European intellectual thought, I benefited from the support of an earlier generation of Asian Americanists. In the form of letters and pats on the back from scholars who had been struggling for years to establish Asian American history, such encouragement has made an essential difference in my intellectual life.[5]

While delivering a lunch time speech to the Association of Asian American Studies (AAAS) in Honolulu in 1998 (and at various other times), I used the image of dwarves or children standing on the shoulders of giants to describe the current state of Asian American studies. I believed the image was apt because it described the gargantuan nature of the scholarly and institutional work that earlier generations of Asian Americanists had done. It was their efforts, and the protests of students who were inspired by them and who agitated for more scholars and teachers like them, who opened the opportunities for younger scholars like me. If Asian Americans have seemed to be belligerent in the fight for more representation in the academy (and metaphorically been carrying a chip on their shoulders when responding to attacks on the credibility of their scholarship), then we entering into the field now are literally the chips off the blocks of their strong shoulders.

The image of standing on the shoulders of those before us also illustrated for me the recent success of so many recently-minted Ph.D's. Academic institutions are hiring Asian Americanists, and it would be easy to attribute such a demand purely to the "intrinsic" worth of new scholarship. Exciting and path-breaking scholarship is being created, and the acquisition of prominent jobs at famous research universities has swelled the academic reputation of younger scholars such as myself. But it surely shows how late in the day it is that children can cast such large shadows. Much difficult work has been done toiling in the harsh heat of the midday sun, when shadows are dwarfed. Those that came before have received scant institutional recognition for the scholarly foundation they have built, and younger scholars have reaped the harvest of such ground breaking. We should remember, however, that we have come at the end of a long day's labor.

Before the giants of the pioneering generation of Asian Americanists appeared, the work of American historians generally focused upon the meaning of Asians to non-Asians in the United States. Gunther Barth, for instance, in his study *Bitter Strength*, argued that white Americans excluded Chinese Americans in the nineteenth century because they considered them impossible to "assimilate." Based almost wholly upon English-language newspapers and other forms of evidence that were produced by non-Asians, Barth argued that Chinese Americans had helped perpetuate this idea by remaining aloof and separate. Barth came under tremendous attack by numerous Asian American scholars in the 1970s, who argued that he had "blamed the victim," and the flaws of his study became the challenge for Asian American studies.[6]

Even when a work of U.S. history was sympathetic to the plight of Asian Americans, for instance, *The Indispensable Enemy*, Alexander Saxton's excellent study of anti-Chinese agitation, it still focused almost exclusively on how non-Asian Americans thought of Asian Americans. Saxton's book detailed how labor unions used racial categories to define and organize those they considered "white workers," excluding those they considered non-white. Still a classic in the field, Saxton's work showed how anti-Asian exclusion arose, but the story of the Asian Americans whose lives were affected still awaited telling.[7]

In the decades since, the professional discipline of U.S. historians has been pulled from both within and without by ethnic studies scholars, prodded to move away from analyses of race that only emphasize white ideas about people of color. Asian American studies expanded beyond documentary sources that only recorded dominant white perspectives.[8] Along with other ethnic studies movements, Asian Americanists led the struggle to open U.S. history to multiple voices.

Asian American historians tried to recover a "buried past," in the words of historian Yuji Ichioka, giving voice to the immigrants and native-born Asian Americans who had been silenced or ignored by mainstream scholarship. Historical research such as Sucheng Chan's *This Bittersweet Soil* painstakingly recovered the forgotten lives of Chinese American laborers and farmers, and the egalitarian legacy of earlier works such as Carlos Bulosan's *America Is In The Heart*, written in the 1930s, inspired the focus of Asian American studies on the lives of common people. The emphasis shifted away from what was inspiring white supremacists in their racism, and towards the hopes and dreams and struggles of Asian Americans in the United States.

In an ironic way, an emphasis on studying the ideas and desires that structured white supremacy has returned to Asian American studies. Through cultural and literary studies in particular, in particular following Edward Said's influential book *Orientalism*, Asian American scholars have been producing a spate of studies showing how white Americans defined the lives of Asian Americans. Said's study showed how scholars in Europe and the U.S. created and reinforced a system in which knowledge about peoples demonized as exotic and inferior "Orientals" was integral to a system which subjugated them. These mostly literary studies had their greatest impact in comparative literature, for instance, in Lisa Lowe's work, but historians of popular culture have also been examining the ways in which "not being Oriental" defined what it meant to be white.

Such work has explained the centrality of "Oriental" depictions for defining whiteness, both for Europeans and Americans. Robert Lee's *Orientals* and the media studies of scholars such as Darrell Hamamoto and James Moy have made powerful arguments about how the power to define and create images has historically been a tool abetting social control and exclusion.[9] In creating oppositions that demonize some people as different, "Orientalist" cultural productions have done a great deal of political work in U.S. history.

At the heart of "Orientalism" has been the process of objectification. In one of my classes at UCLA, I asked the students if there was a difference between an "Oriental" and an Asian American. One of the students answered by stating that an "Oriental" was an object, like a rug or a vase or a plate of food, while an Asian American was a person. Such an answer has been a common way of understanding the difference between the terms because "Orientalism," a process in which people are treated as objects, has been so common. It points to the psychological importance of a term such as "Asian American" in countering the racism and prejudice that dehumanizes people of Asian descent. But it also points to exactly how "Orientalism" as a process works—people and objects are defined in relation to a white desire for the exotic. The dominant meaning that an "Oriental" bears is in relation to the fantasies of someone else.

When I began my study of how a group of Asian American intellectuals in the period between 1924-1965 thought of themselves, I realized that this was impossible to separate from how non-Asians had thought about them. Many of the best works written by historians of U.S. and Asian American history have tended to focus on either one of two concerns: 1) how whites have understood, portrayed and treated Asian Americans, or 2) how Asian Americans have understood their own difficult lives in the United States. I tried to unite both emphases in my research in order to show how the two are so inextricably linked that they cannot be understood apart.

I began my book with an explanation of the Orientalism of elite white thinkers during the 1920s. At the time, politically progressive thinkers such as Horace Kallen argued for a an acceptance of the plural nature of American society. Differences in culture, they argued, could never be totally erased. In fact, pockets of difference within the country might actually be desirable. Such theories later became the foundation of liberal policies of multiculturalism. At the heart of such ideas was an elite appreciation of the exotic. Instead of trying to drive those who seemed different out of the country, cosmopolitan thinkers wanted to learn about the exotic. The acceptance of those who seemed different was politically progressive at that time and seemed by definition to be anti-racist, in particular in opposition to what the elite whites saw as the ignorance and often violent prejudice of working-class and uneducated whites.

However, in my study I tried to show how such a cosmopolitan taste was itself highly racialized. At the heart of this process lay the entwined practices of how to evaluate exotic knowledge and of how to be an elite white. Unlike the value of whiteness described by historian David Roediger, as a metaphorical "wage" from which certain workers benefited by their inclusion into the category of white, the extolling of whiteness in the institutional practices of American Orientalism lay hidden at the center.[10] Professional academics, in defining an interest in the exotic, and at the same time producing knowledge about the unknown, also produced themselves as the expert knowers. Seeing themselves as enlightened and cosmopolitan at the same time they defined working-class racists as ignorant and provincial, progressive and liberal elites crafted themselves as the knowing subject through which others became important.

For much of the twentieth century, analyses of racism have centered upon the working classes. It was economic competition, combined with unenlightened ignorance, that was at the root of all racial conflict and prejudice. Elite ideas of race and culture were understood to be in opposition to working-class racism. As such, they were assumed to be anti-racist. That story has always benefited educated elites in the United States, since their own economic status allowed them the privilege of dabbling in knowledge of the exotic. Part of my project was to see elite definitions of racial and cultural difference from another perspective.

Cosmopolitan appreciation put Asian Americans in the position of being an object of intellectual interest and curiousity. I especially wanted to examine how a fascination with "things Oriental" affected the Chinese American and Japanese American intellectuals who were recruited to study and explain "Orientals" to white American social scientists. How did they survive and sometimes thrive by using these definitions of the "Oriental" to understand themselves and their communities?

American social thinkers defined the "Oriental problem" as they saw it, and in doing so they created what I label an intellectual and institutional construction. By an intellectual construction I meant a framework of theories which defined who "Orientals" were, as well as their place in America. By an institutional construction I meant a network of scholars who produced these ideas, and who were connected to each other through their research on the "Oriental problem" and through academic institutions such as the University of Chicago.

One of the lingering legacies of American Orientalism has been the ways in which Asian Americans continue to define themselves. Protestant missionaries began the connection of the "Oriental" to China and Japan, and American social scientists reinforced it by creating a set of research problems that focussed exclusively on Chinese Americans and Japanese Americans. Within my study I tried to outline how Chinese American and Japanese American intellectuals were drawn into the academic structures of American Orientalism, and therefore, how other Asian Americans, in particular those from the Philippines, were at the same time left out. Those exclusions have continued to plague Asian American history.

Research into the "Oriental problem" came to structure almost all academic thinking about Asian immigrants in America during the first half of the twentieth century. An institutional demand was created for Chinese American and Japanese American informants and researchers. These Asian American scholars, along with their non-Asian colleagues, produced a coherent body of knowledge about "Orientals" in the United States. Distributed by the social networks of Chicago sociology into universities and teaching colleges all across the nation, this knowledge of "Orientals" came to dominate how Asian Americans were defined by others and how they eventually understood themselves.

I split my story into two parts. In the first, a series of white social scientists and reformers come to the West Coast of the U.S. to try and understand what they perceive as the "Oriental problem" in America. In the second part, a series of students with Chinese and Japanese backgrounds come to Chicago in order to study and research various aspects of this "Oriental problem." The two movements were generally distinct in time, with one following the other, but they were also existentially different, involving very different positions in the institutional structure of American academia.

I deliberately chose to focus in the first part on how the stage was initially set by the white Americans who came to learn about "Orientals" on the West Coast. There was a point to telling my story with Asian Americans coming to a stage already set. I wanted to emphasize the constraints that limited the possibilities for Asian American intellectuals in the twentieth century. Asian Americans, like African Americans and other intellectuals of color in the United States, did not (and in many ways still do not) have the freedom of possibilities' that white scholars enjoyed. I could have opened with two simultaneous movements, with Asians coming to America, meeting with white Midwesterners coming to the Pacific Ocean.

Such a setting for my story, however, would have implied that the meeting was between two groups with an equal say in the ways in which the meeting would be defined and understood. The Asian American intellectuals who came to study the "Oriental problem" were given a chance to conduct scholarly research, and they took advantage of the rare opportunity to enter careers in academia. Their understandings of themselves were often profoundly affected by their contact with the theories of the "Oriental problem." However, Asian American intellectuals did not have as much voice in academia as their white colleagues.

This is not to suggest that Asian American scholars did not have as much to say, just that their possibilities for being heard and validated were much more restricted. By giving voice first to the white men who came to understand "Orientals" in the early twentieth century, I hoped to convey the fact that white intellectuals did have first say in defining the meaning of "Orientals" in America. The Chinese American and Japanese American men and women who came to sociology in the twentieth century said and did a great number of things, but they performed upon a stage which was mostly not of their own making.

As an aside on the use of a stage analogy in my discussion of research into the "Oriental problem," I found it fascinating that American social thinkers often explicitly used theatrical metaphors to explain race in the United States. Such a language of performance and costumes and masks has continued to structure many analyses of race in the U.S., and resonates in a curious way with the story about Beulah Ong Kwoh which opened this essay. The reasons for this are many, but first and foremost has been the overwhelming perspective of a white audience in determining cultural and intellectual production, whether for movies, novels, or academic studies.

The rise of Asian American studies as a field has created a new audience for Asian American scholars. One of the healthiest signs of this continuing growth has been the ways in which recent researchers have found the freedom to operate in multiple contexts. Raised with the help of a supportive network of previous scholars, these new intellectuals have also found an institutional home in more traditional disciplines. More importantly, they have been able to begin a process which hopefully will transform not only Asian American studies, but the very ways in which scholarly history is produced.

New Directions In Research
Into Asian American History

Historians must continue to retrieve the silenced stories of Asian Americans. This has been one of the primary goals of Asian American studies since its founding, and it will continue to be the core of its scholarly program. At the same time, understanding the structures of white supremacy that have so thoroughly dominated Asian American history remains an integral part of any such project.

As a wonderful example of how recent work has combined Asian American perspectives with the effects of racism, 1998 Columbia Ph.D Mae Ngai's work on immigration law has managed to listen to the stories of Chinese Americans while at the same time explaining the history of anti-Asian legislation. Ngai's dissertation "Illegal Aliens and Alien Citizens" combined a political history which explained in nuanced ways what lawmakers thought they were doing, with a social history of Chinese Americans who were affected by the laws. An essay which came out of her research won the coveted Peltzer Prize for the best graduate student essay submitted to the *Journal of American History*, and her hiring at the University of Chicago symbolizes the inroads into the institutional practice of U.S. history that recent Ph.D's are making.[11]

In a similar manner, Erika Lee's 1998 Berkeley dissertation on how the implementation of Chinese exclusion played a central role in the formation of the Immigration and Naturalization Service (INS) also combined the everyday lives of Asian Americans with an examination of what anti-Asian discrimination meant to non-Asians. Her work will contribute to a history of how Asian Americans informed the institutional practices of white supremacy. Her hiring at the University of Minnesota, a department that is particularly strong in immigration history and in American studies, also shows the vitality that Asian American studies is bringing to other forms of scholarship.[12]

At a panel in Honolulu, Hawaii, on teaching Asian American history, Scott Wong of Williams College remarked that we cannot make sense of Asian American history if we just start at the moment bodies from Asia arrive. This has been a difficult intellectual leap for many students of Asian American studies, but scholars such as Wong have been at the forefront of this revolutionary expansion of the subject matter of Asian American history. If the field is to achieve a firm intellectual foundation, it is essential to question an unreflective focus on human bodies "Orientalized" by whites.

Asian American history must take into account what happened long before the first migrants from Asia set foot in the U.S., and a number of Asian American scholars are doing just that. This process promises to do more than put our overall scholarly project on a good founding. Asian Americanists have been fighting for decades to insert Asian American history as a legitimate concern of U.S. history in general. The next step is to transform the study of history in general, not only American history and those others chauvinistically defined by nationality, but to use the traditional strengths of Asian American studies to create a transnational perspective.

John K. W. Tchen's groundbreaking new work, *New York Before China-town : Orientalism and the Shaping of American Culture,* is an important step in this process.[13] Like Robert Lee's cultural history of American Orientalism, Tchen's careful and nuanced history of American desire for Chinese goods and "Oriental objects" focuses on the central importance of the idea of exotic "Orientals" to the cultural meanings that defined white America. Taking as his period 1776-1882, Tchen expands the subject matter of Asian American history beyond a focus on Asian American bodies, and by explaining the importance of the China trade to early American culture and society, Tchen's study transforms the way we understand both Asian American and U.S. history.

Kariann Yokota's dissertation work on the early United States as a post-colonial nation builds on Tchen's work. Outlining the importance of post-colonial insecurity in the formation of nationalist definitions for a myriad of early Americans, Yokota traces how Anglo-American cultural insecurity in a trans-Atlantic world of trade and exchange was an important element in their demonization of people of color. Like Tchen, Yokota traces the importance of "Oriental goods" in the attempts of white ex-colonials to prove themselves "civilized." Tying the origins of white supremacy in the early U.S. republic to transnational factors, Yokota details the central role of people of color in the shaping of American society. Also like Tchen, she grounds U.S. history in a wider world of transnational migration, exchange and trade.

Yokota shows how a training and background in Asian American studies can transform the ways in which all U.S. historians understand history. Her masters thesis at UCLA was already groundbreaking in its focus beyond Asian Americans, tracing the relations between African Americans and Japanese Americans in Los Angeles before, during and after World War II.[14] Bringing unique insights that came from her training in Asian American studies, her work in early America promises to expand not only Asian American history, but to rework fields of research that have long ignored the insights of Asian American scholars.

The potential effects of transnational perspectives on history cannot be underestimated. Asian Americans, because they have been defined as both part of the American social body and also in essential ways alien to it, have grounded Asian American studies in the perspectives of the marginalized. But Asian American history at many points has also been best understood as a transnational history, a product of migration flows and the changes in consciousness and culture brought about by physical movement.

As a transnational perspective on history, Asian American studies has already explored many of the problems and issues that other fields of history are tentatively entering in their own scholarship. During a semester at the University of California's Humanities Research Institute, I was among a number of scholars who tried to map out the potential of what we called a "postnational American studies." For us, new scholarship that focuses on transnational perspectives has been uneven, with much of it making fundamental errors of conception. These mistakes are unfortunate and unnecessary, since they result from the idea that transnational scholarship needs to start from scratch. A number of fields, including Asian American Studies and Border Studies, have long been exploring transnational perspectives, and one of the goals of our semester together was to draw upon this history of transnational scholarship.[15]

The importance of seeing history from a transnational view has always marked the work of the best Asian American historians.[16] International politics has often been central to many of these analyses, but there have also been many other exciting possibilities. Madeline Hsu's forthcoming book, *Dreaming of Gold, Dreaming of Home,* based upon her 1996 Yale dissertation examining Taishanese families between the years 1904-1939, will be formative in this regard. In getting away from normalizing notions of family that make the overseas families of Cantonese migrants a pathology, Hsu shows that, though difficult in practice, such transnational familes became the norm. Families began to operate in ways that were founded upon long migration, aided by new methods in communication, transportation, and the transference of capital.

Similar to Hsu's work, Augusto Espiritu's and Arleen deVera's forthcoming UCLA dissertations both take seriously the transnational nature of social and political organizations that have shaped Filipino American history.[17] Such transnational perspectives potentially have the greatest impact in studying the history of recent migration from Asia, and from South and Southeast Asia in particular. Changes in transportation and communication technologies have made the exchange across national borders of physical bodies and intellectual and cultural products more rapid and more common. In response, the rise of transnational perspectives in scholarship are not just an academic fashion, they are the explanatory device of both the past and the future.

There is a danger, however, in thinking about transnational connections in ways that reify racial identity. Conceptions of a "Chinese diaspora," for instance, often trade a political marking of human bodies for a highly racialized notion of nationality. Diasporic writings have sometimes been careful to avoid too physical a notion of diaspora—for instance Jonathan Okamura's recent book on the Philippine diaspora emphasized the forms of consciousness that Filipino migrants developed in different places—but in some ways a physical foundation for diasporic studies is almost unavoidable.[18] After all, the metaphor of diaspora, of seeds being spread widely, is essentially organic and emphasizes the human bodies that make up something labelled a "Japanese" or a "Korean" diaspora. Whether such a focus is somehow justified by appeals to a shared culture or consciousness, it rests ultimately on a categorization of physical bodies that remains to be thoroughly conceived.

It might be tempting, for instance, to think of Asian immigration to the United States in mythic terms, of migrants from the Far East coming to the West Coast of the United States and crossing the continent eastwards, passing fleeing Indians and westering white settlers. Figuring Asian immigrants as a sort of anti-frontier myth would be appealing, a powerful way (along with the story of Hispanics who were in California, Texas and New Mexico long before it was the American West) of subverting Frederick Jackson Turner's conception of the "Western frontier." Turner's 1892 thesis placed white European Americans at the center of history, situated at a frontier moving steadily westwards, occupying the boundary between civilization and savagery.

Telling a story about Asians from a different shore, crossing the Pacific instead of the Atlantic and creating their own eastern frontier, might seem a welcome corrective to Eurocentric American history.[19] But the notion of an Asian diaspora spreading outwards from China and Japan or Southeast Asia, into Australia, Hawaii, South America, and finally Canada and the United States, would only place Asians instead of Europeans at the center of history. Though laudable in the attempt to renarrate U.S. history, it cannot be the ultimate story.

It would be more interesting to talk about locations, about points between which people move. Getting away from the metaphors of homeland and destination that make America the end of long journeys, I told a story in my book about various sites. These places were the central nodes for the production and distribution of knowledge, the founts for creating the forms of consiousness that result from contact. Theories about racial and ethnic identity were defined during the early twentieth century, a subset of a larger phenomenon labelled "cultural consciousness." My study placed ideas about "Orientals" in this context of the rise of cultural identity. I tried not to assume that something called "Oriental" or "American" existed outside of the definitions and social practices that arose to deal with the movements of human bodies.

The concept of culture was a way of getting away from biological theories of race that had served a similar function of categorizing similarities and differences between humans. For theoreticians of the "Oriental problem," cultural theory was a knowledge system arising from the categorization of differences—between American and Chinese, between American and Japanese, between Japanese and Chinese, between "Negro" and "Oriental," between "white" and "colored." At the same time, it created a sense of similarity among people who purportedly shared the same culture.

These systematic comparisons were made at certain locations. And thus Honolulu, Seattle, San Francisco, Los Angeles, and Chicago were sites for the production of knowledge. The knowledge that was created was linked to other theories about the geographic origin of cultural differences: Where did difference arise? Who brought it from where? Questions were asked and knowledge was constructed. The locations were meeting points, sites from which and to which people moved. Migrating intellectuals carried ideas between places—they also transformed ideas, moving from one way of seeing the world to another.

Diasporic studies, no matter how carefully they define their subject matter, have a hard time dealing with the difficulties of presuming the existence of that for which they are searching. By trying to define some phenomenon that somehow unites different people at disparate locations, an assumption of some essential cultural consciousness becomes a binding agent that is often little more than a shorthand for racial theory. Such difficulties do not reflect some lack of thinking on the part of the scholars, but arise from the pervasive nature of racial formations based upon continuing social and political practices. It is the history of those historical practices upon which we must focus, not on some ephemeral object called "culture."

As a concluding note to this essay, much of the intellectual fervor I have described has also reflected the rise of new institutions in producing Asian Americanists. The first strongholds in the study of Asian American history tended to be on the West Coast, where most Asian Americans lived. With the rising numbers of Asian Americans who live elsewhere around the U.S., and more importantly, the increasing enrollments of Asian American students in every single college and university in the nation, interest in Asian American history has spread. Consequently, the training of scholars has also widened beyond schools such as Berkeley, UCLA, and San Franscisco State. New concentrations of faculty in places such as UC San Diego, Washington State, and Stanford have increased the opportunities for the training of graduate students in the west.

The East Coast and Midwest have also been slowly transformed from institutions where scholars often worked alone, far away from others with like interests. Gary Okihiro, for a long time teaching Asian American history at Cornell, was the founder and one of the primary patrons of East of California, a network of disparate Asian American scholars in the east that echoes of early immigrant mutual benefit associations. Okihiro has now taken on the task of building Asian American studies at Columbia University. He joins Jack Tchen, who has been working in the New York area for years. Tchen was recently tenured at NYU and is the founding director of a new Asian Pacific American research center there, after years at Queens College and before that the New York City Chinatown Project (now the Museum of the Chinese in the Americas). Robert Lee, as an associate professor at Brown University, has provided an important institutional voice in the east that has affected not only Asian American historians, but scholars of American studies in general.[20] Each of them, along with scholars such as Peter Kwong at Hunter College and Scott Wong at Williams, have provided a supportive network for the study of Asian American history outside the West Coast.

Asian American history has been an essential part of U.S. history, and the number of scholars studying that history will continue to grow. The challenge ahead is to use our potential strength to change the overall practice of academic history. U.S. history can be transformed by the insights of Asian American studies, and one of the exciting possibilities is a transnational perspective that escapes the limited boundaries and perspectives of nationalist histories. Already, women's studies has so changed the practice of history that gendered analysis is an integral part of any decent historical study. Hopefully, analyses of racialization and nationalization will someday be recognized in a similar manner as an inextricable element in the historical process.

Because one of the concerns in my own research has been how institutions produce knowledge, I am fascinated by the future consequences of the spread of Asian American studies. East Coast institutions have played a large role in recent intellectual production, producing Ph.D's and also providing a spate of new jobs for recent Ph.D's. There are great rewards for the increasing stature of Asian American studies in the traditional powerhouses of American academic life; however there are also potential dangers with the "Ivy-fication" of the study of Asian American history.

One danger is a return to an earlier structure of evaluation in which knowledge about Asian Americans is mainly for the perspective of an academic, and therefore overwhelmingly white, audience. Because the structure of East Coast institutions still make Asian American scholars lone or isolated entities, they are constrained in the need to produce knowledge interesting and important to a general audience. It is a credit to those scholars who have been educated in such institutions, and to those who are currently teaching there, that they have survived and often thrived in such settings.

It would be a shame, however, if in coming so far, we are also returned somehow to a world in which the most interesting qualities we have are defined by the points of view of whiteness. Scholars of Asian American history have much to research and they have much to say, not only about Asian Americans but about history in general. If an academic structure continues to marginalize Asian Americans, however, the clarity of our accents will be defined not by the content of our histories, but by the desires and pleasures of an "Orientalist" audience.

Notes

1. The themes of this talk were first aired as part of the plenary session on "Post-Colonial Histories" at the 1998 Association for Asian American Studies conference in Honolulu, Hawaii. Many thanks to the organizers of that conference and of the plenary session panels in particular.

2. Yu, *Thinking "Orientals": A History of Knowledge Created About and By Asian Americans* (New York: Oxford University Press, forthcoming).

3. Another current term for people who can trace their ancestors back to Asia or the Pacific Ocean is "Asian Pacific Islanders." "Asian American" still works as a useful label for many of the people who were formerly known as "Orientals," yet its emphasis upon "Asian" is seen to marginalize Pacific Islanders who are not from the continent of Asia. For race in American society, Michael Omi and Howard Winant, *Racial Formation in the United States* (New York: Routledge, 1986). On "whiteness" as a social, legal, and economic category, George Lipsitz, *The Possessive Investment in Whiteness* (Philadelphia: Temple, 1998); Matthew Frye Jacobson, *Whiteness of a Different Color: European Immigrants and the Alchemy of Race* (Cambridge, Massachusetts: Harvard University, 1998); Tomás Almaguer, *Racial Fault Lines: The Historical Origins of White Supremacy in California* (Berkeley: University of California, 1994); David Roediger, *The Wages of Whiteness: Race and the Making of the American Working Class* (London: Verso, 1991); Alexander Saxton, *The Rise and Fall of the White Republic* (London: Verso, 1990); Virginia Dominguez, *White by Definition* (New Brunswick: Rutgers University, 1986).

4. For instance, Yuji Ichioka studied Chinese and East Asian history at Columbia; Franklin Odo also began as an East Asianist, and Gary Okihiro originally studied African history; Ronald Takaki was an Americanist, but his dissertation was on antebellum pro-slavery arguments.

5. For instance, Sucheng Chan, Art Hansen, Shirley Hune, Yuji Ichioka, Peter Kwong, Frank Ng, Frank Odo, Gary Okihiro, Michael Omi, Ronald Takaki, Jack Tchen, Ling-chi Wang, Scott Wong, and Judy Yung. Community historians Philip Choy and Him Mark Lai were also crucial in their help and encouragement.

6. Gunther Barth, *Bitter Strength: A History of the Chinese in the United States, 1850-1870* (Cambridge: Harvard University Press, 1964). Barth's book on the whole was sympathetic to the plight of Chinese immigrants, although it reflected the cosmopolitan appreciation of ethnicity of white racial liberals of the late 1950's and early 1960s. As a student of Oscar Handlin, the great historian of immigration at Harvard, Barth's book was one of a slew of Handlin influenced works that detailed immigrant groups that had come to the U.S. In a

strange way, the period of the Great Migrations of the nineteenth century was understood to be aberrational by scholars in the 1950s and 1960s, writing and living in a time when immigration exclusion was federal policy. Now that mass migration has again become a fact of life in U.S. society, many historians are just beginning to realize that it was the Exclusion Period of 1924-1965 which was the aberration.

7. A recent book that details the political origins of Chinese exclusion, Andrew Gyory, *Closing the Gate: Race, Politics, and the Chinese Exclusion Act* (Chapel Hill: University of North Carolina Press, 1998) disagrees with Saxton's argument that labor was behind Chinese exclusion.

8. Community-based historians outside of academic institutions were crucial in this process. For instance, Him Mark Lai, who founded the Chinese Historical Society in San Francisco, compiled large volumes of Chinese language newspapers and other materials virtually unused by earlier scholars.

9. Robert Lee, *Orientals: Asian Americans in Popular Culture* (Philadelphia: Temple University Press, 1999); Darrell Hamamoto, *Monitored Peril: Asian Americans and the Politics of TV Representation* (Minneapolis: University of Minnesota Press, 1994); James S. Moy, *Marginal Sights: Staging the Chinese in America* (Iowa City: University of Iowa Press, 1993).

10. Roediger, *Wages of Whiteness.*

11. Mae Ngai, "Illegal Aliens and Alien Citizens: United States Immigration Policy and Racial Formation, 1924-1945," Columbia Ph.D, 1998.

12. Erika Lee, "At America's Gates: Chinese Immigration During the Exclusion Era, 1882-1943," University of California, Berkeley Ph.D, 1998.

13. John Kuo Wei Tchen, *New York Before Chinatown: Orientalism and the Shaping of American Culture, 1776-1882* (Baltimore: Johns Hopkins University Press, 1999).

14. Yokota worked at UCLA with Valerie Matsumoto, Don Nakanishi, and Yuji Ichioka on her MA research.

15. See the forthcoming essay collection from the UCHRI research group on *A Post-National American Studies,* edited by John C. Rowe and published by the University of California Press, and my essay for the volume, "How Tiger Woods Lost His Stripes."

16. For instance, in the work of earlier historians such as Yuji Ichioka and Sucheng Chan, and in more recent work such as that of Steffi San Buenaventura, Renqiu Yu, Gordon Chang, and Scott Wong.

17. Espiritu and deVera work with Michael Salman and Valerie Matsumoto at UCLA. Under the guidance of professors such as Salman at UCLA, a number of graduate students studying Philippine-American history from a transnational perspective are in the institutional pipeline, and promise to address a long standing marginalization

of Filipino American history in the discipline of history.

18. Jonathan Okamura, *Imagining the Filipino American Diaspora: Transnational Relations, Identities, and Communities* (New York: Garland Publishing, 1998).

19. Ronald Takaki, *Strangers From A Different Shore* (New York: Penguin Books, 1989).

20. Matthew Jacobson of Yale University's Department of American Studies, credits Lee as an important influence in his recent book *Whiteness of a Different Color*, an important study on how ethnic immigrants became "white" through a process that made them distinct from blacks and other "people of color."

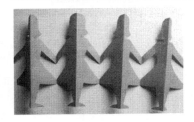

Amerasia Journal 26:1 (2000): 163-180

Reclaiming Chinese America:
One Woman's Journey

Ruthanne Lum McCunn

I published my first book, *An Illustrated History of the Chinese in America*, on April 1, 1979.

I had submitted the manuscript to at least two dozen New York publishers, all of whom had rejected it—most with form letters, a few with compliments for the writing, but regrets that there was no market for a book about Chinese Americans for young people. But I knew from eight years of teaching in California elementary and junior high schools that there was a need for a book like mine. Indeed, it was the absence of information about the Chinese American experience in Social Studies texts that had prompted me to research and write the book.[1]

"Let's publish it ourselves," my husband Don said when I quit the San Francisco Unified School District over an educational dispute. "You have almost ten thousand dollars in your retirement fund. That's enough to cover the costs for five thousand copies."

Jobless and with no other cash reserves, I quailed.

"If *you* don't trust your claim that there's a market for a book about Chinese in America for young people, why should a New York publisher?" Don came back.

Acknowledging he was right in principle, I met his challenge. But my fears that the enterprise would fail prompted me to select April Fools Day for the book's publication date.[2] Even after the book received excellent reviews and we returned to press for another five thousand copies after six months, my fears did not recede. What if we had already saturated the market that we could reach with our limited resources?[3]

RUTHANNE LUM McCUNN has published seven books on the experiences of Chinese in America. Her work has won critical acclaim and has been translated into eight languages and adapted for the stage and film.

Lalu Nathoy/Polly Bemis on steps of her cabin at the Salmon River.
Courtesy of Idaho Historical Society. From *Thousand Pieces of Gold* (Boston: Beacon
Press, 1988).

While researching the Chinese in Idaho for *An Illustrated History of the Chinese in America*, however, I had come across the story of Lalu Nathoy, later known as Polly Bemis, and I wanted desperately to write about her. So I allowed Don to convince me that we should at least try supporting ourselves through a combination of part-time jobs and self-publishing.[4]

According to Sister Mary Alfreda Elsensohn's *Idaho Chinese Lore* (Cottonwood: Idaho Corporation of Benedictine Sisters, 1970), Lalu Nathoy was born in a northern Chinese village in 1853. During a long, hard drought, her parents sold her to bandits who, in turn, sold her to a brothel in Shanghai. The brothel's Madam shipped Lalu to San Francisco, where she was auctioned off to Hong King, a saloon keeper in the Idaho mining camp of Warrens. Lalu, renamed Polly by the European American miners, eventually won her freedom through a poker game and ran her own boarding house. In 1894, she married Charlie Bemis, and they settled by the Salmon River, which remained her home until her death in 1933.

I wanted to write about Lalu/Polly for several reasons. From Elsensohn's sketch, Lalu/Polly seemed extraordinary, and I believed a book about her would not only reveal a little known area of U.S. history but be an exciting read. Moreover, Lalu/Polly broke the prevailing stereotype in America that Asian women are passive, and her story would be an antidote to the popular sagas of poor immigrants who become huge successes by building empires on the backs of other people. Here was a woman who had overcome great hardships, and although she had never become wealthy financially, she had been rich and generous in spirit.

Since Lalu/Polly was illiterate in both Chinese and English, she left no personal records, so I had to piece together her story through oral histories and archival research. Because she was so unusual, there was no shortage of photographs or print material: her exploits—such as her digging a bullet out of Charlie's cheek with a crochet hook—were written up in the newspapers; and when pioneers wrote their memoirs, they usually included an anecdote or two about her. But I soon discovered glaring inconsistencies in the various accounts. Some articles and stories had almost no basis in fact. Some seemed fairly accurate. Almost none agreed. There were also huge gaps, especially about her childhood in China.

Even the few facts I did find about Lalu as a girl didn't make sense. Why had her feet been bound, then unbound? Since the persons who had bought her were bandits, why had they given her father two bags of seed? Most confusing was the jewelry in St. Gertrude's Museum that Sister Mary Alfreda claimed Lalu had brought from China. If her family was so poor that they had been forced to sell her, why had she arrived in America with jewelry?

Unless I passed over her years in China, I clearly could not write a nonfiction book about Lalu/Polly. Yet I felt very strongly that in order to understand Polly's life in America, it would be crucial for the reader to know and understand Lalu's life in China. So I decided to write a biographical novel. That did not mean I was willing to take liberties with the truth. Rather, it meant that I threw myself into the kind of intensive research that would help me fill in the gaps and sort through the disparate facts.

I read dozens of books on nineteenth century China, particularly those books dealing with village life, bandits, and the flora and fauna of Northern China. I studied the crops, when to plant, when to harvest, the various cycles of cultivation and holidays, the farm implements used, daily routines, and the folklore of the area until I knew it as intimately as if I had lived there myself. Then and only then did I begin to reconstruct Lalu's first eighteen years.

Similarly, I steeped myself in the history and geography of Idaho, especially the Salmon River area. I located people who had known Polly and went to Idaho to interview them. I visited Warrens and her cabin at the Salmon River.

Everything I read and everyone I interviewed claimed that after Charlie's death, Polly gave the deed to her ranch at the Salmon River to her neighbors in exchange for their taking care of her needs until she died. This puzzled me because Chinese at that time were forbidden by law from owning land. I didn't dismiss the possibility, though. Chinese weren't allowed to become citizens either, yet I had come across instances where judges in small towns either weren't aware of the law or chose to disregard it and approved applications for citizenship anyway. So I did search for the deed that Polly was supposed to have given her neighbors, but I failed to find one. Then I learned a mining claim entitled the claimant to a property so long as s/he continued to mine it, and when I looked for a mining claim Polly might have given her neighbors, I found it.

This discovery of a mining claim in place of a property deed may seem like hairsplitting—hence insignificant. But it provided me with important insights into Charlie's intellect and character as well as his feelings for Polly. Everyone—including Polly—said Charlie was lazy. Yet he had always mined his claim on the Salmon River, and when I checked the date on Charlie's claim, I realized it coincided with the nearby Buffalo Hump rush. By taking out the claim, then, Charlie cleverly circumvented the discriminatory property law and protected his wife. That Polly had the claim to give her neighbors also indicated that both she and Charlie recognized its importance because their entire cabin burned down, yet two pieces of paper survived: the mining claim and their marriage certificate.

In writing my book, *Thousand Pieces of Gold*, about Lalu/Polly, I was fearful that footbinding, the sale of a child by her own father, and the enslavement of Chinese women for prostitution would reinforce negative Asian images. So without taking away from the horror of what Lalu's father did, I tried to show the social order under which they lived really gave him little choice. I was also careful to draw the father's character sympathetically. But I was afraid that readers might still think: Chinese men are the villains; Charlie Bemis—hence European American men—are the heroes. So I created the fictitious and positive character of Jim, the Chinese packer, making certain, of course, that he was plausible within the context of history.

Similarly, where the European Americans in Warrens are appalled by Polly's tiny feet, I have *her* shocked by the willingness of European American women to bind their bodies in corsets. And in a scene between Charlie and Polly, I try to make clear that the slave trade Chinese men engaged in would have been impossible without the collusion of the European American power structure.

Finally, I felt it important for the reader to understand that although Polly loved Charlie deeply, he was *not* her whole life. So I did not end the book with his death although in terms of traditional dramatic structure, the active, page-turning elements stop at that point. For ending the book with Charlie's death would have implied that Lalu/Polly's life ended with him. And that would have been, I believe, a terrible betrayal of the strong, independent woman she was.

I finished writing *Thousand Pieces of Gold* in 1981, and Don and I published it that fall. The second printing of *An Illustrated History of the Chinese in America* had been selling just as slowly as I had feared, and people in the book trade had warned us that publishing fiction, in particular a biographical novel about a Chinese pioneer woman, would be very risky. But Don had written and published a book about the new personal computers, *Computer Programming for the Complete Idiot*, that was selling well enough to finance a printing of five thousand copies of *Thousand Pieces of Gold*, and we were both too committed to Lalu/Polly not to take the risk.

We had almost no prepublication sales. Excellent reviews and the selection of *Thousand Pieces of Gold* as an alternate by Book of the Month's Quality Paperback Book Club, however, not only fueled sales but stirred the interest of New York publishers, and we sold reprint rights to Dell.[5]

While looking for information about Chinese packers in the Pacific Northwest, I had found the story of Pie-Biter in Fern Cable Trull's unpublished masters thesis, "The History of the Chinese in Idaho from 1864-1910" (University of Oregon, 1946). According to the pioneers Trull interviewed, Pie-Biter had earned his nickname from his love for American pies. He had come to America to work on the railroad, become a very successful packer with his own pack train, and on the lead horse that Pie-Biter rode, he had two boxes, one for each side, which held the sixteen pies he purportedly ate every day. None of the pioneers knew Pie-Biter's true name or what happened to him after he returned to China. But when my mother was a girl in Hong Kong, her father used to take her to a pie shop owned by a Chinese American baker who made delicious pies, and it seemed to me that coupling these stories together would make a wonderful tall tale in the tradition of John Henry and Paul Bunyan. The profit from selling close to forty thousand copies of *Thousand Pieces of Gold* and the advance from Dell could not finance the exorbitant costs of producing a children's picture book, however. Luckily, the margin of profit from Don's second computer book *Write, Edit, and Print* was sufficiently high to cover the expenses for publishing *Pie-Biter*, beautifully illustrated in full color by artist You-shan Tang.[6]

I have ever sought variety in my life, and the moment I stumbled on Marjorie Lew's article, "Faith, Hope and Survival," about Poon Lim, the world's champion survivor, in a Los Angeles Chinese New Year commemorative magazine, I knew I had found the subject for my next book. Mr. Poon's experiences as a castaway would give me the opportunity to research and write about a man, a person in very different circumstances from those of Lalu/Polly. More importantly, Mr. Poon's amazing achievement challenged the stereotype that Asians don't value life.

Briefly, the merchant ship on which Mr. Poon was working as a second steward sank on November 23, 1942 within two minutes of being torpedoed some 750 miles east of Brazil. Mr. Poon had no knowledge of the sea. Yet he was the only member of the crew to survive, and when he was finally rescued by fishermen at the mouth of the Amazon River 133 days later, he was in such excellent physical and mental condition that the U.S. Navy asked him to reenact his experiences in New York harbor for their survival training section.

Through a special act of Congress, Mr. Poon was able to remain in America, and he settled in Brooklyn. He continued to go to sea as a steward, and in 1982, I began interviewing him each time his ship came into the Port of Oakland.

Mr. Poon's memory of his 133 days on the raft was excellent. He also gave me news clippings, the report from the U.S. Navy, photographs from his reenactment, and other miscellaneous articles. In order to recreate his experiences for the reader, however, I needed to know the layout of British ships of that period, the conditions under which stewards worked, details about the part of the Atlantic Ocean in which Mr. Poon drifted, such as the weather conditions and types of fish, how the war was being waged, and the like. I also had to find out as much as I could about Mr. Poon himself in order to understand what gave him the will to go on day after day. This meant learning about his family and his life as a boy on Hainan Island, what his feelings and thoughts were as a child, a seaman, and then a castaway.

Since much of the information I needed was British, I had to write libraries and archives in England, and I contacted the Ben Line, the shipping company for which Mr. Poon had worked. Once again I uncovered conflicting "facts." U.S. Intelligence

Poon showing how he rigged the canvas awning to catch rain water. Courtesy of Poon Lim. From *Sole Survivor* (Boston: Beacon Press, 1999).

Poon Lim an hour after landing in Belem, Brazil. The Brazillian fishing family that picked him up gave him the clothes he is wearing in this picture. He had been adrift for 133 days.
Courtesy of Poon Lim. From *Sole Survivor.*

reports claimed that Mr. Poon's ship, the *Benlomond*, had been sunk by an Italian submarine. This was based on Mr. Poon's description of the white, red, and green colors on the conning tower of the submarine. The British claimed that the submarine was a German U-172. That made more sense to me since it was the Germans who were waging intense submarine attacks in the Atlantic at that time, but how could I prove it?

At a loss, I consulted military historian Col. William Strobridge, who told me the National Archives had all the logs from World War II German submarines as spoils of war. So I sent for a photocopy of the log for the U-172 for November 23, 1942, the day the *Benlomond* was torpedoed. The log was, of course, in German. Charles Burdick, a World War II submarine buff who translated the log for me, gave me the address for the German commander of the submarine, D. Carl Emmermann, who sent me a photograph of the insignia that was painted on the conning tower: a white neptune on a green sea. This explained the colors Mr. Poon saw and the basis for the error.

Because I chose to write about Mr. Poon's experiences in the style of a novel, I published *Sole Survivor* as fiction. But when *Reader's Digest's* International Division bought condensation rights for their overseas' magazines, they employed a fact checker to double check my account which they then published as nonfiction in Australia, Belgium, Denmark, France, Germany, Great Britain, Hong Kong (in two editions, one for the Chinese reading public in Asia, the other for the English), Portugal, Scandinavia, and Singapore. *Sole Survivor* was also a nonfiction selection of Book of the Month's Dolphin Book Club, and it won the 1985 Southwest Booksellers Award for nonfiction.[7]

As publishers, Don and I had to show our books at one or two national trade conventions a year. As a writer, I was invited to speak at schools, libraries, universities, and conferences around the country. Wherever I went, I would try and make time to do some research in the local archives, and the larger my collection of photographs and stories grew, the stronger I felt the need to publish a collection of biographical profiles—embedded in a mosaic of photographs—that would show the diversity within Chinese America.

From the questions and comments of people I met as I went around the country, it seemed to me that in communities where Chinese were few in number, most people believed Chinese had come to America for the gold rush and/or to build the railroad, then returned to China; in places with large populations of Chinese immigrants, all Chinese—even those who were third and fourth generation Americans—were too often regarded as newcomers. What I also hoped to convey, then, was the long, continuous history of Chinese in America.

The result was *Chinese American Portraits: Personal Histories 1828-1988*, which contains seventeen biographical profiles divided into three sections—Pioneers, Generations, and Contemporaries—and over 150 photographs. My criteria for selection were that each person I profiled would illuminate a certain aspect of Chinese American history, and the photographs—together with their captions—would provide additional texturing. For example, the chapter "Mary Bong, Frontierswoman" includes photographs and miniprofiles of other pioneer women, "Arlee Hen and Black Chinese" includes photographs and miniprofiles of other Chinese of mixed ancestry as well as interracial couples, and so on.

The production quality that I wanted for *Chinese American Portraits* was well beyond our means. I was also becoming increasingly impatient with the time and energy publishing stole from research and writing. In the ten years since I had sent out *An Illustrated History of the Chinese in America*, however, the only Chinese American titles that had met with commercial success were Maxine Hong Kingston's *Woman Warrior* and *China Men*, and when

Lue Gim Gong shortly before his death.
Courtesy of Him Mark Lai. From *Chinese American Portraits: Personal Histories, 1828-1988* (Seattle: University of Washington Press, 1996).

I sent a proposal package for *Chinese American Portraits* out to publishers in 1986, I was told repeatedly that there was no market for the book. One publisher even claimed that Maxine Hong Kingston had already exhausted the topic of Chinese in America! Fortunately, Jay Schaefer at Chronicle Books in San Francisco disagreed, and he accepted *Chinese American Portraits* for publication in 1988.[8]

That same year, Beacon Press in Boston reprinted *Thousand Pieces of Gold* and Scholastic Books in New York accepted *Sole Survivor* for reprint (as nonfiction biography) in 1989, allowing me to give up self-publishing.[9] But I couldn't support myself or my research and writing from my royalties, so I periodically accepted guest lectureships at universities to supplement my income.

The pioneer whose life I wanted to explore further was Lue Gim Gong. Lue had accompanied his uncle from Lung On, their village in Toishan, China, to San Francisco when he was ten years old. Two years later, in 1870, Lue was one of seventy-five Chinese boys who were duped into going to North Adams, Massachusetts, to break an ugly strike at a shoe factory. Lue's Sunday School teacher in North Adams gave him the education he had always longed for, and together they settled in DeLand, Florida, where he developed a hardy, frost-resistant orange that was named after him and earned him national renown.

Because Lue did become famous, there were many articles about him that were published in magazines and newspapers between 1911, when his orange won the Wilder Silver Medal from the U.S. Pomological Society, and 1925, when he died. Every single one of these articles referred to his Sunday School teacher, Fanny Burlingame, as a cousin of the diplomat who negotiated the Burlingame Treaty of 1868. Many of these articles even attributed Fanny's sympathetic attitude towards Chinese to this "cousin." What I discovered from reading the North Adams' newspapers for that period, however, was that Fanny's sympathetic attitude was quite typical for people of her class background in North Adams. And when I located the Burlingame genealogy in an archive in Rhode Island, I found there was no connection between Fanny and the diplomat; the supposed relationship was simply a fanciful fabrication that had been repeated over and over until it became "fact."

Fanny's attachment to Lue was actually so strong that he's included in her family genealogy. His own family in China, however, struck his name from their family genealogy, or *ga bo*. The first person who told me this was Lew Yew Huan, a clansman of Lue's who lived in San Francisco. And when I went to Lue's village in Toishan, I discovered that he's remembered there as a *mo been yun*, man without a queue, a man who had been scorned because he had brought home ideas and books instead of money or technology, a man who had run away the night before his wedding even though he knew that according to Chinese tradition, his betrothed would be married to him in absentia, making her a living widow for the rest of her life.[10] It was for this betrayal of his family and people that his name was struck from the *ga bo*, and it was not restored even after he developed the orange that won him the Wilder Medal and national attention in America.

Nor did Lue's fame and the millions his orange brought to the citrus industry in Florida bring him any personal wealth or happiness in DeLand, where I interviewed a half dozen people who had actually known him. Citrus growers spoke glowingly of Lue's accomplishments, as did members of the local historical society. He was a genius, they said, a plant wizard whose orange had contributed millions to the state's citrus industry. Yet he had died a pauper. And although everyone spoke of Lue with admiration and respect, every anecdote about him seemed to take place outdoors. The closest he got to being invited within a house seemed to be the front porch. Moreover, Lue—a devout Christian—stopped attending church after Fanny died, creating a prayer garden on his property instead.

Since I was told he had kept a diary and that at least one volume had survived, I hoped that Lue himself would explain his behavior in China, his relationship with Fanny and her family, the reason he might have been held at arms' length by people in Florida.

Ruthanne Lum McCunn between Lue Gim Gong's grandnephews Lew Duk Sum and Lew Duk Gwong (in black) in Lung On (Dragon Peace Village) December 1985.

Lung On (below).

Unfortunately, while I was still trying to pinpoint its location, the person in possession of the volume offered it to a university archive and was told the diary had no value, so he burned it.

Profiling Lue's life in *Chinese American Portraits* and then writing a footnoted account for *Chinese America: History and Perspectives* (San Francisco: Chinese Historical Society of America, 1989) made me realize that his life provided a means to examine the impact of migration on both the person who emigrates *and* the family left behind. Lue's story also provided an opportunity to explore the issue of misperceptions due to cultural, racial, gender, and religious bias.

The structure of my novel about Lue, *Wooden Fish Songs*, was inspired by the destruction of his diary and the wide divergence in the oral histories about him. Just as Lue was silenced in life, neither did he receive his own voice in the book. I retained the disparate points of view expressed in the oral histories by writing about Lue from three radically different points of view: his mother, Sum Jue, in China; his Sunday School teacher, mentor, and would-be lover, Fanny, in Massachusetts; and in Florida, Sheba, an African American woman who was Fanny's cook and Lue's friend. While telling Lue's story, these three women reveal their own personal histories and the ethnic, cultural, and religious biases that determine how they view him. Thus, the truth about Lue can only be found when *all* their stories are combined.[11]

While working on *Wooden Fish Songs*, I had been invited to Lincoln, Nebraska, to speak at a conference, and I had discovered a fascinating story in the state archives about Edward Day Cohota. Cohota, a Chinese man in Valentine, Nebraska, fought in the Civil War as a union soldier, yet was denied the right to homestead, since Chinese were not permitted to become naturalized citizens during Exclusion and only citizens could homestead. Years before, historian Him Mark Lai had given me an article about another veteran, Hong Neok Woo, and as I came across the names of other veterans, I would add them to my "Civil War" file. By 1994, there were ten names in the file, and through a combination of military records, pension files, newspapers, family papers and reminiscences, archival documents, and published accounts of the Civil War, I painstakingly set about reconstructing their lives.

Although several of these veterans would make fine heroes for a Civil War novel, I merely documented what I recovered in an article "Chinese in the Civil War: Ten Who Served," which was published in the Chinese Historical Society of America's annual journal in 1996,[12] for my imagination had been seized by the independent spinsters of Sun Duk, a county in China's Pearl River Delta.

As a girl in Hong Kong in the 1940s and 50s, I had been familiar with these spinsters who had migrated from Sun Duk in search of work and were laboring as servants.[13] Indeed, I had been deeply influenced by their courage in resisting the norm of marriage, their strength in committing themselves to lives of independence. And since these independent spinsters had successfully won acceptance, admiration, and respect in Sun Duk as early as the 1830s, I believed a novel about them could help dispel the popular American misperception that women throughout China have always been victims.

By the time I embarked on this project in 1994, most of the independent spinsters of my childhood had died or retired to their villages in China. Luckily, my friend Tsoi Nu Liang made my quest hers, and one of her cousins, a retired women's welfare worker, located four independent spinsters in an old people's home in Shiqiao who agreed to be interviewed.

As Janice Stockard points out in her book *Daughters of the Canton Delta* (Stanford: Stanford University Press, 1989), accurate recovery of the past frequently rests on constructing the right questions. So before I went to Shiqiao, I read and reread Stockard's book on the independent spinsters as well as the work of Marjorie Topley and Andrea Sankar. I also read diverse articles from Chinese newspapers, magazines, and county gazettes that Judy Yung and Him Mark Lai shared from their personal archives.[14]

Everything I read suggested that at least some of the self-combers were lesbians. And every person I talked to in Hong Kong about the self-combers inevitably muttered in a hushed aside, "They were lesbians, you know." But I could never get anyone to elaborate.

I had no desire to focus on this one possible aspect of the self-combers' lives. At the same time, I didn't want to ignore it. What I wanted to know was whether some of the self-combers were, in fact, lesbians, or were people suggesting the self-combers were lesbians because they insisted on lives of independence just as some people in this country maintain that women who are feminists are lesbians. I also wanted to know how the lesbian spinsters, if there were any, were perceived by the heterosexual spinsters and the larger community, whether the lesbian spinsters lived as couples or in community with the heterosexual spinsters, and so on. But all my Chinese relatives and friends confirmed my own fear that I would offend my interviewees by bringing up the topic, telling me bluntly, "You can't ask about lesbians. Chinese don't even speak openly about heterosexual sex with each other, and you'll be a stranger with a white face from America."

Although my white face does set me apart in China, I am fluent in Cantonese and I learned excellent Chinese manners from my mother. So I brought plenty of small gifts to Shiqiao and passed them out as my friend and I had tea with her cousin, lunch with the women's welfare workers who had helped locate the spinsters, then tea with the directors of the old people's home.

By the time we finally sat down with the four spinsters to yet more presents and tea, several hours had passed, and with conversation flowing freely, everybody seemed relaxed. Since it was a very hot day, we were outside in a sort of breezeway where other residents were playing *mah jong*, chatting, or dozing, and as I posed my questions and the spinsters answered, some of the other residents began drifting near and chiming in.

Suddenly, my friend's cousin said, "You know, there were spinsters who lived together as man and wife." The women's welfare workers, who looked like they were in their late twenties and early thirties, gasped. Laughing at their shock, the elderly spinsters confirmed that there had been women who had lived as couples, sometimes in their own houses, sometimes in community with other spinsters.

"So long as the two didn't have the same surname, it was alright."

Eager to educate the women's welfare workers, my friend, and myself, the spinsters, other residents, cousin, and directors became increasingly animated in their talk, giving me much more than I had dared hope for.

Now, writing my novel, *The Moon Pearl*, about the first girls in the Sun Duk district to resist marriage, I realize I was right to choose April Fools Day for publishing my first book. Not because I was abandoning economic security, but because I failed to see how profoundly my life, once committed to reclaiming Chinese America, would be enriched.[15]

Notes

Author's Note: My journey has been made possible through the generous support of many people, some of whom are named in this article. Many more are named in the Acknowledgements of my books. I am profoundly grateful to them all.

1. Neither my professors nor my textbooks in my university U.S. History courses had mentioned Chinese. It was only during a 1974 Summer Institute for Chinese Bilingual teachers sponsored by San Francisco State College and the San Francisco Unified School District that I was finally introduced to the history of Chinese in America through *Outlines: History of the Chinese in America* by H. Mark Lai and Philip P. Choy (1971) and *A History of the Chinese in California: A Syllabus*, Thomas W. Chinn, Editor, H. M. Lai, Philip P. Choy, Associate Editors (San Francisco: Chinese Historical Society of America, 1969).

2. Don McCunn, who had written and published *How to Make Sewing Patterns* (New York: Hart Publishing Company, 1973), had taken back the rights in 1977 and published it himself under the imprint of Design Enterprises of San Francisco. This was the imprint under which I published *An Illustrated History of the Chinese in America*. Don produced the camera-ready copy for both books with rub-off type and a proportionally spaced typewriter.

3. The only bookstores willing to sell *An Illustrated History of the Chinese in America* were San Francisco's left-wing bookstores, such as Everybody's, China Books, Modern Times, and Revolutionary Books. Gift/souvenir stores in San Francisco's Chinatown also carried the book. The major sales were to schools and libraries.

4. Except for marketing and promotion, Don took care of every aspect of our publishing business, from production to billing. Personal computers were just becoming available and he charged a TRS-80 on our Mastercard, confident he could teach himself how to program it, computerize our business, and write a book on programming that would not only repay our investment but keep us afloat.

5. The good reviews also attracted a lot of offers from movie producers, and in 1991 *Thousand Pieces of Gold*, the film, was released by American Playhouse.

    In print since its publication, *Thousand Pieces of Gold*, the book, was published in 1983 by Dell's Laurel line in a mass market edition, and has been available from Beacon Press in trade paperback since 1988. It has also been translated into Chinese, Mongolian, French, and Danish.

    The first Chinese translation, by Ellen Lai-shan Yeung, ran as a serial in San Francisco's *East/West* newspaper in 1983. The second, by Tsoi NuLiang, was published by Guangdong People's Publishing in the People's Republic of China in 1985, and it should be noted that in answer to inquiries by Tsoi Nuliang, the Research Department on Northeastern and Inner Mongolian Nationalities at the National Institute for Minorities in Beijing identified Lalu Nathoy as a Mongolian name. So Lalu Nathoy's family—although living among Han Chinese—was most likely either Mongolian or Daur, a minority in Mongolia that is related culturally and linguistically to the Mongols and Tungus-Manchu-speaking peoples. Although no confirmation of Lalu's exact origins is possible, the Mongolians claimed her as one of their own, and the *Inner Mongolian Magazine* published a Mongolian translation of *Thousand Pieces of Gold* in serial form. Then through Tsoi Nuliang, the Inner Mongolian Writers Association invited Don and me for a visit in 1987. The delegation hosting us was certain I had been to Northern China before because they found the details of Lalu's childhood years too authentic to believe they came from print research alone.

According to the June 1987 *Idahonian*, Lalu/Polly's last cabin on the banks of the Salmon River is now the Polly Bemis Historical Museum. Open to the public, the museum is listed in the National Register of Historic Places.

6. In addition to excellent reviews, *Pie-Biter* won the 1984 Before Columbus Foundation's American Book Award. Because the story is multicultural, I had wanted to publish the book in English, Chinese, and Spanish, but our limited resources only allowed for English and Chinese. After selling out the 10,000 copies we printed, I began searching for a publisher willing to publish a trilingual edition. Finally, in 1998 Shen's Books redesigned *Pie-Biter* and published it in English, Chinese, and Spanish.

7. In the years since *Sole Survivor* was first published in 1985, the use of fiction techniques in writing nonfiction has become so common that in 1999, I revised the Epilogue and Author's Note for a new nonfiction edition published by Beacon Press.

8. In 1990, *Chinese American Portraits* was selected by *Choice* as an "Outstanding Academic Book." In 1996, University of Washington Press brought out a new edition of *Chinese American Portraits: Personal Histories 1828-1988*. Except for the cover, nothing was changed.

9. Don, also tired of self-publishing, returned to working in the theatre.

10. It was through Him Mark Lai that I met Lew Yew Huan, who gave me the letters of introduction to the Lew/Lue clan in Lung On Village. The visit to Toishan was made possible through Tsoi Nuliang, who secured a travel grant from Flower City Publishing in Guangzhou, where she was the director of the Foreign Literature Department, and additional support from the China International Exchange Center and the Overseas Chinese Affairs Office of Toishan.

11. While I was writing *Wooden Fish Songs*, Peter Ginsberg, President of Curtis Brown, Ltd., agreed to become my agent, and he sold the book to Dutton/Plume for publication as a hardback in 1995, paperback in 1996. The book was shortlisted for the Bay Area Book Reviewers Award in 1995 and won the Women's Heritage Museum's Jeanne Farr McDonnell Award for Best Fiction in 1996.

    In 1997, Don and I adapted *Wooden Fish Songs* for a fifty-minute "Concert Reading" performed by three actors playing Sum Jue, Fanny, and Sheba. This concert reading has toured over twenty universities, libraries, and museums in the San Francisco Bay Area, New York, New England, Washington D.C., and Hawaii. In October

1999, Florida's West Volusia Historical Society dedicated a bust of Lue Gim Gong (made from his death mask) in a garden gazebo at the Henry A. DeLand House Museum and a new headstone for Lue's grave in DeLand's Oakdale Cemetery. *Wooden Fish Songs: A Concert Reading* was performed as part of the ceremonies honoring Lue, and Bill Dreggors, director of DeLand House, has since arranged for the planting of several Lue Gim Gong trees on the museum grounds.

12. A new edition of *Wooden Fish Songs* was published by Beacon Press in June 2000. My hope, as expressed in the final sentence of the article, was that "others will continue to explore this scarcely mined area of the Chinese experience in America." And with "Chinese in the Civil War" by Thomas L. Lowry and Edward S. Milligan in *North & South* (Volume 2, Number 4, 1999), the count of Chinese Civil War veterans has mounted to forty-seven.

13. I was born in San Francisco's Chinatown to a mother of Chinese descent from Hong Kong and a father of Scottish descent from Idaho. My mother could not become accustomed to life in America, and when I was one year old, she took my middle sister and me back to Hong Kong to live with her family. (My eldest sister, who is profoundly retarded, remained in the U.S., where she would have access to better care.) I didn't return to America until 1962, when I was sixteen, to go to college.

14. I relied on Marlon Hom and Ellen Lai-shan Yeung to translate these articles for me. I'm deeply indebted to them—and to Tsoi Nuliang, Judy Yung, and Him Mark Lai—for their generous assistance during every one of my projects.

15. *The Moon Pearl* will be published by Beacon Press in September 2000.

Amerasia Journal 26:1 (2000): 181-205

Asian American Labor History:
"What *Do* You Do?"

Chris Friday

An Opening Line

"I am a historian," I answer to queries as to what I do. "Really, I just love history (though I hated it in school)," the person who asked me about my job generally says, followed by "What kind of history *do* you do?" I know they expect me to offer an answer that will fit on some shelf of a giant chain bookstore or appear on history channel—those marketplace histories that are nearly always constructed as wars, formal politics, biographies of "famous" people, or long, synthetic, and celebratory narratives. When I answer, "My specialization is Asian American labor history," the response is quizzical. It takes a moment for most people who are not Asian Americans themselves to get past their assumptions about Asian Americans (immigrant and American-born alike) as "natural" entrepreneurs and "model minorities."[1] After processing my unexpected reply, for I am what most would construct as "white," I most often get back, "Oh, that's right. There used to be lots of *them* working on the railroads around here." (Depending upon the place, the nearby mines, fields and orchards, laundries or restaurants, or canneries are inevitable substitutes for the railroads.) A few might mention undocumented Southeast Asian immigrants working in sweatshops as near slaves or others, Fujianese stowaways in cargo containers. After those sincere, but still obligatory attempts at connecting to my specialization, most will turn the discussion to the travesty of Japanese American internment,

CHRIS FRIDAY is a professor of history and director of the Center for Pacific Northwest Studies at Western Washington University, Bellingham. His focus is on racial formations in the American West and Pacific, Asian American and American Indian Studies as well as labor history.

particularly any recent Hollywood version. Others who find no connection to Asian American history sometimes quiz me on some arcane aspect of a famous union leader or labor heroics (the "Wobblies" are a favorite).

These exchanges are equally inspiring and depressing. It *is* a great feat to have the general public recognize the very real role of Asian Americans in the nineteenth- and twentieth-century capitalist transformation of the United States. Current narratives still shunt Asian Americans aside as bit players and sojourners in the grand triumph of American industrialization but at least they have some role. It is also heartening when people recognize the problems created by late twentieth-century global capitalism and that coerced labor exists in American society. One can even find pleasure in that Japanese American internment has found a place in the public's historical consciousness. It is depressing, though, that three decades of Asian American Studies has only managed to carve out so little in the historical narrative and that the understanding of Asian Americans is so episodic.[2] I am also discouraged by the fact that the pressure to construct Asian Americans as "perpetual foreigners" (note the "them" in the response) still wins out over the reality of sustained struggle of Asian Americans as a part of American history. I am frustrated by the refusal to admit that Asian Americans are not the only peoples in North America who currently and historically face the complexities of transnational lives.[3] In American history narratives as well as in popular culture, Asian Americans are sojourners, not immigrants, or immigrants, not settlers. On some fundamental level, such constructions reduce Asian Americans to people who "don't want to stay here" and even "don't belong here." As for the history of workers, Asian Americans remain faceless hordes and outside the realm of heroic union struggles for most people. One can be too harsh and glib in judging the "popular mind." There are many historical narratives among many different peoples, but the assumptions illustrated in the exchange I outline above are insidious and creep into the very fields of scholarship that might benefit most from looking more carefully at the juncture of Asian American Studies and labor history, at Asian American labor history.

There is one small problem with this assertion: Asian American labor history as a consciously articulated field of study does not exist either within Asian American Studies or labor history. That is a bold, and perhaps to some, insulting and surprising statement. It is clear that while scholars within Asian American Studies have given the working lives of Asian immigrants and Asian Americans attention over the years, attention to working lives is more often than not a byproduct of their research agendas.[4] Labor historians have also occasionally looked at Asian American labor, but as a whole they tend to see it as a sidelight or addendum to the main story-line.[5] The separate pursuits have helped academics recognize that in the very real lives of the peoples they study, the constructions of race, class, and gender have been conjoined in what can only be understood as oppressive layers—a point that did not and has not escaped the people in those studies. For the most part, though, academics have not built bridges between Asian American Studies and labor history and have stayed within one or another of the respective camps.

This is no small question. Should Asian American labor history be part of either of those bodies or something separate? Segregating various ethnic, racial, class, or gender groups threatens to marginalize them. Incorporating them into the metanarratives—as they now stand—seems only to subsume these "different" histories, and the people end up as exotics and exceptions. Those of us who might hope to take up distinct Asian American labor history are up against stiff odds. Broadly speaking, Asian Americanists have seen little of value in labor history and labor historians have been blind to the decentering model that Asian Americans present to them. Both have either subsumed or marginalized the "story" to one degree or another and with unfortunate consequences for all. But there is hope. I firmly believe that a separately defined Asian American labor history holds great potential because it stands in an interstitial space.[6] A brief glimpse at the historical trajectories of Asian American Studies, labor history, and American history suggests how and why that space emerged. Once that space has been "named," it becomes easier to see what value and role Asian American labor history can play.

Crises and Emergence

Asian American Studies began in crisis, matured in crisis, and continues to grow in crisis. At the risk of oversimplifying a complicated story and telling it to an audience that already knows it well, sketching out the development of Asian American Studies reveals how it might be linked to other areas of scholarly endeavor, especially labor history. In the late 1960s and early 1970s, the Asian American movement spawned the first significant inclusion of Asian American topics in academe.[7] Asian American students and activists demanded relevant histories, literatures, and social analyses. These they wanted taught in colleges and universities. Through the new curricula, the proponents of Asian American Studies hoped to change the political discourse about race and power in American society. At least some institutions heeded those calls and a new generation of Asian Americanists created new courses and published new studies. Much of the effort focused on reconstructing what Asian Americans themselves had done historically and contemporarily rather than just focus on what had been done to them, though highlighting oppression and injustice remained important political tools. *Amerasia Journal* emerged as the primary site for the articulation of the struggle as well as some of the internal tensions. Shortly thereafter, a handful of sociology and history journals began to publish articles related to Asian American experiences, too, and, with the growth of *Amerasia,* marked the emergence of Asian American scholarship.[8]

At least in the historical literature within Asian American Studies, because many nineteenth-century Asian Americans had migrated in international labor markets, the writings produced often revealed the lives of workers.[9] In spite of the focus on laborers, no significant or sustained connections between established labor historians and Asian American studies emerged. With the exception of authors like Alexander Saxton and Herbert Hill, most labor historians continued much earlier trends of either ignoring Asian American labor or blaming Asian immigrant workers for degrading "American" labor, especially organized labor.[10] Understandably, Asian Americanists found little of relevance in the labor history's focus on organized labor. The fact that unions had their own dark histories of exclusion, sometimes even gaining power at the expense of Asian Americans, made any tight association nearly unbearable.

The focus on Asian American working lives might have provided a "logical" scholarly link to labor history and built important academic and political coalitions. Instead, Asian Americanists read hostility and disinterest from labor and labor historians and expended their scholarly efforts locating and examining Asian American communities and the lives of individuals therein.[11] Those historical and sociological studies formed an important base of information and proved helpful to scholars seeking legitimacy within academe during the establishment of Asian American Studies programs and centers. These efforts to recapture community histories, to understand what Asian Americans have done, and to build programs within academic institutions, although still incomplete, continue to the present.

By the mid-1970s, a new crisis emerged. In order to secure a place for Asian American Studies in academe—by obtaining and then retaining tenure-track positions in traditional departments as well as newly created programs and centers—Asian Americanists had to "produce" works recognizable to those in an institution that had for decades denied them entry and legitimacy. What had started as a drive to serve "the community" quickly got mired in the reality of what academic bureaucrats demanded as "real scholarship."[12] To their credit, Asian Americanists produced on both fronts but their efforts to satisfy two very different agendas contributed to a growing rift between an academic "intelligentsia" and a vocal body of political activists. The former often found itself in the "publish or perish" conundrum, while the latter sought to create *an* Asian American identity for political and social action. By the 1970s, it was increasingly clear that not only were there many different Asian American communities but also that their interests were often distinct and sometimes in conflict with each other. As valuable as a panethnic Asian American identity might be, it was not easy to create or maintain.[13]

Asian Americanists were not alone in their difficult circumstances, for a similar tension between serving academe and the public wracked labor historians, too. In the late 1960s and 1970s, the New Left's focus on conflict rather than consensus in American society gave labor history a vigor it had lacked prior to that time.[14] Flowing from the belief that top-down institutional histories of unions did not reflect working-class lives, some labor historians responded in a fashion much like Asian Americanists and moved into community studies. Joined by others dissatisfied with the grand celebratory narratives of inexorable American progress toward "good" liberal ends, these were the practitioners of the "new social history."[15] As a group, they eschewed broad generalizations and argued that only by uncovering the specific and previously hidden or ignored details of various communities could the basic building blocks of a new historical analysis emerge. By the mid-1980s, however, a growing number of historians (led in some cases by labor historians) called for the injection of politics back into these community studies and asked how studies of isolated communities forwarded the political agenda of the present in any fashion.[16] They feared the loss of political connections to working-class lives in ways very similar to those expressed by Asian Americanists who worried that the drive to institutionalize Asian American Studies in academe watered down its connections to the politics of daily life in Asian American communities. For both areas of study, this tension between serving curricular and community ends continues to the present and, for Asian American Studies in particular, gets overlaid on top of the earlier desires to demonstrate an Asian American presence in American society.

The renewed focus on "community" politics pushed scholars to think more carefully about how they characterized and categorized people. Of course, the people examined by academics knew at least intuitively and often explicitly how contingent and ill-fitting categories of race (Asian American) or class (workers) could be. No matter whether they were immigrants, workers, or both, they identified with their extended families or their emigrant district and national origins, perhaps more often than they did with the broader categories of Asian American or working class. This did not mean that people could not or did not hold individual and group identities rooted in class or race, but rather that their identities were always situational and relational, always contingent.[17]

In academe, the people engaged in ethnic and racial studies as well as working-class history were among the vanguard of those whose works revealed that categories of analysis such as race, ethnicity, class, and gender were all social constructions. They were among those whose works fed into the emergence of cultural studies because their studies examined situations in which colonialism, imperialism, and coercion were most apparent and broadly recognized. Given those shared interests one might assume that Asian Americanists and labor historians could find common ground. Instead, the growth of cultural studies has generated new splits among and between Asian Americanists and labor historians. It is ironic that people from both these areas of study had been among the first to call earlier metanarratives of history into question. In the late 1980s and through the 1990s, the unraveling of what many had held to be essential categories brought strained results and forced some into absolute corners where they defend the primacy of race as a "deep culture" or class as a function of "real" material conditions.[18]

Asian American Labor History: Interstitial Studies

Rather than assert the primacy of one category of analysis over another or agonize about the "loss of history" and the "descent into discourse" that this latest crisis has generated, it is more instructive to see what openings it has provided. While I cannot speak to the broad questions it raises for academic enterprises,[19] much less for Asian American Studies, history, or labor history,[20] in this essay I do believe that Asian American labor history can draw on existing studies and embrace the changes of the last three decades.

Directly engaging a separate Asian American labor history demands, not just bringing Asian American Studies and labor history together, it requires connecting various "projects" that are in conflict with each other over the purpose and conceptualization of their efforts as well as how they might periodize their respective histories. Immigration historians have been telling Americans for years that immigrants built America, that this is a nation of immigrants. Given this paradigm, Asian Americans have been hard pressed to overcome the notion that peoples of Asian ancestry have been a part of the building of America; that Asian Americans are not sojourners or "perpetual foreigners" simply waiting for the right time to "go home."[21] The Cold War and post-Cold War ethos that Western democracy and market capitalism represent the zenith of human progress further contributes to the alienation of class-conscious workers from that narrative. The nation-of-immigrants metanarrative thus holds little room for those who by their actions, or by actions attributed to them, question the rise of the American nation by daring to return "home" or by standing in opposition to the unfettered growth of capitalism. This is a seductive narrative, as seductive as its forerunner the frontier thesis, which also had no real place for Asian Americans or for labor. [22]

Alongside the nation-of-immigrants mythos stands a second pervasive notion that the American story is an "American Dilemma" between open democratic ideals (social and political) and very real racial oppression.[23] Indeed, as astute observers like W.E.B. Dubois have noted, race was a central theme in the twentieth century. One problem of many with the "American Dilemma" thesis, at least as it is often practiced and articulated, is that it has been rendered as a black-white binary. In it there is really no room for Asian Americans (or Native Americans, Mexican Americans, or any other group however constituted) other than as bit players in that larger drama. Thus one can see the emergence of the "model minority" thesis in the postwar epoch as a tool in those debates, but nothing substantive about Asian Americans outside that position or regarding earlier periods. Like the nation-of-immigrants, the black-white paradigm has no distinct place for Asian Americans, much less for labor history.

Being caught up in projects of claiming legitimate space in American society and challenging hegemonic narratives is entirely understandable and is certainly not the sole province of Asian Americanists. Labor historians have been so enmeshed in their projects of finding class consciousness and a redeemable union movement, and in searching for a class consciousness that can tear down the wall of racial discrimination against African Americans, that they have scarcely noticed Asian Americans.[24]

While difficult to counter, metanarratives can be attacked, even rebuilt, in meaningful ways.[25] Gary Okihiro, in a forthcoming book, argues that the Asian American subject in American history destabilizes the comfortable binary of black or white, the East (North/South) and West regional split in the United States, and the citizen-noncitizen dichotomy.[26] He points out that Asian Americans are central to understanding American history. In doing so, he makes a case for hybridity and multiplicity, and he recognizes difference while embracing the possibility of common ground. This is an optimistic vision. In it, Okihiro provides a model for all to have social space in "American History." He challenges the nation-of-immigrants narrative because his model does not project a unified "American" as an end result or a pluralism devoid of the exercise of power among the various groups so typical of much "multicultural" rhetoric of the present.

On a related, but somewhat different line of argument, Lisa Lowe argues that the racialization of Asian Americans is situated "within the context of national state institutions and the international forces of global economy" and is a site of a "'state of emergency.'"[27] Constituted by others as "not belonging" forces Asian Americans to live transnational lives whether or not it is how they live their daily lives. This factor, coupled with the rise of global capitalism, according to Lowe, generates particular political formations and requires "new modes of organizing and struggling" at each turn.[28] Looking at and for an Asian American labor history—and by that I mean the history of how peoples of Asian ancestry, be they immigrants or descendants of those immigrants, organized their working lives—helps to reconstitute those modes of organization and struggle. It assists in measuring agency against structure. It helps to reconfigure understandings of racialization, transnational networks, and the politics of liberation.

Yet this task is made no easier by three recent developments in the historiography of American labor represented in the widely acclaimed and important works of Peter Way and Lizabeth Cohen as well as by the recent calls for an institutional synthesis in labor history. Peter Way's corrective to what he perceives as too much focus on the agency of workers, though valuable, remains troubling.[29] In his examination of early nineteenth-century canal workers, Way does not dispute that workers had cultures or some semblance of class consciousness. Instead, he rightly chides the unquestioned celebration of workers' cultures and assumptions of nearly unlimited agency in many of the New Social History's studies. His skepticism about the meaningfulness of workers' resistance and scholars' assumptions that it was ubiquitous and effective is useful. But his thesis that capitalism easily overwhelmed workers' fragmented cultures together with any class consciousness is an over-corrective. It threatens to take us back to the days of culture-less drones in factories and fields, of culture-laden but still nameless, faceless, and powerless coolies whose differences mattered not in the least.[30]

Lizabeth Cohen is linked to Way by her attention to the impact of capitalism on workers and immigrants. With a more nuanced and measured examination of how various cultures confronting twentieth-century consumer capitalism, she demonstrates the uneven and gradual undermining of ethnicity and community cultures.[31] She finds that cultures affected how workers engaged capitalism and that they did so selectively. In her final analysis, she leaves readers with the argument that the culture of consumer capitalism in the United States eventually assimilated and subsumed or incorporated immigrants' cultures, leaving unions the most powerful remaining institution through which workers and immigrants could confront capitalism.

As provocative as Cohen's argument is, it falls woefully short on at least two counts. First, Cohen only hints at the ways in which the interaction of race and capitalism generated an outcome different than that of ethnicity and capitalism. Recent work by George Lipsitz on "the possessive investment in whiteness" in combination with the study of Southern and Eastern European immigrants as "in-between peoples" by James R. Barrett and David Roediger suggest how whiteness and capitalism conjoin in systematic and institutionalized ways to perpetuate oppression based on race.[32] Rather than subsume or obliterate race, consumer capitalism has perpetuated it as a meaningful, if painful, social category.[33] As Michael Omi and Howard Winant point out, most groups are left to fight for position amongst each other and *below* whites in this racialized capitalist society.[34] Neil Foley's study of African Americans, Mexican Americans, and poor whites in south Texas offers one example of how to negotiate issues of race, class, and gender, how to avoid the "binarism trap," and how to see capitalism as affecting social relations while not forcing all "workers" into one tight-fitting mold.[35] Cohen's focus on the insidious, assimilative nature of consumer capitalism and privileging of unions as a primary vehicle for response to it is important, but it underplays the centrality of race in supporting unions and consumer capitalism as a feature of white privilege.[36]

Second, Cohen's recreation of workers and immigrants lives as existing only in the United States makes it very difficult for her to trace out any transnational influences. While it is relatively "easy" to see how immigrants' lives and perspectives remain "transnational,"[37] literature in African American studies suggests fruitful avenues for pursuing how subsequent generations continue to see their lives in transnational perspectives by linking their experiences with anti-colonial movements overseas. For example, in the twentieth century, African Americans saw Ethiopia's struggle for independence as linked to their lives on very real as well as symbolic levels.[38] While Asian Americanists *have* noted this for immigrant generations, the literature is much less developed for subsequent generations especially in the context of work.[39] Moreover, scholars in Asian Studies still resist accepting Asian American Studies as a legitimate field and not "really" Asian, while Asian Americanists get caught up in claiming a legitimate space in the United States. Likewise, labor historians have eyes only for Europe and simply neglect Asia as anything more than some continually recast "yellow peril" for organized labor. International components of racialized identities, whether those be ascribed or taken up by those populations, remain vital long after the first generation's arrival. Race, and racial nationalisms, continue to be constructed in light of the relationships between the United States and the ancestral homelands of emigrants.

Transnational labor markets of the immigrant and subsequent generations provide much of the conduit for these exchanges. In my own work in progress on Pacific maritime labor markets, I find that events like the Hong Kong General Strike of 1922 or the Philippines student unrest of the late 1920s and the early 1930s affected Asian American "community" politics and workers' frames of reference as well as their actions. The inroads of capitalism and imperialism created oppositional cultures that migrated back across the Pacific via transnational labor markets.[40] U.S. consumer markets did not always define "culture" for Asian Americans. Those authors who choose to limit their focus on how capitalism transforms any group of workers' lives to a very narrow locale and who do not trace out these transnational influences will see only a portion of the processes at work. This is not just the story of assimilative U.S. capitalism and consumer culture.

Perhaps even more disturbing than these formulations of the ubiquitous power of capitalism is the recent call among some labor historians for a new institutional synthesis by focusing on the formation and maintenance of unions.[41] The desire to find broad implications for labor studies and to move away from the fragmentation so apparent in the "New Social History" is understandable. Giving primacy to class, to white male organizations, to "national" narratives threatens emergent hybrid narratives of history at a critical moment. Falling back on a flawed narrative that does not "see" race and gender is troublesome.[42] At the same time, the frustration with recovering detail for detail's sake by proponents of synthesis is justified. Details in and of themselves carry little meaning. We must, as cultural historian Phil Deloria recently observed, strive toward finding "new" detail and meanings at the same time.[43] We must use fields like Asian American labor history to investigate the ways in which the lived lives of people interact with, and sometimes against, larger structures of power.

What Would an Asian American History Look Like? Periodization and Conceptualization

As Alexander Saxton once astutely and gently reminded me, "Periodization follows conceptualization."[44] I admit to not fully understanding his comment at the time. Now, it makes more sense to me. At present, historians of Asian America follow the "immigrant" paradigm and punctuate and periodize that history using sequential waves of migration and successive immigration exclusions or openings. Open immigration prior to the 1880s, repeated exclusions between the 1880s and the 1920s, several long decades of restrictive immigration and wartime internment then precede the epoch of new openings after 1965. In the most recent time frame, "old" Asian American immigrant groups have added to their numbers through renewed migration streams and a host of "new" Asians and Pacific Islanders have begun to surpass the earlier migrants in number and influence.

Historians of American labor tend to see the world of nineteenth-century artisans under assault and decay with the "fall of the house of labor" sometime during the 1920s. In the 1930s, industrial unionism surges forward, splinters, and then is hamstrung by the forces of anti-communism in the 1950s. By the 1970s, deindustrialization catches the labor movement unawares. Up through the 1990s, the labor movement—always the focus of labor history syntheses—plays a game of catch-up to meet the needs of its many new immigrant workers, to the scores of women now in its ranks, and to emergence of "new" sectors of work.[45]

Whether or not these rough periodizations "work" for Asian American labor history remains to be seen. It may work fine, but in my recent and still unpublished attempts to understand Filipino labor history, for example, the traditional overlay of successive waves of immigration or various exclusions, while important, does not fully capture the complexities.[46] In the maritime and dock work of the nineteenth and early twentieth century, for example, Asian Americans, African Americans, and European Americans—immigrants and the American-born—vie with each other for position and control of the labor markets long after exclusion of respective Asian Americans. African Americans leverage citizenship to gain control especially at the moment of the "house of labor" struggles in the 1920s and early 1930s. At the same time, European Americans use citizenship to bludgeon Asians, especially Chinese and Filipinos, out of the labor market. This research forces me to add the separate labor histories of diverse peoples—Chinese, Filipinos, African Americans—in ways that threaten to make an entirely different periodization than that put forward by either Asian American Studies or labor historians. While we can use the current periodizations in Asian American Studies and labor history to explain much, it is not yet the time to rebuild a narrative structure for Asian American Labor History based on that alone. I suspect that the few of us who might label ourselves "Asian American labor historians" do not want to do it alone. In three decades of Asian American Studies and an equal time frame for the "New" labor and social history, one has not yet emerged. Judging by the dissertations now nearing completion, those about to be or just recently published, and new studies in progress by established scholars, I believe we soon will have much more to discuss about formulating Asian American labor history as a field of research, study, and teaching.[47] For now, it would be presumptuous and premature to offer a periodization. Aside from the fact that it would undoubtedly be "wrong"—we have much more basic research to do—it would also fly against the sage advice Alex Saxton offered. For now, let us proceed with the conceptualization while we amass the details.

What Should an Asian American Labor History Look Like?

If Asian American labor history was a consciously constructed field of study, it could decenter nationalist narratives and deflect the institutional imperative. Latin American labor historian Charles Berhquist offers a cogent and compelling argument for internationalizing labor history that would serve any attempt to create an Asian American labor history well.[48] Berhquist argues that control, gender, globalism, and "postmodernism" should be key elements for labor historians. By focusing their studies on the struggle for control of work places and many different levels of politics, Berhquist holds that labor historians can illuminate how the motives of diverse groups are linked. Those instances of unity, not only reveal coalition politics, but also are sites of a democracy that are not subservient to capitalism or the state (however the latter may be constructed).[49]

Gender analysis helps break down the dichotomies of productive and reproductive labor, or public and private spheres of action so often constructed by labor historians. Berhquist notes that labor history has focused "almost exclusively on work in the formal economy of patriarchal societies, and on the expressions of workers' experience, consciousness, and action."[50] But attention to gender should direct scholars to the ways in which households[51] mediate productive and reproductive labor. Gender analyses, he notes, also promise a means to examine the intersection of the work place with community mobilization.[52] For an Asian American labor history, connecting communities (however formed and maintained) and the workplace not only falls squarely within this model, but offers a means to alleviate tensions between academics and community activists and to maintain those important alliances.[53]

The globalization to which Berhquist refers speaks against the parochialism so common in American social history.[54] In spite of the fact that the world capitalist system is oppressive and coercive, it potentially connects workers and their struggles to each other. He urges labor historians to look for the ways in which workers create and maintain networks and organizations in this context. Thinking in global terms contributes, too, to understanding the ways in which "free labor. . .is inextricably bound up with coerced labor."[55] The traditional labor history focus on trade union development and white privilege, as a growing number of labor historians are recognizing, is thus linked to various colonial and imperialist acts.[56] Contesting that privilege thus takes on much greater meaning than what some have criticized as the "micropolitics of identity."[57]

Finally, Berhquist observes that labor history has been tied to the "masternarratives" of both Liberalism and Marxism. For Berhquist, "Postmodernism" (by which he means the discourse analysis of cultural studies) makes it possible to "discover and decenter the social bias in hegemonic discourse and legitimize understandings of the past generated by groups of the oppressed."[58] Berhquist does not mean to promote a relativist position or to argue that all knowledge or any reality is "knowable" only on an individual basis. Instead, he contends that labor history still needs to expose oppression and to pinpoint progress in history toward "good," democratic[59] ends such as those movements where workers reap the full benefits of their labors.

Berhquist's call to action is important because it reflects the direction that some of the best of American labor history is moving. Among many, the works of Elizabeth Faue, Neil Foley, Robin Kelley, Earl Lewis, David Roediger, Dana Frank, and Elizabeth Jameson, while each markedly different in scope and focus, demonstrate how labor history can be pursued with great reward in just the arenas Berhquist outlines.[60] Furthermore, Asian American Studies has been moving in similar directions. Attention to coalition politics, antiracist struggles, and the maintenance of a panethnic identity stand close to the idea of "control."[61] Asian Americanists also have forcefully engaged the issues of gender in a fashion similar to that which Berhquist suggests, even if much more waits to be done.[62] Likewise, globalism is not a new theme to Asian American history; it is a perennial question and one that continues to call for attention. The influence of discourse analysis on Asian American Studies has been good, especially when it does not deny the very real material conditions under which many people suffer and relatively few benefit. In the past decade, it has not created a quagmire of relativist positions, but instead has helped illuminate Asian American Studies as a "project" bent on exposing a hegemonic order and seeking ways to generate new discourses to counter oppression. With the goals and possibilities of labor history and Asian American Studies so close and similar to each other, the links between the two beg for attention. Thinking of Asian American labor history as a systematic endeavor and not as some by-product of Asian American Studies or as the story of yet one more group of "others" in labor history, promises to build mutually productive bridges between those heretofore separate fields. Its focus on workplaces promises to link public and private lives through those sites where people interact with one another and where lines of power and authority are often most painfully visible.

Notes

1. Cliff Cheng, "Are Asian American Employees a Model Minority or Just a Minority?" *The Journal of Applied Behavioral Sciences* 33: 3 (1997), 277-290, provides a useful review of the literature surrounding the "Model Minority Thesis."

2. This is reminiscent of the now famous statement that American Indians are generally treated as an episode rather than as peoples in syntheses of American History.

3. Perhaps Latino/as are the only group that bears this onus to the same degree as Asian Americans.

4. I review the historiography of Asian American labor in "Asian American Labor and Historical Interpretation," *Labor History* 35:4 (1994), 524-546

5. *Ibid.*

6. I admit to being fascinated and influenced by, as well as frustrated with, Homi K. Bhabha, *The Location of Culture* (London and New York: Routledge, 1994), and readers will no doubt recognize those areas in this essay.

7. William Wei, *The Asian American Movement* (Philadelphia: Temple University Press, 1993), provides a good introduction to this topic, as does Keith Osajima, "Pedagogical Considerations in Asian American Studies," *Journal of Asian American Studies* 1:3 (1998), 269-282.

8. I have not explored this assertion systematically, but even a quick glance at the tables of contents in regional history journals such as *Western Historical Quarterly* and *Pacific Historical Review* reveals a growing willingness to consider Asian American history as a part of the "regular" scholarly discourse.

9. See Friday, "Asian American Labor and Historical Interpretation."

10. Alexander Saxton, *The Indispensable Enemy: Labor and the Anti-Chinese Movement in California* (Berkeley: University of California Press, 1971); and Herbert Hill, "Anti-Oriental Agitation and the Rise of Working-Class Racism," *Society* 10:2 (1973), 43-54. The literature blaming Asian American labor for degrading "American" labor took at face value the arguments many in organized labor put forward. Thus for many years, history and historiography were closely entwined. Some recent scholarship seeks to extend and revise the earlier literature. For examples, see Carlos A. Schwantes, "From Anti-Chinese Agitation to Reform Politics: The Legacy of the Knights of Labor in

Washington and the Pacific Northwest," *Pacific Northwest Quarterly* 88:4 (1997), 174-184; and Chris Friday, "'There are Chinese and there are Chinese': An Illustrated Essay and Review of *This Coming Man*," *Pacific Northwest Quarterly* 89:2 (1998), 98-104. Other authors have focused on women's roles and activities to chart out new territories. See Margaret K. Holden, "Gender and Protest Ideology: Sue Ross Keenan and the Oregon Anti-Chinese Movement," *Western Legal History* 7:2 (1994), 222-243; Martha Mabie Gardner, "Working on White Womanhood: White Working Women in the San Francisco Anti-Chinese Movement, 1877-1890," *Journal of Social History* 33:1 (1999), 73-95; and Constance Backhouse, "The White Women's Labor Laws: Anti-Chinese Racism in Early Twentieth-Century Canada," *Law and History Review* 14:2 (1996), 315-368.

11. Hyung-chan Kim, ed., *Asian American Studies: An Annotated Bibliography and Research Guide* (New York: Greenwood Press, 1989), provides a thorough overview of the literature published up to the mid-1980s. The tendency to essentialize communities has created problems. Historians need to pay more attention to "community" as historical phenomena.

12. Don Nakanishi's tenure battle at UCLA during the last half of the 1980s is perhaps the most widely known case that illustrates the difficulties of negotiating "academic" and "community" concerns. See Larry Gordon, "Asian-American Wins Fight for Tenure at UCLA," *Los Ángeles Times*, May 26, 1989; and Don T. Nakanishi, "Linkages and Boundaries: Twenty-five Years of Asian American Studies," *Amerasia Journal* 21:3 (1995/1996).

13. Asian American is a recently constructed and problematic social category. But as troublesome as the label may be in the ways it differentiates peoples of some Asian or Pacific Islander ancestry as "perpetual foreigners," and simultaneously obscures very real differences among peoples, it remains a useful term to employ. The "lumping" or ascriptive, non-agentive components of identity have played no small part in identity formation and the reception of Asian immigrants and their descendents in American society. Labeled as Asian Americans, Asiatics, Orientals, immigrants, or sojourners, these markers of difference from the naturalized norm of white, citizen, settler, or American, people who migrated from Asia and the Pacific as well as their descendants in the United States had to contend with being lumped together even as they claimed to be distinctive from other migrants or "minorities" in order to claim social and legal space in American society. Thus South Asians might claim Aryan or Caucasian descent, Chinese might argue a dual nationalism in opposition to as singular Japanese nationalism in World War II, or Filipinos might argue that theirs was the only "Christian" country in all of Asia in order to maneuver for better position in American society. All were still "non-white" even if "non-black." Their position between whiteness and blackness—the principle narrative of race in American society—not only destabilized racialization in American thought, it also means that the category is useful as an organizing

concept when applied to the past so long as one does not assume that there really was *an* Asian American identity to be had prior to the 1960s in spite of brief moments of cross-ethnic solidarity.

14. Eric Arneson, "Crusades Against Crisis: A View from the United States on the 'Rank-and-File' Critique and other Catalogues of Labour History's Alleged Ills," *International Review of Social History* 35 (1990), 110.

15. *Ibid.*, 112; Richard Price, "The Future of British Labour History," *International Review of Social History* 36 (1991), 250.

16. Sean Wilentz "Land, Labor, and Politics in the Age of Jackson," *Reviews in American History* 14:2 (1986), 200-209.

17. This is not to argue that material conditions do not matter, for they do, as does the institutionalization of racism. For an excellent discussion of the latter, see Eduardo Bonilla-Silva, "The New Racism: Racial Structure in the United States, 1960s-1990s," in *Race, Ethnicity, and Nationality in the United States: Toward the Twenty-first Century*, ed. Paul Wong (Boulder: Westview Press, 1999). Joan Wallach Scott, *Gender and the Politics of History* (New York: Columbia University Press, 1988), forcefully calls historians to task on the issue of gender.

18. Herbert Hill, "The Problem of Race in American History," *Reviews in American History* 24:2 (1996), 189-208, harshly criticizes labor historians such as Eric Arneson for privileging class over race and for making the former an essential category. For responses to such arguments, see Price, "Future of British Labour History," 250; Arneson, " Crusades Against Crisis," 115-116; and Eric Arneson, "Race, Party, and Packinghouse Exceptionalism," *Labor History* 40:2 (1999), 207-213.

     This debate is one of the more prominent ones at the conjunction of race and labor studies and is interestingly linked to issues raised in the 1995 Association for Asian American Studies (some of which appeared in *Amerasia Journal* 21:1-2 [1995]). This debate amply demonstrates the tensions wrought by cultural studies on the more traditional fields of history, sociology, and political science within Asian American Studies. The ascension of Asian American literary studies and an "Asian American" literature (some would even argue canon) imposed new questions and called to question the neat essentializations frequent in many earlier studies. For a discussion of "deep culture" see Paul Wong, Meera Manvi, and Takeo Hirota, "Asiacentrism and Asian American Studies?" *Amerasia Journal* 21:1-2 (1995), 137-147.

19. Bhabha, *Location of Culture*, 19-40, in his chapter "Commitment to Theory," defends the academic pursuit of topics as a form of political engagement.

20. Larua L. Frader, "Dissent over Discourse: Labor History, Gender, and the Linguistic Turn," *History and Theory* 34:3 (1995), 213-231, provides a helpful discussion.

21. Adam McKeown, "Transnational Chinese Families and Chinese Exclusion, 1875-1943," *Journal of American Ethnic History* 18:2 (1999), 73-110, complains that the effort to challenge this notion makes it

nearly impossible to recognize the transnational lives of Asian immigrants and difficult to see the roles that women played in emigration. In terms of women, questions need to be redirected from "why were there so few Asian immigrant women (with the notable exception of Japanese)" to "how did the prolonged absence of men affect women, children, and families in the sending country." See Maruja M.B. Asis in *Asian and Pacific Migration Journal* 3:4 (1994), 641, in which she notes that the focus on immigrant women has obscured women's homeland roles in immigration for far too long.

22. For intriguing discussions of the relationship between the Frontier and Asian American Studies, see Shirley Hune, "Introduction: Pacific Migration Defined by American Historians and Social Theorists up to the 1960s," in *Asian American Studies: An Annotated Bibliography and Research Guide*, ed. Hyung-chan Kim (New York: Greenwood Press, 1989), esp. 23-28; and Sucheng Chan, "Western American Historiography and Peoples of Color," in *Peoples of Color in the American West*, ed., Sucheng Chan, Douglas Henry Daniels, Mario T. García, and Terry P. Wilson (Lexington, Massachusetts: D.C. Heath and Company, 1994), 1-14.

23. George J. Sanchez, "Race, Nation, and Culture in Recent Immigration Studies," *Journal of American Ethnic History* 18:4 (1999), 66-84, provides an insightful discussion of the various metanarratives and links Latino/Latina history and Asian American history to immigration history more generally and in a fashion that pushes immigration historians toward a more thoughtful consideration of race than they have heretofore attempted in any systematic fashion. Donna R. Gabbaccia, "Is Everywhere Nowhere? Nomads, Nations, and the Immigrant Paradigm of United States History," *Journal of American History* 86:3 (1999), 1115-1134, critiques the ways in which historiography has contributed to constructions of "nation" through the study of global Italian migrations. Also see Osajima, "Pedagogical Considerations"; and Yen Le Espiritu, "Colonial Oppression, Labour, Importation, and Group Formation: Filipinos in the United States," *Ethnic and Racial Studies* 19:1 (1996), 29-48.

24. Friday, "Asian American Labor and Historical Interpretations"; Edna Bonacich, "Editorial Forum: Reflections on Asian American Labor," *Amerasia Journal* 18:1 (1992), xxiii-xxiv; and Sucheng Chan, "Asian American Labor History," *Radical History Review* 63 (1995), 174-188, reviews Gary Y. Okihiro, *Cane Fires: The Anti-Japanese Movement in Hawaii, 1865-1945* (Philadelphia: Temple University Press, 1991), Renqiu Yu, *To Save China, to Save Ourselves: The Chinese Hand Laundry Alliance of New York* (Philadelphia: Temple University Press, 1992), and Chris Friday, *Organizing Asian American Labor: The Pacific Coast Canned-Salmon Industry, 1870-1942* (Philadelphia: Temple University Press, 1994). In spite of the title of that review, these works originate from Asian American Studies, not labor history quarters.

25. The "project" need not simply be one of unraveling the existing metanarrative(s), or as one colleague recently put it: "The metanarrative of tearing apart the metanarrative." Historians build narratives,

but they must do so with more self-reflection than they have to present.

26. Gary Okihiro, *Common Ground: Reimagining American History* (Princeton, forthcoming). Okihiro provocatively titled an early draft of the manuscript "American History" which is fitting, if challenging. Okihiro argues that "social constructions. . .serve particular purposes and functions for specific relations, societies, and times." Using chapters arranged thematically on space (region, nation, and the East-West binary) he employs the Asian and Asian American subject not only to decenter simplistic binaries, but also to unravel and expose the "projects" that created them. Also see Gary Y. Okihiro, *Margins and Mainstreams: Asians in American History and Culture* (Seattle: University of Washington Press, 1994).

27. Lisa Lowe, *Immigrant Acts: On Asian American Cultural Politics* (Durham: Duke University Press, 1996), 174.

28. *Ibid.*, 175.

29. Peter Way, *Common Labor: Workers and the Digging of North American Canals, 1780-1860* (Baltimore: Johns Hopkins University Press, 1997).

30. Sherry B. Ortner, "Resistance and the Problem of Ethnographic Refusal," *Comparative Study of Society and History* 37:1 (1995), 173-193, offers an extremely useful discussion of how to conceptualize resistance.

31. Lizabeth Cohen, *Making a New Deal: Industrial Workers in Chicago, 1919-1939* (Cambridge: Cambridge University Press, 1991).

32. George Lipsitz, *The Possessive Investment in Whiteness: How White People Profit from Identity Politics* (Philadelphia: Temple University Press, 1998); and James R. Barrett and David Roediger, "Inbetween Peoples: Race, Nationality and the 'New Immigrant' Working Class," *Journal of American Ethnic History* 16:3 (1997), 3-44.

33. Also see Bonilla-Silva, "The New Racism."

34. Michael Omi and Howard A. Winant, *Racial Formation in the United States: 1960-1990,* 2nd ed. (New York: Routledge, 1994).

35. Neil Foley, *The White Scourge: Mexicans, Blacks, and Poor Whites in the Cotton Culture of Central Texas* (Berkeley: University of California Press, 1999).

36. Elizabeth Faue, *Community of Suffering and Struggle: Women, Men, and the Labor Movement in Minneapolis, 1915-1945* (Chapel Hill: University of North Carolina Press, 1991), is another significant study of the 1990s which deserves careful consideration. Faue offers the important argument that organized labor had, at specific moments, an opportunity to embrace a community focus, most often called for by women, but that at times of crisis organized labor fell back on patriarchy and privileged men's work at the job site. By the 1940s this left unions with a history, and increasingly a historiography, that was institutional and male. By implication, it was also largely white. Faue's study points to the need to consider race and unionization much as she has focused on gender.

37. Michael P. Hanagan, "Labor History and the New Migration History: A Review Essay," *International Labor and Working Class History* 54 (Fall 1998), 57-79, provides a helpful discussion of how labor historians need to understand the ways in which transnational politics, labor markets, and social networks are all embedded in larger social structures created under global capitalism and imperialism. These issues remain an important aspect of understanding Asian American Studies, which in much of the newer literature, does a better job of considering gender than many labor and immigration histories that focus on European migration streams. For examples, see Lowe, *Immigrant Acts* along with discussions by Delia Aguilar San Juan, "The Philippine Century: Urgent Feminist Questions," *Amerasia Journal* 24:3 (1998), 27-35; and Anne E. Lacsamana, "Academic Imperialism and the Limits of Postmoderist Discourse: An Examination of Nicole Constable's *Maid to Order in Hong Kong: Stories of Filipina Workers*," *ibid.*, 37-42.

38. Gail Plummer, *Rising Wind: Black Americans and U.S. Foreign Affairs, 1935-1960* (Chapel Hill: University of North Carolina Press, 1996); Winston James, *Holding Aloft the Banner of Ethiopia: Caribbean Radicalism in America* (London and New York: 1998); and Penny M. Von Eschen, *Race Against Empire: Black Americans and Anticolonialism, 1937-1957* (Ithaca: Cornell University Press, 1997), extend the understanding of a "Black Atlantic" outlined by Paul Gilroy, *The Black Atlantic: Modernity and Double Consciousness* (London and New York: Verso, 1993). Also see Robin D. G. Kelley "'But a local phase of a world problem': Black History's Global Vision, 1883-1950," *The Journal of American History* 86:33 (1999), 1045-1077.

39. For examples, see Sucheng Chan, "European and Asian Immigration into the United States in Comparative Perspective, 1820s to 1920s," in *Immigration Reconsidered: History, Sociology, and Politics,* ed. Virginia Yans-McLaughlin (New York: Oxford University Press, 1990), esp. 47-60; L. Eve Armentrout Ma, *Revolutionaries, Monarchists, and Chinatowns: Chinese Politics in the Americas and the 1911 Revolution* (Honolulu: University of Hawaii Press, 1990); and Nancy Abelmann and John Lie, *Blue Dreams: Korean Americans and the Los Angeles Riots* (Cambridge, Massachusetts: Harvard University Press, 1995). For studies that give attention to workers more directly and to subsequent generations, see Yuji Ichioka, "Japanese Immigrant Nationalism, the Issei, and the Sino-Japanese War, 1937-1941," *California History* 69:3 (1990), 260-275; idem, "An Instance of Private Japanese Diplomacy: Suzuki Bunji, Organized American Labor, and Japanese Immigrant Workers, 1915-1916," *Amerasia Journal* 10:1 (1983), 1-22; idem, "A Buried Past: Early Issei Socialists and the Japanese Community," *Amerasia Journal* 1:2 (1971), 1-25; Judy Yung, *Unbound Feet: A Social History of Chinese Women in San Francisco* (Berkeley: University of California Press, 1995); and Him Mark Lai, "To Bring Forth a New China, to Build a Better America: The Chinese Marxist Left in America to the 1960s," *Chinese America: History and Perspectives* (1992), 3-82.

40. The literature on the 1905 Boycott, for example, suggests how trans-national oppositional cultures can emerge, even if in that case the merchants were the driving force. See Silas K.C. Geneson, "Cry Not in Vain: The Boycott of 1905," *Chinese America: History and Perspectives* (1997), 27-45; Delber L. McKee, "The Chinese Boycott of 1905-1906 Reconsidered: The Role of Chinese Americans," *Pacific Historical Review* 55:2 (1986), 165-191; and Shih-Shan H. Tsai, "Reaction to Exclusion: The Boycott of 1905 and Chinese National Awakening," *Historian* 39:1 (1976), 95-110.

41. Arneson, "Crusades Against Crisis," 122, attacks those calling for a new institutional labor history. Price, "Future of British Labour History," 91, calls for a focus on institutions, but wants to give attention to power struggles within them. Jerry Lee Lembke, "Labor History's 'Synthesis Debate': Sociological Interventions," *Science and Society* 59:2 (1995), 137-173, wants a synthesis of class relations and not the "micropolitics of identity" as he calls it. Joseph A. McCartin, "Industrial Unionism as Liberator or Leash? The Limits of 'rank-and-filism' in American Labor Historiography," *Journal of Social History* 31:3 (1998), 701-711, calls "rank and filism"—the focus on workers' agency (which is akin to community politics)—an interpretive *cul de sac* and wants to focus on the ways workers function within institutions.

42. For a rather cantankerous assessment of the "New Labor History," see Robert Zeiger, "Books that Didn't Influence Me," *Labor History* 40:2 (1999), 177-189.

43. Deloria made these comments in a session at the 1999 Western History Association Meeting in Portland, Oregon.

44. I had the good fortune to have Alex Saxton as the instructor in my first graduate seminar at UCLA in 1983. His patience with me and his abilities to guide seminar discussions have been a major influence in my own development. I owe him and a great many other faculty and students at UCLA in those years a huge intellectual debt.

45. Among the stronger studies are David Montgomery, *The Fall of the House of Labor: The Workplace, the State, and American Labor Activism, 1865-1925* (New York: Cambridge University Press, 1987); Dana Frank, *Purchasing Power: Consumer Organizing, Gender, and the Seattle Labor Movement, 1919-1929* (New York: Cambridge University Press, 1994); and Robert H. Zieger, *American Workers, American Unions, 1920-1985* (Baltimore: Johns Hopkins University Press, 1986).

46. "Color Lines, Citizenship, and Organized Labor: Asian Americans and African Americans in the Marine Cooks and Stewards Union, 1930 to 1950," in the session "Race, Ethnicity, and Organized Labor in Twentieth-Century America: Beyond Black and White," Association for the Study of Afro-American Life and History Annual Meeting, Charleston, South Carolina, October, 1996; "The Marine Cooks and Stewards Union on a Narrowing Path: Race, Gender, Work, and Politics in the Cold War Epoch," prepared as a paper for the 1996 Organization of American Historians Annual Meeting; expanded

as a public lecture for the Northwest Center for Comparative American Cultures and Race Relations, Rockefeller Humanities Lecture Series, Washington State University, April 1996; and "'Yellow' or 'White': What Color the Pacific? Race and Maritime Labor, 1880s-1920s," for the "Crossings" Symposium in honor of Alexander P. Saxton, UCLA Department of History and William Andrews Clark Memorial Library, Los Angeles, California, September 1998.

47. Among the emerging works are: Nayan Shah, "San Francisco's 'Chinatown': Race and the Cultural Politics of Public Health, 1854-1952," Ph.D. dissertation, University of Chicago, 1995; Linda Espana Maram, "Negotiating Identity: Youth, Gender, and Popular Culture in Little Manila, 1920s-1940s," Ph.D. dissertation, University of California, Los Angeles, 1996; Dorothy Fujita Rony, "'You Got to Move Like Hell': Trans-Pacific Colonialism and Filipino/a Seattle, 1919-1941," Ph.D. dissertation, Yale University, 1996; Catherine Ceniza Choy, "The Export of Womanpower: A Transnational History of Filipino Nurse Migration to the United States," Ph.D. dissertation, University of California, Los Angeles, 1998; and the work now underway by Josephine Fowler at the University of Minnesota who seeks to locate race *and* class in transnational perspective.

48. Charles Berhquist, "Labor History and Its Challenges: Confessions of a Latin Americanist," *American Historical Review* 98:3 (1993), 757-764. For a more recent discussion, see Marcel van der Linden, "Transnationalizing American Labor History," *Journal of American History* 86:3 (1999), 1078-1092, who articulates three modes of institutional transnational labor forms (1. solidarity with a labor movement outside the United States; 2. the United States labor movement as a model for those in other countries; and 3. international labor relations such as those between the movements in the United States and Canada where the two are nearly inseparable during certain time frames) and non-institutional transnational connections (1. "multiple border connections" in which people see their lives as fitting into several places while also falling outside those same places; 2. third party mediators such as the International Labor Organization; and 3. "material and symbolic practices" that create "multiple identities" for workers). Especially in the latter van der Linden argues that historians must move away from trying to give primacy to either race, class, or gender and instead should investigate how they have "shaped each other" (1092, citing David Thelan, "Making History and Making the United States," *Journal of American Studies* 32 [December 1998], 380). While van der Linden's points are helpful, they are not as encompassing as Berhquist's and while the former does give some attention to Asian Americans (mostly through attention to institutional relations to the labor movements in their respective ancestral homelands), his focus is still largely on the Atlantic world.

49. David Roediger, "What If Labor Were Not White and Male? Recentering Working-Class History and Reconsidering the Debate on Unions and Race," *International Working Class and Labor History* 51 (Spring 1997), 72-95, points out that a world where organized labor

and workplaces are not automatically white and male, we can begin to "see" a different past, we can begin to see a "postwhite labor history" which involves many different coalitions, some of them strikingly antiracist.

50. Berhquist, "Labor History and Its Challenges," 760. Also see Price, "Future of British Labour History," 252; and Sarah Deustch, "Gender, Labor History, and Chicano/a Ethnic Identity," *Frontiers* 14:2 (1994), 1-22.

51. Such households should not be constructed on heterosexist norms and should include a wide spectrum of arrangements including all male (or female) "bachelor" households, those made up of real and fictive kinship groups, and those that are transnational in nature.

52. Berhquist, "Labor History and Its Challenges," 760. Faue, *Community of Suffering*, details how much can be accomplished when the workplace and community are linked and how much is lost when they are not.

53. Some of the issues explored in *Amerasia Journal* 18:1 (1992) suggest how workers organizations, community concerns, and academic studies can be linked productively.

54. Berhquist, "Labor History and Its Challenges," 764; Donna R. Gabaccia, "Worker Internationalism and Italian Labor Migration, 1870-1914," *International Labor and Working Class History* 45 (Spring 1994), 63-79; Espiritu, "Colonial Oppression." Indeed, as Berhquist suggests, it is important to recognize the similarities and connections across various immigrant destinations. Legacies of colonialism and capitalist development link Canada, the United States, and Mexico along with other sites in Latin America. This is not an encouragement of "diaspora studies," which African American historian Clarence Walker points out too often "prettifies oppression" by celebrating the spread of peoples without recognizing the horrific coercion and oppression that accompanies that spread (Clarence Walker session comments at the 1996 Organization of American Historians meeting, San Francisco, California). For a broad discussion of human migration and coerced labor, see Philip D. Curtin, "Migration in the Tropical World," in *Immigration Reconsidered: History, Sociology, and Politics*, ed. Virginia Yans-McLaughlin (New York: Oxford University Press, 1990). John Kuo Wei Tchen, "A New Agenda for Chinese Americans," in *Origins and Destinations* (Los Angeles: Chinese Historical Society of Southern California and UCLA Asian American Studies Center, 1994), 13, draws attention to the relationship between free and coerced labor. Xinyang Wang, "Economic Opportunity, Artisan Leadership, and Immigrant Workers' Labor Militancy: Italian and Chinese Immigrant Workers in New York City, 1890-1970," *Labor History* 37:4 (1996), 480-499, attempts to link U.S. workers and their homelands but overdraws immutable cultural traits.

55. Berhquist, "Labor History and Its Challenges," 761. Eiichiro Azuma, "Racial Struggle, Immigrant Nationalism, and Ethnic Identity: Japanese and Filipinos in the California Delta, 1930-1941," *Pacific His-*

torical Review 67:2 (1998), 163-199, suggests that we must also pay attention to the overlapping sites of these transnational histories for there we can see how many different channels of power play out. Arleen de Vera, "Without Parallel: The Local 7 Deportation Cases, 1949-1955," *Amerasia Journal* 20:2 (1994), 1-25, demonstrates how precarious life for workers on the edge of transnationalism can be. For discussions of contemporary workers in transnational settings, see Paul Ong, Edna Bonacich, and Lucie Cheng, eds., *The New Asian Immigration in Los Angeles and Global Restructuring* (Philadelphia: Temple University Press, 1994); Ivan Light, Richard B. Bernard, and Rebecca Kim, "Immigrant Incorporation in the Garment Industry of Los Angeles," *International Migration Review* 33:1 (1999), 5-25; Mark Ellis and Richard Wright, "The Industrial Division of Labor among Immigrants and Internal Migrants to the Los Angeles Economy," *ibid.*, 26-54; Tania Das Gupta, "Political Economy of Gender, Race, and Class: Looking at South Asian Women in Canada," *Canadian Ethnic Studies* 26:1 (1994), 56-73; and Mark Moberg and J. Stephan Thomas, "Class Segmentation and Divided Labor: Asian Workers in the Gulf and Mexican Seafood Industry," *Ethnology* 32:1 (1993), 87-99.

56. Roediger, "What If Labor Were Not all White and Male?"; and Ronald Bailey, "The Other Side of Slavery: Black Labor, Cotton, and Textile Industrialization in Great Britain and the United States," *Agricultural History* 68:2(1994), 35-51. Unfortunately, those links are still portrayed as largely tied to Europe and an "Atlantic world" and seldom take into account anything stretching across the Pacific.

57. Lembke, "Synthesis Debate."

58. Berhquist, "Labor History and Its Challenges," 764.

59. Berhquist, in *ibid.*, endorses no particular state or political system when he uses the term democratic. For a discussion of democratic labor movements, see Glenn Omatsu, "To Our Readers: Asian American Workers and the Expansion of Democracy," *Amerasia Journal* 18:2 (1992), v-xix.

60. Faue, *Community of Suffering*; Foley, *White Scourge*; Elizabeth Jameson, *All that Glitters: Class, Conflict, and Community in Cripple Creek* (Urbana: University of Illinois Press, 1998); Dana Frank, *Purchasing Power: Consumer Organizing, Gender, and the Seattle Labor Movement, 1919-1929* (Cambridge: Cambridge University Press, 1994); Robin D.G. Kelley, *Race Rebels: Culture, Politics, and the Black Working Class* (New York: Free Press, 1996); David R. Roediger, *The Wages of Whiteness: Race and the Making of the American Working Class*, rev. ed. (London: Verso, 1999); David R. Roediger, *Towards the Abolition of Whiteness: Essays on Race, Politics, and Working Class History* (London: Verso, 1999); Earl Lewis, *In Their Own Interests: Race, Class, and Power in Twentieth-Century Norfolk, Virginia* (Berkeley: University of California Press, 1993).

61. Yen Le Espiritu, *Asian American Panethnicity: Bridging Institutions and Identities* (Philadelphia: Temple University Press, 1992); Karin Aguilar-San Juan, ed., *The State of Asian America: Activism and Resistance in the 1990s* (Boston: South End Press, 1994).

62. For telling examples, see Lisa Lowe, *Immigrant Acts*; Evelyn Nakano Glenn, "From Servitude to Service Work: Historical Continuities in the Racial Division of Paid Reproductive Labor," *Signs* 18:1 (1992), 1-43; Evelyn Nakano Glenn, "The Dialectics of Wage Work: Japanese-American Women and Domestic Service, 1905-1940," *Feminist Studies* 6:3 (1980), 432-471; and Asian Women United of California, eds., *Making Waves: An Anthology of Writings by and About Asian American Women* (Boston: Beacon Press, 1989).

III.

THE ALEXANDER SAXTON HISTORY AWARD ESSAY, 1999-2000

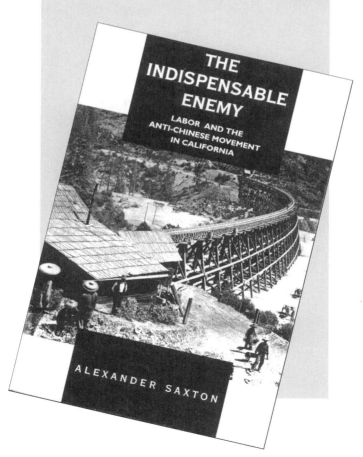

THE INDISPENSABLE ENEMY

LABOR AND THE ANTI-CHINESE MOVEMENT IN CALIFORNIA

ALEXANDER SAXTON

Amerasia Journal 26:1 (2000): 208-231

Beyond Random Acts of Hatred:
Analyzing Urban Patterns of Anti-Asian Violence

Scott Kurashige

When the topic of anti-Asian violence is broached, the tragic death of Vincent Chin is usually recounted. In a climate where Japan was being scapegoated for the economic woes of the American automobile industry, Chin, a Chinese American living in Detroit, was murdered by two unemployed autoworkers. Chin's assailants, whom he'd never met, confronted him at a striptease club and held him personally responsible for their plight. The thrust of the narrative is that Chin was unquestionably an innocent victim, caught in the wrong place at the wrong time, and that his beating was testament to how a wave of prejudice had overtaken rational thought.[1]

The portrayal of anti-Asian violence, as random, haphazard, unpredictable, and targeting innocent bystanders, represents, in my opinion, the dominant discourse on the subject within Asian American Studies. It points specifically to the fact that all Asians in America wear a "racial uniform" that makes us a target of group prejudice and individual acts of hatred. As Yen Le Espiritu has pointed out, organized response to anti-Asian violence became an important vehicle for pan-ethnic "reactive solidarity" in the 1980s.[2] The reasoning is that since racist antagonists can't tell us apart, we'd all better stick together. The general political response has been to demand "justice," usually by ensuring that perpetrators of anti-Asian violence receive criminal convictions and that the prosecution of hate crimes becomes formally incorporated into the judicial system.

SCOTT KURASHIGE is an assistant professor of history and American culture at the University of Michigan, Ann Arbor.

While I recognize the importance of such reform efforts, my goal is to place the study of anti-Asian violence into a broader context that recognizes the patterns of antagonism and violence ingrained within the process of class formation and the construction of systematic forms of racism. One prominent trend in Asian American Studies posited as a systemic response to racism has been the assertion of "anti-essentialist" notions of racial identity.[3] "Anti-essentialist" critics proffer that race is a fluid construct, whose malleability renders its subjects agents of cultural resistance. Racial identity, like sexual identity, is "performed" and those "performances" which transgress boundaries are thus seen as acts contesting the status quo.[4] However, the prevalence of racist violence points to "the limits of cultural resistance" divorced from material practice and grassroots organizing.[5] Building movements of resistance and transformation requires more than rearticulating identity. It entails confronting the material bases of oppression.

In this article, I argue that patterned forms of anti-Asian violence have been the product of reactionary social movements that have been sponsored, legitimized, and/or tolerated by the repressive apparatus of the state. I propose two main goals for analyzing patterned forms of anti-Asian violence: (1) to understand how structures of racism and white supremacy shape the everyday experience of Asian Americans; and (2) to comprehend the means by which communities confront the systemic sources of oppression at the root of anti-Asian violence. The body of this article focuses primarily on the first goal. While the conclusion touches upon the latter issue, I have addressed it in greater detail elsewhere.[6]

As the analysis of "patterned" violence must go beyond recounting individual acts of injustice and hatred, my case study draws upon the historical construction of urban community formation, political economy, and racial conflict in Philadelphia. The article begins with a theoretical discussion of Alexander Saxton's contributions to the study of Asian American history and how insights derived from Saxton's work may be applied to the analysis of anti-Asian violence. It then focuses on anti-Asian violence in twentieth-century Philadelphia. After outlining how patterns of racist violence developed, I document how Vietnamese refugees became integral to the patterns of antagonism in Southwest Philadelphia, an area of town which underwent immense transformation but remained home to a cadre of faithful seeking to keep the

Amerasia Journal

210

neighborhood true to its all-white origins. In particular, I examine the McCreesh Park incident, where after a white youth was killed, Asians became the target of a venomous white backlash and a racially-motivated court case.

Alexander Saxton and the Materialist Conception of History

Starting with *The Indispensable Enemy* in 1971, Alexander Saxton's work has represented the best example of writing in the historical materialist tradition within Asian American Studies.[7] By bridging labor, political, and social history, Saxton proved the importance of anti-Asian ideas and actions to the construction of white supremacy in the American West and ultimately the nation at-large. In this way, *The Indispensable Enemy* perfectly complemented the work of pioneering Asian American historians of the late 1960s and early 1970s, who built archives of primary language and community-oriented materials and sought to uncover in (Yuji Ichioka's words) the "buried past" of previous generations.[8] Such work told a "bottom-up" story of immigration focused on Asian Americans as the central actors of history. Saxton helped provide the context in which the struggles of Asian immigrants took place.

The Indispensable Enemy is a classic book that belongs near the top of every reading list in Asian American history. I wish to draw three contributions from that work that are relevant to this article. First, rejecting the notion that racism was the mere product of individual frustration or group pathology, Saxton showed how hostility towards Asian immigrants was tied to intra-class conflict structured by capitalist social relations. He demonstrated how and why white workers and labor organizations in nineteenth-century California used anti-Chinese crusades as "a powerful organizing tool" to generate a (politically reactionary) social movement. "Anticoolieism" became the rallying cry of white skilled workers, who gained hegemony over the labor movement and instituted an exclusionary craft union structure.[9] In my case study of anti-Asian violence, it will become clear that a similarly antagonistic movement of working-class whites developed in Southwest Philadelphia.

Second, Saxton demonstrated why the construction of anti-Asian racism must be properly analyzed in a multiracial context. Racist campaigns against Chinese Americans in nineteenth century California were not an entirely new phenomena but were derived from a history of anti-black ideology. With slavery no longer viable as a central organizing principle in the aftermath of the Civil War, Democrats seeking to rebuild a political base found that "Chinese fitted readily enough into that mental compartment which in the East had been reserved for blacks."[10] To understand the situation of Asians in twentieth-century Philadelphia, we must appreciate the degree to which they inherit a landscape that has been infused by decades of black-white contradictions.

Third, racism must be placed at the center of the study of dominant ideology. Saxton cautions that racist conflict and violence cannot be explained (or excused) away as the rational product of "job competition." Nor is racism simply a residual product of ruling-class dictate and manipulation. Moving beyond the orthodox "base-determines-superstructure" formula, Saxton challenges us to view class rule and class struggle as arising through the construction of what Antonio Gramsci calls a hegemony that encompasses the ensemble of social relations.[11]

This last point is more fully developed in *The Rise and Fall of the White Republic,* a broader study of politics and culture in the nineteenth-century U.S.[12] In this book, Saxton demonstrated how the American theory of white supremacy—that originated in the rationalization and justification of colonial-era slavery and national oppression—continued to serve the successive hegemonic blocs that sought to legitimize class rule. *The Rise and Fall of the White Republic* documented how racism maintained its essential utility by changing form over time. For instance, as the Enlightenment undermined the authority of the church, notions of white supremacy emanating in Christian theology yielded to biological conceptions of racial order. Likewise, as non-elite whites gained greater political clout, racism became increasingly tied to mass culture and populist vehicles.

By extending the study of racist ideology into the twentieth century, this article seeks to understand the changing function of anti-Asian violence. First, as both the U.S. economy and Asian American labor patterns have become urbanized, so has anti-Asian violence become an increasingly urban phenomenon.[13] Second, as Asian Americans have become integrated into mainstream society, they have gained the protection of state action and jurisprudence. In the era of Asian exclusion movements, violence against "unassimilable" Asian immigrants was often promoted and tolerated by the state. By contrast, in the post-Civil Rights era, violent white supremacist ideas have been pushed to the margins of societal discourse. As a result, incidents of anti-Asian violence are often viewed as exceptional acts (albeit still occurring alarmingly too often), and the liberal response to such phenomena is primarily concerned with ensuring that the state provides equal protection to victims of racist violence and hate crimes.

As the dominant ideology does not consciously promote overt acts of racial hatred (e.g., those in the realm of the Klan), we must be conscious of the most disenfranchised groups in society to appreciate the degree to which violence against Asian Americans continues to be accepted as normal. For instance, the legitimizing synthesis undergirding hegemonic class rule today draws in part from neo-liberal economic theory, "law-and-order" policing, the criminalization of immigration, and heterosexist and misogynist ideas. Consequently, violence against Asians continues least abetted in cases of labor under sweatshop conditions; police brutality; the disciplining of undocumented immigrants; and homophobic, sexual, and domestic violence.

My focus here is on the relationship between anti-Asian violence and urban community formation. Thus, the remainder of this article focuses on one particular form of marginalization: Asian Americans living in blighted urban areas that have been devastated by economic deindustrialization. It is here where they have encountered working-class whites (and sometimes other people of color) embittered by the undermining of blue-collar work and their "normal" way of living.

Patterns of Racist Violence and Exclusion in Southwest Philadelphia

The wave of racist violence that erupted in the early 1990s against Asians in Southwest Philadelphia was an attempt by longtime white residents to control their "turf" against residential "invaders." Thus, to place these events into proper historical context, it is necessary to understand three factors: (1) how violence contributed to the construction of urban racism; (2) how white privilege became identified with white neighborhoods (or "places"); and (3) how the experiences of Asians took place in a multiracial context shaped by a history of black-white relations.

In *How the Irish Became White*, Noel Ignatiev used a case study of antebellum Philadelphia to demonstrate how racist violence, particularly in the form of race riots, proved indispensable to the creation of the white supremacist social order of Northern cities. Predominantly indigent laborers, Irish American immigrants were considered a "lower" race than American-born whites and became the targets of nativism and discrimination. Through mob violence, the Irish were able to "earn" their way onto the white race team by proving their value as oppressors of African Americans and defenders of white supremacy. Although white supremacist mobs comprised only a small but vocal minority of the community, "that organized force of hundreds was able to batter those who opposed it, or even those who held back, into silence and submission, so that in time it came to speak for the entire community."[14]

As a structure of racial inequality became ingrained within the social fabric of the industrial city, the role of white supremacist violence began to shift towards defense of privilege. In the densely settled city that was colonial and pre-industrial Philadelphia, African Americans and whites had lived in close proximity; hence, violence served to confer status upon the dominant race by keeping minorities in their place *metaphorically*. With the rise of industry, beginning with the textile mills of the 1820s, racial inequality was to a greater degree produced and reproduced by spatial segregation. Over the course of industrial Philadelphia's history, all-white neighborhoods were built around all-white factories, which led to the simultaneous creation of "ghettoes of opportunity" for whites and "ghettoes of last resort" for African Americans.[15] In this context, defense of white privilege became equated with keeping minorities in their place *literally*.

Segregation advanced further at the turn of the century with the formation of "streetcar suburbs" in Philadelphia and the subsequent development of electric-powered industries.[16] The further decentralization of the city accelerated the creation of all-white suburbs. By now the pattern had been established, whites had solidified themselves as a hegemonic racial grouping, established a hold on the factory jobs and labor organizations, and built racially exclusive communities around the factories. The construction of all-white, "streetcar suburbs" represented then a form of what Saxton calls "soft" racism, whereby inequality is reproduced more by the stable functionings of the political economy and aversion to people of color predominates over direct conflict. In this context, it is important to recognize the way in which racial and class privilege can become synonymous with place, and hence, defending privilege becomes inseparable from controlling spatial relations.[17] Thus, the "hard" racism of whites came into play largely in the maintenance of segregated communities against nonwhite intruders.

There is perhaps nothing which exemplifies this historical process more than the history of Southwest Philadelphia—or just "Southwest" as it is called by local residents. Though still part of the hinterlands when the core of Philadelphia experienced its tremendous nineteenth-century industrial growth, Southwest emerged as an industrial, "streetcar suburb" in time for the Second Industrial Revolution of the early twentieth century. Southwest was a densely settled neighborhood designed for second-generation white ethnics, mostly Irish and Italians. The move to the suburb represented a case of relative upward mobility for its new inhabitants, whose class status ranged from the less well-off strands of the middle-class to the relatively stable sectors of the working-class. This class dimension of the neighborhood was and still is reflected in the architecture of Southwest, whose landscape is dominated by two-story rowhouses. Rowhouses, still extremely common in lower-middle/working-class neighborhoods throughout Philadelphia, served as a cheap (since land usage is maximized) source of family residences which could be built in a relatively short period of time.[18]

Through repeating the practice of asserting white privilege and excluding African Americans, white Southwest residents reinforced an ideology of white supremacy throughout the twentieth century. Yet, by the 1970s, the rules had begun to change. Economic restructuring dramatically changed the face of northeastern, industrial cities like Philadelphia due to two simultaneous processes. First, capital on a national level shifted from the Northeastern Frostbelt to the South/Southwestern Sunbelt. Second, within cities, capital relocated from urban centers to suburban peripheries (and beyond). This restructuring exacted a demanding toll on Philadelphia and is the reason it remains mired in an economic quagmire.[19] From 1955 to 1975, Philadelphia lost 75 percent of all manufacturing jobs citywide.[20] For sixteen straight years from 1969 to 1984, Philadelphia experienced a decrease in manufacturing jobs, as the total plummeted from 252,500 to 108,400.[21]

As corporations shifted their priorities to meet the demands of flexible accumulation, communities like Southwest that were tied to the old, industrial order found themselves left out of the equation.[22] Historically, communities in Philadelphia had been linked to the industrial economy. Businesses had a stake in the community and thus invested in them. However, in post-industrial Philadelphia, high-tech jobs and service-sector jobs replaced factory jobs. Corporations either abandoned factories or relocated to the newest suburbs, building state-of-the-art, automated production facilities and taking advantage of lower rents and taxes. Moreover, the globalization of the economy led corporations to eschew community ties in favor of more profitable national and international links. The limited development that took place in Philadelphia was incredibly lopsided and benefited only a select few communities, such as the financiers in Downtown Center City, while others were neglected.[23]

As the jobs moved to the new suburbs, so went many white residents of Philadelphia. Southwest was no exception. The population of Southwest declined as the American Tobacco Company shut down its plant, Purex fled, and General Electric scaled down its workforce from 5,000 to 450. Meanwhile, the second Great Migration saw large numbers of African Americans from the South moving into Philadelphia. The "white flight" to the new suburbs left a vast supply of affordable housing in Southwest, which African Americans quickly occupied. From 1960 to 1970, the African American population of Southwest tripled from 11 percent to 33 percent of the total population. During the 1960s and 1970s, Kingsessing, the northernmost neighborhood of Southwest and the one closest to the core of the city, went from being nearly all-white to all-African American. By 1980, whites were no longer a majority in Southwest.[24]

Whites in the heart of Southwest, fearing a repeat of the next-door Kingsessing transformation from white to black, committed a series of atrocities against African Americans that swelled in the late 1970s and early to mid-1980s. In 1979, two white men crawled onto the roof of a factory "looking for a 'nigger' to shoot," then shot and killed thirteen-year-old Tracey Chambers, the first African American who passed by. In 1980, white youths from Southwest stabbed an African American youth on a trolley. In response, a group of African American youth went into Southwest and stabbed a white youth to death.[25] While these incidents point out the racial tensions, a series of events directed at an African American home-owning family in 1985 best exemplify the white homeowners' attempt to keep Southwest racially pure. Soon after the family moved into an all-white block, a bottle was thrown through their window. Three weeks later, 400 whites demonstrated on the front lawn of the family's home, demanding that they get out. One month later, arsonists broke into the house and burned it to the ground.[26]

As a result of economic restructuring, the Southwest of the 1980s and 1990s was no longer a prosperous suburb but a buffer zone between the disproportionately poor and African American inner-city and the white and middle-class suburbs. The economic basis for the white neighborhood of Southwest as a "ghetto of opportunity" all but vanished with the sharp decline in manufacturing jobs. Moreover, housing values plummeted as a result, and this factor was compounded by attempts to keep the neighborhood all-white, thus effectively reducing demand within the housing market.[27] While neighborhoods on the eastern and western ends of Southwest transformed from predominantly white to black, the geographic core of Southwest (roughly between 61st and 68th Streets) remained predominantly white.[28]

In 1990, the typical white resident in Southwest had the following profile: working-class; Irish descent; high school education or less; household income just above the poverty level at $18,000 to $24,000; home owner; and living in a rowhouse built in the early twentieth century. We can see how the typical white resident possessed little of the human capital necessary to compete in the new job market of the global economy, which created an increased premium on higher education. In the areas adjacent to McCreesh Park, only 6.9 percent of all whites age twenty-five and above had a bachelor's degree while 41.5 percent did not finish high school.[29]

As the economic advantages of white privilege were negated by post-industrial decay, many whites in Southwest opted to maximize what David Roediger has labeled the psychological "wages of whiteness."[30] They defended their sense of place and community that was informed by decades of racism and rooted materially in the one thing which stands out as an asset in this profile—the ownership of homes. In their research on Philadelphia neighborhoods, Adams et al. found that white working-class "urban villages" like the one in the heart of Southwest were most likely to be the sites of racial hostilities when confronted by the migration of people of color. Specifically, the factors relating positively to racial tension were identified as areas with a stable and predominantly white population, where median family income was lower, jobs had been lost, and residents were older.[31] These whites who were unable to flee Southwest and who were decimated by the neighborhood's economic downturn chose to vent their frustrations on the newcomers. African Americans were the initial targets, but Asian Americans were added to the list as demographics shifted.

Sources of Anti-Asian Violence
in Southwest Philadelphia

To make sense of racist violence directed at Southeast Asian refu-gees during the process of primary and secondary resettlement in Philadelphia, we need to be in tune with how these historical processes of white privilege and racial exclusion still reverberate today and how patterns of anti-black racism have constructed the rules of the game by which all in Philadelphia must play. As Southeast Asian refugees entered American society, they en-countered the historically constructed race/class hierarchy. The overwhelmingly working-class refugees represented to capital a new source of cheap laborers, who by definition are to be disen-franchised and impoverished. For some white working-class com-munities, the introduction of refugees provided a new scapegoat but also a new "other" against which whites can and must pro-claim and assert their "whiteness." As Etienne Balibar points out, the new postcolonial conditions, arising without a transforma-tion of relations of power within the core nations, lead to "new" racisms to fit the old structures of domination. As the world wit-nesses "the reversal of population movements between the old colo-nies and the old metropolises," systems and ideologies rooted in imperialism are transformed into markers of difference based on nativism and added to the mix of racist definitions.[32]

To this day, Philadelphia remains a city highly segregated in terms of black and white. Yet, locating Asian Americans challenges us to look beyond this binary opposition. As Ellen Somekawa has demonstrated, Southeast Asian refugees resettled in Philadelphia in the late 1970s and 1980s found themselves living "on the edge" in marginal areas between predominantly African American and predominantly white neighborhoods. As a result, simply affirm-ing a common, everyday sense of place in the city has been an uphill fight for Southeast Asian refugees. Somekawa writes:

> Struggling for space is part of the lived experience of getting up and going through each day, especially for recent immigrants. To wear what one wants and to speak the language of one's choos-ing, to sit on the front steps, to hold a public celebration, to ob-serve one's religion and to use a library or walk on a sidewalk are forms of struggling for space. . . . Fighting for "turf" is of-ten represented by the media and the police as the petty and ju-venile concerns of young gang members, but in actuality it can mean contending for the right to participate in basic human ac-tivities.[33]

That Vietnamese Americans first relocated to a particular all-white neighborhood within Southwest was due to more than just happenstance. Not coincidentally, the period in the 1980s of white animosity toward African American newcomers also represented the beginning of Asian American community formation in Southwest. For whites looking to get out of Southwest (proto-typical "motivated sellers"), selling their houses clandestinely to Asians allowed them to escape or at least reduce the social stigma attached to selling to African Americans that emanated from whites "stuck" in Southwest. Thus, the construction of "whiteness" out of the black/white dialectic facilitated the entrance of Asian Americans into Southwest. Yet, the eruption of contradictions between whites and Asian Americans was lingering around the corner.[34]

The Vietnamese community in Southwest derived mainly from the second wave. In contrast to the first-wave "refugees" in Philadelphia, who tended to possess the connections, education and financial resources to make the uneasy transition to life in American society, refugees from the second and third waves were initially resettled into areas of economic decline or transition. A significant portion of the refugees ended up in West Philadelphia, where as Somekawa notes, they were housed in "vacant and deteriorating" complexes by landlords whose desire "to milk their properties as their strategy for making profit... coincided with the needs of the resettlement agencies who had to place large numbers of refugees in a short period of time."[35] A glimpse at the 1980 Census statistics for a West Philadelphia census tract with a concentration of refugees reveals the severe poverty in which the refugees lived. Average household income for Asians was but $7,828. In addition, 36.2 percent of the Asian households had an annual income below $5,000, while 85.6 percent of Asian households had an annual income below $15,000.[36]

The Asian migration to Southwest was spearheaded by Vietnamese refugees from inner-city West Philadelphia, particularly those who came to the U.S. with some skills, perhaps as entrepreneurs or urban workers, that allowed them to build savings and escape what they viewed as a harsher environment.[37] Like the white immigrants before them, the Vietnamese who came to Southwest were the successful ones who had "made it" (albeit by inner-city refugee standards). Like the African American migrants before them, they were attracted to Southwest Philadelphia because of the abundance of cheap houses, most selling at prices between

$15,000 and $20,000.[38] From 1980 to 1990, the Asian American population of Southwest skyrocketed 459.2 percent, rising from 174 to 973. Moreover, the growth of the Vietnamese population of Southwest dwarfed this figure as it jumped 853.4 percent from 58 to 553. In 1990, Vietnamese made up some 58.6 percent of the Asian American population in Southwest with Cambodians and ethnic Chinese comprising much of the remainder.[39]

Southwest was appealing to Vietnamese because it was predominantly white (and in the eyes of many Asian Americans, white neighborhoods were more attractive than heavily African American inner-city neighborhoods), near public transportation, and extremely affordable. For Vietnamese Americans, Southwest was the best choice of a limited range of options. Whites in Southwest, desperate to sell their houses but aware of the fierce neighborhood campaign to keep out African Americans, began to sell their houses to Asians in the early to mid-1980s. Houses were sold under the table. In other words, in order to circumvent fair housing laws, whites did not officially post their houses with real estate agents. Debbie Wei, a founding member of Asian Americans United and formerly an ESOL (English for Speakers of Other Languages) teacher for many Southwest youth, remarked that "The first Asians that moved in, moved in very quietly. There was no big 'FOR SALE' sign. There was no big triumphant thing. So I think it sort of took the neighborhood by surprise."[40]

Initially, Vietnamese in Southwest were spared the firebombings and attacks that African Americans suffered. But as encounters between whites and Asians increased, so did white hostilities towards Asians. In fact, by 1990, the number of Asians living in the predominantly white central area of Southwest had surpassed the number of African Americans, who clustered around the edges of Southwest. In the racist discourse and actions of whites in Southwest, Asians began to supplant African Americans as the "other" in the dialectic through which "whiteness" was reasserted. Though Asians were found mainly in "white" sections of Southwest, an examination of demographic characteristics for the area reveals that Asians came far closer to resembling African Americans than whites. For instance, based on 1989 income, the poverty rate for whites in Southwest was 13.5 percent, slightly above the citywide white poverty rate of 11.1 percent. However, that rate paled in comparison with the Asian American poverty rate in Southwest, which stood at 48.6 percent. The Asian American rate just surpassed the African American poverty rate of 44.1 percent. Statistics for unemployment, household income and educational attainment told a similar story.[41]

The demographic changes, slowly being reflected in the cultural landscape of Southwest, did not sit well with long-time, white residents. On Woodlawn Avenue, the central retail strip that flanks the streetcar line, older neighborhood storefronts were displaced by ethnic businesses. From the mid-1980s to the early 1990s, racist harassment and violence by whites were built into the daily lives of Asian Americans in Southwest. Older adults attempted to stay in their homes and hoped the problems would subside. In the words of one resident, "We had to borrow money to buy this house. We have nowhere to move. So at night we now stay inside."[42] However, their children were a different story. Despite parental attempts to keep youth (especially girls) inside the house, the routine of going to school and hanging out with friends kept Asian American youth outside the home.

The lack of public space and recreational outlets in Southwest meant that youth tended to congregate around a few areas. One was Dennis Pizza, a small storefront where fifty Asian American, African American and white youth could be found crowded around four video games, and the steps of a nearby church.[43] The lack of recreational outlets also gave rise to young men of all races (as young as middle school age) grouped around these hang outs smoking and drinking as a form of common social activity. These places then became the contested sites of the struggle to control space. In this struggle, intimidation was commonly used by whites to teach new Asian residents to stay in their place, as the following story of a Southeast Asian youth attests:

> He explained that when he first moved to Southwest Philadelphia, he didn't know where it was safe to go. He went to rent a video and walked by a whole bunch of white guys. They started to harass him and proceeded to chase him all the way home where he escaped inside. However the group stayed outside, throwing rocks until they broke a window.[44]

Given the dearth of recreation outlets, McCreesh Park, a multiuse facility in the central area of Southwest, was one of the only public recreation areas in Southwest. The park could be found in the middle of the overwhelmingly white and most segregated area of Southwest. However, contiguous to the east end of the park lay the largest concentration of Asians in the neighborhood, including two hundred living in the four blocks closest to this east end.[45]

McCreesh Park's large size and central geographic location made it a highly visible battleground for the racialized struggles over space in Southwest. In an interview, Trang, a high-school-aged youth from Southwest, easily maps out the park along racial lines, defining boundaries that are self-evident to all: "Baseball field would have been for the whites, and half of the other field would have been for the Asians playing soccer. On the basketball court, two of them belongs to, like, you know, the white side, and two of them for, like, the black or the Asian." These boundaries were mediated by relations of power reflecting the racial hierarchy. As Trang notes, "If we were there playing basketball and, you know, white people start coming at us, then, you know, I guess we would leave. 'Cause we wouldn't want any trouble from them. If we're smart enough, we would just leave."[46]

Although all were forced to live in the hostile racist environment of Southwest, the experiences of Asian Americans ruptured along gender lines, conforming to the traditional (but not unproblematic) public/private split. Women and girls by nature of their economic roles and family obligations were more likely to be at home than men and boys. Hue Tran's parents' roles were representative of Vietnamese Americans in Southwest. Her father worked as a janitor in a large hospital, while her mother either took care of the home or did piecework at home to supplement the family income.[47] For girls, as Tran notes, parental concern for safety conspired with a patriarchal assignment of chores to keep them home most of the time:

> Because more of the families are here, the Asian teens, especially the guys, are out on the street more. [To] the girls, the parents can say, "No you can't go out. And, you have to cook, you have to clean. You have to take care of the kids." That's all the girls' jobs. The guys, though, they're allowed to go out. I see a lot of them out on Woodland Avenue just hanging out. Most of them are about sixteen and under.[48]

Girls were also schooled by their parents to avoid confrontation. In Trang's case, "My parents, they would just say, 'Ignore them 'cause they have no manners.'"[49] The above quotes help us to understand why confrontations between young men became the most visible outward manifestation of the fight by white Southwest residents to reproduce a white supremacist order and the struggle of Asian residents to resist such oppression.

What Tragedy? Whose Tragedy?

As racial contradictions heightened in a neighborhood where residents were crowded literally side-by-side into rowhouses, the possibility of a serious altercation between white and Asian American youth in Southwest loomed larger and larger. August 4, 1991 was the day that tragedy struck. It marked the date when David Reilly, an eighteen-year-old white male, was killed at Southwest Philadelphia's McCreesh Park. On that night, a group of whites in their late teens and twenties, some belonging to a neo-Nazi group called the "White Power Boys," were drinking beer in McCreesh Park after midnight. When the whites spotted a group of Asian American youth, they moved to drive them out of "their" park. Even the prosecution's own witnesses testified that David Reilly's friends threatened the Asian American group. Brian Parker, referred to in court as the "fat guy," went up to the Asian Americans with his dog and said, "I have a pit bull. He's gonna bite you." Another warned, "I have a gun behind my back."[50] This type of event had occurred many times before in Southwest with one exception. This time, the Asian American youth fought back. One of them escaped to retrieve knives. A fight ensued, and Reilly, reportedly in an attempt to break up the fight, was caught in the crossfire.

The death of David Reilly was a tragedy for numerous reasons. First, there was the obvious tragedy recognized by the public, that the life of a young man had been claimed. Sympathy overflowed from all over the city of Philadelphia. The second tragedy was that the same public had scarcely recognized the plight of the Southeast Asian community, particularly the youths, who faced constant harassment, intimidation, and discrimination. Just as in the nineteenth century, the complicity of state institutions gave rise to rule by mob, consisting here of the young white men, who anointed themselves the foot soldiers of white supremacy in Southwest and organized themselves into white supremacist gangs. These problems were not alleviated but intensified by state intervention. For instance, in what has become a common practice against youth of color nationwide, Philadelphia police in the 1980s began stopping young Asian males at random and taking their pictures for "mug books." In some instances, police beat and/or arrested Asian Americans that they stopped at random. According to John Fong, former Executive Director of Asian Americans United, the use of the mug books led to "cases of Asians being arrested and kept in jail for several days simply because someone had mistakenly picked them out from these mug books."[51] The sentiment of many Asians in Southwest was that an Asian youth could have easily been the one lying dead on the ground, and yet there would have been no public sympathy and no motions for justice from the state institutions.

The third tragedy was that Asians in Southwest were forced to endure a vigilante response marked by an eruption of race hatred. On the night of Reilly's death, Ty Truong, a twenty-four-year-old Chinese-Vietnamese resident of Southwest, was arrested. Truong had been out at the movies all night and only drove by McCreesh Park on his way home. Nonetheless, Brian Sciarrillo, a friend of David Reilly's and one of the prime instigators of the altercation which led to his death, pointed at Truong and said, "That's one of the motherfucking gooks."[52] On that basis, the Philadelphia Police arrested Truong on the spot as a crowd of whites chanted "Gook, get the gook."[53] After holding him for fifty-five days, the police finally acknowledged Truong's alibi, released him and dropped all charges.

For numerous whites in Southwest, Reilly's death served as a justification for all of their racist beliefs and practices. And indeed, many whites were anxious to have their voices heard. One white youth told the city's largest newspaper: "I'm racist. Being racist to me means being proud of your heritage. I don't believe in mixed couples. [There are] a lot of people like me. I'm a skinhead."[54] Moreover, the sentiments of whites were inscribed upon the landscape as white supremacist graffiti appeared all over the neighborhood, particularly in McCreesh Park. Nearly a year after the McCreesh incident, Thoai Nguyen, a member of Asian Americans United, walked through McCreesh and the neighborhood surrounding it. He found "Fuck the Nips" etched on a power box near the basketball court, "White Power" spray painted on the concrete bleachers along with neo-Nazi symbols, and "Be proud to be White, Never Surrender" scrawled across the bridge adjacent to the park.[55]

Even a community meeting arranged by the Philadelphia Human Relations Commission to "ease tensions" was overrun by the white vigilante mentality. Due to fear, only about ten Asian American residents attended. Speaker after speaker in the predominantly white crowd of five hundred people issued angry calls for frontier justice. As members of Asian Americans United who attended the meeting note, "It was the most bitter irony that this meeting, called by the Human Relations Commission to encourage 'healing,' turned out to be more like a racist free-for-all against people of Asian descent."[56]

Again, since no one knew exactly how David Reilly was killed, these white vigilantes drew upon their community's decades of racist practice and sought to punish Asians as a group. One group of adult white males went out to beat up "slant-eyes" when they heard that David Reilly was killed. A white man who with fourteen others randomly dragged Asian Americans off the local streetcar described his actions like this:

> We'd kick the shit out of them. Really hurt them bad. When I felt the tire iron smashing his head, it felt good. I got one for David. . . . When I went to David's funeral, I felt great. I thought I'd done something good. Now David can to go to heaven resting easier.[57]

The final tragedy was the unjust treatment of the Southeast Asian youth defendants accused of murdering Reilly and the message this sent about how little the criminal justice system understood, respected, or valued Asian communities. After Ty Truong was finally released, authorities arrested seven other Vietnamese youth: Minh La, Tho Tran, Dieu Nguyen, Khoa Ho, Manh Hoang, Tuan Huynh and Khanh Lam. All were charged with first degree murder and held on bail ranging from $150,000 to $1.1 million (rates that were inflated out of fear that the *refugees* might go back to Vietnam).[58] Six were tried together in a racially-tinged case which saw the defendants tried and convicted in the media before opening arguments began. Despite the fact that the prosecution never identified who actually stabbed David Reilly, three of the defendants were found guilty of third-degree murder and six of criminal conspiracy. Their sentences ranged from one-to-ten years to twelve-to-thirty years imprisonment.[59]

Conclusion

In this article, I have argued that racist violence must be understood not only as random acts of terror that strike unexpectedly but must be seen as constitutive elements of the racial hierarchy and class rule in the U.S. I have used a case study of the recent history of the Southeast Asians in Southwest Philadelphia to show the enduring legacy of these historical patterns amidst changing conditions and the continued injustices against Asian American communities.

The continued effects of racist violence, particularly impacting the most marginalized segments of Asian American populations points to the necessity to transcend the liberal response to anti-Asian violence. It is important to recognize that the "random occurrence" phenomenon resonates primarily with middle-class Asian Americans, for whom anti-Asian violence is an aberration which disrupts their otherwise safe and secure living environments, rather than working-class Asian Americans for whom patterned racist violence can be an everyday life experience. In confronting both "random" and "patterned" forms of racist violence, it is necessary to fight to ensure that Asian Americans and all aggrieved minorities are protected by Constitutional principles which are ensconced in the U.S. legal system. But this is only a tactical step, for overcoming patterned racist violence will require a profound transformation of social relations—something which can only be accomplished by sustained social movements which transcend the liberal order of bourgeois democratic society.

The work of organizations like the Philadelphia-based Asian Americans United and New York City-based Committee Against Anti-Asian Violence serve as models of activist work which stems from a materialist analysis of anti-Asian violence. Such an analysis points out the necessity to develop a class-conscious response to racist violence and hate crimes. Asian American activists have learned that to confront the sources of racist violence rather than just the symptoms, it is necessary to attack the pressure points of the interconnected system of white supremacy, capitalism, and imperialism. They understand that it is always necessary to be in touch with the real people whose lives are most impacted by racist violence, to comprehend their experiences and struggles, to stay in tune with changing conditions and movements, and most of all to organize campaigns which resonate with the sentiments of community members. The goal of this activist work is not only to use education and agitation to demystify the racist ideology which legitimizes such systems, but also to organize at the grassroots community level, challenge the repressive elements of state power, and ultimately transform societal relationships so that racist violence is *eliminated*.

Notes

This article is a revised version of a paper submitted for the Alexander Saxton History Prize. It draws upon research conducted for my master's thesis in Asian American Studies ("Locating Oppression and Resistance: Asian Americans and Racist Violence," M.A. Thesis, UCLA, 1996). I would like to thank Kyeyoung Park, Yuji Ichioka, Russell Leong, and Glenn Omatsu for their comments and assistance.

1. Chin's story and the community struggle to hold his killers accountable is best recounted in Christine Choy and Renee Tajima's brilliant
    documentary *Who Killed Vincent Chin?* (1988).

2. Yen Le Espiritu, *Asian American Panethnicity: Bridging Institutions
    and Identities* (Philadelphia: Temple University Press, 1992), 134-160.

3. The most often-cited work of this nature is Lisa Lowe, "Heterogeneity, Hybridity, Multiplicity: Asian American Differences," *Immigrant
    Acts: On Asian American Cultural Politics* (Durham and London: Duke
    University Press, 1996), 60-83. Though in fairness to Lowe, it should
    be pointed out that her stated intention is to argue for the material
    origins of such differences.

4. The notion of "peformativity" is most associated with Judith Butler's
    work problematizing gender and sexuality. See Judith Butler, *Gender
    Trouble: Feminism and the Subversion of Identity* (New York: Routledge, 1990).

5. I am borrowing the notion of "the limits of cultural resistance"
    from the title of Jinqi Ling's paper delivered on a panel we shared
    at the 1997 Association for Asian American Studies Conference. See
    also, Jinqi Ling, *Narrating Nationalisms: Ideology and Form in Asian
    American Literature* (New York: Oxford University Press, 1998).

6. Scott Kurashige, "Panethnicity and Community Organizing: Asian
    Americans United's Campaign Against Anti-Asian Violence," *Journal
    of Asian American Studies* 3:2 (in process).

7. Alexander Saxton, *The Indispensable Enemy: Labor and the Anti-Chinese Movement in California* (Berkeley and Los Angeles: University
    of California Press, 1971).

8. Yuji Ichioka, *A Buried Past* (Berkeley: University of California Press,
    1974).

9. Saxton, *Indispensable Enemy*, 261. Saxton's work placed the economic
    analysis of the "split labor market" into a broader ideological context. The idea of the "split labor market" as an economic basis for
    attacks on Asian immigrants by white workers has been most developed in Asian American Studies by Edna Bonacich. See Edna
    Bonacich, "A Theory of Ethnic Antagonism: The Split Labor Market," *American Sociological Review* 37: 5 (October 1972), 547-559; see
    also, Lucie Cheng and Edna Bonacich, "Introduction: A Theoretical Orientation to International Labor Migration," in Lucie Cheng
    and Edna Bonacich, eds., *Labor Immigration Under Capitalism: Asian
    Workers in the United States Before World War II* (Berkeley and Los
    Angeles: University of California Press, 1984), 1-56.

10. Saxton, *Indispensable Enemy*, 260.

11. In this sense, Saxton's work answers the concern voiced by Paul
    Gilroy that "the primary problem for analysis of racial antagonism
    which occurs within the broad framework of historical materialism must be the manner in which racial meanings, solidarity and
    identities provide the basis for action." See Paul Gilroy, *"There Ain't
    No Black in the Union Jack": The Cultural Politics of Race and Nation*

(Chicago: University of Chicago Press, 1991), 27. Following in Saxton's footsteps, my intention is to discuss racist practices as consciously material phenomenon so as to sharply distinguish my analysis of race from those Marxists who view it solely as "false consciousness."

12. Alexander Saxton, *The Rise and Fall of the White Republic: Class Politics and Mass Culture in Nineteenth-Century America* (London: Verso, 1990).

13. Although Sucheng Chan cites the Los Angeles massacre of 1871 as the "first documented instance of a spontaneous outbreak against a Chinese community," the bulk of her accounts of violence against Asians during the nineteenth and early twentieth century period of immigration and settlement are situated in rural locales. See Sucheng Chan, *Asian Americans: An Interpretive History* (Boston: Twayne Publishers, 1991), 45-61.

14. Noel Ignatiev, *How the Irish Became White* (New York: Routledge, 1995), 130.

15. Carolyn Adams et al., *Philadelphia: Neighborhoods, Division, and Conflict in a Postindustrial City* (Philadelphia: Temple University Press, 1991), 11.

16. Sam Bass Warner, Jr. dates the rise of the "streetcar" suburb to the period between 1870 and 1900, coinciding with the vast expansion of American capitalism that gave rise to large-scale Fordist production. Warner, *Streetcar Suburbs: The Process of Growth in Boston, 1870-1900*, 2nd ed. (Cambridge: Harvard University Press, 1978).

    See also Kenneth Jackson, *Crabgrass Frontier: The Suburbanization of the United States* (New York and Oxford: Oxford University Press, 1985) for a discussion of the general suburbanization process, especially 289-290 for the racial motives behind suburbanization and 209-215 for the discriminatory impact of Federal Housing Agency "redlining."

17. My conception of the connection between place and white privilege has been influenced by the brilliant work of Mike Davis on twentieth-century Los Angeles. See Mike Davis, *City of Quartz* (London: Verso, 1990); and Mike Davis, *Ecology of Fear: Los Angeles and the Imagination of Disaster*, paperback edition (New York: Vintage Books, 1999).

18. Warner, 88-93 and 141; Adams et al., 73-74.

19. Allen Scott, *Metropolis: From the Division of Labor to Urban Form* (Berkeley and Los Angeles: University of California Press, 1988), 9-25.

20. Adams et al., 81.

21. Taken from U.S. Department of Labor, Bureau of Labor Statistics in Scott, 19. Although the numbers end in 1984, there should be little doubt that the trend continued.

22. Neighborhoods similar to Southwest Philadelphia are the focus of study in Thomas Sugrue's insightful analysis of postwar Detroit that

demonstrates the connection between deindustrialization, segregation, racial inequality, and neighborhood conflict. See Thomas J. Sugrue, *The Origins of the Urban Crisis: Race and Inequality in Postwar Detroit* (Princeton: Princeton University Press, 1996).

23. Adams et al., 30-99.

24. Paul Keegan, "SouthwestSide Story," *Philadelphia Magazine* (October 1992), 78.

25. *Ibid.*

26. Adams et al., 22.

27. *Ibid.* Moreover, redevelopment of Southwest was rendered difficult by the presence of rowhouses requiring that entire city blocks be redeveloped. This means first that redevelopment requires a substantial investment (and thus risk) of capital, and second, that developers must have the cooperation of numerous residents simultaneously. The reduced attractiveness for redevelopment (i.e. future value) served further to deflate the property values in Southwest.

28. Based on examination of block-group data from the 1990 U.S. Census. Data extracted from the U.S. Bureau of the Census at www.census.gov.

29. *Ibid.*

30. David Roediger, *The Wages of Whiteness: Race and the Making of the American Working Class* (London: Verso, 1991).

31. Adams et al., 25.

32. Etienne Balibar, "Is There a Neo-Racism?" in Etienne Balibar and Immanuel Wallerstein, eds., *Race, Nation, Class: Ambiguous Identities* (London: Verso, 1991), 20-21.

33. Ellen Somekawa, "On the Edge: Southeast Asians in Philadelphia and the Struggle for Space" in Wendy L. Ng et al., *Reviewing Asian America: Locating Diversity* (Pullman: Washington State University Press, 1995), 33.

34. This was part of a social context where the growing population of Asian Americans in Philadelphia was met with hostility on a citywide level. Statistics from the Philadelphia Commission on Human Relations reveal that Asian Americans were the victims of 25-30 percent of all reported interracial attacks in the late 1980s and early 1990s. The population of the Hmong community in Philadelphia declined from over 3,000 in the early 1980s to around 450 by 1991 after, as one researcher describes, "a series of violent racial attacks and pervasive crime in their neighborhoods led most of them to pack up and leave the city by 1984." In 1990, Heng Lim, a Cambodian refugee, was murdered in South Philadelphia by a white man who called him a "fucking chink" and beat him on the head with a piece of lumber. Despite being identified by witnesses, Lim's killer was allowed to go free for five weeks before being arrested by police, who refused to charge him with "ethnic intimidation," the state's hate crime law. Robert Thayer, "Who Killed Heng Lim?" M.A. thesis, School for In-

ternational Training, 1990, 14, 53-58.

35. Somekawa, 41.

36. Philadelphia Census Tract 87, U.S. Census, 1980. Note: figures are not broken down by ethnicity. Vietnamese represented 259 of 738 Asian and Pacific Islanders in this tract. Cambodians were not listed as a separate ethnic group.

37. Hue Tran's family moved from West to Southwest Philadelphia. She describes the West Philadelphia neighborhood, where family origi- nally settled and why they were compelled to move:

We were one of the first few Asian families there. It was predomi- nantly a black neighborhood and we had a lot of problems there. Also, the housing wasn't good. They resettled us in a really bad area. It's something that you would want to get out of. Kids would pick fights with you. We couldn't play outside because several times when we did, the little boys would come down the street, and they would throw rocks at us. And so from that time on, we just stayed inside the house, and my mom said, "You're not going out anymore." And so we were homegirls. Hue Tran, personal interview, Septem- ber 15, 1992.

38. Thayer, 12.

39. Tract-level data, U.S. Census, 1980, 1990. Due primarily to immi- gration and refugee resettlement Philadelphia's Asian Pacific Is- lander population grew 145 percent between 1980 and 1990. Accord- ing to 1990 Census counts, there were 43,522 Asians and Pacific Is- landers in Philadelphia, or 2.7 percent of the population, and 82,035 when the four counties surrounding Philadelphia are in- cluded. Vietnamese comprise 13.1 percent of the Asian Pacific Is- lander population in Philadelphia. Vietnamese are the fourth largest Asian group behind Chinese (11,691), Koreans (6,969) and Asian Indians (6,293).

40. Interview with Deborah Wei, September 15, 1992.

41. Tract-level data, U.S. Census, 1990.

42. Anonymous quote taken from Neeta Patel, Ellen Somekawa and Dao X. Tran, "Racial Violence in Southwest Philadelphia: Asian Lives Do Not Come Cheap," *Forward Motion* 11:3 (July 1992), 30.

43. Interview with Trang (pseudonym), September 15, 1992.

44. Patel, Somekawa and Tran, "Racial Violence in Southwest Phila- delphia," 24.

45. Block-level data, U.S. Census, 1990.

46. Interview with Trang.

47. For a more detailed discussion of gender relations within the Viet- namese American households in Philadelphia, see Nazli Kibria, *Fam- ily Tightrope: The Changing Lives of Vietnamese Americans* (Princeton: Princeton University Press, 1993), 73-166. Kibria argues that the man- ner in which household income is constructed by diverse members

of extended family in a "patchwork" manner leads to both a subversion of the traditional patriarchal household and generational conflict.

48. Interview with Hue Tran.

49. Interview with Trang.

50. Quoted in Assistant D.A. Joseph Casey's opening statement, *Commonwealth* vs. *Minh La,* et al., Court Transcript (First Judicial District of Philadelphia: Court of Common Pleas, June 5, 1992) 43-44. This came out in both trials. I was in attendance of *Commonwealth* vs. *Khanh Lam,* when Tuiet Mac testified to this on February 11, 1993. As an interesting side note, at the trial on that date, I also observed the sheriff in the court attempt to handcuff the Vietnamese American translator when the court adjourned. This "inadvertent" episode reveals how racial discourse truly pervaded every aspect of the trial and everyone involved.

51. John Fong, "How Are the Police Serving Asians?" *Asian American Justice Watch* 1:2 (July 1992), 6.

52. *Commonwealth* vs. *Minh La,* et al.. 50.

53. Robin Palley, "Uneasy Truce in White-Asian Feud," *Philadelphia Daily News* (August 5, 1991).

54. Jeffrey Fleishman and Martha Woodall, "Tension High after Teen Slain in City," *Philadelphia Inquirer* (August 4, 1991).

55. Thoai Nguyen, "Learning From Our Tragedies," *Asian American Justice Watch* 1:2 (July 1992), 6.

56. Patel, Somekawa and Tran, "Racial Violence in Southwest Philadelphia," 24-25.

57. Keegan, 77.

58. Linda Loyd and Thomas J. Gibbons Jr., "Suspect in Reilly Killing Gets Bail," *Philadelphia Inquirer* (October 19, 1991); Raoul V. Mowatt, "Trial for 6 in Reilly Slaying," *Philadelphia Inquirer* (November 26, 1991).

59. Susan Caba, "Six Defendants in Reilly Slaying Sentenced to Jail," *Philadelphia Inquirer* (November 20, 1992).

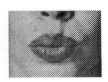

N.V.M. GONZALEZ

A GRAMMAR
OF DREAMS

UNIVERSITY OF THE PHILIPPINES PRESS

N.V.M. GONZALEZ
THE NOVEL OF JUSTICE
Selected Essays
1968-1994

In Memoriam
Nestor Vicente Madali Gonzalez
1915-1999

Kalutang

N.V.M. Gonzalez

IT IS SAID THAT AMONG THE HANUNOOS the body and the soul are not readily separated.

But the body is not too easily fooled. Nor is it even misled or ill-directed.

I have lived with the Hanunoos; I grew up among them. I have watched them walk down the jungle trail, interminably making song with two wooden sticks. The song helps the soul know where the body is.

Through stretches of fern and embankments of vine, across clearings and second growth, the music travels. Its maker pauses, looking idly up at the sky or swatting a stubborn leech off his leg.

The beating of sticks changes the rhythm from slow to fast; it may even dissolve altogether into silence, coming through again, in a lilting, graceful theme or as a trembling against the stillness of sun-mottled leaves. And then there is a scuffing of dry twigs or the crunch of tree bark.

For our Hanunoo is once more on the move, now with body and soul together.

What follows is an account of my own journey, with my own two wooden sticks. At first I did not know where I was going. Eventually, I did and I continued on, assured not only of the direction I was taking but also of the presence of a self entire.

Excerpted from WORK ON THE MOUNTAIN by N.V.M. Gonzalez (University of the Philippines Press, 1995).

N.V.M. Gonzalez from the Heart:
A Tribute to His Life and Work

N.V.M. GONZALEZ, National Artist for Literature, wrote most distinctively of a Filipino way of life even as he spent many years in the United States and abroad. He was a mentor to students on both sides of the Pacific—in the Philippines and in the United States; he was a writing colleague to writers internationally, from Southeast Asia to Europe. Through his writing, N.V.M. Gonzalez shaped, chiseled, and interpreted the metaphors of Filipino life and brought forth its unique expression to the world. As a lover of words, N.V.M. was truly a Filipino in the world. Together with his beloved wife and partner in life, Narita, the two traversed the world of literature and the world of nations for more than half-a-century.

As N.V.M. Gonzalez once said, "Literature is an affair of letters." Thus, true to his word and to his calling, he wrote, including the unforgettable collection of stories, *Bread of Salt,* and the novels, *The Winds of April* and *The Bamboo Dancers,* and collections of essays including *Work on the Mountain* and *The Novel of Justice.*

N.V.M. Gonzalez was born Nestor Vicente Madali Gonzalez on 8 September 1915 in Romblon, Romblon. The son of a school supervisor and a teacher, he grew up in the remote barrio of Wasig, Mindoro surrounded by a lush countryside that would leave its mark on his work. He studied at Mindoro High School from 1927 to 1930. He had decided very early that he wanted to be a writer, writing his first published essay for the *Philippine Graphic* and getting his first poem published in *Poetry* in 1934. In Manila, he studied briefly at National University but never obtained a degree. In 1934, together with future national artist Francisco Arcellana, he became part of the influential group of writers called the Veronicans. He also wrote for the *Philippine Graphic* and won in several contests, writing in Tagalog and English. He would also edit for the *Evening News Magazine* and the *Manila Chronicle.*

He went to the United States with a Rockefeller Foundation Fellowship in 1948. Returning to the Philippines, he taught at the University of Santo Tomas, Philippine Women's University and the University of the Philippines. He would teach at UP for 18 years, one of only two people to teach there without a college degree. He traveled and wrote on various international grants. He began a long stay in the United States while teaching in California in the 1960s, becoming visiting professor at the University of California in Santa Barbara, professor emeritus at California State University, Hayward and at UCLA's Asian American Studies Center and the Department of English.

He is the author of fourteen books and received many awards, including the Don Carlos Palanca Memorial Award for Literature, the Philippine Republic Merit Award for Literature in English, the Republic Cultural Heritage Award, the Jose Rizal Pro Patria Award, and the City of Manila Medal of Honor.

N.V.M. Gonzalez received an honorary doctorate from UP in 1987, and in 1989 the university named him international writer in residence. For the 1998-1999 year the University of California selected him as the Regents Professor, where he taught and lectured at the UCLA Asian American Studies Center. He returned to teach at UP in the late 1990s. He was named National Artist for Literature in 1997.

N.V.M. leaves behind his wife Narita and children Ibarra, Selma, Michael, Lakshmi, inlaws Cezar Cortes, Patricia Araneta-Gonzalez and grandchildren Bang, Chitty, Huggy, Sierra and Nicky.

—WRITTEN AND COMPILED BY
Ruel S. De Vera, Russell Leong, and Prosy delaCruz

Amerasia Journal 26:1 (2000): 239-254

book reviews

FACE. By Aimee Liu. (New York: Warner Books, 1994. 356 pp. softcover $10.99).

A subtly nude woman photographer graces the cover of Aimee Liu's first novel, *Face*. Curiously, her face is hidden, while remaining at the forefront are the woman's back and her camera. One might surmise that Liu's marketing team became overly ambitious with exoticism. This might be the case, but nonetheless, the cover is indicative of what lies inside the book—snapshots of secrets, dreams, nightmares, and buried realities. Liu utilizes this wall of skeletons to develop slowly a recovery of her protagonist's lost Chinatown culture. She seems to be asking, "Does "The Face" even matter?" by creating an elusive image of protagonist Maibelle Chung via photographs of life in New York's Chinatown through her lens. Yet there is more to Liu's social critique of Chinatown than just Maibelle's mere search for her heritage; Liu dives into an inquiry of what Maibelle does not anticipate on encountering—an even darker past connected to those who have shaped her identity.

From the start, Liu acquaints the reader with Maibelle's sense of displacement in Chinatown. As a flight attendant, she was able to escape the ghosts of her past—a past that Liu paints as a hazy picture, even to Maibelle. Eventually, however, Maibelle is called back to face her ghosts, as Tommy Wah asks Maibelle to be his photographer for his creative commentary on New York's Chinatown. Though she's intrigued, the offer still strikes some chord of hesitation and fear. Along with Tommy Wah's correspondence, Maibelle also considers other matters of circumstance, such as a near accident on the plane and the death of a photographer in New York: "Tommy Wah's letter. The landing in Pensacola. Marge Gramercy. Too many signs, I decided. Or warning" (9). Liu's fragmented syntax offer more pictures for her album, as Maibelle describes key factors in her decision to return to New York.

The novel's plot development centers around Maibelle's craving for cohesion in her mysteriously disjointed life. Consequently, Liu has her assume the recently departed Marge's life in the quest to piece together the puzzle: "Living in her tracks, I thought, might make her achievement seem real to me. Attainable. It might bring both my life and my work back into focus" (10). With the help of her friend Tommy (with whom Maibelle also shares a long-forgotten past) and the dead complete stranger, Marge, she will embark on an otherwise forbidden journey through memory and experience. Maibelle's return to New York's Chinatown is also greeted by those who will help recover the missing links to her haunting recurring nightmares—her family.

Aside from her indifferent brother and sister, Maibelle's Mum has her motives for resurfacing and reviving her husband's claim to fame and its hidden mementos, while Dad would rather have it all disappear. Despite Mum's neurotic and sometimes psychotic schemes and manipulation, one thing is clear: Mum is undeniably a catalyst in Maibelle's return to photography. Maibelle describes how she appropriates Mum's careful teachings and develops it into a picture of her own design:

> My mother began teaching me practically from birth to watch the world through an imaginary viewfinder. Using the magic of the camera, she said, I could stop time cold, yet keep it alive. Through the alchemy of the darkroom, I could float the ghosts of moments I'd live through back into shadow and light, and when I finally mastered the magic, I would feel the photograph as though I were watching myself watch the world—and seeing the world look back. (25)

Liu's otherwise amusing portrayal of Mum gains some sensitivity as Maibelle recounts how she mystically regards the world behind the camera in the above example. This is one moment out of many in which Liu subtly connects seemingly unrelated characters in order to complicate further Maibelle's repressed past. Flying up to "watch the world" is something she learned from a close childhood friend—someone who the reader also learns is Maibelle's guardian angel through her journey of nightmares. Yet it is Maibelle's mother who paves the path for association, and hence, remembrance.

Maibelle's father is the primary source of the mystery that's to be unraveled in the course of the text. Scraps of carefully chosen vignettes are either put out on the table by him or randomly picked up along the way due to Maibelle's probing sense of curiosity. Liu portrays her father as the key to unlocking the family album, though Maibelle is unsure of why or how. Yet everything in the shadows, no matter how unrelated, seems connected through him. Liu poignantly describes how Dad casually tells Maibelle that she had been named after his sisters. Maibelle reacts:

> I'd never even seen a picture of my aunts, and yet I bore their names. That seemed to make them a part of me, or vice versa. A fact of my life almost since I was born, yet no one had ever bothered to tell me. It was a minor thing, but it gave me a sense of what an amnesia victim must experience on being told he has a name he doesn't recognize, that total strangers are his dear friends and family. A sense of existing on two planes at once, with no connection between them. (87)

This brief reflection embodies the feel of the entire text. Liu, like a mystery novelist, drops clues here and there, and by the end of the novel, the picture is *almost* complete. And as Maibelle shoots pictures of the residents of a Chinatown senior citizen center, she realizes that even these people with whom she thought she had no relation are projecting memories of her childhood. One of the most important characters is old Li, the shopkeeper who captures the young Maibelle in his enthralling storytelling ways. Nearly forgotten, he is remembered as Maibelle chats with interesting elders at the center who knew Li. Once again, Maibelle is faced with yet another level of recovered broken memories of a childhood from which she ran away. Fragments conjoin, and missing pieces find their way back home to the master puzzle, but can the reader figure out Maibelle's face?

Aimee Liu has written an intriguing debut novel. Today's collection of Asian American texts grapple with issues of recovering lost identities, piecing together the dark secrets of previous generations, and bridging cultural rivers between continents. However, Liu's text stands out in its pristine juggling of time and place—all framed within the eyes of a camera. Her placement of striking photographic images of Chinatown between sections of the novel also adds to the intrigue and depth of the words between the pages. As Maibelle's father tells her, "Photographs are like mirrors. They can always be manipulated and distorted, no two people use them the same way" (135). After all, that is what appears to be Liu's point—that it takes much more than a thousand words to tell the story of a single picture.

Brandy Worrall
University of California, Los Angeles

ASIAN/AMERICAN: HISTORICAL CROSSINGS OF A RACIAL FRONTIER. By David Palumbo-Liu. (Stanford: Stanford University Press, 1999. 534 pp. hardcover $65.00, softcover $24.95).

"[W]e will ask," explains David Palumbo-Liu, "not whether Asians have become assimilated, but, 'to what, exactly, are they to be assimilated?'; 'how does the history of Asian America demonstrate the centrality of Asia to the imagining of modern America'; and 'what have been the various historical incarnations and precise contents of the Asian/American dynamic?'" (1-2). With this set of inquiries, Palumbo-Liu launches *Asian/American: Historical Crossings of a Racial Frontier*, his ambitious study of the dynamics between "Asian" and "American" in the twentieth century. By questioning *not whether*, but *to what* Asians have been assimilated, Palumbo-Liu establishes the grounds for critical interrogation of how America works in the construction and maintenance of its identity and ideologies. This broad-reaching and thoroughly researched book details the manifold ways that America's imaginings of Asia have centrally informed the changing configurations of modern America. The specificity with which Palumbo-Liu conducts his study marks the significance of this important contribution to contemporary Americanist and Asian Americanist discourses on national identity formation and the relationship of that process to the U.S.'s racialized, minoritized groups. This particularity provides for scholars engaged in these discourses precise, grounded knowledge that successfully challenges Eurocentric ideas about American modernity, thus indelibly shifting the grounds for inquiry into the cultures and apparatuses of the nation.

Asian/American is a big book: divided into five sections of two chapters each, with introduction, conclusion and an appendix additional, that the hefty size of this volume is necessary becomes quickly evident as Palumbo-Liu unfolds his argument. The complexity of understanding modern America in its relationship to Asia (as foreign region) and "Asia" (as conceptual entity), requires a study that reaches in multiple directions—to the historical and cultural, to the political and economic, to the relationship between the national and the global, to the interplay among race, class, and gender, and to the differences between Asian Americans and other racialized minorities. Palumbo-Liu's great accomplishment here is that he engages with and clarifies this intricate complexity without being reductive. Our understandings of what constitutes national culture and identity are productively complicated by this attentiveness to the multitude of factors that participate in the production of the nation.

The argument of the book is signaled by the construction, "Asian/American" of its title. Palumbo-Liu explains that "[a]s in the construction 'and/or,' where the solidus at once instantiates a choice between two terms, their simultaneous and equal status, and an element of indecidability, that is, as it at once implies both exclusion and inclusion, 'Asian/American' marks *both* the distinction installed between "Asian" and "American" *and* a dynamic, unsettled, and inclusive movement" between them, or over that distinction (1). "Asia" in the American frame neither can be completely segregated out of the national imaginary, nor has been absorbed into and by "America" such that distinctions do not remain. Modern America has come into being through ongoing negotiations of the figure of Asia as a signifier of foreign nations and interests and as that figure is recognized already to be within America. Thus, according to Palumbo-Liu, since especially the 1930s, the U.S. has negotiated both the conditions of its interiority (i.e., Asian peoples already in residence and participating in the nation) and global relations, a double mode of introjection and projection at work within a field of interplay between U.S. racial ideology and its economic interests.

Three interrelated analyses organize this study: body, psyche, and space. Focus on corporeality enables a grounding in the material histories of immigration and economics, especially as they precipitate certain understandings of gendered and racialized bodies, while attention to the psyche, the mind and mentality of the (Asian) American, allows us to examine the rationale behind and ideology of those understandings. Pointed consideration of the nation through the analytic of space registers the deployment of these understandings of the Asian and American body and mind within both literal and figurative conceptualizations of American territory. The constellation of these analyses makes possible to see that the modern American legal, sociological, and cultural texts that Palumbo-Liu considers take up the project of "inventing the terms upon which to negotiate the hybridization of the modern nation feeling its very interior penetrated by the formerly foreign" (105).

Anchored by consistently insightful analyses of key sociological studies, legislative maneuverings, newspaper and other media accounts, and centrally, by literary and filmic narratives, *Asian/America* explores both the terms and consequences of this negotiation. Representations of Asians in such disparate texts as Sax Rohmer's 1936 novel, *President Fu Manchu*, Chang-Rae Lee's contemporary work, *Native Speaker*, and popular films like Frank Capra's *The Bitter Tea of General Yen* are examined (each in separate, historicized chapters) alongside analysis of *Time* and *Newsweek* magazine covers that provide evidence of the nation's continuing preoccupation with "the foreign within" throughout the twentieth century. Demonstrating dissimilarities among, or the very unevenness of these representations, is an important part of the work of this book: doing so makes impossible simplistic, homogenous conceptualization of either the nation or of Asian America. This unevenness signals the dynamic movement of the solidus Palumbo-Liu describes—the unsettled, indecidable state of the relationship between "Asia" and "America." Palumbo-Liu moves us, in other words, through the twentieth century, through modern (and to postmodern) America, in his tracing of the multiple, varying roles that Asia/"Asia" has played in national identity formation. This book moves us, that is, to understanding the present function of the Asian in America, or the Asian American, as conditioned both by the ways in which modern America has come into being, and by the specific characteristics of the present historical moment.

Palumbo-Liu's persuasive explanation of how "Asian American social subjectivity now vacillates between whiteness and color," and how "its function is always to trace a racial minority's possibilities for assimilation" (5) signals the contemporary importance of his project for Asian Americanist and Americanist scholars. In mapping the uniqueness of the Asian/American dynamic, this book charts significant differences among the processes of racialization experienced by various minoritized groups in the U.S. As especially Part III ("Modeling the Nation") and the closing chapters detail, analyzing the specifics of these differences exposes the anatomy of contemporary American nationalist and internationalist discourses. By the book's end, we understand both how and why it is that Asian American social subjectivity, unlike other racialized American subjectivities, bears these particular functions of being at once a signifier of possible assimilation and of the limits proscribing that possibility.

Asian/American is a timely book. As scholarly inquiry continues to turn attention to mapping the contours of twentieth century America, and as both popular and academic discourse continues to herald the importance of the "Pacific Rim" in the twenty-first century, this study's decisive establishment of the centrality of Asia to American modernity, and as well, its multi-disciplinary orientation and framing, provides both the substantive knowledge and the critical means for researching what present incarnations of the Asian/American dynamic may reveal about the nation. Practitioners not only of Asian American and American Studies, but of contemporary cultural studies, will find *Asian/American* to be of critical interest.

Kandice Chuh
University of Maryland, College Park

MASKING SELVES, MAKING SUBJECTS: JAPANESE AMERICAN WOMEN, IDENTITY, AND THE BODY. By Traise Yamamoto. (Berkeley: University of California Press, 1999. 329 pp., hardcover $45.00, softcover, $17.95).

As the first book-length study of Japanese American women's writing, Traise Yamamoto's *Masking Selves, Making Subjects: Japanese American Women, Identity, and the Body* will doubtless be measured against a tradition of Asian American feminist scholarship that includes such voices as King-Kok Cheung, Elaine Kim, Dorinne Kondo, Amy Ling and Sau-ling Wong. Certainly Yamamoto builds on previous feminist scholarship in her concern with the narrative and ontological effects of silence, which she conceives as the practice of "masking" in Japanese American women's writings. Her study establishes the complex means by which "masking" their purposes or selves served these women writers who, despite the racialized and gendered discursive networks in the west that curtailed their articulation, nonetheless often succeeded in envisioning a sense of agency for themselves. Attentive to "the specific ways in which Japanese American women construct themselves as subjects and their simultaneous construction as objects in an orientalist discourse" (65), *Masking Selves* offers an important reappraisal of poststructuralist theories of subjectivity in her analysis of Japanese American women's development of a complex dynamic of concealment and revelation in their writings.

The book is built around "the grammatical doubleness" of the title phrase, "masking subjects," which "suggests both a process enacted by an agency separate from the socially defined self as well as a self whose agency is enacted in the process of masking." Thus the readings of Japanese American women's writings are located "in the awkward juncture between two claims," or between postmodernism's arguments against the totality of selfhood referenced by concepts of subjectivity and the political and material urgency of subjectivity for marginalized subjects.

The "phrasal ambiguity" of the title is chiefly explored as a symptom of the interrelationship between the racialized and gendered Japanese/American female body and text within U.S. history and Japanese American women's conflation with Japanese women and a feminized Japan in the broader Western imagination, as Yamamoto points out in the opening essay on Pico Iyer's travel narratives. Without denying either the unique contingencies of Japanese American women's identities or the instability of the body as the site of the construction of race and gender, Yamamoto offers a nuanced argument for "how the combination of the geisha stereotype and the visually based racial economy of the United States results in the invisibility of the Japanese American female subject" such that "her invisibility as a [national] subject is paired with her hypervisibility as a sexualized, racially marked body" (5). In order to trace the effects of this contradiction, the book draws on a number of related genres and areas—white western male travel writing; popular films; and, in the last half of the book, Japanese American women's autobiographical and creative works, including travel memoirs, fiction and poetry. Yamamoto's purpose is "to discuss modes of agency that disrupt and cannot be causally or directly traced to the social or discursive constructs that would seem to determine the subject in all its modalities"(3).

The most compelling arguments here engage with the importance and elusiveness of the body as a necessary, though unstable, site for the negotiation of subjectivity and selfhood for women and racialized subjects. What emerges is a familiar, but often still unheeded, critique of the limitations of postmodernism for the racialized and gendered writer: postmodernism's conceptualization of the fragmented self as a recent "discovery" ignores both the histories of disenfranchised groups and the risks of a "disempowered" stance for racialized and gendered subjects. While Yamamoto acknowledges the body's indeterminacy as a bearer of identity and difference, she maintains that in "vacating the body as an irredeemable site of fetishization," Japanese American women writers find themselves "at a problematic site of psychic disembodiment" (77). In their writings, they are often forced to redefine the relation between form and function, between the body, as a marker of abjection, and the self, as a still powerful source of agency. *Masking Selves, Making Subjects* reevaluates apparent acts of abjection or disavowal to inquire how Japanese American women writers are nevertheless able to experience a degree of agency, however provisional or obscured. The body is reclaimed as a disjuncture that is nevertheless experienced as itself the ground of a viable subjectivity" (81).

Throughout her discussion the author returns to the question of "the ways in which the body is visually conscripted into structures of difference" (91). She finds that the agency assumed by the "masquerade" of social performance in a poststructuralist sense must be revised to account for the "mask" of "the racial markedness of the body/face" that Japanese American women writers must deal with as they attempt to shape resistant subjectivities (100). In Japanese American women's autobiographies of the internment period, the relation between what Yamamoto deems "that other, private self" and the racial "mask" haunts the permission to speak and challenges our expectations about the functions of self-revelation. In *Nisei Daughter*, Monica Sone's image of her body as a metonym for the community, "like a two-headed monstrosity" (Sone 236) split between the pressures to disclaim any relationship to Japanese culture and the continuing sense of a connection to a Japanese self. This image, by now legendary in Asian American studies, indicts the restricted circumstances of representation for Nisei autobiographers, circumstances that led them to express a self through concealment, a body clearly marked by a racial difference that must be at once denied and asserted in the climate of post-World War II America (103).

Although Yamamoto focuses on the works of Japanese American women, her book also challenges the scholarly conventions of reading or interpreting Asian American women's writing in general. In a chapter on the trope of maternal absence, she argues that intergenerational approaches often ignore the fact that Japanese American women "must both differentiate from and identify with the mother in order to construct a viable subjectivity in which gender and race are mutually constitutive" (143). Instead, Yamamoto argues we must examine maternality in relation to particular and unstable political or historical contexts that determine the value and circulation of the ethnic or racialized mother. It is in this last regard that Yamamoto reveals her keen sense of the problematics of "masking" as a means of subjectivity, as a process that simultaneously enables and limits the articulation of self for Asian/American women (255). Yamamoto's concluding points about the failure of language also awaken us to the complex nature of all forms of representation, rooted as they are in contingent social processes and negotiations: "that memory [no less than narrative] evokes presence but is not itself presence" (260). Still, as Yamamoto so eloquently argues, it is perhaps in attending to this critical distinction that Japanese American women succeed in speaking a self that mediates between the urgency of expression and the constraints of an art that is always rife with political risks.

Caroline Chung Simpson
University of Washington

SONGS OF THE CAGED, SONGS OF THE FREE: MUSIC AND THE VIETNAMESE REFUGEE EXPERIENCE. By Adelaida Reyes (Temple University, 1999. 218 pp. hardcover $59.50, softcover $19.95).

"Where people go, music goes. They are inseparable" (15). This is the guiding tenet that is at the core of ethnomusicological studies and Adelaida Reyes' (New Jersey City University) engaging book on music and the Vietnamese refugee experience. Analyses of music in immigrant communities and cultural diasporas are abundant and wide-ranging within the ethnomusicology landscape, a field which seeks to understand music as human behavior in social, cultural, and historical context. What makes Reyes' methodology unique is her focus on the "forced migration" aspects of the refugee musical experience. Reyes argues that, as opposed to voluntary immigrant communities, refugees who must flee from their homelands out of fear and terror of persecution produce and experience music differently as a consequence of their forced migration. In support of her argument, Reyes has composed a textured and colorful account of how music can be held as a revealing mirror by which to study the Vietnamese refugee journey.

Over a period of more than ten years (1983-1993), Reyes observed and collected data on different groups of Vietnamese refugees, tracing their exodus along a trajectory beginning at a camp of first asylum, proceeding to a refugee processing camp, and ending with resettlement in the United States. Along the way, Reyes demonstrates and concludes from her findings that deeply-embedded sentiments of nostalgia for pre-1975 Vietnam and vehement feelings of anticommunism are reflected in the music of Vietnamese refugees.

The composition of *Songs of the Caged, Songs of the Free* is structured into two major segments. In part one, Reyes develops the *cantus firmus*, or leading melody, of her book by following the journey of Vietnamese refugees from Vietnam to camp life in the Philippines. She provides in these first few chapters an ethnographic sketch of musical life in two specific refugee camps: Palawan (a camp of first asylum for many Vietnamese after their escape from Vietnam), and Bataan (a processing center that served as the last stop before resettlement in another country). Reyes analyzes the prominence of Vietnamese "sad songs" and "love songs" in the camps in the context of loss and separation suffered by asylees from warfare and escape. She illustrates that as these refugees moved toward resettlement, they increasingly insisted on making clear distinctions between Vietnamese music made "before 1975" and "after 1975." These expressions, Reyes contends, were taken to be synonymous with respective distinctions between "non-communist" and "communist" Vietnam. Indeed, the music that was played in the camps was exclusively pre-1975 music, highlighting the intense longing for a non-communist Vietnam and corresponding feelings of fierce anti-communism held by the refugees.

Reyes' discussion of "public" versus "private" or "localized" production of non-communist music within the camps is also interesting and noteworthy. Her analysis is particularly insightful as it captures the nuances of camp musical life, giving the reader a detailed understanding of how different genres or types of Vietnamese music such as *cai luong*, *vong co*, or *tan nhac* were featured in different camp settings.

In the second half of the book, Reyes moves beyond the camp settings and examines music in the context of the transplanted lives of resettled Vietnamese refugees in New Jersey and California. In the chapter on New Jersey, Reyes focuses on *Tet* (Vietnamese New Years) public celebrations as localized windows into the musical expressions of Vietnamese resettlement experiences in the 1980s. In studying the musical performances at these public celebrations, Reyes concludes that the Vietnamese community in New Jersey, "as a transitional or emergent community, one in the early stages of defining itself both to itself and to others" (101), shared a *preoccupation* with surviving in their new home and grappling with challenging identity issues. Reyes explores this resettlement process in much more detail when she examines the Vietnamese community in Orange County, California.

Having the largest Vietnamese community outside of Vietnam, Orange County provides a polychromatic and dynamic background for Reyes' study of music through the prism of refugee circumstances. This section of the book is the most comprehensive and absorbing, as Reyes documents various music venues and different genres of Vietnamese music that have been transplanted to the United States. In turn, she gives the reader a revealing passageway into understanding the various impacts of U.S. society and political and economic pressures on Vietnamese American musical life.

In general, one of the many strengths of Reyes' accounts of refugee musical experiences is that she consistently provides relevant historical, sociopolitical, and economic contexts for her multi-layered ethnomusicological analyses. She also often includes the voices of refugees themselves, showing how their views on life are often reflected in their choice of music. For Reyes, music does not exist in a vacuum; it is interwoven with people and their lives and changes with the flux of time. In the last two chapters of the book, Reyes discusses changes in the Vietnamese American musical scene after the lifting of the trade embargo and the "normalization" of relations with Vietnam. Using an inductive approach, Reyes thus expands her discussion of musical contrasts between forced and voluntary migrants to include broader themes of variation, discontinuity, displacement, cultural heterogeneity and identity, and marginality.

These complexities, that are integral and defining features of the Vietnamese refugee experience, inevitably present methodological challenges that tend to limit Reyes' explorations of stories of forced migration. However, Reyes, deftly weaves the various components of her narrative together by providing analytical commentaries that probe the deeper meanings of musical renderings. She demonstrates that music is an illuminating medium for studying the emotional and psychological undercurrents of ethnic communities. This is especially true for those communities, such as the Vietnamese refugee community, that have undergone traumatic tribulations and, as a result, turn to music to communicate experiences that may not find expression through other means. For those who want to learn more about the sonorous complexities of Vietnamese American life and identity, Reyes's study on the musical passages of this refugee community is an eloquent and informative recital. Through *Songs of the Caged, Songs of the Free*, Reyes has given us not only an innovative and insightful perspective on what it means to be a refugee; she has also shown us how "to see at close range the persistence and power of musical expression under the most trying conditions" (175).

Tu-Uyen Nguyen
Los Angeles, California

THE POLITICAL ECONOMY OF RACISM: A HISTORY. By Melvin M. Leiman. (East Haven, Connecticut: Pluto Press, 1992. 421 pp. hardcover $63.00, softcover $18.95).

Leftist scholars have struggled to explain "race" in ways that do not trivialize the lived experience and history of people of color, yet maintain the primacy of their Marxist critique of capitalism—that is, class-based exploitation. Leiman takes on this Marxist task utilizing economic, historical, sociological and political analysis to develop a complex multidisciplinary explanation of the relations between class and black racism in the United States. He asserts that racism is fundamental to the historical development of capitalism and that the end to racism can only occur with the dismantling of the "unplanned" capitalist market economy. This dismantling, however, will occur only when working class whites and blacks recognize their shared labor/class consciousness and subordinate their racist (in the case of whites) and racial (in the case of blacks) interest.

Leiman weaves his argument with an intricate historical and economic discussion of capital formation. He creates the stage for the enduring resiliency of racism against blacks in the U.S. In the early chapters, the author examines why, how, and under what circumstances black discrimination, bolstered by racism, serves the interest of the capitalist system and is itself fundamental in the structure of the capitalist mode of production. Leiman demonstrates that black discrimination impacts working class whites and capitalist, and is neither monolithic nor static. Leiman explains how racism was used at each phase of capitalist development in U.S. history. He carefully outlines the oppressive consequences of this historical process on the contemporary economic and political reality of blacks in the U.S., which include poverty and a polarized black elite—the processes and conditions whereby racism is "rooted in the historical structure of capitalism and helping to reinforce the system" (191).

The author argues that racism and black discriminatory policies (state and private), from slavery to affirmative action to glass ceiling, ultimately serves the capitalist system, first, by artificially controlling labor supply and creating economic multipliers that foster capital accumulation. Second, racism and black discrimination inhibits interracial labor organizing and class-consciousness, a prerequisite for overcoming capitalism. The strength of Leiman's analysis lies in his ability to show that capitalists (competitive and monopolist) and white working classes (skilled and unskilled) are not monolithic. Each segment's interest has influenced the maintenance or dismantling of racial discrimination over time in relation to differing capitalist developmental periods and market cycles. Thus, not all capitalists benefit from racial discrimination in all conditions, nor do all white workers.

Capitalist development, however, does not occur in an economic vacuum. For Leiman, the government exists to protect the interest of the capitalist class. He synthesizes political and sociological explanations with economic processes. Government's distance from capitalists, however slight, allows the government to foster long run perspectives that enforce or relax racial discrimination based on the material needs of capitalism and the need for social order (whose disruptions can materially harm capitalism) at any particular moment. Leiman uses numerous examples throughout U.S. history, from slavery to the civil rights movement, and the economic expansion the 1960s, to illustrate the relationships among economic cycle, technological advancement, social unrest, and political economy.

His historical and political economic explanation is followed by a critical analysis of radical and orthodox critiques of racism. In examining radical (Marxist) critique, Leiman offers to fill in the gaps of existing critique by tackling the complex relationship of capital, white workers, and economic cycles. In short, he argues that the more recognized radical approaches lack the complexity for empirically based theoretical explanation. Orthodox critiques of race fall short because they attempt to explain racism as an aberration from the norm of capitalism, thus its eradication can occur through transformation of the capitalist system. Such thinking, for Leiman, fails to recognize that racism, through the historical process of capitalist development, is now an integral part of capitalism. Thus the elimination of racism is impossible without the deconstruction of capitalism.

In the final three chapters of the book, Leiman critiques the black responses to racism, and switches his stance from a scholar offering explanation to an advocate of a specific radical solution. This perhaps is where Leiman is most vulnerable. His critique of

various black responses to racism includes analysis of Black Capitalism, Black Nationalism and Black Radicalism. None is adequate
for Leiman inasmuch as each of the black responses emphasizes
race consciousness first, which only impedes class-consciousness.
Even Black Radicalism falls short because it focuses on organizing the black masses rather than black labor and for emphasizing
race over class. In advocating his solution, Leiman calls on the
black working class to join with white labor as the vanguard for
progressive change. Though Leiman has taken great pains to explain the "realness" of racism and its role in the capitalist structure, he ultimately subordinates race to class. "Institutional racism and exploitation confronting the black is a higher development of institutionalized exploitation facing *all* workers, and the
race question is ultimately only part of the class question" (313).

For Leiman an interracial labor movement remains the only
hope for structural change from a capitalist unplanned economy
to a democratic planned economy, because labor remains the "only
institution capable of setting up a party genuinely independent
of the capitalist class" (332). And, it is only through the elimination of capitalism that we can eliminate racism.

Despite Leiman's convincing articulation of racism as fundamental to the capitalist structure, his call for class solidarity is the
heart of this book. The final chapters' critique of black responses
to racism left me perplexed. Who was his intended audience? It
seems as though Leiman wants to make clear that any emphasis
on race over class is folly or wrong, i.e., energy spent traveling
down a dead-end road, and that while black responses have raised
black consciousness and self-esteem, their usefulness has run its
course. Leiman's dismissal of the organizing of black masses is also
unsettling. Somehow, the tone of his approach sounds like a military general discussing "acceptable casualties." "The overwhelming problem remains how to raise the revolutionary consciousness from the lumpen level to the working-class level since this is
the only level that has the potential of structurally transforming
the dominant capitalist mode of production" (294). Is Leiman trying to convince the Black scholar, philanthropist or radical activist of their wrong-headedness and lead them to the light of labor
organizing? While Leiman does warn against the potential elitism
that labor vanguard can foster, he seems to romantically trust that
labor will have the consciousness to overcome the temptation.
Leiman's understanding of race is virtually silent on non-black minorities, though he acknowledges that the labor movement needs

to be international in scope due to capitalist exploitation of Third World countries. The failure to at least mention Asian Americans in his analysis or at least a statement outlining his omission as a matter of resources makes me wonder if he feels that Asian Americans are tangential to our understanding of the political economic history of the U.S. as well as forays into Asian Third World countries. For Asian American scholars interested in examining a model for complex multidisciplinary work on political economy and race, Leiman offers a challenging and thoughtful read. If you are looking to find out how Asian Americans fit into the U.S. political economic history or how focus on class can overcome racism you will be disappointed.

Curtiss Takada Rooks
San Jose State University

canadian ethnic studies
études ethniques au canada

An interdisciplinary journal devoted to the study of ethnicity, immigration, inter-group relations and the history and cultural life of ethnic groups in Canada.

Une revue interdisciplinaire consacrée à l'étude de l'éthnicité, de l'immigration, des relations entre groupes, et de l'histoire et de la vie culturelle collective au Canada.

SPECIAL ISSUES AVAILABLE/NUMEROS SPECIAUX EN VENTE

1992, Vol. XXIV, no. 3	– Multicultural Education: Directions for the Nineties
1993, Vol. XXV, no. 3	– Ethnicity and the Family
1994, Vol. XXVI, no. 3	– Racial and Ethnic Inequality
1995, Vol. XXVII, no.3	– From Russia with Love: The Doukhobors*
1996, Vol. XXVIII, no.1	– Ethnic Themes in Canadian Literature

RECENT REGULAR ISSUES INCLUDE/NUMERO REGULIERS RECENTS COMPRENNENT

1994, Vol. XXVI, no. 3	– "Deconstructing the Categorical Reality of Race and Gender"
1995, Vol. XXVII, no. 1	– "Racial Supremacism under Social Democracy"
1995, Vol. XXVII, no. 2	– "Les modes d'organisation collective des Lao à Montreàl: un contexte socio-politique structurant"
1995, Vol. XXVII, no. 3	– "Doukhobor Survival Through the Centuries"
1996, Vol. XXVIII, no. 1	– "Neither Here nor There: Canadian Fiction by the Multicultural Generation"

$18.00 for individual issues/$18.00 pour un seul numéro. Outside Canada $18.00US/hors du Canada $18.00US.

For all issues prior to 1996, enquire at the Calgary journal address below/pour let numéros avant 1996 disponibles adressez vos demandes au bureau du journal à Calgary à l'adresse ci-dessous.

Issues also include book and film reviews, opinions, immigrant memoirs, translations of primary sources, books received, an index and annual bibliography.

Chaque numéro comprend des recensions de livres et de films, des opinions, des mémoires d'immigrants, des traductions de sources primaires, livres reçus, et des bibliographies.

Subscription rates/frais d'abonnement:	One year/un an	Outside Canada/hors du Canada
Individuals/particuliers	$50.00	$50.00 US
Students/étudiants	$20.00	$20.00 US
Institutions/institutions	$60.00	$60.00 US

Above rates include membership in the Canadian Ethnic Studies Association/Les frais comprennent la qualité de membre de la Societé d'études ethniques au Canada.

Articles for publication, books for review and general correspondence should be addressed to CANADIAN ETHNIC STUDIES, c/o The University of Calgary, 2500 University Drive N.W., Calgary, Alberta, Canada T2N IN4. Single orders and back issues can be obtained from this address.

Subscription Orders and Inquiries should be addressed to CANADIAN ETHNIC STUDIES ASSOCIATION, Centre for Ethnic Studies (CEETUM), Université de Montréal, C.P. 6128, succursale Centre-ville, Montréal, Québec H3C 3J7.

Tout les articles, les recensions, et la correspondance générale doivent etre adressés aux ETUDES ETHNIQUES AU CANADA. The University of Calgary, 2500 University Drive N.W., Calgary, Alberta, Canada T2N IN4. Tout numéro courant et ancien de la revue peut être commandé à l'adresse ci-dessus.

Pour les abonnements et les informations prière de vous adresser à la SOCIETÉ d'ÉTUDE ETHNIQUES AU CANADA, Centre d'études ethniques (CEETUM), Université de Montréal, C.P. 6128, succursale Centre-ville, Montréal, Québec H3C 3J7.

ASIAN
AMERICAN
POLICY
REVIEW

Volume VII, Spring 1997
"Transnationalism"

Established in 1989, the *Asian American Policy Review* is an independent journal published annually by graduate students of the John F. Kennedy School of Government at Harvard University.

The mission of the *Review* is to provide scholars, elected officials, policy analysts, and community leaders a forum to discuss contemporary issues and events affecting Asian Americans.

As the first non-partisan, scholarly journal devoted to public policy issues affecting the Asian American community, the *Review* encourages public dialogue and promotes leadership within the Asian American community.

FEATURES
Articles and studies on the impact of transnationalism on public policies of concern to the Asian American community
--Frank Wu and M. Nicholson with media perspectives on the John Huang controversy
--Interviews with Connie Chung and Hawaii Governor Benjamin Cayetano

PERSPECTIVES
Commentaries by notable policymakers and practitioners on the recently passed welfare legislation
--Andrew Leong
--Karen Narasaki
--Rep. Patsy Mink

STUDENT NOTES
Outstanding submissions by graduate and undergraduate students

BOOK REVIEWS
Reviews of recent publications of policy significance to the Asian American community

SUBSCRIPTIONS
Individual: $12, Institution: $28. Volumes II, III, IV, and V, and VI are available for purchase. Please make all checks payable to: Asian American Policy Review.

CALL FOR PAPERS
Deadline for Volume VIII is November 1, 1997.

VOL. VI - SPRING 1996 "AFFIRMATIVE ACTION"
Dana Takagi • Paul Igasaki • Frederick F.Y. Pang • Dennis Hayashi & Christopher Edley, Jr. • Lance Izumi • Ling-chi Wang • Corinne Kodama • Helen Hyun • Kent Wong • Susan Lee

Asian American
Policy Review
John F. Kennedy School of
Government
Harvard University
79 John F. Kennedy Street
Cambridge, MA 02138

PHONE: (617) 496-8655
FAX: (617)496-9027
E-MAIL: aapr@
ksg1.harvard.edu
WEB: http://
www.ksg.harvard.edu/~aapr

*The **Review** is committed to the following principles in selecting papers for publication: timeliness of topic to current policy discussions; originality and thoroughness of research & ideas; cohesiveness & sophistication of arguments; contribution to scholarship and policymaking; style, tone, & coherency of language; and overall effectiveness. Please contact the Review office for further information regarding the Review's submissions and editorial policy.*

The Journal of Religion and Film

Edited by:

William L. Blizek
and **Ronald R. Burke**

Department of Philosophy and Religion

CALL FOR PAPERS

JR&F invites manuscripts on a wide variety of topics related to religion and film. JR&F is published on the internet twice a year at the following address: http://www.unomaha.edu/~wwwjrf

Manuscripts should be approximately 3500 words in length and should include a 100-word summary of the content. Manuscripts will be peer-reviewed and may be submitted for consideration either via e-mail or by mailing a 3.5 inch disk to the editors. Footnotes should be numbered in the text and listed at the end of the manuscript. Manuscripts may be submitted to:

William L. Blizek and Ronald R. Burke
The Journal of Religion and Film
Department of Philosophy and Religion
University of Nebraska at Omaha
Omaha, Nebraska 68182-0265
internet: rburke@unomaha.edu or blizek@unomaha.edu

Journal of Popular Culture

Ray B. Browne, editor

· Subscription includes membership in the Popular Culture Association.
· Joint subscription with *Journal of American Culture:* $65.00.
· Published quarterly.
· $35.00 yearly, $65.00 for two years.
· Institutions: $45.00 yearly, $80.00 for two years.
· Outside USA: add $4.00 per year postage fee.
* The JPC is in its twenty-seventh year of publication.

Journal of American Culture

Ray B. Browne and Tom Towers, editors

· Subscription includes membership in the American Culture Association.
· Published quarterly.
· $35.00 yearly, $65.00 for two years.
· Institutions: $45.00 yearly, $80.00 for two years.
· Outside USA: add $4.00 per year postage fee.

Journal of Cultural Geography

Alvar Carlson, editor

· Published bi-annually.
· $12.50 yearly, $23.00 for two years.
· Institutions: $15.00 yearly, $28.00 for two years.
· Outside USA: add $2.00 per year postage fee.

Clues: A Journal of Detection

Pat Browne, editor

· Published bi-annually.
· $12.50 yearly, $23.00 for two years.
· Institutions: $15.00 yearly, $28.00 for two years.
· Outside USA: add $2.00 per year postage fee.

Popular Music and Society

Gary Burns, editor

· Published quarterly.
· $25.00 yearly, $45.00 for two years.
· Institutions: $30.00 yearly, $55.00 for two years.
· Outside USA: add $4.00 per year postage fee.

Popular Press
Bowling Green State University
Bowling Green, OH 43403
To order: 1-800-515-5118

Available Back Issues
of Amerasia Journal

Single Issues: $13.00 each
(Please circle issue number and fill out order form on back)

Get the Amerasia Journal 1971-1998 Cumulative Article
Index! $5.00 (plus $3.00 shipping and handling).

UCLA Asian American Studies Center Press

3230 Campbell Hall • Box 951546 • Los Angeles, CA 90095-1546
(310) 825-2968 • Fax # (310) 206-9844 • email: ku@ucla.edu

PUBLICATIONS—Order Form

Name

Street Address

City   State   Zip

Signature   VISA/MASTERCARD/Discovery/Diners/JCB accepted: (add 3% credit card charge)

Card Number   Phone #   Expiration Date   Total

(please circle the items you wish to order)

An Asian American Internet Guide. ($5.00 paper)

2000-01 Asian Pacific Community Directory. ($15.00 paper)

A Buried Past II: A Sequel to the Annotated Bibliography of the Japanese American Research Project Collection. ($20.00 paper)

Confrontations, Crossings and Convergence: Photographs of the Philippines and the United States, 1898-1998. (text + 100 photographs, $15.00 paper)

Emergence of the Vietnamese Communities in America. (Bibliography, $10.00 paper)

Executive Order 9066: The Internment of 110,000 Japanese Americans. (Catalogue, $15.00 paper)

Pilipino America at the Crossroads: 100 Years of U.S. Philippine Relations. (Bibliography, $15.00 paper)

Emergence of the Vietnamese Communities in America. (Bibliography, $10.00 paper)

Fading Footsteps of the Issei: An Annotated Check List of the Manuscript Holdings of the Japanese American Research Project Collection. ($24.95 paper)

Filipino American Scholars Directory 1998. COMPILED/EDITED BY ELIZABETH A. PASTORES-PALFFY, HERMINIA MENEZ, TANIA AZORES ($15.00 paper)

A History Reclaimed: An Annotated Bibliography of Chinese Language Materials on Chinese in America. ($25.00 cloth)

History of the Okinawans in N. America. ($25.00 cloth)

2000-01 National Asian Pacific American Political Almanac. ($15.00 paper)

Prism Lives/Emerging Voices of Multiracial Asians. (Bibliography, $10.00 paper)

Rappin' with Ten Thousand Carabaos: Poetry by Al Robles. ($13.00 paper)

Between a Rock and a Hard Place: A History of American Sweatshops, 1820-Present. Peter Liebhold and Harry R. Rubenstein. (text + photographs, $12.00)

Views from Within: The Japanese American Evacuation and Resettlement Study ($15.00 paper)

Handling charges: $4.00 per copy on first and $2.00 each on next up to four. $8.00 on small box and $15.00 on large box ❖ California residents add 7.75% and L.A. County residents add 8.25% Sales Tax.

⊞ subscribe ⊞

MAKE CHECKS PAYABLE TO:
"UC Regents"

MAILING ADDRESS:

Publications/UCLA Asian American Studies Center Press
3230 Campbell Hall ⊞ Box 951546
Los Angeles, CA 90095-1546
(310) 825-2974/2968 ⊞ FAX (310) 206-9844

email: ku@ucla.edu

I would like to order _____ @ $_____.____.

I would like to order _____ @ $_____.____.

I would like to order the **Amerasia Journal 1971-1998
Cumulative Article Index!** @ $5.00
(plus $3.00 shipping and handling)

I would like a 1-year subscription to *Amerasia Journal*

☐ $35.00/year (individual)

☐ $55.00/year (institution)

Subscriptions: three issues/year ⊞ All Amerasia Journal subscribers
receive a free subscription to **CrossCurrents**, newsmagazine of
the UCLA Asian American Studies Center.

Back issues $13.00 each, plus $4.00 shipping and handling.

California residents add 7.75% sales tax, Los Angeles residents 8.25%.
No shipping charges on **Amerasia Journal** subscriptions in U.S.
Foreign subscriptions to **Amerasia Journal** add $8.00 per year.

Handling charges: $4.00 per copy on first and $2.00 each
on next up to four. $8.00 on small box and $15.00 on large box.

Students—20% (photocopy of current student identification required).

Terms: Dealers and Agencies—20% discount.
No discounts on **Amerasia Journal** subscriptions.

Name _____

Address _____

State _____ Zip _____

Signature VISA/MASTERCARD/Discovery/Diners/accepted: (add 3% credit card charge)

Card Number _____ Phone # _____ Expiration Date _____ Total